TOWARDS KOREAN RECONCILIATION

Towards Korean Reconciliation
Socio-Cultural Exchanges and Cooperation

GABRIEL JONSSON
Stockholm University, Sweden

LONDON AND NEW YORK

First published 2006 by Ashgate Publishing

Reissued 2018 by Routledge
2 Park Square, Milton Park, Abingdon, Oxon OX14 4RN
605 Third Avenue, New York, NY 10017

First issued in paperback 2021

Routledge is an imprint of the Taylor & Francis Group, an informa business

© Gabriel Jonsson 2006

Gabriel Jonsson has asserted his moral right under the Copyright, Designs and Patents Act, 1988, to be identified as the author of this work.

All rights reserved. No part of this book may be reprinted or reproduced or utilised in any form or by any electronic, mechanical, or other means, now known or hereafter invented, including photocopying and recording, or in any information storage or retrieval system, without permission in writing from the publishers.

A Library of Congress record exists under LC control number: 2006922670

Notice:
Product or corporate names may be trademarks or registered trademarks, and are used only for identification and explanation without intent to infringe.

Publisher's Note
The publisher has gone to great lengths to ensure the quality of this reprint but points out that some imperfections in the original copies may be apparent.

Disclaimer
The publisher has made every effort to trace copyright holders and welcomes correspondence from those they have been unable to contact.

ISBN 13: 978-0-815-39852-3 (hbk)
ISBN 13: 978-1-351-14440-7 (ebk)
ISBN 13: 978-1-138-35848-5 (pbk)

DOI: 10.4324/9781351144407

Contents

List of Tables		*vii*
Acronyms		*ix*
Acknowledgements		*xi*

1. Introduction		1
1.1	Purpose	1
1.2	Theoretical framework	4
1.3	Organization and scope	7
1.4	Spelling of Korean names	9

2. Lessons from German and Yemeni Unification		11
2.1	Introduction	11
2.2	Divided Germany	12
2.3	Gorbachev comes to power in the Soviet Union	20
2.4	The Berlin Wall falls	23
2.5	Causes of German unification	28
2.6	Consequences of German unification	30
2.7	Divided Yemen	33
2.8	Yemeni unification	38
2.9	Causes and aftermath of Yemeni unification	40
2.10	Conclusions	46

3. Inter-Korean Relations		49
3.1	Introduction	49
3.2	Unification policies of North and South Korea	50
3.3	The development of inter-Korean relations, 1953-1997	55
3.4	President Kim Dae Jung's unification policies	58
3.5	Steps forward in inter-Korean relations, 1998-1999	61
3.6	Steps backwards in inter-Korean relations, 1998-1999	66
3.7	Official contacts and developments in North Korea	68
3.8	Historic North-South summit and its aftermath	72
3.9	Inter-Korean relations, 2001-2002	79
3.10	The North Korean nuclear crisis re-emerges in 2002	85
3.11	Conclusions	94

4. Inter-Korean Socio-cultural Exchanges and Cooperation		97
4.1	Introduction	97
4.2	Legal foundations of inter-Korean socio-cultural exchanges and cooperation	98
4.3	Development of inter-Korean socio-cultural exchanges and cooperation	100
4.4	Types of socio-cultural exchanges and cooperation	108
4.5	Characteristics of inter-Korean socio-cultural exchanges and cooperation	130
4.6	South Korean NGOs and unification	140
4.7	The impact of socio-cultural exchanges and cooperation on North Korea	142
4.8	Conclusions	148
5. Case Studies of Inter-Korean Socio-cultural Exchanges and Cooperation		151
5.1	Introduction	151
5.2	North Korean defectors to South Korea	152
5.3	Adaptation of North Korean defectors to life in South Korea	162
5.4	Humanitarian aid from South to North Korea	179
5.5	Divided families	184
5.6	Conclusions	187
6. Views of North Korea, Unification and the Great Powers		189
6.1	Introduction	189
6.2	Views of North Korea and accommodation of North Korean Culture	190
6.3	Views of unification in South Korea, 2000-2001	196
6.4	Views of unification in South Korea, 2002-2003	208
6.5	Implications of the great powers' policies towards Korea	215
6.6	Conclusions	220
7. General Conclusions		223
7.1	Inter-Korean socio-cultural exchanges and cooperation	223
7.2	Obstacles to Korean unification	226
7.3	Lessons from German and Yemen unification	230
7.4	Towards closer inter-Korean relations and a unified Korea?	232

Chronology   *235*
Bibliography   *265*
Index   *283*

List of Tables

Table 6.1	Cognitions of North Korea, 1996	191
Table 6.2	Experiences of North Korean culture, 2001	191
Table 6.3	Experiences of lectures on North Korea, 2001	192
Table 6.4	Types of North Korean culture experienced, 2001	192
Table 6.5	Opinions of North Korean films, 2001	193
Table 6.6	Reasons for liking North Korean films, 2001	193
Table 6.7	Reasons for disliking North Korean films, 2001	194
Table 6.8	Opinions of North Korean arts, 2001	194
Table 6.9	Reasons for liking North Korean arts, 2001	194
Table 6.10	Heterogeneity between North and South Korean art and literary works, 2001	195
Table 6.11	The impact of North Korean art and literary works, 2001	195
Table 6.12	Discussion on unification, 2000	196
Table 6.13	Reasonability of unification, 2000	197
Table 6.14	Time for unification, 2000	197
Table 6.15	Obstacles to unification, 2000	198
Table 6.16	Main tasks for unification, 2000	199
Table 6.17	Reasonability of unification, 2001	200
Table 6.18	Interest in unification, 2001	200
Table 6.19	Obstacles to unification, 2001	201
Table 6.20	Main tasks for unification, 2001	202
Table 6.21	Opinions on unification education, 2001	203
Table 6.22	Perceived heterogeneity between the two Koreas, 2001	203
Table 6.23	Perceived impact of tradition in the two Koreas, 2001	204
Table 6.24	Explanations of the deepening of heterogeneity, 2001	204
Table 6.25	Perceptions of North and South Korean youth's way of thinking, 2001	205
Table 6.26	North Korea's main tasks to promote homogeneity, 2001	205
Table 6.27	South Korea's main tasks to promote homogeneity, 2001	206
Table 6.28	Interest in unification, 2002	209
Table 6.29	Reasonability of unification, 2002	209
Table 6.30	Time for unification, 2002	209
Table 6.31	Formula for unification, 2002	210
Table 6.32	Time for unification, 2002	210
Table 6.33	Obstacles to unification, 2002	211
Table 6.34	Prerequisites for unification, 2002	212
Table 6.35	Formula for unification, 2002	213
Table 6.36	Cognitions of North Korea, 2003	213

Table 6.37	Communization of South Korea, 2003	214
Table 6.38	Discussion on unification, 2003	214
Table 6.39	Main tasks for unification, 2003	215
Table 6.40	Opinions of great powers' attitudes on Korean unification, 2002, 2003	215

Acronyms

APEC	Asia-Pacific Economic Cooperation
ARF	Association of South East Asian Nations Regional Forum
BAPUF	Buddhist Association for a Peaceful Unification of the Fatherland (North Korea)
CDU	Christian Democratic Union (East Germany)
CIA	Central Intelligence Agency
CNN	Cable News Network
COMECON	Council for Mutual Economic Assistance
DCRK	Democratic Confederal Republic of Korea
DM	Deutsche (West German) Mark
DMZ	Demilitarized Zone
EC	European Community
EU	European Union
FAO	Food and Agricultural Organization
FEER	Far Eastern Economic Review
GDP	Gross Domestic Product
GDR	German Democratic Republic
GFKC	General Federation of Korean Churches (South Korea)
GNP	Gross National Product
GPC	General Popular Congress (North Yemen)
IAEA	International Atomic Energy Agency
IFRC	International Federation of the Red Cross
IOC	International Olympic Committee
KBS	Korean Broadcasting System (South Korea)
KCNA	Korean Central News Agency (North Korea)
KCT	Korean Central Television (North Korea)
KECC	Inter-Korean Economic Cooperation Committee
KEDO	Korean Peninsula Energy Development Organization
KINU	Korea Institute for National Unification
KNCC	Korean National Council of Churches (South Korea)
KNRC	Korean National Red Cross (South Korea)
KWP	Korean Workers' Party
LDC	Least Developed Countries
MBC	Munhwa Broadcasting Corporation (South Korea)
MoU	Ministry of Unification (South Korea)
NATO	North Atlantic Treaty Organization
NGO	Non-governmental Organization
NKCF	North Korean Christian Federation

NKFB	North Korean Federation of Buddhists
NNSC	Neutral Nations Supervisory Commission
NPT	Non-Proliferation Treaty
NSL	National Security Law
OM	Ost (East German) Mark
SBS	Seoul Broadcasting Station
SED	Socialist Unity Party (East Germany)
SNCC	South-North Coordinating Committee
SNU	Seoul National University
UN	United Nations
UNCHR	United Nations Commission on Human Rights
UNDP	United Nations Development Programme
UNEP	United Nations Environment Programme
UNESCO	United Nations Educational, Scientific and Cultural Organization
US	United States
WCC	World Council of Churches
WHO	World Health Organization
YCIMOR	Yemen Company for Investment in Mineral and Oil Resources
YRG	Yemeni Reform Grouping
YSP	Yemeni Socialist Party (South Yemen)

Acknowledgements

Firstly I wish to extend my gratitude to those who have been kind enough to offer their assistance during the preparation of this book. This stimulating project would never have reached completion without a pair of one-month research visits to South Korea during both 2002 and 2004. I therefore would like to acknowledge Stockholm University, the Center for Pacific Asia Studies at the Institute of Oriental Languages for providing financial support for both of these fact-finding sojourns.

In addition, I wish to express my gratitude to Professor Staffan Rosén at Stockholm University, Head of the Korean Department at the Institute of Oriental Languages, and to Professor Masako Ikegami-Andersson, Head of the Center for Pacific Asia Studies, for their invaluable assistance during the course of the project. I have also drawn great encouragement for the project from seminars held at both the Korean Department and at the Centre for Pacific Asia Studies. In particular, I wish to express my thanks to Doctor Linus Hagström at the Swedish Institute for International Affairs and Doctor Anders Uhlin at Lund University's Department of Political Science, for their kind advice and assistance.

In Korea, I wish to especially thank the former President of the Korea Institute for National Unification, Doctor Seo Byung-Chul, and his successor Doctor Park Young-Kyu for permitting me to study at the institute. As a guest researcher, I benefited greatly from my affiliation with the institute in terms of collation of relevant material and of course in terms of establishing valuable contacts. I also wish to thank my wife, Lee Hee-Sook, and my daughter, Rebecka Ye-mi, for their extraordinary patience towards me during the preparation of this book. Noel McCarthy has my thanks for editing the English as does Roberto Menkes for his assistance concerning technical matters related to the project. Finally, Liber Kartor AB [Liber Maps Ltd.] deserves my thanks for letting me use their map of the Korean Peninsula reprinted in *Bonniers Stora Världsatlas* [*Bonnier's Great World Atlas*] from 1994 with a few additions. Thank you one and all.

Stockholm, 24 January, 2006

Gabriel Jonsson

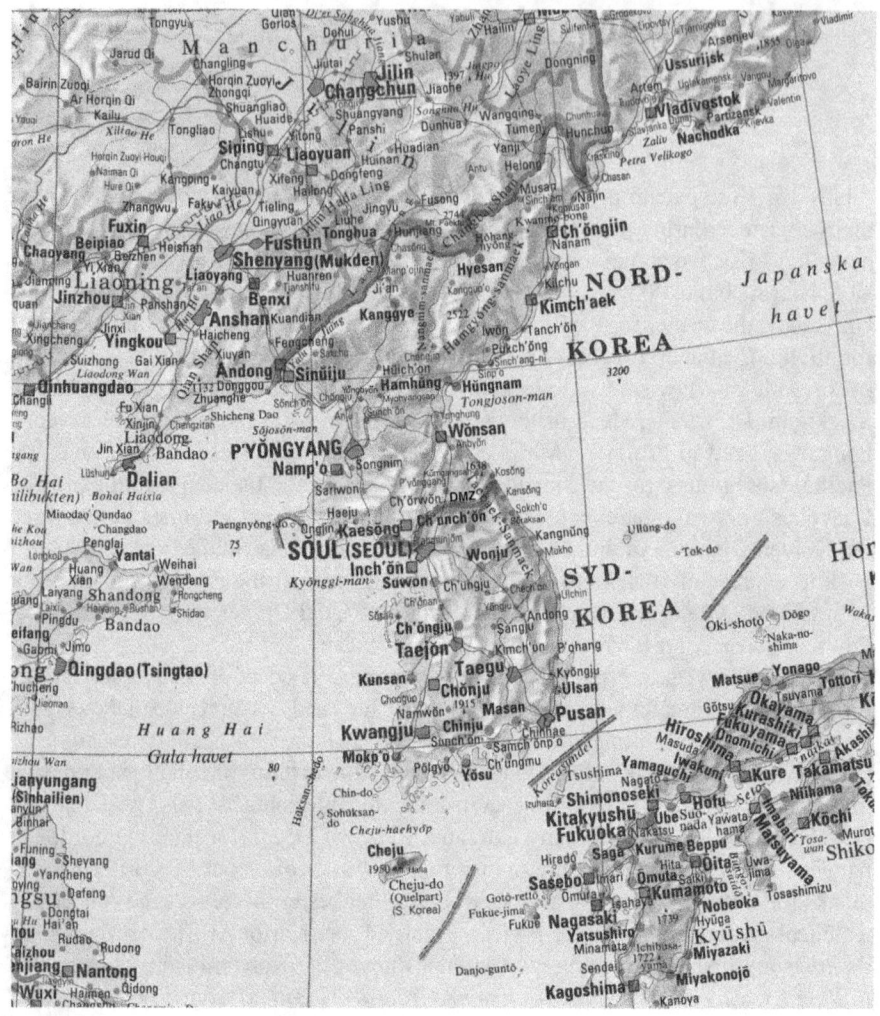

Map of the Korean Peninsula

Chapter 1

Introduction

1.1 Purpose

Korea is generally considered to be the world's only divided nation following on the unification of both Germany and Yemen, in 1990. According to the South Korean scholar O Ki-sông (1999), Korean unification remains an aspiration due to unique forms of nationalism singularly inherent to both states. The South Korean scholar Park Young-Ho and his associates wrote in (2002) that unification is asserted primarily, as a should-do task whereby the myth of "One People, One Nation" has become a widely popularized catch-cry. The former North Korean diplomat defector Hyôn Sông-il writes (1998) that unifying North and South is the greatest wish of the Korean people.[1] Whether this aspiration for unification is actually reflected in the detail of public policies or not will be a primary subject for investigation in this book.

Political and economic issues dominate amongst the vast body of literature concerning eventual Korean unification. However, there can be no doubt that in addition to these, socio-cultural exchanges and cooperation encompassing the fields of science, culture as well as the arts, religion, sport, media and publishing, popular culture, tourism, South Korean aid to North Korea, exchanges of divided families, all in their totality, amount to a multi-faceted patchwork which actually characterizes inter-Korean relations.[2] Firstly, the South Korean scholars Cho Han Bum and Ko Yong-gwôn (2002) argue that such contacts contribute to an overcoming of the heterogeneity created by partition and which more specifically contributes towards a sense of statist and indeed collective homogeneity. Neither of these authors define in concrete terms what they mean by "heterogeneity" and "homogeneity" however, as their compatriot scholar Choi Jinwook and his associates point out (2003), Koreans'

---

[1] Harrison, *Korean Endgame: A Strategy for Reunification and US Disengagement* (Princeton: Princeton University Press, 2002), p. 348; Hyôn, "T'ongir-ûl wihan Namhan-ûi chôngch'i sahoejôk pyônhwa panghyang", in Yi (ed.), *T'ongir-ûl wihae Namhan-do pyônhae-ya handa – Pukhan ch'ulsin hakcha-dûr-ûi chujang-gwa Namhan hakcha-dûr-ûi nonp'yông* (Seoul: Orûm, 1998), p. 13; O, *Nambukhan munhwa t'onghamnon: munhwa-ûi kujo punsôg-e ûihan t'onghap kwajông yôn'gu* (Seoul: Kyoyuk kwahaksa, 1999), p. 90; Park et al., *T'ongil sinario-wa t'ongil kwajôngsang-ûi chôngch'aek pangan: ironchôk model-gwa chônmunga insik chosa* (Seoul: T'ongil yôn'guwôn, 2002), p. 59. Original quotation marks.

[2] Definition from O, "Nambuk kyoryu hwalsônghwa-rûl wihan mingan tanch'e-ûi yôkhal – sahoe munhwa kyoryu-rûl chungsim-ûro", *T'ongil munje-wa kukche kwangye* 10 (December 1999), p. 75.

long experience of living as a unified people within a unitary culture has contributed towards a certain familiarity in terms of homogeneity. In this study, homogeneity and heterogeneity refer only to opinions regarding socio-cultural characteristics as experienced in the context of the two Koreas.

Cho argues that to overcome heterogeneity as a social factor, common characteristics have to be recalled and replenished so as to create a lasting basis for a new, unified society. Socio-cultural exchanges and cooperation it is argued, must be seen to break away from the kind of constraints inherent to government-led contacts and economic cooperation. This, it is argued, is necessary so as to overcome socialized heterogeneity and in the final analysis, create a socio-cultural community on the peninsula, prior even to actual systemic reunification. A successful outcome from socio-cultural exchanges and cooperation are in themselves vital stepping stones for the establishment of peaceful relations as well as contributing to a wider sense of social unity, nation-wide. In his view such contacts offer the most realistic prospects of ultimately overcoming the Cold War structures pertaining on the Korean Peninsula, in the pursuit of peaceful coexistence.[3] Whether this opinion holds water or not will also be the subject of some considerable investigation here.

Nonetheless, scholars' opinions on homogeneity versus heterogeneity in the Korean context tend to differ considerably. The American anthropologist Roy Richard Grinker (1998) argues against the concept of "homogeneity" (*tongjilsông*), which he claims is one of the most important, as well as one of the most taken-for-granted concepts pertaining to eventual unification. Since unification is often presented as "recovering homogeneity" (*tongjilsông hoebok*); progress on unification is hindered: North and South Korea are after all not homogeneous, he argues. He even claims that, while admittedly it would probably cause intense disagreement, "Koreans have never been homogeneous and never will be". The word used to explain cultural and political difference (*ijil*) contains a negative connotation which implies weak interest in or acknowledgment, of diversity. He also argues that while South Korean politicians frequently boast that South Koreans are themselves homogeneous, there remain long-standing regional tensions within the wider nation.

However, in spite of partition, Korea may indeed be a more homogeneous society than the aforementioned views would appear to imply: O (1999) argues that a combination of a lengthy joint history from 668 to 1945, as well as the usage of a common language ultimately contributes towards not only a sense of unity, but indeed a unified culture. This common language and these shared historical traditions create a symbolic mechanism for eventual re-integration of the currently

---

3 Cho, "Chôngsang hoedam ihu sahoe munhwa kyoryu-ga Pukhan sahoe-e mich'in yônghyang", in T'ongil yôn'guwôn, *Nambuk kwangye palchôn-gwa hanbando p'yônghwa chôngch'ak* (Seoul: T'ongil yôn'guwôn, 2002), pp. 2, 12-13; Choi et al., *Nambuk kwangye-ûi chinjôn-gwa kungnaejôk yônghyang* (Seoul: T'ongil yôn'guwôn, 2003), p. 263; Ko, "Nambuk sahoe munhwa kyoryu hyômnyôg-ûi hyôn-hwang-gwa kwaje", in Kunsan taehakkyo hyôndae inyôm yôn'guso & T'ongil munje yôn'gu hyôbûihoe, *Nambukhan kyoryu hyômnyôg-ûi hwalsônghwa pangan* (Kunsan: Kunsan taehakkyo hyôndae inyôm yôn'guso, 2002), pp. 47-8.

heterogeneous ways of life pertaining on both sides of the border. The influence of Buddhist culture for more than 1,000 years as well as Confucian culture for hundreds of years constitutes, in itself, a homogeneous cultural layer. North and South Korea maintain mostly without exception, common traditional values such as an acceptance of patriarchal authority, the maintenance of the family as a social institution, children's respect for their parents and the prioritization of parental ambitions regarding the next generation's educational development. Other common cultural characteristics include acceptance and respect for authority, a sense of interdependence among neighbours widely identified as a social virtue, and is further typified through the culinary culture and a widespread pride over *Hanbok* (national dress). While acknowledging these characteristics, he argues that regardless of whether heterogeneity has come about as a result of capitalism versus socialism or as a by-product of inevitable albeit separate processes of modernization; the two Korean states have, nonetheless, become heterogeneous through a process of socialization stemming from an illusionary sense of heterogeneity.

The South Korean scholar Kim Pyông-no (2000) diverges from Grinker and O's analyses and argues that both North and South Korea need to confront and acknowledge that culture, arts and sports in the two states have indeed developed differently throughout recent history, providing an obstacle for those who oppose notions of heterogeneity. Values and attitudes that recognise heterogeneity as a valuable form of diversity need to be established and indeed be promoted to a level whereby genuine coexistence begins to emerge. At the end of the day, the differing characteristics of North Korean art need not be rejected or be disregarded as being inferior, but need to be understood as being simply different.[4] We will return later to many of these differing views on the socio-cultural basis for unity.

Secondly, we should recall that German unification in 1990 was facilitated by the expansion of people to people exchanges on many different levels. The Basis of Relations Treaty signed by East and West Germany in 1972, promoted in the words of the South Korean scholar Kang Suk Rhee (1993), "value integration". The term describes promotion of a feeling of a common race, language, culture, history and set of customs and traditions revolving around shared concepts of peace, freedom and prosperity. He argues that both North and South Korean leaders have by and large, ignored the question of value integration at the expense of structural integration.[5] The author shall return to this point later in the book.

---

4 Grinker, *Korea and Its Futures: Unification and the Unfinished War* (New York: St. Martin's Press, 1998), p. xiii; Kim, "Nambuk munhwa yesul-mith sûp'och'û kyoryu-ûi hyônhwang-gwa kwaje pôp chedo changbi sigûphada", *T'ongil Han'guk* (2000), 7, p. 43; O, ibid., 1999, pp. 260, 263, 264, 276, 291, 347-49; Song, *The Rise of the Korean Economy* (New York: Oxford University Press, 2003), pp. xxii, 36.

5 Rhee, "Korea's Unification: The Applicability of the German Experience", *Asian Survey* 33 (1993), no. 4, pp. 365-66.

Although value integration was indeed an important factor in the case of Germany, we should remind ourselves of the interpretation applied by Grinker (1998) who wrote that:

> South Koreans risk repeating two mistakes made by the former West Germany prior to German unification: failing to discuss practical and specific dimensions of unification until after it occurs, and ignoring the extent to which half a century of division can produce significant social and cultural differences between the two sides of a nation.[6]

Consequently, preparing for unification and encouraging human exchanges are indeed important tasks; however, whether Grinker's writing is congruent with current social realities, has yet to be fully put to the test.

In the context of this background, the book aims to contribute to the literature on Korean unification through focusing on socio-cultural exchanges and cooperation between the two Koreas, so as to find out what actual impact they have had on cross-border relations, what concrete results have stemmed from them and how these could eventually contribute to the creation of closer contacts with unification in mind. Inter-Korean socio-cultural exchanges and cooperation have been extensively studied by South Korean scholars, in particular by Cho Han Bum whose works have indeed been indispensable on the subject, in addition to several other studies which have also been disseminated. However, there are but a few studies published in English in this field, and this book aims to fill this glaring gap.

1.2 Theoretical framework

Since functionalism was promoted by the Kim Dae Jung Government (1998-2003) as a means of theoretically legitimizing public policy towards North Korea, it has naturally constituted this study's essential theoretical framework.[7] Functionalism was conceptualized by Professor David Mitrany (1888-1975) in the 1930s and 1940s, in the aftermath of the disastrous experiences of the First World War and the Great Depression. He explained functionalism as an approach to the problems of international relations primarily; it has since become central to the study of international integration theory. Thus, transforming formerly tense inter-state relations into peaceful ones is a matter of long-term concern not alone on a practical level but of course also on a theoretical one.

Functionalism's primary concern is with the development of a "working peace system" or, to quote from his book *The Functional Theory of Politics,* "The historical task of our time is not to keep the nations peacefully apart but to bring them actively together". The core of functionalism's agenda is the prioritization of human needs or public welfare in contrast to the supremacy of the nation-state or the celebration of any particular ideology. In Mitrany's view, the organization of the world into states

---

6 Grinker, ibid., p. xv.
7 From Choi et al., ibid., p. 37.

generated damaging dogmatic tendencies. Instead, a functionalist mantra has come to be summarized in the belief that, "form follows function": since human needs change over time and vary across space, institutional solutions have to be both open-minded as well as flexible.

Functionalism's central principles are grounded in the belief that man can be weaned away from his loyalty to the nation state by the experience of beneficial international cooperation, stemming from international organizations and regimes in accordance with mutually agreed areas of activity which ultimately increase common welfare rewards to individuals beyond the level, obtainable within the context of the nation state. This shift away from loyalty towards the nation state, he believed, would ultimately reduce the risks of international conflict.

If individuals and groups began to recognize the benefits of this cooperation, they would become increasingly enmeshed in international cooperation; mutual interdependencies would develop and in turn be sustained by expanding international cooperation. These interdependencies have, over time, been seen to promote the impetus for further integration in other fields, which ultimately undermine the most fundamental basis for the nation state. The successful application of the functional approach could ultimately spell the death knell for national governments, as a dense network of interlocking cooperative ventures evolve, as witnessed partially in the context of the European Union. In addition, the loyalties of the citizens as an important pillar for the nation state would be progressively weakened through the development at the popular level, of a social-psychological community stressing overlapping "cooperative" goals. Nonetheless, these goals posed no apparent threat to the existent cultural attachments of groups and individuals, Mitrany acknowledged.

He recognized that economic development created interdependencies between groups which could indeed bind them together more closely. Through the establishment of cooperative ventures across national frontiers the dangers stemming from the intrinsic isolation of states could yet be avoided. Instead, it was suggested that states could be brought closer together, further reducing the risk of inter-state conflict. In the mid-1970s, it could be questioned if the experience of common activity really served to change attitudes radically and indeed if international cooperation really encouraged those who were affected by it, to question their sense of loyalty towards their national governments or other symbols of the nation state. Yet it has been frequently claimed that the available evidence regarding the outputs and benefits of this type of cooperation as it impacts upon public attitudes offered no decisive challenge to functionalism theoretically.[8]

---

8 Mitrany, *A Working Peace System: An Argument for the Functional Development of International Organization* (London: The Royal Institute of International Affairs, 1943), pp. 6-7, 19, 26-7, 32, 51; *The Functional Theory of Politics* (Bristol: Western Printing Services Ltd., 1975), pp. 136, 240; Rosamond, *Theories of European Integration* (Houndmills: MacMillan Press Ltd., 2000), pp. 31, 32-4, 36, 39, 199; Taylor, "Introduction", in Mitrany, ibid., 1975, pp. ix-xi, xx-xxii. Original quotation marks. "Cooperative" is quoted from Taylor, ibid., p. x.

Notwithstanding this, functionalism has, nonetheless, been criticized on a number of grounds. The first criticism relates to the theory's basic assumption that the determination of needs is an objective and technocratic exercise. As a political task, it is in the final analysis an inherently unstable basis for progress. Administration of public communications is one thing, however, coordination of production, trade and distribution is made incomparably more complex due to the intensely competitive nature of their practice. Mitrany disliked laissez-faire capitalism. He endeavoured to apply functionalist principles to the multi-faceted spheres of production, finance and trade, claiming that there was a requirement for fundamental alterations to the behavioural logic of firms, markets and financiers.

The second criticism criticises the very functionality of functionalism in terms of being hopelessly naïve and resting upon unreasonable assumptions about the ability of people and governments to move in rational directions. Functionalists' technocratic emphasis led to an underestimation of the continuing salience of politics: technocracy is of course a deeply political process. Functionalist reasoning contains universal assumptions about the capacities and probable outcomes in terms of cognitive change. This indicates that the objective fulfilment of needs will almost always automatically generate support for the institutional forms used to address those needs. But the mechanisms through which needs are identified in the first place are often underestimated and tend to be poorly identified. Further, a communicative theory of how actors come to believe certain things about the world is entirely absent. The ultimate recourse to an objective rationality is not sufficient in itself, in terms of cognitive application of current social science.

A third criticism is that functionalism has a poor record of prediction: things have not turned out the way Mitrany envisaged. But it should be noted that his work concerned advocacy rather than prediction extending a theoretical context which offered a possible systemic solution. Until his death, Mitrany advocated a functionalist world order using his working theory as an active form of political intervention rather than a theory based one on the production of law-like generalizations: to this extent there was a predictive element within his understanding of functionalism. By emphasizing the progress and nature of social change, Mitrany's recommendations for international organization reflected assumptions about the evolution of human needs and the tendency of different forms of governance to reform and adapt normatively.

The fourth criticism concerns the lack of scientific rigour: functionalism has no foundational theoretical statement. Actually, Mitrany's position as a public figure meant that his audience tended to be, more often than not, a more general public audience as opposed to an exclusively academic one. For Mitrany, theoretical rigor was a problematic aspect in terms of denoting practical rigidity and creative closure.[9] In the context of these strengths and weaknesses, the applicability and relevance of functionalism in the Korean case is to be tested here.

---

9   Rosamond, ibid., pp. 39-42.

1.3 Organization and scope

When observed as a divided nation, there is a not uncommon opinion prevalent that Korea may well yet learn from earlier experiences of German and Yemeni unification during the 1990s (Vietnam is excluded from the study on the grounds that it was reunified by war). Consequently, the methods of unification recorded by the South Korean scholars Ok Tae Hwan and Kim Soo Am (1998) – "absorption" in the case of Germany and "agreement" in the case of Yemen – are primarily of interest in the context of Korea.[10]

Chapter 2 therefore investigates the lessons of the German and Yemeni unification experiences with particular emphasis on Germany which has of course attracted the lion's-share of scholarly attention, heretofore. Three issues are analyzed essentially here: What characterized relations between the two Germanys and the two Yemens before unification? What factors enabled unification? What have the consequences of their unification been? The first issue is investigated through an account of inter-German and inter-Yemen relations, including major developments within the spheres of politics, economics and socio-cultural contacts through previous decades. The periods investigated are, in the case of Germany, 1949-1990 and in the case of Yemen, 1967-1990. East and West Germany were created in 1949, whereas North Yemen was established in 1918 and South Yemen in 1967. The explanations and consequences of unification are later investigated in detail and interpretations of their respective developments are looked at comparatively.

Chapter 3 analyzes inter-Korean relations since the end of the Korean War, in 1953. The three issues to be investigated here are: What has characterized and underlined North and South Korea's unification policies? How have inter-Korean relations developed? What are their primary characteristics? The first issue is studied through an account of major characteristics of unification policies, between 1953 and 1997. The two other factors are investigated through reviewing the primary developments within the context of political, economic and socio-cultural contacts. In particular, the context in which socio-cultural exchanges and cooperation have taken place is closely examined. Trade basically differs from political contacts by being conducted through non-governmental channels but is anyhow presented in the same context due to the definition of socio-cultural contacts on p. 1. The main emphasis is focused on the period from 1998 onwards because relations since then have become much more frequent and comprehensive. Socio-cultural contacts are studied in greater detail than political and economic issues to give as accurate a view as possible of their extent. Socio-cultural events recorded in Korean, appear here (and elsewhere), resting on the author's own translations; indeed this also applies to the quotations and book titles supplied. References to and comparisons with

---

10 Ok & Kim, *The Initial Phase of Unified Korea* (Seoul: Korea Institute for National Unification [KINU], 1998), pp. 1-2. 31 scholars believed in absorption to unify Korea and nine in an agreed unity. Yemen [and Vietnam] are not mentioned but "agreement" [and "by force"] refer to the two nations.

Germany and Yemen are also drawn in terms of their relationship with the intrinsic theory of functionalism as applied to the analysis.

Chapter 4 investigates inter-Korean socio-cultural exchanges and cooperation in some detail, with particular emphasis on the 1990s when contacts began to expand. Socio-cultural exchanges and cooperation, which additionally includes, environmental cooperation and women to women exchanges, which are also referred to from some other studies in order to as accurately as possible reflect the universality of inter-Korean contacts. These are examined from five different points of view. These are: In what legal context have these socio-cultural exchanges and taken place? How have these contacts developed? What kinds of exchanges and cooperation have actually taken place in practice? What are the characteristics of the socio-cultural contacts? How is North Korea affected by these contacts? These issues are investigated with particular consideration being taken to the opinion that socio-cultural exchanges and cooperation in their very application, contribute substantially to the restoration of national homogeneity and indeed the functional approach to political theory.

In selecting actual examples, the basic principle has been to record only accomplished contacts and of these only the most frequently recorded ones. But for the pre-1990 period proposals to hold exchanges are included in addition. For the post-1990 period some other events than those which are the most frequently recorded ones are included because of the broad scope of contacts and their differing characteristics. In analyzing the characteristics of socio-cultural exchanges and cooperation, the number of people involved in those contacts and the length of meetings held are recorded in detail so as to contribute to an understanding of the diffusion effects of contacts that are hardly ever investigated in the wider literature. For the sake of convenience, a chronological record of socio-cultural contacts and other major events appears as a result, at the end of the book.

Chapter 5 investigates three specific areas of socio-cultural exchanges and cooperation: (1) the position of North Korean defectors in South Korea, (2) the impact of South Korean humanitarian assistance on North Korea and (3) the situation of divided families in an effort to provide a more detailed overview. The period of time dealt with will primarily govern the period from the mid-1990s onwards, however some previous developments are also included in the review of the fallout surrounding the situation of the defectors.

The importance of the first issue becomes clear from the opinion expressed by Grinker (1998) to the effect that over 700 North Korean defectors then living in South Korea were "...the only available model for assessing potential social and economic problems in a unified Korea...". He also goes on to argue "...that the defectors are a model for the potential costs of unification, whatever the peace dividend".[11] South Korean humanitarian aid to North Korea creates people-to-people contacts which contribute to socialized notions of each other. Divided families obviously contributed to the trauma created by the partition of the two Koreas: this issue is

---

11 Grinker, ibid., pp. xv, 226.

regarded by the British scholar James A. Foley (2003) as "...one of Korea's most urgent and pressing humanitarian problems...". A similar opinion is expressed by the South Korean scholar Suh Jae Jean (2002), who regards the divided families as "the most important humanitarian case" among the many issues to crop up as a consequence of Korea's partition.[12]

Chapter 6 investigates a few aspects of South Koreans' opinions on North Korea and eventual unification which could affect the impact of socio-cultural contacts bilaterally, the number of opportunities to develop closer ties generally and ultimately influence the prospects for actual Korean reunification. In addition, North Korean defectors' opinions of South Korea are investigated albeit less extensively, and comparisons are made in an effort to present a more complete picture of Koreans' views of each other and unification in general. As Rhee (1993) notes, "The reunification of Korea remains an international issue that cannot be settled outside the context of global political and economic realignments".[13] South Koreans' perceptions of the views and interests pertaining to eventual Korean unity held by the United States, Japan, China and Russia as well as the actual impact of these powerbrokers' policies towards the two Koreas, are analyzed in some detail. In this way, the perceived positive impact of socio-cultural contacts on relations is investigated.

Chapter 7 identifies the studies main findings with particular attention being paid to the opinion created as a consequence of the positive impact of socio-cultural contacts on inter-Korean relations as well as the functional theory of politics: How do they actually relate to currently prevalent perceptions? The relevance of "value integration" in embedding closer relations through "absorption" and "agreement" as methods of unification, are also investigated. The prospects for establishing closer relationships in the interests of unifying Korea are also discussed in the conclusion.

1.4 Spelling of Korean names

Throughout the book Korean names and terms are transliterated according to the McCune-Reischauer system, however, some exceptions are made for the names of politicians in both Koreas that are written in accordance with widely accepted international practice. Examples include South Korean Presidents Park Chung Hee (1963-1979), Chun Doo Hwan (1981-1988), Roh Tae Woo (1988-1993), Kim Young Sam (1993-1998), Kim Dae Jung (1998-2003) and Roo Moo-hyun (2003-) and of course the North Korean leaders Kim Il Sung (1945-1994) as well as Kim Jong Il (1994-). When private Korean names are transliterated, writers' own punctuation is applied when published in English.[14] If the names of Korean scholars are referred to

---

12 Foley, *Korea's Divided Families: Fifty Years of Separation* (London & New York: RoutledgeCurzon, 2003), p. 1; Suh, "The Reunion of Separated Families under the Kim Dae-Jung Government", *The Journal of East Asian Affairs* 16 (2002), no. 2, p. 352.

13 Rhee, ibid., p. 365.

14 See KINU, *Korea Institute for National Unification 2002* (Seoul: KINU, 2002), pp. 9-18: ibid., *2004* (Seoul: KINU, 2004), pp. 9-11, 13-18. When possible, spellings have been

in works by other Korean scholars in English, the Korean method of transliteration is applied. The order of names follows the Korean practice, that is by placing the surname first before the forenames. Exceptions are made only when scholars write their names in the Western naming order and when they have been published jointly with foreign scholars. If Korean scholars have taken foreign names, these names appear according to the Western naming order. In the case of newspapers, and newspaper companies, their preferred punctuation is applied.

---

checked against businesscards. Businesscards have also been used when available for South Korean scholars not affiliated to KINU whose spellings differ from the McCune-Reischauer system.

Chapter 2

Lessons from German and Yemeni Unification

2.1 Introduction

The unifications of both Germany and Yemen in 1990 have provided Korea with two case examples of how unification can be achieved with some degree of success, as well as providing pointers towards the experiences likely to be thrown up in the aftermath of an eventual reunification. In order to shed further light on these complex issues, characteristics governing the relationships between East and West Germany as well as North and South Yemen prior to unification are examined, in addition to the causes for their unification which are also analyzed here; with particular focus on the consequences and basis for the political, economic and socio-cultural factors which underlined developments there.

Since most scholarly attention has been devoted to the case of German unification, more emphasis is placed on the German case, rather than that of Yemen. Germany is also far more populous, is wealthier, and the historical background to the division contains similarities with that of Korea. Important focus points for investigation relate to the preunification period 1949-1989 incorporating which policies East and West Germany pursued in an effort to manage the circumstances thrown up by partition, how these policies changed over time, what impact the policies had on cross-border relations, as well as in what geopolitical context contacts developed and not least with regard as to how internal and external factors affected relations in terms of both positive and negative developments.

Further, the economic power of the two Germanys' are looked at, as well as the impact of the respective political leaders on the process of unification alongside the development of socio-cultural exchanges which are, also discussed in depth. The more positive and indeed some of the more negative developments throughout the process of German reunification are weighed against each other in order to give a balanced and fair account.

Developments during 1989 and 1990 as well as the economic, political and social consequences of unification are investigated in greater detail as they constitute the particular experiences that can be of greatest value to a re-unified Korea. My purpose thus incorporates an explanation on the process that enabled unification and the developmental trends which followed afterwards in preference to a recounting of all events that preceded unification with the exception of some major ones which are, of course, included. This discussion also includes an examination of the respective population ratios for the two former Germanys.

Which internal and external factors enabled unification? How did they differ from previous developments? What policies exactly, have been pursued to establish a unified Germany? All of these questions are analyzed. Explanations as to how unification occurred are presented and compared with each other in an effort to provide a broader and fairer view of the process towards German unification in the context of its relevance to the Korean experience. In particular, the question of whether the term "absorption" is appropriate to explain and characterize German unification is analyzed in the light of previous developments and subsequent evaluations of the unity process. Indeed, evaluations of the consequences of unification are illuminated, both in terms of those that were made both prior to as well as, of course, in the aftermath of 1990. Whether the overwhelming weight of pre-unity expectation with regard to unification were met or not is also the subject of investigation. In addition, the question of how pre-unity power relations affected the unification process is examined.

The sections dealing with Yemen essentially follow the same approach as that of Germany, however, the period of time investigated commences in 1967 since both North and South Yemen as separate entities were founded in 1918 and 1967, respectively. Focus is also directed here on the "unification period" of 1989-1990. What factors enabled unification? How was the process towards unity implemented? What policies were pursued afterwards? Each of these questions is investigated. Particular emphasis is put here on evaluating whether the term "agreement" provides an accurate account of the unity process through reviewing pre-1989 issues of relevance and analyzing explanations and evaluations of Yemeni unification. Just as in the case of Germany, both positive and negative developments are compared with each other in the interests of balance. Whether post-unity developments matched pre-unity expectations is also the subject of investigation in addition to power relations both prior to and in the aftermath of unification.

Comparisons are not infrequently made between the unification processes in Germany and Yemen as well as the post-unity developments which were to follow in an effort to identify both relevant similarities as well as actual differences. In this sense, the project focus is discussed in terms of what model should be considered as being the most relevant one in the Korean context. What lessons may Korea draw from the German and Yemen experience are noted in some detail and will be analyzed later in the book.

2.2 Divided Germany

In accordance with the 1945 Potsdam agreement, Germany came to be governed by the allied nations of the United States, the Soviet Union, the United Kingdom as well as France. However, the West-East division became permanent in 1949 due to a growing US-Soviet Cold War confrontation. The four allied nations governed Germany by means of direct rule for a decade.

However, German unity was not dropped from the domestic political agenda. The 1949 West German Constitution proclaimed "the unity and freedom of Germany" as being the supreme national goal. The 1949 East German Constitution asserted that "Germany is an indivisible democratic republic". In 1956, East Germany (The German Democratic Republic; GDR) presented the first of what would become all but one of numerous proposals for the eventual formation of an all-German "confederation" (the earlier proposals for unification would of course have copper fastened Eastern dominance). Reunification was even described by the Socialist Unity Party's (SED) chief Walter Ulbricht as the "main question of the German people".[1] However, since the country had not completed the passage into socialism and was far behind West Germany (Federal Republic of Germany; FRG) economically, the SED emphasized domestic transformation.

Whereas West Germany after division actively promoted mutual visits to preserve national homogeneity, East Germany actually restricted human contacts. Visits from the West for family purposes were permitted on a limited scale. However, until the 1953 workers uprising it was, due to defections, virtually impossible for East Germans to visit West Germany unless carried out for business purposes. Afterwards travel restrictions were eased somewhat, enabling on average 250,000 East Germans visitation rights to West Germany between 1954-1957, this in comparison with 2.7 million West Germans visiting East Germany during 1957 alone. In any event, defections continued, primarily via the greater Berlin district. The East German government attempted to prevent a brain drain of students and skilled labour. In the period between the 1949 division and the completion of the Berlin Wall on 13 August, 1961 some 2.7 million East Germans – 20 per cent of the original population – had managed to flee to West Germany. Many people felt neither comfortable in their own land, nor did they feel loyal towards it. The policy impetus to speed up socialist transformation in the late 1950s was reflected in massive shortages of basic staple products making everyday life intolerable for many citizens.[2]

While much of this large-scale emigration was taking place, West Germany adopted the Hallstein doctrine refusing to recognize the legitimacy of the East German government and the other Warsaw Pact governments, with the exception

---

1 Quotations from Marsh, *Germany and Europe: The Crisis of Unity* (London: Heinemann Ltd., 1994), p. 23; McAdams, *Germany Divided: From the Wall to Reunification* (Princeton: Princeton University Press, 1993), pp. 28, 41; Pond, *Beyond the Wall: Germany's Road to Unification* (Washington, D.C.: The Brookings Institution, 1993), p. 24.

2 Kim, *Tong sôdok injôk kyoryu silt'ae yôn'gu* (Seoul: Minjok t'ongil yôn'guwôn, 1996), pp. 7, 11-15; Marsh, ibid., pp. 23-4, 38; McAdams, ibid., pp. 3, 28, 43-4, 48-9; Pond, ibid., pp. 24-5; Rhee, "Korea's Unification", p. 361. Interestingly, McAdams writes: "...it is noteworthy how little we still know about the erection of the Berlin Wall". The reason is that very few individuals were involved in the decision (ibid., p. 49). Pond records that Erich Honecker in his capacity as Central Committee secretary in charge of security was the erector of the wall but gives no further details (ibid., pp. 20, 21).

of the Soviet Union, with whom it maintained diplomatic relations. A majority of the West German population regarded reunification as an indefeasible national obligation. East Germany did not recognize the West German government on the other hand, although Ulbricht throughout 1963-1964 made persistent efforts to establish closer contacts.

One short term outcome was a staggering 1.2 million visits by West Berliners to East Berlin during the 1963-1964 Christmas holidays as part of the first substantial contacts between the two divided sides of the city since the wall was completed. In the aftermath, the East German government reversed its policy allowing business travel only for its favored citizens, a policy continued during the 1960s in an effort to control visits by West Germans. One method utilized for instance, was to permit only one annual visit between relatives per family. Nonetheless, approximately 1.7 million East Germans visited West Germany between 1961 and the first half of 1966. The great majority of them happened to be pensioners. Another 5.5 million visited West Berlin. As noted previously, more West Germans visited East Germany some 600,000 by 1962, a figure which rose to about 2 million annually by the mid-1960s.

At the SED Congress in 1967, Ulbricht even emphasized that "the unification of the German states" remained his government's primary objective. On the other hand by 1963, West Germany had begun to pay for the repatriation of East German political prisoners to the West, as part of a policy of which the aim was to further isolate East Germany and force it into accepting a unification process based on the principle of "free elections". Due to the larger population, elections would likely have resulted in West Germany dominating any unified Germany on a de facto basis.[3]

By the late 1960s, many West German ministers had given up any hope of an East German collapse through a policy of open hostility. In 1967, the Hallstein doctrine was jettisoned and East Germany declared itself to be a sovereign and separate state. The new West German government, led by Chancellor Willy Brandt, adjusted the previous policy of limited contacts with East Germany and the surrounding communist countries, by engaging in negotiations. The only qualification was that the Brandt government would never be willing to treat East Germany as a separate nation. In fact, Brandt emphasized that there were "two German states, but only one German nation". The new "Ostpolitik" also hinged on the continuation of "Westpolitik", that is a firm commitment towards the Atlantic Alliance.

In spite of initial domestic and foreign criticism that Ostpolitik was a "one-sided concession to the Communists", as well as a "weak appeasement policy"; the West German government applied itself to the new policy. It did so in the belief that expanded contacts would work to its own advantage in the long run by reducing regional tensions and in turn, by strengthening its international position vis-à-vis the East, that is achieve "change through rapprochement". Yet, the Germans never

---

3 Hart-Landsberg, "Korean Unification: Learning from the German Experience", *Journal of Contemporary Asia* 26 (1995), no. 1, p. 68; Kim, ibid., 1996, pp. 20-25; McAdams, ibid., pp. 6-7, 19-20, 35, 41, 67, 73, 76-7; Pond, ibid., p. 25. Quotations are from Hart-Landsberg (ibid., p. 68) and McAdams (ibid., p. 77).

advocated any official formula towards a reunification process: peaceful coexistence was considered more important.⁴

This policy should be regarded as a strength rather than a weakness as: *Financial Times*' European Editor David Marsh (1994) writes: "Had an overt strategy existed to change a state of affairs accepted as a principal outcome of the Second World War, it would have crumbled under an onslaught of suspicion at home and abroad".⁵

Ostpolitik was facilitated by the global détente process and contributed towards the signing of bilateral treaties between West Germany and the Soviet Union as well as Poland in 1970. The use of force against each other was renounced and the borders between the two Germanys; as well as between East Germany and Poland, were formally recognized.⁶ In 1970, Ostpolitik led to the first face-to-face heads of government meetings between the West's Willy Brandt and the East's Willy Stoph aimed at discussing the pre-requisites for an inter-German agreement. At the first meeting, Stoph expected Brandt to greet such demands as an abandonment of the policy of giving a "special" character to the inter-German relationship. He himself did not respond at all to Brandt's twenty-point plan on formal relations at the second meeting. However, following on Ulbricht's replacement as SED chief by Erich Honecker in 1971, the level and frequency of dialogue improved substantially.

This was largely thanks to the latter's black-and-white perspective on policy-making instead of the nature of the maximalist positions previously adopted by Ulbricht. In May, 1972, a Transit Treaty was signed allowing West Germans to make regular private visits to their relatives and friends in the East. To a more limited extent, the same opportunity was extended to East Germans in cases of "urgent family need". In July, of that year, the West German government introduced legislation to facilitate ordinary East Germans' journeys to the West by even providing welcome money as well as travel expenses. Actually, East Germans could only bring with them five Ost Mark (OM) which made them dependent on financial support from their West German relatives during their stays. In October, the SED announced a general amnesty for all of its citizens who had fled to West Germany prior to 1972.

More significantly, a Basis of Relations Treaty, which stemmed essentially from Brandt's twenty-point plan, was agreed and signed on 21 December, 1972 following on six-months of hard negotiations. In spite of opposition, the treaty was accepted

---

4   Hart-Landsberg, ibid., p. 68; McAdams, ibid., pp. 69, 79-80; Pond, ibid., p. 26; Rhee, ibid., p. 367; Steininger, "The German Question, 1945-95", in *Germany since Unification: The Domestic and External Consequences* (ed. Klaus Larres, Houndmills & London: MacMillan Press Ltd., 1998), pp. 16-18; Yang, "Kim Dae-jung Administration's North Korea Policy", *Korea Focus* 6 (1998), no. 6, pp. 55-6. Quotations are from Steininger (ibid., pp. 16, 18) and Yang (ibid., p. 55).

5   Marsh, ibid., p. 25.

6   However, West Germany afterwards maintained that final legal recognition of the Oder-Neisse border would have to await a united German government. The issue became increasingly urgent in 1990 since it was the one great postwar reconciliation still pending. It was finally decided in July 1990 that Germany and Poland would sign a treaty guaranteeing the Oder-Neisse line. From Pond, ibid., pp. 192-93, 223.

by the West German Parliament in May 1973. Although Bonn and East Berlin still interpreted the national question differently – East Germany wanted Bonn to show due respect for its sovereignty, while West Germany claimed that inter-German relations would always differ from those reigning over relations between any other states – the treaty contributed, nonetheless, to transforming the nature of the German question.[7]

Kang Suk Rhee (1993) notes that the treaty served as the the basis for "value integration" between the East and West German people primarily through interpersonal contacts, the flow of information, ease of travel, assistance with regard to humanitarian issues in addition to cooperation in other matters of mutual interest. The latter included, socio-cultural contacts, of which TV was the most notable, indeed by the 1960s it became possible to watch the TV coverage of both jurisdictions reciprocally. From 1972 onwards, correspondents were permanently stationed in each state respectively. East German correspondents had, however, been stationed in West Germany since the 1950s. Implementation of the treaty was guaranteed by the Allies. East Germany was recognized as an independent state through the terms of the treaty. Permanent missions (not embassies) were established in Bonn and East Berlin in 1974. West Germany insisted in its relations with the European Community (EC), that intra-German trade was not international trade but domestic trade, which made it exempt from Common Market tariffs. East Germany thus became a stalking member of the EC.

In September 1973, both states became UN members. By the end of 1974, 110 countries, including the world's major industrial powers the United Kingdom, France, the United States and Japan, had established formal relations with East Germany, this in contrast with a figure of only 13 nations, five years earlier. Consequently, East Germany's trade relations also began to diversify from the Council of Mutual Economic Assistance (COMECON) to the West: trade with the Soviet Union had accounted for 39.1 per cent of total exports in 1970 but that trade share fell to 31.4 per cent by 1974. The proportion of trade with the West rose during the same years from a level of 24.4 per cent of total trade to 30.9 per cent. East Germany also found it easier to access loans from Western lending institutions in an effort to purchase Western technology and consumer goods. This was an additional feature added to the benefits gleaned by East Berlin already which had enjoyed the fruits of receiving special overdraft credits from Bonn that saved it millions of Marks in annual interest payments, not forgetting the substantial transfers enjoyed by means of the annual payments for transit fees.[8]

---

7 Kim, ibid., 1996, p. 52; McAdams, ibid., pp. 83, 86, 88, 92-101; Rhee, ibid., p. 365; Steininger, in Larres, ibid., pp. 17-18. "Special" and "urgent family need" are quoted from McAdams (ibid., pp. 86, 88).

8 Kim, ibid., 1996, pp. 35-6; Marsh, ibid., p. 34; McAdams, ibid., pp. 103-105, 107, 111-112; Pak, "Nambuk munhwa kyoryu-ŭi hô-wa sil", *Pukhan* (October 2000), pp. 54, 56; Pohl, "Farewell to Model? German Experiences with Unification and Its Implications for Korean Strategies", in *Exploring New Areas for Multi-lateral Inter-Korean Cooperation*

One concrete change in East-West contacts could be seen in the fact that as much as a third of the West German population had been to East Germany or East Berlin at some point and time.⁹ Yet, in November 1973, fearing the influence of eased travel restrictions on the communist society and seeking further economic benefit, from the amount of currency that Westerners had to exchange for East German marks when crossing the border, the currency tariff was doubled to ten Marks for day visits and 20 Marks per diem for visits lasting more than one day (this policy was originally introduced in 1964 at a lower rate). Consequently, the number of short-term or extended visits by West Germans to East Germany amounting to nearly 2.8 million in 1973 had dropped by more than 350,000 visits by 1974. The number of West Berliners travelling to East Germany rose from 3.3 million in 1972 to 3.8 million by 1973, falling again to 2.56 million by 1974. However, when in the same year the minimum exchange rate was lowered by about one-third following West German protests, the figures rose again.

As seen before, the lightening of travel restrictions for East Germans mainly benefited pensioners. Now the visiting period permitted was extended. Other visitors often remained loyal to the political system and usually travelled in groups accompanied by secret police agents. As witnessed earlier, East Germans did not receive passports but travelled under the auspices of travel certificates. In contrast, West Germans needed a passport and a travel permit issued by East German authorities when travelling into the East.

Other signs of improved relations were seen through the operation of postal and telephone communications which were upgraded in 1972-1973, this in sharp relief to previous policy whereby there were no official telephone links at all between Berlins' two sides as late as 1970. The first inter-German agreement on cooperation with regard to health care and medicine was signed in 1974. It was followed by a roughly equivalent accord on sporting contacts. There were additional exchanges in the fields of drama and music primarily dominated by East German performances in West Germany as it was hard to get permits for Western performers from the inflexible East German authorities.

Knowledge about West Germany spread in the East thanks to the influence of West German TV even among those who were unable to travel. Political, social and economic organizations in the West established contacts with their counterparts in the East. These developments worried an East German government who had sought to cultivate a monopoly on the truth. In late 1974, all of the earlier references to the German nation and their goal of reunification were excluded in the new East German Constitution.¹⁰

(Seoul: KINU, 1998), p. 8; Pond, ibid., p. 23; Rhee, ibid., pp. 364-66; Steininger, in Larres, ibid., p. 18.

9   Rhee, ibid., p. 366: fn. 8. Unfortunately, Rhee does not say what years the figure refers to and how it is calculated.

10   Kim, ibid., 1996, pp. 21, 34-5, 37, 51, 53, 56-7, 66; McAdams, ibid., pp. 100, 101, 102-103, 110-112; Pohl, ibid., p. 8; Rhee, ibid., p. 366: fn. 8.

Ostpolitik was pursued less assiduously by Chancellor Brandt's successors, in spite of their previous criticism. When Helmut Schmidt came into power in 1974, due to his political background and changes in the policy environment he put far less emphasis on inter-German relations than Brandt had done. The agreements pursued by the Schmidt government with East Berlin were primarily uncontroversial and were technical in nature for example, the construction of the new Autobahn between Hamburg and Berlin.

Throughout the 1970s an increasing number of high-level West German politicians visited East Germany. But the extent of détente should not be overexaggerated. West German journalists who had published critical articles on East Germany were expelled and severe restrictions were placed on journalists who rocked the boat and endeavoured to remain in the East. In 1975, the *Der Spiegel* correspondent Jörg Mettke was the first journalist to be expelled due to an article on the forced adoption of children in East Germany. Famous East German literary and cultural figures critical of the government were forced into silence or into permanent exile. The most prominent case occurred in 1976, when the out-spoken songwriter and satirist, Wolf Biermann, was shorn of his citizenship during a concert tour in West Germany. In October 1980, the Honecker government announced that all West Berliners and West Germans, including children and retirees who had previously been exempted from surcharges when making extended visits to East Germany would now have to exchange twice as much currency as before and four times as much if making day-long visits to East Berlin. Not surprisingly, travel into East Germany declined in the ensuing months.

When the new exchange requirements went into effect, Honecker also called into question the essential compromises of the Basis of Relations Treaty. He demanded that Bonn recognize East Germany's separate citizenship, agree to an immediate exchange of fully accredited ambassadors, settle the Elbe boundary dispute and lastly abolish a monitoring station used for recording human rights violations. West Germany rejected all of these demands.[11]

Following the slow down in diplomatic relations experienced in the late 1970s, Ostpolitik in the 1980s comprised largely of direct economic support for the East. This included bailing out political prisoners by paying around DM (Deutsche Mark) 200m annually during the late 1980s. A turning point in relations came in December 1981 when Honecker and Schmidt met in East Germany to discuss the restoration of normal ties between the two states (they also had had brief encounters during 1975 and 1980). Schmidt stressed the view that some form of stable relations should be maintained regardless of what happened between the opposing superpowers; however, he stressed he did not want a recurrence of the irritation caused in 1980, by the raising of the minimum currency exchange to 25 Marks.

For Honecker, Schmidt's visit was proof apparent that West Germany had indeed come closer to accepting East Germany as its' equal. Following on the meeting,

---

11 Larres, "Germany in 1989: the Development of a Revolution", in Larres, ibid., p. 37; Marsh, ibid., p. 35; McAdams, ibid., pp. 113-117, 127, 130-32, 138-40.

the duration of single-day visits by West Berliners to East Berlin underwent an extension and the East German government promised to facilitate citizens travelling West Germany in the event of "urgent family necessity".

However, the compulsory exchange requirements were to remain at record high levels and after some delay West Germany agreed finally in June 1982, to a new, several year extension of loan credits to East Germany. The financial assistance West Germany extended to East Germany after the Basis of Relations Treaty had been signed in 1972 annually amounted to approximately DM 2 billion (about $ 1.2 billion), reaching an estimated 7-10 per cent annual value of the East's actual economic output. This policy would later serve to facilitate unification since it promoted East Germany's dependence on West Germany and thereby made it even more difficult for the East to resist West German efforts towards unification. In fact, by 1983 the SED was willing to make a number of key concessions on issues involving inter-German contacts in return for West German credits and an upgrading of East Germany's status in terms of Bonn's foreign policy priorities.[12]

The East German government eased the passage of West Germans crossing border control points and drastically reduced the number of vehicles on the transit routes to and from Berlin. The compulsory exchange requirement for children under the age of fourteen was lifted in return and the 60,000 pre-programmed weapons along the border were decommissioned (there had been armed guards previously). In 1984, East Germany allowed over 20,000 of its most disenchanted citizens to emigrate to the West. In return, the West German government sealed off the inner offices of its mission in East Berlin at a time when other would-be East German emigrés had sought to use the building as a center for seeking asylum.

In 1983-1984, West Germany provided new loans of DM 2 billion to East Germany, which by 1984 had reciprocated by reducing the compulsory minimum exchange requirements for retirees and by extending annual visits for West German citizens travelling to the East from a maximum of 30 to 45 days. West German support also contributed significantly to making East Germany one of the world's top ten industrial nations, a fact that West Germany took a certain pride in.[13] However, in reality, East Germany had already, by the 1970s, spurned the opportunity to modernize its industry.

An inter-German treaty on cultural cooperation, which had been envisioned in the Basis of Relations Treaty of 1972, was finally concluded in 1986. The primary reason for the delay was essentially that East Germany believed whatever cultural

---

12 Hart-Landsberg, ibid., p. 68; Kim, ibid., 1996, p. 43; Marsh, ibid., p. 34; McAdams, ibid., pp. 116, 138, 147-50, 155-56, 166: fn. 76; Pohl, ibid., pp. 13-14; Pond, ibid., p. 23. "Urgent family necessity" is quoted from McAdams (ibid., p. 150).

13 The scholars Wagner and Kang even write on the effects of West German economic support to East Germany: "That is the whole secret why the GDR is so much better economically than the rest of the socialist countries in Europe". From "Introduction", in *Korea and Germany: Lessons in Division* (eds Myoung-Kyu Kang & Helmut Wagner, Seoul: Seoul National University Press, 1990), p. 22. In the author's opinion, this view is grossly exaggerated; how could economic development be explained by only one factor?

exchanges which would be established as a consequence would ultimately serve to undermine the ruling regime. According to the South Korean scholar Kim Kook Sin (2001), the treaty contributed greatly to enhancing national homogeneity through the expansion of civilian exchanges in the spheres of music, film, theater and publishing although he provides no concrete examples. Other forms of socio-cultural contacts occurred through youth, sports and religious exchanges, city partnerships and cooperation in the fields of science and technology. Rhee (1993) notes that an important byproduct of Ostpolitik was the philosophy of a "general welfare", what Chancellor Brandt came to call "human unity", a reference to the harmony between ordinary Germans, East and West, thanks to the process of value integration over a number of decades. Improved knowledge in East Germany of West German society contributed to protests against their own government's failure to satisfy peoples' real needs and served to underline the lack of basic freedoms such as freedom of speech, travel, assembly, association and the press.[14]

2.3 Gorbachev comes to power in the Soviet Union

Mikhail Gorbachev's rise to power in March 1985 gave official legitimacy to reform policies in both the Soviet Union and within the Eastern European communist countries, particularly in Poland and Hungary, during the 1980s. However, the SED chief Honecker, who in September, 1987, finally made a long-delayed official visit to Bonn that in its turn spawned a variety of cooperation agreements and strengthened East Germany's position as an independent state, actively began to resist reform. This was due to a growing awareness on his part that reforms would open the door for reunification by changing the perception of the socialist state as an alternative to capitalist West Germany and undermining the highly centralized economic system. The economy would no longer be the recipient of massive subsidies to enhance the SED's communistic policies. East Germany was experiencing growing debt pressures from the West and failed to undertake necessary investment in industrial upgrading and infrastructure. Meanwhile, high spending on internal and external security were maintained. The economic situation merely deteriorated further. By the time of unification, income per-capita in East Germany was two-thirds of West Germany's average. The value of their economy was after all, "only" five to six times larger than the East German economy.[15]

---

14 Kim, ibid., 1996, pp. 43-4, 45, 48-9, 83; Kim, "Togil, Pet'ŭnam, Yemen t'ongil sarye", in T'ongil yôn'guwôn, *Pundanguk t'onghap-gwa p'yônghwa hyôpchông* (Seoul: T'ongil yôn'guwôn, 2001), p. 5; Larres, in Larres, ibid., p. 37; Marsh, ibid., pp. 25, 39; McAdams, ibid., pp. 155-56, 161-62, 165; Pond, ibid., p. 292: fn. 9; Rhee, ibid., p. 366.

15 Statistics from *Barclays Capital Asian Special Report,* "What Rating for a Unified Korea?", 13 July, 2000, pp. 2, 5. "Only" is quoted from p. 5. However, according to the South Korean scholar Sung Chul Yang, the West German GNP was about ten times larger than that of East Germany. From Yang, "The Lessons of United Germany for Divided Korea", in *Korea*

East Germans travelling to West Germany were facilitated in the 1980s by a number of measures, for instance, in 1984, by the extension of annual visits from 30 to 60 days while only one journey from the East was permitted for ordinary workers. Yet, by 1986, not only retired citizens but also an additional 573,000 East Germans under retirement age took advantage of a more liberal definition of "urgent family matters" and began travelling westwards. The number of working-age visitors to West Germany was 1.2 million by 1987 and 1.5 million by 1988. Combined together with an estimate of more than two million retirees who travelled regularly, they amounted to a total of no less than 3.5 million visits into West Germany in 1987, comprising between one-fifth and one-quarter of the total East German population.[16]

While the SED continued to reject reforms, there emerged by the late 1980s for the first time, rising popular demands for widespread reform. Such demands were both a result of the new Soviet foreign policy to allow countries of the Soviet bloc to pursue independent policies in addition to increased knowledge about West Germany with its democratic and economic strengths witnessed by a rising number of visitors to the West as well as the influence of West German TV. As many as 90 per cent of East Germans had by the late 1970s, regularly watched the news on West German TV. The economic situation differed diametrically from Honecker's description in 1986 to the Central Committee of the central economic planning system as being "efficient, dynamic and flexible".[17] The government's attempts to reassert its control by suppressing unauthorized protests and organizations by force and, even more remarkably, forbidding Soviet publications only enflamed the opposition. Following solidarity rallies for arrested and expelled activists, many were released and returned to opposition activism. There was even growing disgruntlement detected within the SED and the security agencies.

Public opinion regarded SED insistence on its accomplishments at the nation's 40th anniversary in October, as being nothing short of cynicism. Due to growing frustration, a rising number of discontented East German citizens decided to emigrate during the summer of 1989 via Hungary, which on 2 May had decided to open its borders with Austria; indeed the American Professor A. James McAdams (1993) wrote that: "The beginning of the end of the GDR should be dated May 2nd, 1989, although this fact was by no means self-evident at the time".[18] In September, the

---

and the World: Beyond the Cold War (ed. Young Whan Kihl, Boulder: Westview Press, 1994), pp. 263-64. It is unclear what explains the different ratios.

16 Hart-Landsberg, ibid., p. 60; Kim, ibid., 1996, pp. 43-4; Kim, ibid., 2001, p. 5; Larres, in Larres, ibid., pp. 37-9; Marsh, ibid., pp. 29, 36-9; McAdams, ibid., pp. 165-67, 173-74, 183; Pond, ibid., p. 82; Steininger, in Larres, ibid., p. 20. "Urgent family matters" is quoted from McAdams (ibid., p. 167). Kim (ibid., 1996, pp. 121, 122) records that the two German leaders had met at the funerals in 1984 and 1985 of Soviet leaders and in 1986 at the funeral of the Swedish prime-minister.

17 Quoted from Marsh, ibid., p. 39. In 1981, Honecker had boasted that, one day, socialism would "knock on the door" of West Germany (ibid., p. 98).

18 Quoted from McAdams, ibid., p. 193.

Hungarian government unilaterally renounced the standing travel agreement with East Germany which facilitated unhindered travel to the West.

Later, East Germans also began to flee via Czechoslovakia and Poland as well as via the West German Permanent Mission in East Berlin. By September of 1989, more than 70,000 people had escaped. The migration was witnessed in the East on West German TV and served to encourage the reform movement, ultimately splitting the governing SED.[19]

Migration was greatly facilitated by West Germany's refusal to submit to demands to recognize separate East German citizenship: the refugees were simply not treated as foreigners. The West German government reassured the Honecker government that it had no interest in depopulating East Germany. It now emphasized its wish to help the refugees. However, refugees continued to arrive, and quickly became less welcome among the West German public due to the economic costs involved in their welfare needs and through the perception that they undermined existing social stability.

In early October 1989, large demonstrations took place in several cities as the eyes of the world were fixed on East Germany's 40th jubilee on 7 October. The demonstrations drew encouragement from the Gorbachev speech commemorating the anniversary, in which he cautioned their leaders that "life punishes those who come too late". Initially, demonstrations were met with violence. But the demonstrations in Leipzig on 9 October, in which 70,000 people participated, were peaceful in spite of widespread fears of violence. No specific order to shoot had apparently been given: since East German troops were under Soviet military command they could not ignore their order of command and violently suppress demonstrations. Leipzig marked the beginning of the movement for peaceful mass demonstrations that demanded far-reaching political and economic reforms, including the right of free travel.

Since demonstrations became increasingly frequent and popular in terms of support, it quickly became impossible for the police to hinder them. While demonstrations and the exodus of people continued unabated, Honecker was forced to resign on 18 October.

The Honecker government had already been fatally weakened and now, indisposed as he was due to a gall bladder operation during August and September, he was replaced by his successor designate, Politburo member, Egon Krenz.[20]

---

19 Hart-Landsberg, ibid., pp. 60, 62; Kim, ibid., 1996, pp. 45-6; Larres, in Larres, ibid., pp. 38, 41-4, 46-7; Marsh, ibid., pp. 29, 39, 41, 188: fn. 38; McAdams, ibid., pp. 180, 182-3, 188, 193; Pak, ibid., p. 56; Pond, ibid., p. 101; Steininger, in Larres, ibid., pp. 20-21.

20 Hart-Landsberg, ibid., p. 61; Kim, ibid., 2001, p. 8; Larres, in Larres, ibid., pp. xvi, 47-50; Marsh, ibid., p. 35; McAdams, ibid., pp. 196-97, 200, 202-203; Pond, ibid., pp. 111-115; Steininger, in Larres, ibid., p. 22. The quotation is from Steininger (ibid., p. 22).

2.4 The Berlin Wall falls

West Germany reacted towards the growing and largely spontaneous East German civic movement by aiming to weaken both it as well as the SED, by changing the focus of popular concern from reform to unification: this would enable Chancellor Helmut Kohl's government to bring an end to socialist rule in East Germany. Kohl, who throughout his political carrier had believed in "national unity", but for many years preferred not speak about German reunification, did so for the first time in early September and repeated himself again in November.[21] Then, Kohl praised the courage shown by East German demonstrators and called for "free self-determination of all Germans" in an attempt to encourage the East German people to seek relief through unification. The most decisive event for East Germany ceasing to be an independent state was seen when the Berlin Wall was opened on the next day, 9 November, by a mistake: the public thought that the new travel laws announced meant that they could cross the border without delay, when in actual fact the intention had been to make exit visas available to all who wanted them.[22] The SED, which would never recover from the East German people's seizure of power, had been unable to stop the mass migration. It was forced into granting the right of free travel to the West in an effort to cling to power. More than five million people crossed through the wall during the following four days and socialized with each other.[23] Clearly, there had been a strong pent-up demand for Germans to meet each other across the border.

Kohl's policies and the granting of free travel did not automatically speed up the process towards unification. On the contrary, both the East German government and the civic movement remained opposed to unity. However, by mid-November the first demands for reunification were raised in street demonstrations since domestic conditions deteriorated and the SED failed to meet the growing popular demands for reform. The demonstrations ensured that the people's revolution did not lose its momentum.

The SED began losing most of its members as did the trade union, the Free German Youth. The parliament became for the first time a forum for debate; Honecker even gave up his seat and was arrested for corruption and abuse of power.

Unprecedentedly, Erich Mielke, minister for state security in charge of the Stasi during the previous 32 years, was questioned in parliament. Most of the old

---

21 Paradoxically, according to the former American journalist Elizabeth Pond, Kohl had over the years promoted striving for one Germany as a "life-long delusion" more doggedly than any other politician (ibid., p. 5).

22 McAdams (ibid., p. 3) records that Honecker on 20 January, 1989 had said: "The Wall will remain as long as the reasons for its presence have not been eliminated. It will still be there in 50 and even 100 years". Kohl expressed in October 1988 that he would not live to see the wall fall but said in December 1990 that he meant he would not live to see it as chancellor (Marsh, ibid., pp. 26, 185: fn. 11, 12).

23 Hart-Landsberg, ibid., pp. 60-62; Larres, in Larres, ibid., pp. 50-52; Marsh, ibid., p. 26; McAdams, ibid., pp. 3, 198-99. "Free self-determination of all Germans" is quoted from Hart-Landsberg (ibid., p. 62) and "national unity" from Marsh (ibid., p. 26).

Politburo members were investigated by prosecutors. In November, censorship was abolished and the parliament began probing past corruption and misuse of office. The Parliament voted on 1 December to strike from the constitution Article 1 guaranteeing the leading role of "the working class and the Marxist-Leninist party". While previously claiming "we are the people" demonstrators began to shout "we are one people" but the new Prime Minister Hans Modrow, who took over from Krenz in November, could not respond to these appeals for reunification.

The public in both German states generally supported unity, however, the East Germans were much more enthusiastic than the West Germans. There was, however, widespread scepticism towards unity in both states. In West Germany, a few intellectuals opposed unification and the Social Democrats warned of the consequences of hasty unification. On 28 November Kohl, who, after the unexpected opening of the Berlin Wall had urged the East German government to immediately implement reforms to prevent further emigration, presented a "Ten-Point Plan for German Unity" to stabilize the situation.[24]

According to Kohl's plan, West Germany would provide East Germany with economic aid, but only after the East committed itself to free elections and a market economy. The civic movement such as the New Forum took part in Round Table talks with the government and the political parties in December to find an alternative to unification with the West and retain some structural form of East German socialism. Since they failed, the economic crisis became more aggravated. This speeded up the process towards unification, which in time became a question more of "when" than "if". One reason for the economic difficulties was that two-thirds of the almost 350,000 East Germans who were allowed to leave during 1989 were skilled workers. Comparing this figure with the 616,000 East Germans crossing westwards between 1961 and 1988, among them approximately 30,000 had emigrated during 1988; the economy was clearly in a profound crisis.[25] Another 192,000 East Germans escaped in the first half of 1990, but the increased prospects for reunification eventually stemmed the stream of people across the frontier.

In February 1990, a new government which included the opposition was formed in East Germany. It proposed political and economic reforms and demanded financial assistance from West Germany. But the Kohl government refused to give any aid to the East until after the March elections. It also planned for a German currency union that would require the East German government to agree to a market-based economic transformation supported by the introduction of the West

---

24 Hart-Landsberg, ibid., p. 62; Larres, in Larres, ibid., pp. 52, 53-4; McAdams, ibid., pp. 199-200, 202, 203; Pond, ibid., pp. 8-11; Steininger, in Larres, ibid., pp. 22, 23-4. The quotations are from Pond (ibid., p. 11) and Steininger (ibid., p. 22).

25 Of would-be escapees, more than 200 people were killed between 1961 and 1989. Young people fleeing East Germany in the 1980s could calculate that if they did not get shot while trying to escape they would have to serve some four years in jail before being bought free by West Germany. At their height, the number of landmines in border regions totalled over 700,000. From Pond (ibid., pp. 78, 79). Kim (ibid., 1996, p. 121) writes that the mines had been removed as of 1 November, 1985.

German currency. Not surprisingly, the Round Table rejected the Kohl proposals and demanded economic aid from the West to support economic reforms. It also demanded a gradual unification and additionally that the final treaty should include a social charter to protect the rights of East Germans, but the Kohl government rejected these proposals and reaffirmed its previous position not to provide aid prior to the elections.[26]

West German parties (except for the Greens) sought to control the 18 March election process in East Germany through supporting their sister parties. The elections had been planned for the following May but largely due to the East German people's ferment, they were held earlier. Kohl promised East Germans that by voting for the Christian Democratic Union (CDU) and its allies, which supported unification under the terms of Article 23 of the West German Basic Law which permitted states or regions to rejoin West Germany, they would be guaranteed "instant prosperity". The CDU and its allies won the East's first free elections, heralding the fall of the East German communist regime. The CDU and its allies received roughly 48 per cent of the vote. Party leader Lothar de Maizière became the new prime minister. 22 per cent of voters voted for the Social Democrats, while the revamped communists of the Party of Democratic Socialism received merely 16 per cent. The "Alliance 90" comprising the civic movements against unification received only 2.9 per cent support.

The new government accepted the West German proposal, introducing a currency union to meet the growing chaos and emigration from East Germany which had raised considerable fears in the West. The currency union went into effect on 1 July. In the words of Marsh, (1994), it was "...a decisive step along the road to full-scale unification".[27] This is hardly a surprising view since, in addition to introducing the DM to East Germany, the East now accepted the economic takeover by West Germany, agreeing to abolish socialism, introducing private enterprise and accepting the West German political and legal order. Consequently, large demonstrations took place in Berlin against the union.

According to the currency conversion agreement, current payments such as wages were to be converted at one OM to one DM. The official exchange rate pre-agreement was 4.4 OM to one DM. Consequently, better West German products became cheaper in East Germany. Unemployment rose, which encouraged emigration to the West. Since the average exchange rate used for translating savings accounts was approximately one DM to 1.8 OM, almost half the value of personal savings disappeared. The abolition of state subsidies for basic goods and services made them far more expensive.[28]

---

26 Hart-Landsberg, ibid., pp. 62-3; Larres, in Larres, ibid., pp. 54-5; Marsh, ibid., p. 38; Steininger, in Larres, ibid., pp. 22, 23-4.

27 Marsh, ibid., p. 53. McAdams (ibid., p. 215) calls the union an "economic reunification".

28 Hart-Landsberg, ibid., pp. 63, 64-5, 66; Larres, in Larres, ibid., p. 55; Pond, ibid., p. 199; Steininger, in Larres, ibid., pp. 24-5. "Instant prosperity" is quoted from Hart-Landsberg

Another reason why prices rose was that the East's productive capacity plummeted. East Germans also had to pay new income taxes as well as insurance and retirement contributions. Since both prices and social payments went up, real disposable income fell. Privatization of state firms aggravated the economic situation. Firms' liquid assets were converted at a rate of two OM to one DM and debts were converted on a one-to-one rate resulting in a financial squeeze causing many bankruptcies. West German firms could purchase the best East German firms at attractive prices. Those that were not sold were shut down. The acceleration of the economic decline that resulted from the currency union greatly reduced government revenues while rising unemployment created growing demands for assistance.[29]

When Chancellor Kohl and Prime Minister de Maizière met a few days later after the currency union had been enforced, to negotiate the terms of unification, the latter asked for a "unification treaty". In other words, the states would jointly decide on new constitutional goals and an economic system for a reunified Germany. The West German negotiator responded by saying:

> This is the accession of the GDR to the FRG and not the reverse. We have a good Basic Law that is proven. We want to do everything for you. You are cordially welcome. We do not want to trample coldly on your wishes and interests. But this is not the unification of two equal states.[30]

On a national level, one step towards unification during the very end of partition was to eliminate border checks. Another one was to decide that the new German armed forces would draw 320,000 troops from West Germany and only 50,000 troops from East Germany.[31] Integration took nine months. Bonn and East Berlin signed the Unification Treaty (over 1,000 pages in length) on 31 August. The treaty stipulated that East Germany would accede to West Germany in accordance with Article 23 of the West German Basic Law on 3 October and that unified Germany would be known as the Federal Republic of Germany with Berlin as its capital.[32]

Meanwhile, a favourable external environment for German reunification had been established, not least since the end of the Cold War was announced at the US-Soviet summit held at Malta in December 1989. During Gorbachev's rule the Soviet Union worked harmoniously together with the United States, the United Kingdom and

---

(ibid., p. 63).

29 According to Marsh (ibid., p. 69), economist Holger Schmieding described the effect of the monetary union on East Germany as "probably the gravest economic crisis ever to befall an advanced industrial economy in peace-time".

30 Quoted from Hart-Landsberg, ibid., p. 64. The author has been unable to find any other official statement showing that unification was achieved through West Germany dictating the terms.

31 According to Kim (ibid., 2001, p. 8), the East German army was rather dissolved than integrated into the new German army.

32 Hart-Landsberg, ibid., pp. 64, 65-6; Hwang, "Korean Reunification in a Comparative Perspective", in Kihl, ibid., p. 287; Pond, ibid., pp. 219, 223, 227.

France in the negotiations leading to unification. The United States was the strongest advocate of German unity because of common security interests within Europe. As a huge distant country, the US had nothing to fear from German unification. However, in particular Britain but also France attempted to hold unification up as a concern that Germany would become a stronger actor in European politics at their expense. Contributing to this view was Britain's envy of Germany's post-war recovery and France's experience of three German invasions since 1870. Also the Soviet Union had, prior to 1990, expressed fears that unification could threaten stability across Europe, but no well-coordinated strategy was pursued by Moscow, London and Paris.

As a consequence of the Allies governing Germany for ten years, the legitimate right to decide the future of the two Germanys, lay outside of Germany. The two German states accepted the legality of the Allies' right to participate and sought their cooperation in international negotiations. The two-plus-four talks involving the Allies and the two Germanys were constructed within the umbrella of Gorbachev's "common house of Europe".

Soviet cooperation in the unification process was important, since as the German scholar Manfred Pohl (1998) points out, East Germany was never really a sovereign state because the Soviet Union had had the final say on political decisions. But at this time it decided not to interfere in the unification process. The change in Soviet policy is to a large extent explained by the loss in power due to its vain struggle to match the United States' arms spending under President Ronald Reagan. Economically, East Germany had become a liability for the Soviet Union. In addition, the ties that West Germany had established with other communist countries, especially the Soviet Union, reduced Warsaw Pact opposition to unification through absorption.[33]

In this new political atmosphere, the Soviet Union as well as the United States, supported full German membership of the North Atlantic Treaty Organization (NATO). At a conference of NATO and Warsaw Pact states held in Ottawa in February 1990, full international acceptance of German unification was reached: the Germans themselves would determine the "internal aspects" of unification without outside interference. It was also specified that Germany should have full sovereignty at the moment of unification.

Internationally, guarantees for full German sovereignty from the Soviet Union, the United States, France and the United Kingdom were agreed upon in September. An agreement was reached on the withdrawal of Soviet troops from East Germany by late 1994. Unification took place on 3 October, 1990. Remarkably, no blood had been shed on the way. Considering that only 7 per cent of West Germans had believed in an opinion poll in December 1986, as opposed to 23 per cent in September 1989

---

33 Hart-Landsberg, ibid., p. 68; Larres, in Larres, ibid., pp. 39, 40, 52-3; Marsh, ibid., p. 42-52; Pohl, ibid., p. 9; Pond, ibid., p. 161; Rhee, ibid., pp. 361-62; Steininger, in Larres, ibid., pp. 22-3, 25. "The common house of Europe" is quoted from Rhee (ibid., p. 361).

and 51 per cent in December 1989, that they would ever live to see reunification, the process took place at a remarkable speed.[34]

2.5 Causes of German unification

The above term "absorption" describes well the process towards German unification in 1989-90. On the other hand, Pohl (1998) writes that: "Unification in Germany has certainly not been a planned and orchestrated process, but a historic development which from the beginning was marked by a dynamism on its own...".

In contrast, the German economist Martin Hart-Landsberg (1995) summarizes his analysis by writing that: "...the collapse of the GDR was, to a considerable extent, triggered by deliberate West German state policy" and that "...the West German state pursued unification through absorption because it wanted to ensure, if not actually strengthen, the economic and political hegemony of existing West German institutions in a new united Germany".

The above account supports his analysis but he later modifies it:

> The West was able to absorb the East only because of the prior collapse of the GDR. A viable East German government would not have accepted its own total destruction. It would have demanded, as part of a gradual process of unification, the creation of new German institutions. That is precisely what the West German elite did not want and that is why the West German government repeatedly refused to offer the economic support necessary to stabilize the GDR.

This opinion of the East's collapse concurs with Pohl (1998) writing that East Germany "was already bankrupt long before the actual collapse in 1989/90", a view which also is supported by the above account. Partly in line with Hart-Landsberg's modified opinion but without mentioning the impact of his own policies, Kohl said in an interview with the above Marsh in March 1990: "For a long period, East Germany appeared a monolith. But it was a house of cards, and it simply fell down".

Contributing to the demise was also East Germany's vulnerability to changes in existing geopolitical conditions. These were in 1989 expressed by the German and South Korean Professors Helmut Wagner and Myoung-Kyu Kang as follows:

> It is a curious state indeed that exists in the GDR: the political system is backed by the Red Army, the economy is financed by the Federal Republic, and the Wall only hinders the escape of more than 1.5 million people, mostly young people, from the GDR on the spot. What a handicapped pseudo-nation!

---

34 Marsh, ibid., pp. 185: fn. 7; Pond, ibid., pp. 180-81, 217, 224; Steininger, in Larres, ibid., p. 25.

In addition, the above Kim Kook Sin (2001) expresses the opinion that the main reason for smooth political unity with West Germany was based on East Germany's heavy reliance on the Soviet Union restricting its autonomy.[35]

Also popular demands greatly affected unification. Rhee's (1993) opinion differs from that of Hart-Landsberg: "...the driving force that brought about reunification was the East Germans' desire to live like the people in West Germany". The contribution of influences from preceding developments in Poland, Hungary and the Soviet Union is clear from the German scholar Klaus Larres (1998): "Despite all internal difficulties and dissatisfaction, it is doubtful whether there ever would have been a revolution in the GDR without the external stimuli". On the impact of popular demand, he writes: "Pressure by the East German people was also the main reason why the domestic process and the two-plus-four negotiations between the two German states and the four World War II allies for political unification were completed much more speedily than initially thought feasible".

Marsh (1994) expresses a view similar to that of Rhee: "Unification was fervently desired by the broad mass of the East German people, and when it came, they rejoiced". The views of Marsh and Rhee are similar to what the South Korean political scientist Hwang In Kwan (1994) describes as unification taking place "from below" through democratic processes: popular demonstrations followed by general elections. He notes that the 1972 Basic Treaty, the March 1990 elections in East Germany, the currency union and the Unification Treaty were "substantial preparatory agreements for unification". In addition, Marsh (1994) writes that in West Germany "There was a national consensus in favour of unification". His writing "Reflecting the bonds of history and culture, and the millions of shared re-collections and family ties, many West Germans felt a vague sense of responsibility for their compatriots" implies that there were socio-cultural factors besides knowledge contributing to unification.[36]

These statements clearly show that unequal power relations, geopolitical changes and popular demands for unification enabled German unity. Nonetheless, "absorption" does not give full justice to the process towards unification since pre-1989 developments facilitated it. Consequently, it would be more correct to speak of unification as a gradual process that was finally accomplished through absorption.

---

35 Hart-Landsberg, ibid., pp. 67-8, 72-3; Kim, ibid., 2001, p. 8; Marsh, ibid., pp. 25, 185: fn. 8; Pohl, ibid., pp. 7, 9; Wagner and Kang, ibid., p. 22. Hart-Landsberg (ibid., pp. 66-7) records that all East German universities were forced to close their departments of Marxism-Leninism, to restructure their departments of History, Law, Economics, Philosophy and Education and to fire all staff in these departments as additional examples of West Germany dictating the terms of unification.

36 Hwang, ibid., pp. 291-2; Larres, in Larres, ibid., pp. 33, 35; Marsh, ibid., pp. 5, 27, 53; Rhee, ibid., p. 366.

2.6 Consequences of German unification

After German unification, its economic consequences have been widely discussed. According to Hart-Landsberg (1995), Chancellor Kohl had not only promised that unification would be easily financed through economic growth, and also that East Germans would enjoy "instant prosperity", although there was, as mentioned above, widespread scepticism in both states. Marsh (1994) records that Kohl in May 1990 had said: "In truth everyone will profit from the future economic dynamics of East Germany... When could the Germans ever hope better to master the economic problems of unity than now, when everyone can see the German economy is in such outstanding form?". Marsh also writes that Kohl pledged in a similar fashion that: "...no one will have to give up anything for German unity...".

Kohl's statements imply, to say the least, an overestimation of the West German economy and an underestimation of the East German. In fact, the GDR economy had, in spite of its weaknesses, as late as 1988, been described by the *Encyclopaedia Britannica* as "the most developed and prosperous of the Communist countries of eastern Europe and one of the major industrial nations of the world".

A more realistic opinion than that of Kohl is recorded by Marsh (1994) writing: "On German Unity Day, on 3 October 1990, the pessimists declared it would take a generation to integrate the two parts of the nation". In 1998, the British scholar Christopher Flockton wrote that: "It will not take three to four years for the east to catch up, as was optimistically claimed in 1990, but fifteen or twenty years".[37]

In fact, German unification has turned out to be costly not only as a result of the backwardness of the East German economy but also because of the West German strategy to achieve unification through absorption. The promises that the economic benefits would become apparent relatively quickly proved irredeemable: while the West German economy grew by 7 per cent following unification, the East German economy plunged by 50 per cent from 1989 to 1991 before growing by 9.7 per cent in 1992 and 6.5 per cent in 1993. On top of this, rapid wage rises following unification undermined eastern firms' competitiveness further.

Previously stable export markets disintegrated due to the collapse of the COMECON trading system that had linked the Eastern European communist countries; 70 per cent of East Germany's exports had gone to these regions before unity. As of 1993, 70 per cent of the East's industrial capacity had been shut down and 3.5 million people had become unemployed. However, while industries facing world competition with obsolescent technology or a high-cost labour force suffered severely, sheltered branches and those supplying the large infrastructural projects such as the construction industry prospered. Workers' productivity as measured in GDP per worker was in 1993 about 40 per cent of the West causing, along with an appreciating currency, unit labour costs that were roughly 75 per cent higher.

---

37 Flockton, "The German Economy since 1989/90: Problems and Prospects", in Larres ibid., p. 64; Hart-Landsberg, ibid., p. 66; Marsh, ibid., pp. 31, 52-3, 59, 193: fn. 2; Pond, ibid., p. 20. *Encyclopaedia Britannica*'s opinion is quoted in Pond (ibid, p. 20).

Also social conditions deteriorated: the birth rate per 1,000 people in East Germany fell by 60 per cent between 1989 and 1993. In the beginning of 1991, reportedly nine out of every ten East Germans reportedly felt they had second-class status in the unified country that had 16 million inhabitants in the East, as against 63 million in the West.[38]

Due to the difficult economic situation, large-scale migration of highly skilled labourers westwards continued also after unification while very few West Germans moved eastwards. In the Kohl cabinet formed in 1991, after the first post-unity elections had been held in December 1990, only three out of nineteen ministers were from the former East Germany. All of them were appointed to relatively minor posts. But as an act of conciliation to the East German people Berlin was in 1991 chosen to be the seat of government.

Not surprisingly, although even most unemployed East Germans were better off in material terms than they had previously been when employed thanks to West German social security benefits, they have suffered the most from the consequences of the unification. According to a 1993 opinion poll, because of large-scale unemployment and dashed hopes of rapidly catching up with West German living standards, 57 per cent of East Germans wanted an improved form of communism. But West Germans have also paid a price. Although West Germany was established as Europe's leading economy, due to the fall in government revenues in the East in combination with rising costs for unemployment, problems quickly arose. The Eastern Recovery Program was launched by Kohl in 1991 at a time when the Bonn government paid some DM 200 billion ($ 100 billion) a year, to keep the eastern economy going. Such transfers comprised more than 50 per cent of the East's GDP. The program was financed by an income tax surcharge of 7.5 per cent on West Germans, whereas Kohl had previously rejected tax increases prior to unification not least since elections would be held in December 1990.[39]

Transfers of public sector funds from the West to the East approached DM 600 billion in the first four years of unity, of which 75 per cent was spent on supporting incomes and consumption. Much of the remainder was spent on improving infrastructure and on industrial investments, however, the East faced competition from much cheaper labour, for instance from Hungary to where Audi moved a DM 1 billion motor components project.

The transfers generated enormous spending power in the East that created demand for goods from the West; the West German GDP grew by 5.7 per cent in 1990 – the highest figure since 1969. By fall 1992, 9,000 out of 12,000 state-owned East German enterprises had been privatized through being sold to western companies.

---

38 Flockton, in Larres, ibid., p. 77; Hart-Landsberg, ibid., pp. 64, 66, 67, 79: fn. 8, 9; Marsh, ibid., pp. 4, 6, 65, 81-2, 87-8, 120, 198: fn. 86; Yang, in Kihl, ibid., pp. 267, 274: fn. 25. Yang cites a report on mental disunity recorded in *Newsweek*, 1 April, 1991 and *The Economist*, 23 February, 1991.

39 Hart-Landsberg, ibid., p. 66; Marsh, ibid., pp. 6, 30-31, 56-7, 61, 99-100; McAdams, ibid., pp. 220-222; Pond, ibid., p. 243; Rhee, ibid., p. 372.

However, as of 1998, yet unresolved property titles issues hampered privatization and new investment projects; the two states had agreed in the Unification Treaty that property nationalized by the East German government should be returned to the original owners.

Because of the huge costs of unification which, as of 1998, in aggregate terms based on the costs of labour market support, liquidity credits for Treuhand (privatization) firms, pensions and social security, regional assistance and infrastructure programmes; exceeded the costs foreseen in the 1990 unification treaty by more than three times, it was also financed by large-scale public borrowing abroad and at home. Borrowing abroad between 1990 and 1994 exceeded the total sum West Germany had borrowed during the years between 1949 and 1990. Domestic borrowing forced up interest rates and drove the economy into recession. The current account showed a deficit in 1994. Unemployment then passed the four million level, against two million in West Germany during 1989. Including people on short-time working and in government-run job-creation and training schemes, all of which were concentrated in eastern Germany, the true number of unemployed people in united Germany in 1993 was estimated at 5.8 million. As of 2004, unemployment was at 18 per cent, more than twice as high as in western Germany.[40]

Considering the problems caused by unification, it is hardly surprising that the Austrian scholar Rolf Steininger (1998) writes that Chancellor Kohl in 1991 admitted: "As far as inner unity goes, the economic and social challenges will admittedly take longer and cost more than most, including myself, had originally assumed". Kohl added: "What I hoped to achieve in three to five years will perhaps need twice that time". At the 15th anniversary of the fall of the Berlin Wall in 2004 he admitted: "Four decades of division have sat deeper marks and split the nation more than I had thought at that time".

Marsh wrote in 1994 that: "Unification has bruised the most powerful economy in Europe". He also records that there was great resentment in the East against West Germans' expectations that East Germans should feel gratitude towards the enormous financial transfers they received. Meanwhile, the unequal distribution of new wealth increased the potential for jealousy and ill will. Consequently, it is not surprising that an opinion poll conducted in May 1993 showed that only 22 per cent of Germans in the West and 11 per cent of those in the East expressed a spirit of national "togetherness" across the Elbe. 71 per cent of Germans in the West said they had "opposing interests". The figure for the East was 85 per cent. Frustration over the aftermath of unity remained in both parts of Germany.

In 1998, Steininger wrote: "More than a half decade after unification it is one state but still two societies". Since economic growth was higher in the West than in the East between 1997 and 2000, it is not surprising that Kim Kook Sin in 2001 wrote

---

40 Flockton, in Larres, ibid., pp. 64, 65, 70, 79; Hart-Landsberg, ibid., p. 66; Lundin, "Murens fall gav tysk baksmälla: 15 år efter att Berlinmuren öppnades önskar nästan en fjärdedel av västtyskarna att den stod kvar", *Svenska Dagbladet,* 9 November, 2004; Marsh, ibid., pp. 6, 63-6, 83, 99; Pond, ibid., p. 231; Rhee, ibid., p. 371.

that East Germans still had difficulties in adapting to capitalism, felt psychologically inferior to West Germans and regarded themselves as second-class citizens, although a year before, disposable net income had reached almost 90 per cent of the Western level. Such feelings can only have been reinforced by the fact that, in 1999, 95 per cent of industrial production in the East was produced by companies owned by West Germans. Hence, what German President Richard von Weisaecker called the "human union" remains to be achieved: the German scholar Werner Pfennig (2001) writes: "In contrast to earlier, more optimistic expectations, most people now agree that at least two generations will be needed to achieve true national unity in the sense of greater social integration". Since an opinion poll conducted in November 2004 showed that only 14 per cent of East Germans and 23 per cent of West Germans said that "we are one people" it is a realistic assessment.[41]

Considering the huge unification costs which, as of 2002, according to the then German Ambassador to South Korea, Mr. Hubertus von Morr, amounted to 600 billion euros, it is not surprising that Pohl in 1998 had concluded that the main lesson gained from the German unification for Korea is "...how not to do it...". He adds: "The patient West German approach to intensified relations with the GDR probably is the only lesson which could be learned by the South Korean leadership". In other words, a gradual approach towards unification is highly desirable.[42] It is hard to reject this view, but German reunification shows that political events may take place both unexpectedly and at surprising speed making preparations virtually impossible.

2.7 Divided Yemen

Like Germany, Yemen has historically been a divided nation. The British anthropologist Paul Dresch (2000) has commented upon the division by writing "Since the rise of Islam, if not well before, the idea of Yemen as a natural unit has been embedded in literature and local practice. Unified power has not".[43]

Consequently, it is not surprising that there long was a wish for a single Yemeni nation. This wish emerged in a context shaped by outside powers. In 1839, the British occupied Aden. The Ottomans established themselves along the Red Sea coast in

---

41 *Barclays Capital Asian Special Report*, ibid., p. 3; Kim, ibid., 2001, pp. 9, 10-11, 34-5; Lundin, ibid., 9 November, 2004; Marsh, ibid., pp. 6-7, 56, 67, 124-25, 183: fn. 5; Pfennig, "From Division through Normalization to Unification: A Comparative View on Developments in Germany and Korea", *Korea Observer* 32 (2001), no. 1, pp. 25, 31; Steininger, in Larres, ibid., pp, 27-9; Yang, in Kihl, ibid., p. 265. "Human union" is quoted from Yang, ibid., p. 265. "Togetherness" and "opposing interests" are quoted from Marsh (ibid., pp. 7, 183: fn. 5). Author's translation of Kohl's statement that was made in *Bild* on 8 November, 2004.

42 Morr, from a speech held at the international conference "Inter-Korean Relations and Peace Building on the Korean Peninsula", Seoul, 14 June, 2002; Pohl, ibid., pp. 7, 8, 11.

43 Dresch, *A History of Modern Yemen* (Cambridge: Cambridge University Press, 2000), p. 1.

1849. In 1872, the Ottomans occupied Sanaa. A border was established between North and South in 1905. When the Ottomans withdrew from the North in 1918-19, the country became independent. The 1962 Revolution ended the rule by the Imam (leader of the Muslim community) and established the Yemen Arab Republic, that is North Yemen.

In 1967, the British left Aden, which became the People's Republic of Yemen, that is South Yemen (in 1970 renamed the People's Democratic Republic of Yemen). South Yemen soon formed connections with the Eastern bloc, in particular the Soviet Union, but Northern Yemen did not cooperate with either East or West – military and economic aid was received from both the United States and the Soviet Union. As a consequence of the South Yemeni rulers introducing socialism, in combination with repressive measures against dissidents, perhaps a quarter of the population of less than two million fled to North Yemen, not least the merchant class.[44]

In the North, there were also large numbers of Southern refugees from tribal areas. Many refugees joined organizations that aimed to overthrow the Adeni Government and carried out raids across the border. On the other hand, few people moved south. While there were liberals in the North, some constituencies wished the Southern government destroyed. Although some prominent Northerners in Southern politics were strong proponents of Yemen's integration, it was hardly looming. On the contrary, North Yemen's foreign minister claimed in 1969 that "we are further from unity than we were a year ago".[45] If trade is an indicator of the prospects for Yemeni unity, they even diminished afterwards: the percentage of the North's exports going to the South declined from 52 per cent in 1969 to less than 7 per cent in 1973. The figures for imports fell from almost 30 per cent to 6 per cent.[46]

More important than trade in hindering Yemeni unity became the Northern government's assertion of its historical legitimacy. It argued that due to the superiority in terms of population and economic strength, South Yemen must immediately dissolve its government and become a part of the North. But also the South Yemeni government asserted its own legitimacy and argued that unification should be achieved by its superior advanced socialist system removing the North's feudal capitalist society and integrating it with the South by a communization of the North.

However, it was hard to form domestic consensus on how to achieve unity in both Yemens. The Northern tribes had different opinions on Yemeni unity, which made it impossible for the government to form a distinct policy. In South Yemen, people of Northern origin and hardliners advocated a rapid military unification. On

---

44 Dresch, ibid., pp. 1, 3, 120-123, 124, 217, 219, 220, 242: fn. 10; Europa Publications Limited, "Yemen: Introductory Survey", in *The Europa World Year Book, 2001* (London: Europa Publications Ltd., 2001), p. 4359; Hwang, in Kihl, ibid., pp. 280-281; Kostiner, *Yemen: The Tortuous Quest for Unity, 1990-94* (London: Royal Institute of International Affairs, 1996), p. 1.

45 Quoted from Dresch (ibid., p. 123).

46 Dresch, ibid., pp. 123; Europa Publications Ltd., ibid., p. 4359; Hwang, in Kihl, ibid., p. 281.

the other hand, pragmatists of Southern origin argued for removing the Northern government after a period of peaceful coexistence, during which the South would implement social reforms and achieve economic development. Their view was based on the South having only one-fourth of the North's population, which would make unification by military force difficult. There were also concerns that, after a rapid unification, South Yemen could be culturally absorbed by North Yemen.[47]

While both states argued for unification, exile groups from the South received support from the Sanaa government. Border incidents worsened until a war was fought between the two Yemens in October 1972. The exile groups tried to infiltrate South Yemen, whose armed forces retaliated by attacking bases in North Yemen. But the war, which neither Yemen could win, ended in the same month thanks to mediation by the Arab League. Nor did it stop efforts to achieve unity: the presidents met in Tripoli, in 26-28 November and declared their intention to unify Yemen within 18 months and to draw up a joint constitution within a year (the constitution had been discussed at the first summit held in Kuwait in March 1970). Furthermore, part of North Yemen's President Ibrahim al-Hamdi's message from 1974 onwards was for Yemeni unity. He encouraged work on joint problems.

In February 1977, he met with his Southern counterpart Salim Rubay Ali in the border regions. President Ali then visited Sanaa in August of the same year. But hostilities did not end: just two days before the scheduled return visit by President Hamdi to Aden in October to discuss unity, he was murdered by unknown assassins. In 1978, there was even more violence: in June, North Yemen's President Ahmad al-Ghashmi was blown up by a briefcase bomb carried in the suitcase of an emissary from South Yemen's President Ali, who was executed two days later by opponents within the ruling party. In spite of these setbacks, the new South Yemeni Constitution established in 1978 stated in the preamble "the aim of a united Yemen under the Yemeni Socialist Party (YSP)".[48]

It was also considered that "A united Yemen would be economically viable in a way that the South on its own is not".[49] This view implies a recognition by the leaders that South Yemen was less developed than North Yemen, probably at least

---

47 Kim, *Yemen t'onghap sarye yôn'gu* (Seoul: Minjok t'ongil yôn'guwôn, 1993), pp. 64-7.

48 Dresch, ibid., pp. 124, 130, 147, 149, 221; Europa Publications Limited, ibid., p. 4359; Hwang, in Kihl, ibid., pp. 281-82; Kim, "Yemen t'ongil pangsig-i Hanbando t'ongir-e chunûn sisajôm", in Minjok t'ongil yôn'guwôn, *Yemen t'ongir-ûi munjejôm* (Seoul: Minjok t'ongil yôn'guwôn, 1994), pp. 18-19; Kostiner, ibid., p. 14. The quotation is from Dresch (ibid., p. 149).

49 Quotations from Dresch (ibid., p. 149). Dresch writes on p. 186 that the North in the early 1970s was, in spite of the frequent bankruptcy of the government and the high infant mortality, not a poor nation in most ways and gives sufficient food supply as an example. The South, which was far poorer, subsidized basic foodstuff. This indicates that people may have been better off than one would expect. Perhaps an indication of North Yemen being better off economically than South Yemen in the late 1970s is that the remittances sent home by about one million workers abroad accounted for 40 per cent of the North's GNP. On the contrary,

partly due to the large-scale migration of merchants to North Yemen referred to above (a migration that seems comparable to that of skilled labour from East to West Germany).

In October 1978, a contingent of northern tribesmen supporting the South appeared in Aden. Since North Yemen responded by renewing support for exile groups, clashes erupted again and a second Yemeni war broke out in February 1979. The Southerners invaded the North and took a number of towns beyond the border, but the dispute was brought to an end already in March, by the Arab League.[50] As in 1972, the two presidents – Ali Abdullah Salih in the North and Abd al-Fattah Ismail in the South – met, this time in 28-30 March in Kuwait where they promised to work towards unity. They also decided to draft a constitution within four months. At this time broadcasting began in the North's TV of "Pictures of my Country" portraying a united Yemen and its culture as a sign to many Yemenis that the nation was one, although ruled by two governments. There were also many family ties between the two states, which showed a high level of social and economic homogeneity. Contacts among neighbouring tribes along the border went on pretty easily and some trade was conducted. North and South Yemenis were constantly meeting abroad since both states exported labour (cf. fn. 49).[51] These informal meetings appear to have been the most important socio-cultural contact between the two Yemens.

Nonetheless, tensions remained while steps were taken to improve relations during the 1980s. Peaceful coexistence now became the basis of both states' unification policies. President Ali Nasir Muhammad of South Yemen and Ali Abdullah Salih of North Yemen agreed in September 1981 to refrain from using their respective territories as a base for military actions against each other. At the one-day Aden summit in December 1981, concrete measures to implement unification were announced. A Yemen Council led by the two presidents to oversee the unification process would be formed. The Council would also appoint a Joint Ministerial Committee consisting of the prime ministers, other key ministers as well as the armed forces' chiefs of staff. It was agreed that the council would meet at least once every three months. A secretariat to handle administrative functions of the council and the committee was formed. Important goals set up included the coordination and integration of economic and social development as well as the formulation of a common foreign policy. The leaders promised to facilitate citizens' movements over the border, to integrate school curricula and to promote media cooperation.

---

the estimated share of remittances sent back by 85,000 workers abroad of the South's GNP at the same time was around 70 per cent. Figures from Kim (ibid., 1994, pp. 10, 12-13).

50 No figures of casualties are recorded in the literature for this war either suggesting that they probably were negligible also this time.

51 Dresch, ibid., pp. 149-150, 153, 221: e-mail, 28 February, 2005; Europa Publications Limited, ibid., p. 4359; Hwang, in Kihl, ibid., p. 282; Kim, ibid., 1994, pp. 18, 20; Kostiner, ibid., pp. 14-15. Data differ on when in 1979 war began; Europa Publications Limited (ibid., p. 4359) writes February and March and Hwang (ibid., p. 282) as well as Kim (ibid., p. 20) February but only Dresch (ibid., p. 149) January. Kostiner writes (ibid., p. 14) that clashes erupted again between June 1978 and March 1979.

In January 1982, a 136-article draft constitution for the proposed unified Yemen that had been signed in December, was approved by a joint constitutional committee. The constitution was to be approved by both parliaments and then become the subject of a referendum. Although these targets were not accomplished, talks were until December 1985, held through the Yemen Council, the Joint Ministerial Committee and the secretariat on 19 occasions. Consequently, mutual confidence was created and the states experienced their longest period ever of peaceful coexistence.[52]

A new summit on unification was held in Tripoli in July 1986. In 1987, meetings were held to discuss repatriation of refugees from North to South Yemen after the South's January 1986 civil war. Most refugees had reportedly been repatriated as of July 1987. Following meetings by top officials in early 1988, the two states had by May the same year, agreed to withdraw all military forces from the border area and to establish a demilitarized zone at an area along the border to facilitate oil exploration. They also decided to set a timetable for a draft of the unity constitution and to form a "joint committee for a unified political organization".

Customs dues were in 1983 removed from trade. The economies converged, largely due to the priorities of foreign donors. After the two Yemens had failed to act on an agreement concluded in 1985 to develop oil and gas fields, a common agreement on oil and gas exploration was signed at the summit held in Sanaa 3-4 May, 1988. This led to the joint establishment in January 1989 of the Yemen Company for Investment in Mineral and Oil Resources (YCIMOR). In May 1988, the 1985 agreement on the border area was revived. A joint development company to handle oil matters in a shared zone was set up, a scheme to link the two electricity grids was taken up (accomplished in mid-1997) and it was agreed to facilitate Yemeni citizens' crossborder movement by establishing new border crossing points and demanding only identification cards to cross the border. However, even previously informal exchanges had taken place along the border, which contributed to preventing antagonistic life styles and new ways of thinking to develop. Finally, in June 1989, direct telephone links were established.[53]

Nevertheless, Dresch's writing (2000) that "North and South Yemeni governments alike spent enormous amounts on the police and military" is an indication that mutual suspicion still remained: as late as March 1988 troops massed on each side of the border. This was during a period of renewed tension as a result of the defeat of President Ali Nasir Muhammad in the South's 1986 civil war and his subsequent exile and 40,000 of his followers to North Yemen. There were also North Yemeni tribes opposing closer relations with South Yemen, while the South's President Ali had to consider the opinions of the hard-line pro-Soviet factions in his policies

---

52 Dresch, ibid., p. 152; Europa Publications Limited, ibid., p. 4359; Hwang, in Kihl, ibid., p. 282; Kim, ibid., 1993, p. 79: 1994, p. 20; Kostiner, ibid., p. 15.

53 Dresch, ibid., pp. 157, 161, 181, 221; Europa Publications Limited, ibid., pp. 4360, 4365; Hwang, in Kihl, ibid., pp. 282-83; Kim, ibid., 1993, p. 86: ibid., 1994, p. 21; Kostiner, ibid., pp. 8-9, 12, 15-16. "Joint committee for a unified political organization" is quoted from Kostiner (ibid., p. 15).

towards the North. Meanwhile, a North Yemeni official had declared in October 1987 the so far commonly held opinion: "Except by some historic [or historical] accident, unity will only come about over a long period of time".[54]

2.8 Yemeni unification

That historical accident came about as early as in 1989, following major shifts in both Arab and World politics. For South Yemen, the dissolution of the Soviet empire caused the withdrawal of Soviet patronage, including an exodus of military personnel and advisers as well as economic and technological advisers, which created an impetus for domestic reform to rectify past policies. Such policies had led to poor economic development. Soviet aid averaged $ 133m 1986-1988 but it fell to just $ 50m in 1989. The Soviet Union also announced that there was no need for its base in Aden after the end of the Cold War.

To enhance economic development, one target was to develop the YCIMOR. South Yemen also aimed to join the Arab Cooperation Council founded in February 1989 by North Yemen, Egypt, Jordan and Iraq.[55] But the ultimate target was unity with North Yemen. Just as in East Germany, the South Yemeni leadership began to revise its policies: private and foreign investment was encouraged, government monopolies ended, the YSP ended its monopoly of political life and several political parties were recognized. The leaders realized that unity with North Yemen might be a substitute for the removed links with the Soviet bloc, enhance South Yemen's position in the Arab world, legitimize the ruling class that had grasped power in the 1986 civil war and who still lacked wide-spread popular support contributing to a cessation of inter-Yemeni strife.

In addition, remittances from expatriates in the Gulf states fell by half during the second half of the 1980s, aggravating an already weak economy dependent on aid from the Soviet Union, encouraging the quest for unity.[56] The new post-Cold War era also made the North Yemeni leaders realize that there would be significant advantages in unification, particularly in economic terms: oil-fields containing

---

54 The quotations are from Dresch (ibid., pp. 157, 181). No figures are recorded of military spending on p. 157. The latter statement seems to be consistent with Kostiner's writing (ibid., p. 17) that ideas had evolved in North Yemen advocating gradual unification allowing the two states to become acquainted before taking the final unifying steps and proposing a federal government leaving considerable power to the existing ones.

55 Dresch, ibid., pp. 151, 181-82, 221; Hwang, in Kihl, ibid., pp. 280, 283-84; Kim, ibid., 1994, pp. 20, 22; Kostiner, ibid., pp. 5-9, 12-13, 15; Lawless, "Yemen: History", in Europa Publications, *The Middle East and North Africa 2005* (London: Europa Publications, 2004), p. 1243.

56 Dresch (ibid., p. 134) records that both North and South Yemen depended heavily on aid and loans during the 1970s. No data on the 1980s are recorded but considering his writing on p. 198 that the Yemen Republic in 1990 inherited a debt that was approximately twice the whole country's GNP, also the North was clearly dependent on foreign capital at this time.

reserves with a total estimated value of $ 9.5 billion would be unified and exports augmented via the South Yemeni pipeline to the Indian Ocean. It was also expected that new business opportunities would be created and that an enlarged and peaceful Yemen with potential oil wealth would attract aid from other Gulf states.

Like South Yemen, North Yemen was a poor nation and was undergoing the difficult process of recovering from many years of internal unrest. Yet, the country developed more than South Yemen did prior to unification, thanks to the inflow of modest oil income from 1989-1990 (exports began in 1987), official economic and military aid and workers' remittances.[57] The North's annual average economic growth rate was, thanks to oil-production, 6 per cent during the 1980s. GNP per-capita was in 1988 around $650. On the other hand, the South's economy contracted annually by 3.2 per cent during the years 1980-1988. GNP per-capita was $420 in 1987. By 1987, the South Yemeni GNP rose to $1 billion, while North Yemen's in 1988 was $6.45 billion. Economic decline in South Yemen was particularly severe in 1986 with around 10 per cent caused by the the civil war. Other reasons for the decline were that economic aid from the Arab states stagnated due to falling oil prices as well as a great fall in remittances from workers abroad.[58]

Since North Yemen developed more than South Yemen and had a larger population, it would potentially be possible for the North to dominate a unified Yemen. Meanwhile, North Yemen feared being absorbed into the region's single Marxist state at that time. Nonetheless, from the North's point of view unification with a South Yemen that had relinquished socialism and subversion towards its neighbours would once and for all eliminate the threat from the South to the North. Political reforms aimed to create social tolerance in the South suited the views of the North's leaders.

Unification was also seen as a way to enhance President Salih's position as leader of a large, strategically located country with potential oil wealth and support from major Arab states. In addition, joint Yemeni cooperation in oil exploration, unrestricted passage by Yemeni citizens into each other's territory and a sympathetic attitude towards unity by the Arab states, including Saudi Arabia, as well as the United States, facilitated unification. Actually, Saudi Arabia was the only country which had feared Yemeni unity anticipating that it would make the country stronger. However, the Yemeni leaders projected an image of a peaceful and development-orientated future state. Consequently, Saudi Arabia signalled its support for unity in 1989-90 and communicated this view to President Salih in 1989.[59]

---

57 However, Kim (ibid., 1993, p. 80) records that the pro-Soviet hard-line faction in South Yemen believed that the South was superior both politically and economically to the North during the late 1970s and early 1980s, as well as stronger militarily, but that the economy declined during the rule of Ali Nasir Muhammad. This made it inferior to North Yemen.

58 Kim, ibid., 1994, pp. 11, 13-14, 16, 21-2; Kostiner, ibid., pp. 6-10, 11-12; Lawless, ibid., p. 1243.

59 Hudson, "Bipolarity, Rational Calculation and War in Yemen", in *The Yemeni War of 1994: Causes and Consequences* (ed. Jamal S. al-Suwaidi, London: Saqi Books, 1995), p. 24; Hwang, in Kihl, ibid., pp. 282, 283; Kim, ibid., 1994, p. 22; Kostiner, ibid., pp. 11-13.

With this largely favourable background, in November 1989 the North's President Ali Abdullah Salih and the South's Ali Salam al-Bid signed an agreement to unify Yemen on the basis of recognizing each others' vested interests during a two-day summit in Aden. They announced that the draft unity agreement of 1981 would be the subject of a nation-wide referendum in November 1990. But due to Islamicists' rioting the whole process was moved forward by six months.[60] Although essentially due to the turbulent relationship there would be no institutional merging of the two states, there was little in the way of progress towards unity while the South's rulers faced the prospect of losing power entirely.

Both Yemeni leaders aimed to establish what the Israeli Professor Joseph Kostiner (1996) calls "a strong, economically sound and peaceful unified country", which partly resembles the above considerations of the new South Yemen constitution from 1978.[61] After a six-month period of preparations for unity, during which the states in April agreed on an accord for the republic and the transitional period, on 22 May, 1990, the states unified in Aden as the Yemen Republic. Unification was declared four days earlier than had been planned to blockade opposition from tribal forces in North Yemen and hard-line Stalinists in South Yemen, who had prepared resistance movements. However, most of the Stalinists eventually supported unification because of the principle of equal division of power. Another opposing force was North Yemen's Muslim Brotherhood, who believed that Islamic law should be enshrined in the unified country's constitution, and South Yemeni women who demonstrated fearing that the rising influence of Islamic fundamentalism might jeopardize their freedoms. Nevertheless, unification took place in a state of euphoria: most Yemenis were for unity, although they were almost excluded from the unification process by the authorities, and felt a sense of common identity on a cultural, historical and social level.[62]

2.9 Causes and aftermath of Yemeni unification

The above term "agreement" describes accurately the Yemeni unification process in 1989-90. However, opinions on the impact of pre-unity developments on unification

---

60 On 1 December, 1989 a 136-article draft constitution for the unified Yemen was published but a referendum was not held until 16 May, 1991, when the 128-article draft constitution was enhanced by virtually all voters who, however, comprised only a third of the electorate. From Europa Publications Limited, ibid., p. 4360; Hwang, in Kihl, ibid., p. 283; Kostiner, ibid., p. 30.

61 Kostiner, ibid., p. 1.

62 Dresch, ibid., pp. 181-83, 221; Europa Publications Limited, ibid., p. 4360; Hudson, in al-Suwaidi, ibid., pp. 21, 23-4; Hwang, in Kihl, ibid., pp. 283, 292; Kim, ibid., 1994, pp. 14, 22-3; Kostiner, ibid., pp. 13, 18, 20, 108. It is unclear from Kim (ibid., 1994, pp. 22-3) and Europa Publications Limited (ibid., p. 4360) how strong opposition against unification was. Since women's social activities were restricted after unification, women in the south demonstrated for the restoration of their rights. From Kim, ibid., 1993, p. 105.

differ. That Professor Kostiner (1996) writes: "Before 1989, rapprochement progressed very slowly and cautiously" appears in the light of the above account to be a completely too negative evaluation. On the other hand, his recording that: "... some Arab observers thought that the intra-Yemeni conflict had deeper roots and was more malignant than East-West German relationship..." is difficult to reject.

In contrast, Hwang In Kwan (1994) writes: "Internally, both divided Germany and divided Yemen had agreed on substantial preparatory agreements for unification" and if exemplified in both the 1981 agreement on a unity constitution and the April 1990 accord for the republic and the transitional period. He writes that unification was achieved through hard political struggle and negotiations between the two ruling groups and characterizes Yemen unity as unification "from above" dictated by the more populous North Yemen, in contrast to the "from below" pattern apparent in Germany.[63]

That North Yemen dictated unification distinguishes his thesis from other scholars' views and seems to somewhat contradict the term "agreement". But even the term "from above" accurately describes the unification process since popular participation was discouraged. In the author's view, it would be fair to say that also Yemeni unification was a gradual process that was accelerated by an "historical accident", or rather accidents, that is the end of the Cold War and the resultant prospects for better economic development through unity.

Unification turned out to be difficult to implement. According to Kostiner (1996), the North's President Salih regarded the Yemen laissez-faire approach to unity as superior to the German case, which he saw as West Germany's virtual annexation of East Germany. In fact, both Yemeni leaders "...intended to follow a 'natural course' of unification as set out by 'the people' and not a previously imposed, overbearing state-building system, as had been the case in the unification of East and West Germany". Thus, they believed that the political system would regulate itself. In 1990, President Salih even expressed his vision of a united Yemen by saying: "The new state has removed forever the imaginary borderlines created during partition and is now embarking on a new era". His vision differs from the Yemeni people's scepticism towards the insufficient preparations for unity and sharply contradicts the opinion of the American scholar Michael C. Hudson (1994): "But on the level of the *pays réel,* the two former authoritarian power centers went into the merger lacking good faith and lacking trust in each other". It markedly contrasts also with the leaders' specification of a 30 month transitional period until 22 November, 1992, during which integration would be accomplished.[64]

A serious problem in creating strong administrative foundations was the avoidance of an institutional merger. Instead, the 1990 unity accords prescribed power-sharing and had divided most government posts equally: both leaders prefered unification

---

63 Hwang, in Kihl, ibid., pp. 291-92; Kostiner, ibid., pp. 13, 19.
64 Dresch, ibid., p. 186; Hudson, in al-Suwaidi, ibid., p. 21; Kim, ibid., 1994, p. 22; Kostiner, ibid., pp. 6, 18, 19, 23, 108. The first two quotations are from Kostiner, ibid., pp. 6, 108.

without any concessions within the existing power structure, at a time when North Yemen with about 11 million inhabitants far outnumbered the population of 2.5 million in South Yemen. The population ratio was more uneven than that pertaining in Germany.

The North's General Popular Congress (GPC), Secretary General Ali Abdullah Salih, became president and the YSP Secretary General, Ali Salim al-Bid vice-president. A five-man presidential council divided three posts going to the North and two to the South. The new parliament gave 159 seats to the North and 111 to the South with 31 outside appointees. The 39 minister posts were divided between 20 Northerners and 19 Southerners. The pre-unity parties YSP and GPC remained intact. The third major party was the Yemeni Reform Grouping (YRG) that was strongly based in the North, where it was hardly distinguishable from the GPC.[65]

Largely because Yemen took a pro-Iraqi position after the invasion of Kuwait in August 1990, the economy soon deteriorated, in spite of their hopes for a better future due to unity. This was particularly the case in the South where wages had been raised to the levels of the North in order to reduce the economic gap. At the same time, subsidies for food had been withdrawn resulting in dramatic price rises. The lack of experience in the South in handling a market economy, which involved the privatization of small sized factories and land, created problems with implementation. Social security and health insurance even became worse than it had been before.

A major reason for these economic difficulties was that about one million Yemeni workers in the Gulf region were expelled from Saudi Arabia and other countries which had begun to expel them in September 1990. This was in punishment for Yemen's pro-Iraqi stance in the Gulf War as a consequence of the heavy dependence on trade with and aid from Iraq. This aid was to disappear following the Iraqi defeat. Aid from such countries as Saudi Arabia, Kuwait and the United States almost ceased. Annual Saudi aid, amounting to some $ 500m and an estimated $ 1.8 billion, in workers remittances, collapsed almost simultaneously. The economic situation got worse: in late 1991, the annual inflation rate had risen to 30 per cent and unemployment to 36 per cent. Although oil revenues grew to $ 900m between mid-1990 and late 1991, Yemen suffered from estimated accumulated losses of some $ 4.8 billion between 1990 and 1992 as a result of the general oil-field recession and the Gulf states' boycott of Aden's refineries.

Along with the fall of sales of new oil concessions in 1992, this saw profits from oil revenues decline from $ 700m in 1991 to only $ 100m in 1992. The current account deficit grew and new oil concessions did not reverse the negative economic development, which the unified government was incapable of handling. The parties differed on how to act: the GPC advocated a laissez-faire approach whereas the YSP suggested economic reforms.

Also statistics from the late 1990s suggest that the economic impact of unification remained insignificant. GNP grew in real terms by an average of 3 per cent annually

---

65 Dresch, ibid., pp. 186-87, 251: fn. 4; Europa Publications Limited, ibid., p. 4360; Kostiner, ibid., pp. 13, 20.

during 1990-99, but GNP per capita fell by an annual average of 1.1 per cent, between 1990 and 1998, since the estimated population growth during this period was 4.8 per cent. In 1998, GNP per capita was only $280 but it rose to $490 in 2002, while the aggregate figure for both Yemens in 1989 had been $650.[66]

The principle of equal power-sharing gives some credence to the particular view of Hwang In Kwan (1994) to the effect that, "The unification was by no ways cosmetic". However, rivalry was so strong between the two major parties, which both retained their own forces and sources of funds, indeed some YSP people even were killed.[67] But this was not a new trend: over 150 YSP political activists had reportedly been killed during the unification period in striking contrast to the entirely peaceful German unification process.

Laws had been passed in a joint cabinet meeting in February 1990, to unify customs procedures, taxation, the issuing of passports, banking and diplomatic representation but in reality banking and currency – riyal in the North and dinar in the South – remained separate currencies. In 1996, the riyal became the sole currency. No plan to pacify long-feuding population groups was put in place. The lack of institutional preparation for unity was apparent also in the economic field; no attempts were made to change basic economic structures of the mixed Northern economy and the South's socialist economy or diversification of the sources of revenue, from remittances and oil income. Oil-related commerce was largely controlled by the North, although the South gained significant oil and gas resources after unification. Yet, unlike before unity, oil exploration now tended to separate rather than unite the North and the South. In addition, overall economic conditions did not change after unification that turned out to be very expensive indeed.

Reliance on foreign aid persisted. The conversion from collective to traditional agriculture was expensive. The government could hardly afford to issue new currency in exchange for South Yemeni dinars. GNP fell by some 5 per cent in 1991 alone.[68]

---

66 Day, "Yemen: Economy", in Europa Publications, ibid., p. 1265; Dresch, ibid., pp. 185-86, 191, 221; Europa Publications Limited, ibid., pp. 4363, 4364; Hudson, in al-Suwaidi, ibid., p. 24; Kim, ibid., 1993, pp. 101-103; Kostiner, ibid., pp. 17-18, 31-4, 45. As of early 1998, an estimated 400,000 Yemenis were working in Saudi Arabia (Day, ibid., p. 1275).

67 As of 1991, the number of troops in South Yemen was 27,500 and in North Yemen 36,500 (Kim, ibid., 1994, p. 16).

68 Day, "Yemen: Economy", ibid., p. 1274; Dresch, ibid., pp. 191, 193-94; Europa Publications Limited, ibid., p. 4361; Hebbelstrup, e-mail, 28 April, 2002; Hwang, in Kihl, ibid., p. 283; Kim, ibid., 1993, p. 101; Kostiner, ibid., pp. 17-19, 45. In 2000, Dresch (ibid., pp. 205, 212) wrote that oil revenue accounted for 60 per cent of the state budget and that the country was extremely poor. In fact, de Vylder et al record in *De minst utvecklade länderna och världshandeln* (Göteborg: Novum Grafiska AB, 2001, p. 179) Yemen among the 49 least developed countries (LDC) as defined by the UN. LDC status was given in 1975. Export volume was $ 1,646 billion and foreign debt $ 4,003 billion. Oil and oil products were the main exports (ibid., p. 182). According to Europa Publications Limited (ibid., p. 4365), oil and oil products accounted for 95.5 per cent of the value of total exports in 1999. In 2002, crude oil exports represented 87 per cent of total export value (Day, ibid., p. 1277).

The post-unity economic crisis aggravated political tensions. Due to GPC-YSP rivalry, it became impossible to make decisions and the State weakened accordingly. The outcome of the April 1993 parliamentary elections, which had been postponed from November 1992, increased tensions. The YSP gained only 56 of 301 seats nation-wide, of which 46 in the South, while the GPC gained 123 and the YRG 62, some of them gained at the expense of the YSP. When a vote was later cast in the parliament for the presidential council, the GPC and the YRG gained two seats each, while the YSP held only one. However, in the new government consisting of 29 ministers the YSP was better represented with nine posts, against eleven for the GPC and six for the YRG.

Rivalry did not end with the elections. There was a widespread sense of deprivation and discrimination in the former South Yemen and the YSP felt itself to be an opposition party. The preunification concerns in the South about becoming politically dominated by the North turned out to be not without grounds. Thus, as in unified Germany, there was one dominating part of the country and one dominated, but with incomparably worse consequences to follow. Demands that derived from YSP discontent were brushed aside by the GPC, which argued that they were excessive and out of all proportion to the relative size of the South's population. The YSP wanted a decentralized state with considerable power granted to both regions of the country. But the GPC and YRG stressed maintaining unity and the full reincorporation of the YSP in the unification process. Besides the larger population, the North's dominance can be explained by Sanaa being the traditional centre of culture.[69]

The GPC mobilized for strife throughout 1992-1993 at a time when the armed forces had not yet been integrated (proposals of how to merge them differed). In spite of the GPC-YSP dialogue, mutual distrust and tensions manifested by, for instance, political terrorism and both parties' habits of presenting ultimatums as conditions for discussing important political issues, intensified during the first months of 1994 until the fighting culminated on 27 April. This was after a series of military skirmishes between Northern and Southern units. In contrast to his role during the unity process, President Salih now regarded himself as the enforcer of unity and wanted his state system to govern the whole country in a similar way to the West German Chancellor Helmut Kohl's approach in Germany's unification.

In May, large-scale fighting broke out. To reassert Southern power the YSP announced secession as the Democratic Republic of Yemen on 21 May but the war, which was regarded by Southerners as an invasion of the Northerners or, as the situation was described by a famous pamphlet "from hurried unity to internal colonialism", was soon over: Aden fell on 7 July. The YSP received support from Saudi Arabia but was defeated by the GPC since it was inferior militarily and suffered from a weak leadership; Vice-President Ali Salam al-Bid left Aden soon

---

69 Dresch, ibid., pp. 191-94, 222; Europa Publications Limited, ibid., pp. 4360-4361; Hebbelstrup, e-mail, 4 May, 2004; Hudson, in al-Suwaidi, ibid., pp. 24-5; Kim, ibid., 1993, pp. 98-100; Kostiner, ibid., pp. 35, 45-6, 48-9, 56, 58, 64-5, 71, 73, 112-113.

after declaring secession. Due to intense fighting, large-scale destruction took place in the Southern cities.

The death toll was estimated between 5,000 and 7,000 people (government estimates were lower, opposition estimates much higher). The estimated cost of war for the central government was $ 8bn.[70] Finally, Yemen was reunified by military force, showing that power politics mattered more than the idealistic unification by "agreement". In fact, in spite of President Salih's opinion that the Yemen way of unification was superior to that of Germany, the latter appears to have been a far more realistic process at least in the short term.

In the war's aftermath, President Salih in September introduced amendments to the Constitution intended to strengthen his position further, although he had made commitments to promote reconciliation. The Presidential Council was abolished and in future the president would be elected by universal suffrage. In October 1994, President Salih was re-elected. In the new Council of Ministers, GPC retained the key portfolios and the YRG received nine ministerial posts however, the YSP received none (independents got some posts); southerners continued to feel discriminated against. Other signs of the YSP becoming weaker were that the party was deprived of military power and experienced leadership. A faction of the YSP even joined a new opposition grouping formed in 1995, at a time when the GPC and the YRG were increasingly at odds with each other. The war had a long-lasting impact: the remnants of the YSP boycotted the April 1997 parliamentary elections. The GPC won 188 (123 in 1993) and YRG 53 (62) of 301 seats. In the new cabinet, all but four members were drawn from the GPC.

When the first direct presidential elections were held in Yemen in September 1999, GPC had 226 parliamentary seats and Ali Abdullah Salih, was re-elected president, virtually uncontested. Not surprisingly, the YSP refused to participate in the elections. In January 2001, the Opposition Coordination Council, which included the YSP, was formed as a new opposition grouping prior to the holding in February of the first municipal elections since unification between the GPC and the YRG. Concurrently with the elections, a national referendum was held on proposed amendments to the Constitution. Among those was the proposal to extend the President's term of office from five to seven years. About 77 per cent of the voters endorsed this change. In March, when a new Council of Ministers was formed in March, GPC members held all of the posts; this was also the case after the April 2003 elections. In the same year, there was still heterogeneity between the inhabitants of the former North and South Yemen in terms of family and womens issues as well as in terms of life style but creating a "human union" here does not seem to have been as serious a problem as in Germany.[71]

---

70 Dresch, ibid., pp. 195-97, 222; Europa Publications Limited, ibid., p. 4361; Hudson, in al-Suwaidi, ibid., p. 21; Kostiner, ibid., pp. 67-8, 73-9, 82-5, 90, 112, 113; Lawless, ibid., p. 1246. The quote is from Dresch, ibid., p. 197.

71 Dresch, ibid., pp. 209, 222: e-mail, 28 February, 2005; Europa Publications Limited, ibid., pp. 4361-62, 4363, 4364; Kim, ibid., 2001, p. 34; Lawless, ibid., pp. 1248, 1254, 1255, 1256.

Like German unification, Yemeni unification attracted great interest in South Korea. Since German unification through absorption experienced severe economic and social aftermaths in a country far more developed than South Korea economically, some intellectuals asserted that the Yemeni pattern of unification by mutual agreement would be a more suitable way to unify Korea. But opinions changed due to the 1994 civil war. The editorial of the South Korean daily *Hankook Ilbo* wrote on 9 July: "The Yemen crisis teaches us that a unification achieved by artificial and mere political means will not be successful and that there must be a relatively long transition period to eliminate mutual distrust and antagonism before unification. To that end, steady interaction should be pursued across the divided land to resolve the sense of heterogeneity among ordinary people. What is more, unification must be achieved only by peaceful and democratic means, fully reflecting the wishes of the people".[72] Clearly, Yemeni unification was no easily interpreted project.

2.10 Conclusions

The combination of long-term improvements in relations and favourable "historic accidents" enabled the German and Yemeni unifications in 1990. Relations between the two Germanys reflected both ups and downs and developed more smoothly than those which emerged between the two Yemens. The tendencies in both Germany and Yemen were a gradual expansion and improvement of relations that facilitated the unification processes in 1989-1990. At this time, a "now-or-never" development towards unification had emerged in both states.

Characterizing the unification of Germany as "absorption" and of Yemen as "agreement" is basically correct, however, neither term gives full justice to the unification processes and the factors enabling them. In particular, Yemeni unification turned out to be an idealistic project and it may be described as "power-sharing" followed by division, civil war and power monopolization by North Yemen which came to dominate the country by means of being more populuous. Yemeni unification differs from that in Germany by being decided politically "from above" whereas popular participation "from below" played an important role in the German case.

To give credit to the unification processes in Germany and Yemen, a distinction must also be drawn between the political unifications accomplished in 1990 and the process of "human unity" of citizens who had lived under different circumstances for a long time. The latter process is far more difficult and is not yet over, particularly not in the case of Germany.

A similarity between German and Yemeni unification is that both took place very quickly. East Germany's simultaneous political and economic breakdown in combination with the end of Soviet patronage and West Germany's superior economic power, enabled such a unification. West Germany realized that it must take this now-or-never opportunity to unify Germany on West German terms through absorption,

---

72 Kim, ibid., 1994, pp. 5-6; *Korea Focus,* "Lessons of Yemen's Reunification", vol. 2, (1994), no. 4, p. 143 (translated from *Hankook Ilbo*).

but the long-term consequences of unification were never really considered. Unrealistic statements were made on the economic consequences of unification and the state of the pre-unity East and West German economies, which led to a severe economic decline in East Germany after 1990. West Germany dominated the unified country and East Germans felt that they were second-class citizens.

Also in Yemen, "a now-or-never" opportunity for unification had developed in 1989 due to the end of Soviet patronage to South Yemen and hopes for a common oil exploration policy. Given the often tense relations, Yemen could not have unified as quickly if the two presidents had not decided to unify the nation within six months. However, the unification process did not include a full-scale merger of the different political and economic systems leaving such issues largely to be dealt with afterwards. In particular, the armed forces were not integrated with these disastrous consequences. It turned out to be an overwhelming task to handle political and economic integration while overcoming preunification tensions. Such conditions eventually caused the 1994 civil war. In combination with unforeseeable policies taken by Arab states after 1990, and the following internal chaos explain much of unified Yemen's poor economic performance.

Consequently, the German model of unification appears to be a more attractive model since it largely integrated the political and economic systems during the unification process, prior to actual unity. But this was easier to do in Germany than in Yemen since West Germany dictated the terms of unification based on its superior economy.

In Germany, since the economic and political systems had been integrated the post-unification problems were never threatening the state, in sharp contrast to Yemen. Another striking contrast is that German unification was achieved without bloodshed, whereas South Yemeni politicians had been killed during the unification process.

Lessons from Yemen unification are that the process should take place gradually to reduce tensions and that unification should be achieved ideally by peaceful and democratic means. On the other hand, Yemeni leaders had to consider the particular conditions available for unification implying that a gradual unification at that stage of inception would have been harder to accomplish.

Chapter 3

Inter-Korean Relations

3.1 Introduction

In Chapter 2, we saw that in Germany and Yemen, both developments prior to 1989 and during 1989-90, enabled unification and that there are lessons for Korea, in both of these countries' experiences. This is examined, in order to find out how the development of inter-Korean relations can be interpreted, in the course of this study.

The chapter begins with a survey of North and South Korea's unification policies after the Korean War (1950-1953). The author looks at what has characterized their respective policies, whether they have changed or not over time and what outcomes they have brought about. The influence of West Germany's unification policies on South Korea and the impact of post-unity developments in Germany on the two Koreas are analyzed. In particular, the economic costs of unification in Germany and its impact on South Korean policies are examined. Estimated costs and consequences of Korean unification are also reflected over.

The following section briefly reviews the development of inter-Korean relations during the period 1953-1997. Major political events and the development of economic contacts are noted in order to identify their intrinsic characteristics. President Kim Dae Jung's (1998-2003) unification policies are then examined and comparisons are made with his predecessors' policies, to find out what the similarities and differences actually were. The relevance of functionalism in describing his policies is noted throughout.

Developments in inter-Korean relations since 1998 onwards are then investigated in detail because greater emphasis at the time was directed on the unification issue. The section begins by investigating developments that were considered to be steps forward and backwards in inter-Korean relations. These are weighed against each other in order to give a fair and balanced overview. The survey includes political, military and economic factors that form the context in which the varied socio-cultural contacts took place. Cross-references are made here and heretoafter to identify and compare recurring themes. Again, comparisons are made with Germany but also of course with Yemen.

Socio-cultural contacts are investigated in some detail. Accomplished events are noted and relevant data about them such as where they took place, how long they lasted and, when available, the number of people involved, are presented. If available, evaluations of the events are on the record; this empirical approach is also followed in the subsequent sections. For the sake of convenience, socio-cultural contacts are recorded in the appendix. Official North-South contacts and recent economic and political developments in North Korea are subsequently studied in a separate section since they differ from the previously described developments, while still greatly affecting cross-border relationships.

Attention is then turned to the June 2000 inter-Korean summit. What factors enabled the summit to be held and how contacts in politics, economics and in the socio-cultural field developed afterwards, are examined to evaluate its impact. In this sense, whether the summit was a breakthrough or not in relations is addressed. As previously, most emphasis is placed on socio-cultural contacts, this also includes the divided-families issue.

Finally, developments since 2001 are reviewed in the fields of politics, economics and socio-cultural contacts. Inter-Korean relations are again reviewed from both an internal and external point of view and positive and negative trends are balanced against each other in order to present a fairer picture of the situation. For the sake of convenience, the account is divided into two sections, partly due to the inauguration of a new South Korean president in 2003. Whether developments differ or not from those during the Kim Dae Jung government is also discussed.

3.2 Unification policies of North and South Korea

The South Korean government has long since modelled its reunification policies on those implemented by West Germany. In the early 1970s, the South Korean government began to re-fashion its foreign policy along lines similar to those of West Germany where, as we have seen, the aim was to establish economic and political ties with socialist countries. This new policy is known as "Nordpolitik". By the early 1970s, the South Korean economy had surpassed that of North Korea. This contributed to a change being made in the policy which had been pursued since the Korean War, whereby several proposals from North Korea for increased mutual economic, political and cultural contacts had been rejected by South Korea, with no counterproposals forthcoming.[1] On the other hand, the North Koreans rejected those humanitarian, cultural and economic exchanges offered, as well as a separate UN membership application proposed by the Park Chung Hee government in South Korea, in order to normalize North-South relations at the time. North Korea believed

---

1 As early as mid-1954, at the Geneva Conference, North Korea had made peaceful gestures by proposing the formation of an all-Korea commission and a single Korean legislature through elections, the withdrawal of all foreign troops from the Korean Peninsula and the formal declaration, by outside powers, of the need for peaceful development and reunification of Korea. Reduction of military forces, together with economic and [not exemplified] cultural exchanges were also proposed. From Savada (ed.), *North Korea: A Country Study* (Washington: Library of Congress, 1994), p. 196.

that such a gradual approach to reunification would allow the South eventually to secure a stable division of the Korean Peninsula.[2]

The North's own reunification policy was based, on the contrary, on an approach involving greater immediacy, through the formation of a confederation, to be known as "The Democratic Confederal Republic of Korea" (DCRK). Such a confederation had been proposed by Kim Il Sung already in 1960. At this time, it also called for one-seat representation in the UN. The underlying idea behind this one-Korea policy was that a national government would be formed to be responsible, for instance, for foreign relations and currency management, while each of the two states would maintain their own socio-economic systems. The subsequent expansion of contacts would eventually allow national elections to be organized and the establishment of a re-unified country.[3] The South Koreans rejected this proposal since they feared that, through its implementation, the North Koreans would be able to impose their own social system on the South.

In 1980, North Korea presented a new, and more detailed, proposal for a confederation (DCRK) based on mutual convenience and toleration. Again, a single unified state would be founded on the principle of coexistence. This would leave the two systems intact and federate relations between the two governments. The North Korean proposal was followed in 1982, by a call from South Korean President Chun Doo Hwan, for a Provisional Agreement on Basic Relations between North and South Korea. This proposed first step was to be followed by the establishment of a Consultative Conference for National Reunification, which would draft the constitution for a re-unified country.

In 1989, President Roh Tae Woo, through his Korean National Community Unification Formula, called for the introduction of confidence-building measures, through cultural, social and economic exchanges. Those were to lead to the adoption of a Korean National Community Charter, in which the ground rules for the establishment of a Korean Commonwealth would be included. Eventually, an agreement was to be reached on a constitution for a reunified Korea, which was to be approved through a national voting procedure. Consequently, as long as North Korea continued to maintain its direct approach to reunification and South Korea its

---

2 Hart-Landsberg, "Korean Unification", pp. 68-9; Rhee, "Korea's Unification", p. 360; Savada, ibid., pp. 196, 198. Cultural exchanges proposed are not exemplified by Hart-Landsberg on p. 69.

3 Note must be taken here of the term "national elections" since, from the beginning, North Korea has insisted that an inter-Korean political formula should be based on parity or equality, rather than the relative size of the populations. This is because a supreme Korean council, established on the formula of one-person, one-vote would give South Korea, having a population more than double the size of that of the North, a commanding position under any such arrangement (cf. "single Korean legislature through elections" under fn. 1). From Savada (ibid., p. 195).

indirect approach, it is not at all surprising that this was one major reason why so little progress was made towards reunification during the 1970s and 1980s.[4]

While President Roh Tae Woo was to make Nordpolitik a major feature of his foreign policy, he claimed that, unlike his predecessors, he would not pursue this at the expense of North Korea. Nonetheless, even though this policy contributed to the establishment of diplomatic relations with Eastern European countries, the Soviet Union and China, the basic attitude towards North Korea itself remained unchanged. The result, in terms of diplomacy, was tantamount to the isolation and weakening of North Korea. The simultaneous disappearance of the socialist world also made North Korea's position weaker. This became clear when both the Soviet Union and China supported the admission of both North and South Korea, as separate members, to the UN in September 1991.

In addition, the economic policies of the South also had the practical effect of weakening the North. Although, in October 1988, the South Korean government had lifted its ban on indirect trade with North Korea, it refused, during both the Roh Tae Woo and Kim Young Sam administrations, to allow either large-scale South Korean investments in North Korea or technology transfers, which together would have provided the potential for transforming the economy of the North. Under the National Security Law (NSL), to which there is no equivalent in North Korea, non-governmental contacts with the North were also discouraged.[5] In 1989, law-maker Sô Kyông-wôn and dissident student representative Im Su-kyông were both sentenced to terms in prison because they had made unauthorized visits to North Korea. Also Reverend Mun Ik-hwan, who had been invited by Kim Il Sung to attend a leadership-level inter-Korean reunification meeting, to be held in P'yôngyang during his New Year's address, made an unauthorized visit in 1989.[6]

Both in 1989 and in 1992, the chairmen of the Hyundai group and the Daewoo group visited North Korea but no business agreements were signed since such deals were resisted by the South Korean government. The official reasoning given was related to concerns about the North's nuclear program. The South Korean

---

4 Hart-Landsberg, ibid., pp. 69-70; Rhee, ibid., pp. 366-69; Savada, ibid., pp. 197-98, 199. "The Democratic Confederal Republic of Korea" is quoted from Savada (ibid., p. 199). Proposed cultural, social and economic exchanges are not exemplified by Hart-Landsberg on p. 70.

5 The NSL was first enacted in 1948. Articles 3 and 4 provide long prison sentences and the death penalty for crimes such as "espionage" and "anti-state" activities but these terms are not clearly defined in the law. Under the NSL, North Korea is defined as an "anti-state" organization rather than a country. Article 6 prohibits unauthorized travel to North Korea. Article 7 punishes the act of "praising" or "benefitting" the enemy. From Amnesty International, *Republic of Korea (South Korea): Long-term Prisoners still held under the National Security Law* (London, May 1998), p. 3. Original quotation marks.

6 Hart-Landsberg, ibid., pp. 70-71, 73, 79; Pohl, ibid., p. 7; Rhee, ibid., p. 360; Savada and Shaw (eds), *South Korea: A Country Study* (Washington: Library of Congress, 1992), pp. 262, 263; Suh, "Assessing the Military Balance in Korea", *Asian Perspective* 28 (2004), no. 4, p. 71.

government's policy of limiting, in practice, any economic exchanges with North Korea contradicted its own pronouncements with regard to the need for initiating such economic exchanges and for supporting economic reform in order to prevent the collapse of the North Korean economy.

Instead, South Korean policy-makers began to focus their attention on inter-Korean relations, as a result of North Korea's weakened position and German reunification in 1990, hoping to emulate that experience. Consequently, South Korea actively engaged North Korea in negotiations and promised substantial economic support on condition that the North agreed to accept humanitarian, cultural and economic exchanges with the South. At this time, North Korea in spite of the pursuit of the self-orientated, self-reliant and independent ideology – *juche* – as the basis of its system, was suffering badly following on the collapse of the Soviet Union.

While the South Korean government was thus shifting its policy away from the previous gradual approach to reunification, towards a policy based on the ultimate reunification of Korea through absorption, North Korea remained more unified politically, and more self-sufficient economically, than East Germany had been. Consequently, North Korea maintained reunification through a confederation as its ideal policy. After 1991, however, the North had subsequently modified this stance through the inclusion, as a transitional agreement, of the transfer of diplomatic and defence affairs to regional governments, thus shifting closer to President Roh Tae Woo's reunification plan. Furthermore, in his 1991 New Year address, Kim Il Sung declared that South Korea should have no doubts that their aspiration to achieve a German-style reunification was, in fact, an illusion. In fact, North Korea had studied German unification very carefully and concluded that such a process meant that there was no future for North Korean leaders after reunification.[7]

By late 1991, doubts had already begun to be raised by policy analysts in South Korea as to the desirability of this German-style model, because of the huge financial costs involved. The Korea Development Institute estimated that the implementation of a similar unification in Korea might cost as much as US$ 800 billion over a ten-year period. Thus, by mid-1992, because of this estimate of the high cost of reunification, government officials were publicly announcing their support for gradual reunification through absorption. Even though the German path to reunification had demonstrated, as we have seen, that such a strategy would be impossible, the South Korean government at this time, remained committed to absorption, because it was much more concerned to strengthen existing domestic, political and economic

---

7   Foley, *Korea's Divided Families*, p. 81; Foster-Carter, "History", in *The Far East and Australasia 1999* (London: Europa Publications Ltd., 1998), pp. 529, 531; Hart-Landsberg, ibid., pp. 71-4; Hwang, "A Monumental Step Forward: Two Koreas recognize common ground in reunification plan", *Korea Now,* 17 June, 2000, pp. 12-13; Pfennig, "From Division", pp. 40-41, 43. Proposed cultural, social and economic exchanges are not exemplified by Hart-Landsberg on p. 72. That the collapse of East Germany continues to influence North Korean policy-makers is suggested by the above Pohl (1998): "The North Korean leadership has also learned its lesson from the German unification process – if a socialist regime moves too close to a successful capitalist one, the result may well be destruction" (ibid., p. 11).

institutions than in meeting any potential social and economic costs, associated with a collapse of the North Korean government.[8] Such an attitude towards North Korea can only have contributed to a worsening of relations.

Thus, according to Pohl (1998), even if that policy was to change later, it was and is still to some extent, in South Korea's best interest to help North Korea to keep going. In fact, any sudden collapse would place an enormous burden both on its economic and social structures. Therefore, the gradual approach towards unification is a much preferred option. Pohl's argument gains additional weight from the fact that South Korea, compared to West Germany at the time of reunification, is less affluent, that the population ratio in Korea is less favourable and that South Korea, in 1998, was experiencing an on-going economic crisis.

On the other hand, the fact that this shift in policy has hardly been suddenly adopted is indicated by the following statement from Rhee (1993): "As of early 1993, a consensus had been formed among South Korean intellectuals that Koreans should adopt a 'piecemeal treatment' in managing reunification as opposed to the 'shock therapy' of the Germans". The essence of this idea of "piecemeal treatment" is to lift the North Korean economy to a certain level in order to minimize the cost of reunification, through expanding contacts and helping the North to reform. But still, the reunification cost, through what he terms "applying a *modified* German model to the Korean case", has been estimated to reach US$ 774 billion in such a case.[9] This sum exceeds the 2002 cost of German unification.

Although, according to the American scholar Selig S. Harrison (2002), there is general agreement that the unification costs will steadily rise as a result of the disparity between the two Koreas's growth rates, unification will bring some positive outcomes. In fact, Rhee writes: "In the case of Korea, no one denies that reunification would be good for the country's economy in the long run". The North's abundant mineral resources such as coal and steel would be shared with the South's products. The domestic market would expand and there would be a union of the South's capital and technology with the North's labour force and resources. The South Korean scholar Choi and his associates (2003) agree on these points, but point to added investments in the North and an integration of the unified Korean economy with the regional Northeast Asian area. Unification would also ease political shackles and ideological restrictions and contribute to enhancing Korea's international position.

Negative consequences they point out include concerns regarding the economic effects and costs with problems, such as unemployment, inflation and financial deficits. Opinions on the impact on economic growth are divided: in a survey made by the Korea Institute for National Unification in 2003, 48.2 per cent of the respondents replied that unification would contribute to growth, but 40.9 per cent expected that it would be lowered as a result; 10.9 per cent predicted "no difference".

---

8   Hart-Landsberg, ibid., pp. 72-3.
9   Foster-Carter, ibid., *1998* (London: Europa Publications Ltd., 1997), p. 501: ibid., *1999*, p. 535; Pohl, ibid., pp. 6, 8; Rhee, ibid., pp. 361, 373.

Political integration in terms of dividing power may create acute tensions and social tensions between classes and regions within a unified Korea.[10]

3.3 The development of inter-Korean relations, 1953-1997

It is not at all surprising that inter-Korean relations have been incomparably worse than the examples of preunification East and West Germany, as well as preunification North and South Yemen. The unification policies of North and South Korea have always been diametrically opposed. The Korean War, whose traumatic impact created strong nationalism in North Korea, is undoubtedly an additional reason for these differences. The war ended in 1953 with an armistice agreement that South Korea did not even sign up to.

On the contrary, it wanted to continue fighting. In the view of Sven Juhlin, of the Swedish Foreign Ministry, this was a major mistake on the part of South Korea since it led North Korea to believe that the South was unwilling to bring the war completely to an end. Consequently, North Korea has regarded the US, rather than South Korea, as the opposite party with whom to negotiate a peace treaty. Contributing to this view is also the fact that the US still, as of 2002, exercised operational control over South Korean forces in the event of war. But peacetime operational control was relinquished to Seoul in 1994, due to nationalist pressures. Many leading South Koreans had regarded US operational control as an impediment to a dialogue with the North.

North and South Korea are thus, technically speaking, still at war. That both Koreas, since their foundation in 1948, claim to be the sole legitimate government on the Peninsula and that they, since 1953, have deliberately restricted contacts, has exacerbated the deep mutual distrust that had already existed. Each government has also suppressed negative information about the other. A most tragic humanitarian consequence of this bitter partition is that there were, in 1997, an estimated ten million divided family members who have had no opportunities to contact each other, in stark contrast to the case in Germany prior to unification.[11]

As we have seen above, attempts to open dialogue after the Korean War were doomed to failure. However, following the rapprochement between the US and China, a first period of substantive dialogue began through high-level secret visits in 1971. These talks culminated in the joint communiqué of 4 July, 1972, in which three principles for reunification were identified: reunification must be through peaceful

---

10 Choi et al., *Nambuk kwangye-ûi*, pp. 99, 200, 205, 209; Harrison, *Korean Endgame*, p. 97; Rhee, ibid., p. 372. The survey appears in detail in chapter 6.

11 Foster-Carter, ibid., *1998*, p. 499; Harrison, ibid., 2002, pp. 8, 155, 156, 165; Juhlin, during the lecture "NNSC [Neutral Nations Supervisory Commission] och dess förändrade roll under 1990-talet", Stockholm University, 22 March, 2000; Savada, ibid., pp. 195-6; Savada and Shaw, ibid., p. 261. The source of the figure of divided family members seems to be estimates of the numbers of North Korean refugees arriving in South Korea soon after Korea's division. From Foley (ibid., p. 48).

means only, it must transcend ideological differences and it must be without foreign interference. Following this communiqué, a South-North Coordinating Committee (SNCC) was set up and talks opened with the Red Cross with the aim of re-uniting divided families.

The SNCC meetings dealt with political, economic and cultural affairs. They continued until 1975, and those with the Red Cross until 1978, but they did not, however, produce any results. This was not only because of the differing reunification policies, but also due to the regular acts of aggression, on the part of North Korea, against South Korea, such as constructing tunnels under the demilitarized zone (DMZ) and the attempt to assassinate President Park Chung Hee in 1974 (and President Chun Doo Hwan in 1983). The Red Cross talks failed over the issue of just who would be allowed to visit each other: South Korea wanted to restrict visits to those who were blood relatives while North Korea also wanted to permit the rather vague category of "friends" which created fears in the South. A further brief round of official talks was held in 1979-1980, but they did not produce any results either.

Yet a second period of dialogue was opened in 1984, when North Korea offered rice, textiles and cement in aid to South Korea which then was suffering from severe floods. In a startling reversal of the usual zero sum logic long practiced by both states, South Korea accepted the proposal, which led to further dialogue in 1985, comprising talks on economic, parliamentary and Red Cross matters. The Red Cross talks were the only ones that bore fruit and in September 1985, the first family reunions took place. However, this only covered 100 first-generation family members, of which just 65 were able to meet their relatives. Inevitably, as in the 1970s, inter-Korean relations were soon to worsen again: North Korea suspended all dialogue in 1986, in protest against the annual US-South Korean "Team Spirit" military exercises. Relations deteriorated even further after the shooting down of a South Korean civilian aircraft in 1987.[12]

In 1988, a third period of dialogue began as a result of South Korea's growing economic and diplomatic strength and President Roh Tae Woo's declaration with regard to Nordpolitik. However, North Korea objected, in 1988, to his call for the building of a single "national commonwealth" with the assistance of the US and Japan, claiming that it could only be the agreed three principles for reunification, described above, which should form the basis for improving inter-Korean relations. This dialogue was also hindered by North Korea's objections to "Team Spirit".

Talks with the Red Cross, on reuniting members of other divided families in accordance with the South's unification policies, were resumed in 1988, however without a successful outcome. Less controversially, more progress was made in the field of sports, where the first ever inter-Korean football matches were held in 1990 and joint Korean teams participated in two international events in 1991. Indirect trade, involving raw materials and agricultural products from North Korea and

---

12 Foley, ibid., pp. 76, 77-8, 89; Foster-Carter, ibid., 1998, p. 499; Savada, ibid., pp. 195, 196-97, 199-200; Savada and Shaw, ibid., p. 261. "Friends" is quoted from Foley (ibid., p. 76).

manufactured goods from South Korea, began in 1988, and direct trade emerged in 1990. The volume of trade increased rapidly from US$ 1m, in 1988, to US$ 190m in 1991. As of 1992, South Korea was North Korea's fourth largest trading partner, after China, Russia and Japan. Between 1993 and 1997, the volume of trade grew even further, to a value level of between US$ 200m and US$ 300m. In this way, businessmen from both Koreas were in regular contact, mainly in the context of China.

The first talks between the Korean Prime Ministers were held in 1990. In 1991, after five rounds of meetings, these talks eventually brought two significant results. Firstly, North Korea withdrew its longstanding objections to the two Koreas being members of the UN. In September 1991, both states became UN members.

Secondly, in December 1991, the North and South Korean Prime Ministers signed the Agreement on Reconciliation, Non-aggression and Exchanges and Cooperation (hereafter the Basic Agreement) and the Joint Declaration on the Denuclearization of the Korean Peninsula. Interestingly, the then North Korean Prime Minister Yôn Hyông-muk called the Basic Agreement "the most valuable achievement ever made between the South and North Korean authorities". Under this comprehensive agreement, which was ratified in February 1992, both sides pledged to respect each other's political system and to promote economic, and other, cooperation, as well as to re-unite members of divided families. It also called for the two states to bring the Korean War to a formal closure. Several sub-committees were established to work out how to implement the agreement. At the time it was signed, business talks were also held on, for instance, the joint development of Mt. Kûmgang ("Diamond Mountains") as an international tourist attraction. In July 1992, the North's vice-Prime Minister visited numerous industrial plants in the South.[13]

Although the Basic Agreement had no binding force, in the long run it might well still have provided the impetus for the development of relations similar to those between East and West Germany prior to unification. However, yet again, the period of closer relations did not last very long: Prime Minister Yôn Hyông-muk's statement was not matched by actual developments. Relations worsened again, in particular because of the question of North Korea's suspected nuclear ambitions, despite the fact that President Kim Young Sam essentially continued his predecessor's policies towards North Korea. The nuclear issue was, after many twists and turns, resolved through the 21 October, 1994 Geneva Agreed Framework between North Korea and the US; the North's dialogue partner of choice. According to this agreement, North Korea would freeze its existing nuclear program, accept international inspections and

---

13 Foster-Carter, ibid., *1998*, pp. 499-500; *Inter-Korean Agreement,* 13 December, 1991; Rhee, ibid., pp. 369-70; Savada, ibid., pp. 200-202, 286; Savada and Shaw, ibid., pp. 261-62; Shim, "Spring Thaw? South Korea tries a new, gentler approach to North Korea", *Far Eastern Economic Review* (*FEER*), 11 June, 1998, p. 31. "National commonwealth" is quoted from Savada and Shaw (ibid., p. 261). Yôn Hyông-muk's statement is quoted from Savada (ibid., p. 200).

replace its old graphite-moderated reactors, converting to militarily less dangerous light-water reactors.

By this time, however, relations had already been soured because the Kim Young Sam government had placed the armed forces on a state of high alert, fearing either an attack or the North's rapid collapse. They also had failed to transmit condolences on the death of Kim Il Sung in 1994, and had acted harshly against the few Southern radicals who had done so. President Kim Young Sam, because he had turned from his initial conciliatory approach to a more hard-line stance, was never again to be a welcome partner in any dialogue with North Korea. Nonetheless, exchanges were not completely interrupted: trade continued and, in 1995, thirteen technicians from the Daewoo Concern, who were to supervise a pioneering venture in the North, became the first South Koreans, since 1953, to settle in North Korea with the approval of both governments. In 1995, the North accepted an offer of rice aid from the South and additional aid was provided in 1996.

Besides the nuclear issue and the death of Kim Il Sung, there were two other major setbacks to inter-Korean relations which should be noted here. In September 1996, a North Korean submarine ran aground on the South Korean east coast. However, North Korea subsequently, in December, apologized for the incident. In February 1997, the Korean Workers' Party Secretary, Hwang Jang-yop, sought asylum at the South Korean embassy in Beijing which, after a time in the Philippines, he received. But at the same time, trade continued, relatively unhampered. More significantly, South Korean engineers, albeit representing the multilateral consortium Korean Peninsula Energy Development Organization (KEDO), were in the North, in 1997, for the construction of light-water reactors, South Korean ships continued to deliver machinery and materials and a North-South telephone link came into service.

That such contacts as these took place, while relations were otherwise tense, was in sharp contrast to the previous pattern seen in earlier periods. But the significance of this new process should, nonetheless, not be exaggerated. In fact, following Hwang's defection, the South Korean daily, *Dong-a Ilbo,* went so far as to state that inter-Korean relations were, at the time, in their "worst state" ever.[14]

3.4 President Kim Dae Jung's unification policies

Considering the persistence of the tensions between the two Koreas, it is not surprising that Kim Dae Jung, as early as 1970, when a presidential candidate, spoke out on the unification issue. He had long insisted that trade and investment between North and South Korea would lower the barriers between them, i.e. a functionalist approach to relations. He, therefore, proposed a three-stage model towards reunification which

---

14 *Dong-a Ilbo,* "Nambuk kwangye-ûi wigi", 18 February, 1997; Foley, ibid., p. 82; Foster-Carter, ibid., *1998*, pp. 500-501; Hart-Landsberg, ibid., p. 74; Pohl, ibid., p. 6; Rhee, ibid., p. 364; Shim, "Kim the Cool: South's Reaction to North's Intrusion Signals New Maturity", *FEER,* 9 July, 1998, p. 16.

consisted of a confederation at the first stage, a federation at the second stage and complete reunification at the third and final stage.

During such a first stage, exchanges and cooperation were to be promoted, while peaceful coexistence between these two different political and economic systems was to be copper fastened by institutionalized bilateral cooperation. This idea was subsequently adopted, in 1989, by President Roh. The proposal includes the establishment of a South-North Confederation Council, for the peaceful management of national divisions, which is to provide both Koreas with equal representation, despite the fact that South Korea had a larger population. Although Kim's model differed somewhat from North Korea's own proposal, it was one which, in reality, would in any event be confederal permitting the two states to retain separate armies and control of cross-border movements. North Korea responded favourably because of the principle of parity, which it maintained was compatible with its own position.

During the second stage of Kim Dae Jung's model plan, a true federal government would be formed to handle external affairs, while two autonomous regional governments would retain responsibility for domestic affairs. In the third stage, a reunified and democratic Korea, with a market economy, would be ruled by one centralized government, or several autonomous governments, in a similar pattern to that pertaining in the United States or Germany. After spending half a year, from December 1992, at Cambridge University in Britain, Kim decided to dedicate the rest of his life to the reunification issue. In 1994, he founded the Kim Dae Jung Peace Foundation for the Asia Pacific Region, to function as a research institute on reunification issues.[15]

However, following his election as president in 1998, Kim Dae Jung virtually abandoned his concept of confederation. Instead, his government laid down three principles which were to guide its policies towards North Korea. First, no acts of armed provocation were to be tolerated. Secondly, the absorption of North Korea as a means of achieving reunification was to be ruled out. Thirdly, reconciliation and cooperation were to be promoted in a positive manner. Obviously, there is a clear connection between this third principle and Kim's prior model for reunification. But no specific proposals have been forthcoming from the government on the formulation of policies on reunification, even though it continues to regard the implementation of the Basic Agreement, through dialogue, as one of its policy tools. President Kim has, himself, even refrained from using the phrase "unification policy" but, in contrast to prior governments, he has instead talked of a more general "policy towards North Korea". This approach also differs from the "Nordpolitik" described above, which not only embraced North Korea, but also relations with China and the Soviet Union/ Russia.

---

15 Harrison, "A Path to Peace: President Kim's policies foster improved inter-Korean relations", *Newsreview*, 3 April, 1999, p. 9; Hwang, ibid., 17 June, 2000, pp. 12-13; Kim, *Tasi saeroun sijag-ûl wihayô: saranghanûn chôlmûn-i-wa chongyônghanûn kungmin-tûr-ege pach'inûn iyagi* (Seoul: Kimyôngsa, 1998), pp. 337, 342; Shim, ibid., 9 July, 1998, p. 16.

In practice, Kim's government has declared for a policy of positive engagement – the "sunshine policy" – in the spirit of the Basic Agreement, in order to promote peaceful coexistence, reconciliation and cooperation between North and South Korea, as the first stage towards reunification. The actual task of reunification, a stage that is to be preceded by the preparatory stage of a North-South Confederation for political integration, is considered to be something which is to be tackled by a subsequent administration. Thus, the promotion of immediate reunification is not regarded as being realistic in a situation where both sides, for more than 50 years, have been in a state of confrontation.

However, in the author's view, the estimated, enormous unification costs is also one important reason why the current position is the only realistic one. The basic features of this policy of engagement include the principle of the separation of economic cooperation from politics, in a pattern similar to those relations that exist between China and Taiwan, based on the principle of flexible reciprocity. The target of this policy, apart from peaceful coexistence, is to create an environment in which North Korea is liable to introduce domestic reforms. This is in order to overcome its serious economic difficulties, without fear of government collapse or of absorption by the South; this was to be achieved by the North being assisted in opening up its economy and in introducing features of a market economy. It is clear that such a policy is strongly premised on the judgement that there will in fact, be no collapse in North Korea in the immediate future.

President Kim's sunshine policy differs markedly, in fact, from Nordpolitik, as pursued by Presidents Roh Tae Woo and Kim Young Sam which, as we have seen, were both aimed at promoting reconciliation and but also at pursuing containment policies with the purpose of eventually absorbing North Korea.[16] On the other hand, the sunshine policy displays obvious similarities to the indirect unification policies of Presidents Park Chung Hee and Chun Doo Hwan, although avoidance of the term "unification policy" here constitutes a positive, but nonetheless striking, difference.

The American scholar Harrison (1999) argues that, despite President Kim's pronouncements, North Korea remained suspicious that he was seeking, through the sunshine policy, to bring about the absorption of the North into South Korea, albeit by more refined means than those of his predecessors. An example of such suspicions on the part of the North is provided by Harrison (1999), where he writes that: "'Reform' to North Korean leaders means the replacement of the present leadership with new leaders beholden to the South as a result of dependent economic relations with Seoul, which is just as undesirable to the present leadership in the North as a collapse". The words, spoken by the North Korean Foreign Minister, Paek Nam-sun, at his speech to the UN in September 1999, in which he upheld the confederation model of reunification, would tend to support Harrison's view. Here, he criticized the sunshine policy saying, "it is a conspiracy to absorb North Korea into its democratic system by changing North Korea, on which even South Korean

---

16 Foster-Carter, ibid., *1999*, p. 535; Harrison, ibid., 3 April, 1999, pp. 8-9; Hwang, ibid., 17 June, 2000, p. 12; Yang, "Kim Dae-jung Administration's", 1998, pp. 48, 49-52.

officials commented in public that its present policy is the same as the US peace-transition strategy that caused the Soviet Union to collapse".[17]

3.5 Steps forward in inter-Korean relations, 1998-1999

Whether these words by Paek Nam-sun are true or not, soon after President Kim Dae Jung came into office, in February 1998, his administration began implementing the new sunshine policy. Thus, in March 1998, the government announced the new official policy of allowing South Korean business to negotiate directly. This is, without government consent being required and without government control, with North Korea, concerning trade, investment or aid. It was also now permitted for citizens to travel to P'yôngyang without prior consent from the government, although an official invitation from the North Koreans, along with a written guarantee of safe return, continued to be required.

Such conciliatory policies contributed to the delivery, in June 1998, of a gift to North Korea of 500 cows. The cows had been donated by the founder of the Hyundai Group, Chung Ju Yung. In October, another 500 cows were delivered. Chung Ju Yung now met the North Korean leader, Kim Jong Il, as the first prominent figure from South Korea. The visit led to the agreement to launch the Mt. Kûmgang tourist project, in November. Hyundai would pay $ 942m to North Korea for the project over a six-year period.

According to the South Korean scholar Yang Young-Shik (1998), the meeting constituted a "milestone" in the 50-year history of national division and a sign of the success of the policy of Kim Dae Jung's government, separating economics from politics. Harrison (1999) regards this meeting as a positive response to the sunshine policy.[18]

In November 1998, after many twists and turns, the first South Korean tourists went sightseeing for three days to the world-famous and scenic Mt. Kûmgang, just north of the DMZ, by boat. This historic tour would have been unthinkable earlier, but it was rather a matter of "pre-arranged tours" than "tourism": the 1,300 visitors, of whom most were members of divided families, were required to strictly adhere to three rules during their visit. Firstly, they were not allowed to take pictures outside of the designated areas. Secondly, they were not permitted to have any contacts

---

17 Harrison, ibid., 3 April, 1999, p. 8; Korea Institute for National Unification (KINU), *The Unification Environment and Relations Between South and North Korea: 1999-2000* (Seoul: KINU, 2000a), pp. 159-160. The quotation is from KINU (ibid., p. 159). Whether any South Korean official actually has said so is not known by the author.

18 Brown, "North Korea in 1998: A Year of Foreboding Developments", *Asian Survey* 39 (1999), no. 1, p. 132; Foster-Carter, ibid., *2002* (London: Europa Publications Ltd., 2001), p. 627; Harrison, ibid., 3 April, 1999, p. 9; Park, "South Korea in 1998: Swallowing the Bitter Pills of Restructuring", *Asian Survey* 39 (1999), no. 1, p. 138; Shim, ibid., 11 June, 1998, p. 30; Yang, ibid., 1998, pp. 49, 54. Original quotation marks.

with North Koreans. Thirdly, they were not to criticize North Korea in any fashion whatsoever.

Such tours have continued to be run and, according to a survey conducted in conjunction with the anniversary, in 1999, of the first tour, they have been favourably met by the Korean people. The visitors to Mt. Kûmgang themselves have, unsurprisingly, been particularly favourable towards this policy, believing that it contributes, in several different ways, to the improvement of North-South relations.[19]

While cattle deliveries and tourism were new signs of a thaw in inter-Korean relations, economic exchanges took place also. In 1996, the Daewoo Group had broken new ground by setting up a US$ 10m joint-venture with a North Korean partner, in order to produce garments and plastic bags for export. As of 1998, the value of the joint exports annually amounted to US$ 35m. But, although the establishment of the factory had raised hopes for economic cooperation, in 2000, after five years of operations, it had never made a profit, in contrast to similar Daewoo factories in Indonesia, El Salvador and Burma.

One motive for investment was to try and build up the North Korean economy for eventual unification, an idea which concurred with that of Rhee. The North Korean GDP in the year 2000 was only 4 per cent of the South Korean: the economic gap between them was far larger than those pertaining in Germany and Yemen prior to their 1990 unifications. As of 2003, the figure was a mere 3 per cent. Thus, if there was to be any rise in business exchanges, this would be from a low base line, since inter-Korean trade, having reached a value of US$ 308m in 1997, fell to US$ 222m in 1998, as a result of hikes in the foreign exchange rate and the economic crisis in South Korea. However, by 1999 the volume of trade began to increase again to reach a record level of US$ 333m (cf. p. 57).

The rise was to a large extent due to the growth of what are known as processing-on-commission deals. It is noteworthy that trade balances began changing in South Korea's favour, from 1998 onwards. The trade surpluses were a result of rising trade in non-commercial products such as donations of heavy oil and fertilizer, shipments of machinery and equipment for building light-water reactors and pursuing the Mt. Kûmgang project as well as deliveries of base materials, parts and facilities for the entrusted assembling of manufactured products in the North. But commercial trade was still, in 1999, in the North's favour. The South's trade surplus was thus only nominal. South Korea's rising imports in 1999 were due to purchases of assembled industrial products, mainly textiles, and agricultural commodities. Forest and marine products were also major imports from North Korea. South Korea's main exports were non-metal minerals, chemical products, textiles, machinery and vehicles.

---

19 Kang, "Bridging the Divide: A Survey on the Mt. Kumgang Tour", *East Asian Review* 12 (2000), no. 1, pp. 78-80; *Newsreview*, "Cruising into History", 21 November, 1998, pp. 8-10; "A Mountain of Memories: Tourists Bask in the Grandeur of Mt. Kumgang – and Pray for Reunion with Separated Families", 28 November, 1998, pp. 10-11. Author's quotation marks.

Problems in expanding trade were experienced because of the shortage of foreign exchange in North Korea and high transportation costs.[20]

The processing-on-commission trade, which began on a small scale in 1992, showed a typical trade pattern between an advanced and a developing nation, in which South Korean firms manufactured or assembled their products in North Korea in order to benefit from the lower wage rates. However, in the case of Daewoo, the cost of labour amounting to over US$ 150 a month was higher than in many other low-wage countries due to strict minimum-wage requirements, which offset the advantage of having workers speaking the same language. In addition, shipping costs for a container were, due to the small trade volumes, also higher than the cost of sending goods to Germany!

In 1999, textiles were by far the most important products involved in this expanding trade which, as of October 1999, involved 130 firms and 169 products. Other products made were, with the exception of shoes, more advanced ones, including colour TV sets, auto wiring, computer monitors and audio cassettes. As of 11 November, 1998 about 20 South Korean firms, including the Daewoo and Hyundai Group, had received approval for investing in the North, to a total value of US$ 16.8m.

The North Korean defector, Hwang Jang-yop, while acknowledging the tremendous economic potential of South Korea made in 1999, the following assessment of the possibilities for business cooperation: "If all of the South's idle machinery and facilities were shipped to the North for economic reconstruction, and if major South Korean industries advance into North Korea in earnest, the North Korean economy could quickly develop to the point where it would soon resemble that of the South". On the basis of his having lived in South Korea for eighteen months, he went on to propose that such a transition could well be achieved within a decade.[21] It is hard to determine whether his assessment is true or not, but it neglects the sense of inferiority that North Korea's leaders no doubt would feel by being led by South Korea.

In addition to this business, a US$ 4.6 billion agreement was signed in December 1999, between KEDO and the Korea Electric Power Corporation for the construction of two light-water reactors, in North Korea replacing the Soviet designed graphite-moderated reactors. At the same time the agreement was signed, there were already about 220 South Korean workers in North Korea, preparing for the construction work. The project was scheduled to be completed by 2007-2008 and was expected to greatly expand North-South exchanges. The South Korean magazine *Newsreview*

---

20 Ash, "Economy", in *The Far East and Australasia 2005* (London: Europa Publications Ltd., 2004), p. 507; Kim, "North Korea in 1999: Bringing The Grand Chollima March Back In", *Asian Survey* 40 (2000), no. 1, pp. 161-62; KINU, ibid., 2000a, pp. 123-26, 129-133; Shim, ibid.,11 June, 1998, p. 31; Yoon, "Dollars and Sentiments", *FEER*, 22 June, 2000, p. 20.

21 Hwang, "Strategy for Peaceful Korean Unification", *Korea Focus* 7 (1999), no. 1, pp. 45-6; Kim, ibid., 2000, p. 162; KINU, ibid., 2000a, pp. 127-28, 132-33; Yoon, ibid., 22 June, 2000, p. 20.

regarded the agreement as "another step forward in solving the North's nuclear threat" and a "contribution to securing peace and stability on the Korean Peninsula".[22]

Besides cattle deliveries, tourism and economic exchanges, the policies of the Kim Dae Jung government have contributed to the rise in the number of visits to North Korea and the expansion of socio-cultural exchanges.[23] 3,317 South Koreans visited North Korea during 1998, excluding the tourists to Mt. Kûmgang, which included scholars, journalists and publishers as well as figures from the worlds of art, culture, religion, sports, tourism and environment. In contrast, the total number of South Korean visitors to North Korea from 1989 to 1997 was only 2,408.[24] Nonetheless, the rising number of visitors shrinks into virtual insignificance compared to visits permitted within pre-unity Germany.

Increasingly active socio-cultural exchanges were initiated thanks to the sunshine policy. Between 2-12 May, 1998, the South Korean Children's Arts Troupe, "Little Angels" with 66 members performing traditional music, visited North Korea. This was significant because it was the first civilian arts organization to perform in the North. In November 1998, officials from "The North-South Childhood Friends" visited the North as part of their first campaign launched labelled "Hello! Friend". It delivered 300 self-portraits by school children and received tens of pictures from the Mangyôngdae Female Students' Palace. Cartoons, picture and story books have also been exchanged, facilitating mutual understanding. In early 2004, more than 20,000 South Korean children took part in this campaign.

The photo book *From Mt. Paektu to Mt. Halla – The Fatherland Seen from the Lens* was published, and a photo exhibition was held in Seoul 29 May until 11 June, 1998. A measure to open up to the North Korean media was taken with the decision of the South's government, in October 1999, to allow public access to North Korea's satellite TV broadcasts. In October 1998, South Korean musicians were, for the first time, granted permission to participate in "The Yoon Yi-sang Unification Concert" in P'yôngyang. In addition, the Hankyoreh Unification and Culture Foundation staff, a total of 14 people, were permitted to take part in the concert.

In December 1999, the jointly organized "Peace and Friendship Concert 2000", with popular singers from both Koreas, was held in P'yôngyang. The South Korean Seoul Broadcasting Station (SBS) TV broadcast recorded programs from the concert

---

22 Kim, ibid., 2000, p. 162; *Newsreview*, "Kudos for KEDO: Contract signed to facilitate construction of n-reactors in N.K.", 18 December, 1999, pp. 5-6.

23 However, in 1998, students and activists continued to be arrested, under the National Security Law whose Article 7 provides shorter sentences for the act of "praising" or "benefitting" the enemy, in seeming contradiction to the sunshine policy, for discussing reunification, publishing socialist materials or for simply holding views considered to be similar to those of the North Korean government (cf. p. 52: fn. 5). From Amnesty International, *Republic of Korea (South Korea): Amnesty International calls for prisoner releases and a halt to National Security Law arrests* (London, July 1998), pp. 1, 2. Original quotation marks.

24 KINU, ibid., 2000a, pp. 134-36; Ministry of Unification (MoU), *Kim Dae-jung's Policies on North Korea: Achievements and Future Goals* (Seoul: MoU, 1999), pp. 20-21.

afterwards. Later in December 1999, "The National Unification Concert" was held in P'yôngyang with a joint performance by popular singers from both Koreas.[25]

A number of religious and scientific conferences also took place during 1999, such as "The Role of Religionists for the Unification of Korea" held 24-27 April in Beijing which was attended by five representatives from North Korea and 29 from South Korea. The participants, who also hailed from Japan, announced "the 1999 Beijing Declaration" which urged believers to make efforts for unification. Students from both Koreas attended between, 25-29 July, their fifth joint seminar in Beijing under the topic "The Role of Youth for Establishing a Unified Fatherland".

The scientific meetings held in China during 1999, included the international conference "Situation and Future of the Korean Race Toward the New Millennium" held between 22-24 July to commemorate the 50th anniversary of the foundation of Yônbyôn (Yanbian) University. "The Fourth International Seminar on the Computerization of the Korean Language" was held 13-15 August. A conference of environment specialists on protection of forests in North Korea was held in September and "The Fifth Conference on Unification Issues" was held 26-27 October. Significantly, the August conference attracted attention as an exemplary event in the field of academic cooperation. An inter-Korean common dictionary of computer terminologies containing 2,500 words and an index written in Korean, Japanese and Chinese was published, as the outcome of a joint research project which had taken five years to complete. A reception with scholars from both Koreas was held in Yônbyôn to celebrate the publication. Finally, the first visit ever to North Korea by eleven leading figures from South Korean cultural and artistic circles, took place between 31 August-7 September, at the North's invitation.[26]

A number of sporting exchanges took place during 1999, for the first time since 1990. In August 1999, national umbrella organizations for trade unions held the first workers' football matches ever in P'yôngyang. Thirty-seven South Koreans went North on this occasion. In September 1999, men and women's basketball teams from Hyundai, who were building an indoor sports complex in P'yôngyang, and North Korea played goodwill matches, hailed as the "Unification Basketball Games" which were also broadcast on South Korean TV, in the first live broadcast of a joint cultural event from North Korea. Seventy-nine South Koreans on this

---

25 Cho, *NGOs-rûl t'onghan Nambuk sahoe munhwa kyoryu hyômnyôk chûngjin pangan yôn'gu* (Seoul: Minjok t'ongil yôn'guwôn), 1998, pp. 25-6, 31; Cho, *Nambuk sahoe munhwa kyoryu hyômnyôg-ûi p'yôngga-wa palch'ôn panghyang* (Seoul: T'ongil yôn'guwôn, 1999), pp. 32, 34; Cho, "Chôngsang hoedam", 2002, pp. 4-5; Cho, "NGOs and Inter-Korean Socio-Cultural Exchanges and Cooperation", *International Journal of Korean Unification Studies* 11 (2002), no. 1, p. 111; KINU, ibid., 2000a, pp. 136-7, 140; Lee et al., *Nambukhan p'yônghwa kongjon-ûl wihan sahoe munhwa kyoryu hyômnyôg-ûi hwalsônghwa pangan* (Seoul: T'ongil yôn'guwôn, 2001), pp. 116, 117; MoU, ibid., p. 20; Yi, "Nambuk ôrin-i-ga hamkke hanûn t'ongil madang-ûl", *Minjok hwahae* 2004 (1/2), p. 67.

26 Kang et al., *Nambukhan p'yônghwa kongjon-gwa Nambuk yônhap ch'ujin-ûl wihan chigôp kyoyuk hullyôn punya-ûi yôn'gye pangan yôn'gu* (Seoul: T'ongil yôn'guwôn, 2001), p. 151; KINU, ibid., 2000a, pp. 136, 137, 138-39.

occasion travelled northwards. These games were reciprocated when a North Korean delegation, consisting of a total of 62 people, visited Seoul in December 1999. *Newsreview* considered this visit by the North Korean basketball team to be of considerable significance since it was a "...departure from the established pattern of unilateral visits to North Korea, by South Koreans". In fact, it was the first visit by North Koreans to South Korea, since 1993.[27]

In spite of these contacts, it is worth asking whether socio-cultural exchanges would have become more frequent if the North Korean regime had not been, as the Korea Institute for National Unification (2000) observed, "...concerned about the possibility of social instability caused by the influx of new culture from outside...". A sign that party officials and security personnel seriously feared the consequences of an eventual reunification, is noted by the South Korean scholar Suh Byung-Moon in 1997, who wrote that more than two million North Koreans thought that they might get punished by their own people. Including their families, four to five million North Koreans had such worries.[28]

But North Korea was unable to completely close its doors to the outside world, not least because of its reliance on foreign aid. During 1998, the South Korean government continued to provide humanitarian aid, including food, fertilizer, clothes and medicine, in cooperation with international relief agencies. This aid was continued throughout 1999. In February 1999, the South Korean government allowed diversified support channels to encourage support to North Korea on a civilian level. Civilian organizations would provide direct aid without being required to work through the Korean National Red Cross. By the end of 1999, the total amount of aid provided since June 1995, by South Korea to North Korea, had reached a value of US$ 360.4m, that is 25 per cent of the total support received by the North.[29] These figures imply, along with the trade statistics, an increasing North Korean dependence on South Korea that somewhat resembles the case in Germany, prior to unification. More significantly, this took place between two states with considerably poorer relations and where North Korea's pursuit of juche did not correspond with economic realities.

3.6 Steps backwards in inter-Korean relations, 1998-1999

While the developments described above were considered to be steps forward in inter-Korean relations, there were also events which drove the process backwards. Thus, the first meetings between North and South Korean government officials for

---

27 Cho, ibid., 2002a, pp. 3-4, 9; Cho, ibid., 2002b, p. 113; KINU, ibid., 2000a, pp. 139, 140, 163; Lee, *Pukhan munhwa-ûi suyong silt'ae chosa* (Seoul: T'ongil yôn'guwôn, 2001), p. 45: fn. 62; Lee et al., ibid., p. 117; *Newsreview*, "Inter-Korean Full Court Press: N.K. basketball giant visits Seoul for historic games", 25 December, 1999, pp. 8-9.

28 KINU, ibid., 2000a, p. 142; Suh, "Hyanghu t'ongil chôngch'aek panghyang I", Minjok t'ongil yôn'guwôn, *1997 nyôndo ch'och'ông seminar kyôlgwa pogosô* (Seoul: Minjok t'ongil yôn'guwôn, 1998), p. 142.

29 KINU, ibid., 2000a, pp. 146-48, 150-151; *Newsreview*, ibid., 21 November, 1998, p. 9.

nearly four years, which were held in Beijing, at the North's suggestion in April 1998, ended in failure. South Korea rejected a request from North Korea for 200,000 tons of fertilizer due to the prior refusal of the North Korean government to modify its approach to the issue of allowing members of divided families to meet.[30] The reason for the P'yôngyang government's stubborn resistance on this latter point was due to the fear that this sort of humanitarian action through the principle of reciprocity, could undermine support for Kim Jong Il. Another reason was the fear that family reunions as a socio-cultural exchange would lead to an influx of outside information. Yet, South Korea eventually delivered 100,000 tons of fertilizer to North Korea so as to induce the North to resume negotiations.

However, even the second meeting on family reunions, held in June and July 1999, in Beijing, held on the same terms as the previous meeting, ended in failure. The reason given this time was, firstly, the attitude held by North Korea, that the very fact that it was participating at all in the talks was an indication of its generosity towards South Korea, since this was to implicitly recognize the success of the South's policy of engagement. Secondly, North Korea had demanded an apology for the recent clashes in the West (Yellow) Sea. Thirdly, while South Korea regarded this issue of reunion to be a humanitarian matter, for North Korea, it was a political one.[31]

Besides the failure of these talks; there were also incursions by submarines and spying incidents. A North Korean mini-submarine with an infiltration team carrying firearms and infiltration equipment on board was accidentally caught up in a fishing net, close to Sokch'o, on the eastern coast, in June 1998. This, only one week after Chung Ju Yung had travelled to North Korea with his cows, was not a deliberate provocation. Nine members of the crew were found dead inside the submarine. President Kim called on the P'yôngyang government to "accept responsibility" and prevent any recurrence. Not long after the incident, three weeks later, in July, an armed North Korean agent was found dead washed up on the east coast. But contacts, nevertheless, did continue, as outlined above. In November 1998, a third incident occurred when a speedboat evaded pursuit along the western shore. Since this incident coincided with the Mt. Kûmgang tour, the explanation may be that hard-line elements in the North Korean armed forces now were attempting to undermine

---

30 MoU (ibid., p. 25) records that in 1998 there were 377 cases where dispersed families confirmed the family members' fates and 108 actual cases of reunion, but unfortunately does not record how, when and where these took place. KINU (ibid., 2000a, p. 153) records higher figures for 1999: 461 against 181 cases. The total number recorded for the period 1990 to 30 November, 1999 is 1,852, with 444 cases taking place in third countries. How and when the reunions took place is unclear.

31 Brown, ibid., p. 131; KINU, ibid., 2000a, pp. 151; *Newsreview*, ibid., 21 November, 1998, p. 9; "Stalemate: Family reunion talks stalled again", 10 July, 1999, p. 9; Shim, ibid., 11 June, 1998, p. 31.

the sunshine policy.[32] In December 1998, a third spy boat made an incursion off the southern coast, but on this occasion the intruder was sunk.[33]

In early June 1999, North Korean vessels crossed the Northern Limit Line, intruding on South Korea's territorial waters, in the Western Sea. In stark contrast, the Mt. Kûmgang tours continued as usual along the Eastern Sea. In these ways, the North Korean military created tension, with the aim of raising pressures prior to the North-South talks and elevating North Korea's position in negotiations with the US. In the clashes that took place on 15 June, 1999, after nine days of tensions, at least thirty North Koreans were killed in what the South Korean scholar Samuel S. Kim (2000) calls "...the most serious naval clash and P'yôngyang's most humiliating military defeat since the 1953 armistice...". A North Korean warship was destroyed and several other ships were seriously damaged, while South Korea only suffered a few lightly wounded seamen. That the battle just lasted for 14 minutes can only have reinforced the North Korean military's shock. A few days later the North Korean authorities detained a tourist, a South Korean housewife. She had allegedly attempted to entice a tour guide to defect to South Korea. As a consequence, the Hyundai Concern cancelled the Mt. Kûmgang tours but the tourist was released within a week, although only after having been forced to write a "confession".

But such incidents could not bring about the collapse of South Korea's engagement policy and the tours were resumed. In addition to the incidents described above, serious concerns about security were roused in Seoul as well as in Washington and Tokyo when North Korea, on 31 August, 1998, surprised observers by launching its first multi-stage missile. The missile splashed down 1,380 kilometres away in the Western Pacific, to the east of Japan. With this range capacity, North Korea potentially had most of the region's capitals in its sights.[34]

3.7 Official contacts and developments in North Korea

Although no other South Korean President had ever made efforts to improve relations with North Korea similar to those established by Kim Dae Jung, official contacts remained in stalemate ever since the failed talks, of April 1998. This was in sharp contrast to the rise in non-official North-South contacts throughout the year. However, in February 1999, despite the setbacks described above, North Korea proposed to hold high-level political talks in the latter half of the year on the issues relating to the Basic Agreement, inter-Korean exchanges and as well as the issue of the divided families. But North Korea attached difficult conditions to a resumption

---

32 This argument is from Harrison (ibid., 3 April, 1999, p. 9).

33 Brown, ibid., p. 132; *Newsreview*, ibid., 21 November, 1998, p. 10; Park, ibid., p. 138; Shim, ibid., 9 July, 1998, p. 16. "Bear responsibility" is quoted from Shim, ibid.

34 Brown, ibid., pp. 129-130; Kim, ibid., 2000, pp. 160-161; KINU, ibid., 2000a, pp. 80, 84-5, 106-107; Park, ibid., p. 138; Shim, "Fire, Backfire: Missile test threatens overtures to Pyongyang", *FEER*, 10 September, 1998, p. 22. "Confession" is quoted from Kim (ibid., p. 161).

of talks including a condition that South Korea abolish its National Security Law and suspend joint South Korea-US military exercises; the talks therefore did not materialize. Nor did President Kim's proposals soon afterwards for an exchange of North Korean spies and South Korean war prisoners and citizens kidnapped by the North. North Korea rejected the proposal and denounced it as a merchant's theory.

However, a major step forward in official contacts was taken when President Kim in March 2000, launched in a policy speech what became known as the "Berlin Declaration". Here he declared that the South Korean government was "...ready to help North Korea tide over its economic difficulties". Assistance to develop the North's infrastructure was also offered. Besides economic cooperation, the issues he suggested to be raised in the North-South dialogue were to re-unite divided families, to bring an end to the Cold War structure and to secure peace. When returning to Seoul, President Kim made the forecast that widened economic cooperation would enable South Korea to benefit from inexpensive but trained manpower in North Korea and to earn large amounts of money. But he declared it was more important that such cooperation would prevent war and thereby protect the lives of 70 million Koreans. He also predicted that, during his term in office, there might well be a conclusion to the border structure along the Korean Peninsula remaining from the Cold War era. North Korea soon responded positively to the Berlin Declaration by interpreting it as an opportunity to acquire more economic aid.[35]

When the Berlin Declaration was delivered, it was at a time when North Korea had become more active with regard to attempts, through diplomacy, to join the international community and to find solutions to their severe economic difficulties. Another step in this direction was that North Korean officials in the late 1990s were sent abroad to receive training from the International Monetary Fund and the World Bank.

It should be noted that these economic difficulties had, as early as 1995, and onwards, led ordinary people, party members, teachers, doctors, security officials and soldiers to cross the border from North Korea into China in search of food, although North Korean authorities had imposed stricter border controls to preserve the governments' political control over its own citizens, by keeping them in and holding foreign influences out. Yet, this migration was an indication both of the faltering ability of Kim Jong Il to control the movement of his people and of the threat posed to the very survival of his government from people who returned to North Korea, bringing with them new ideas about the world.

The total number of what became known as the "food migrants" were estimated to be between 100,000 and 400,000 people in 1998 alone, but most of them only

---

35 Kim, "North Korea in 2000: Surviving through High Hopes of Summit Diplomacy", *Asian Survey* 41 (2001), no. 1, pp. 14-15; KINU, ibid., 2000a, pp. 104-105, 110-111, 157; Shim and Edwards, "No Turning Back", *FEER*, 22 June, 2000, p. 16; T'ongil yôn'guwôn, *T'ongil hwangyông-mith Nambukhan kwangye-wa chônmang* (Seoul: KINU, 2000b), p. 86; Yun, "Imgi-nae naengjôn chongsik kanûng", *Digital Chosôn Ilbo*, 11 March, 2000. The quotation is from Kim (ibid., p. 14).

spent a few days in China. Another 100,000 people were estimated to have crossed the Chinese border throughout 1999. Hundreds of them stayed in the border regions, while 10,000 to 20,000 people were observed defecting to China. This migration even led to some casual meetings, in the border region of Yônbyôn, between a few North and South Koreans, something which, as we have seen, was not possible in North Korea itself. But since it was impossible to discuss life in the North, such interaction might not have had much impact on relations.

Another indication of the growing social discontent in North Korea was the fact that, in 1999, the number of defectors to the South reached a total of 136 individuals, doubling the 1998 figure. It is also worth adding here that, in 1995, North Korea, after a series of natural disasters issued, given the juche idea, an unprecedented appeal for humanitarian assistance. The appeal resulted in food aid being provided by the global humanitarian community, including South Korea, the United States and Japan. The presence of this community in North Korea has contributed significantly to what the British scholar, Hazel Smith (1999), has termed a "de facto opening up of the country to the outside world". In 1998-1999, the death toll from the food crisis was by some observers estimated to be as high as two or three million North Koreans.[36]

The expansion of the role and function of the market for farmers' products and the emergence of black markets were indications that the North Korean government had begun to tacitly acknowledge private economic activity. At the beginning of 2000, farmers' markets, of which there were about 300 to 350, accounted for around 60 per cent of grain purchases and for 70 per cent of purchases of the daily necessities of life. Several hundred products were sold at free-market prices. The authorities could no longer control citizens' frequent travels to find food and free exchanges of information about the economic hardships. This situation weakened control over the population and the role of ideology as a force for social integration was, as a result, undermined.

The Articles contained in the new Kim Il Sung Constitution, from 1998, that relate to the economy, recognize, in constitutional terms, changes in the economy that had already taken place during the past few years and provided yet another indication of the manner in which the North Korean government was becoming increasingly aware of its economic difficulties. These Articles establish, or confirm, an expansion of the scope of private ownership, the recognition of the right of freedom to travel and to change one's place of residence, encouragement for the establishment, and operation of businesses in special economic zones, the extension

---

36 Eberstadt, *The End of North Korea* (Washington, D.C: The AEI Press, 1999), pp. 46, 88, 99; Foley, ibid., pp. 58, 65; KINU, ibid., 2000a, pp. 78-9, 144; *Korea Now*, "Full Tilt on the Diplomatic Front: N.K. warms up to international community to stay clear of total collapse", 25 March, 2000, p. 12; Lawrence, "North Meets South", *FEER*, 29 April, 1999, p. 14; Shim, "A Crack in The Wall", *FEER*, 29 April, 1999, pp. 10-12; Smith, "'Opening up' by default: North Korea, the humanitarian community and the crisis", *The Pacific Review* 12 (1999), no. 3, pp. 453-4, 456-7, 476: fn. 26. "Food migrants" is quoted from Shim (ibid., p. 11).

of the operations of independent enterprises as well as adopting the concept of cost, price and profitability, as well as the expansion of foreign trade and the elimination of the right of "state supervision". In addition, that part of the state apparatus concerned with the economy was reduced, from 32 to 23 organs, while those remaining were strengthened through the appointment of economic specialists, as a new class of technocrats.

However, the significance of such steps should not be exaggerated, since the Supreme People's Assembly, during the session in April 1999, stated that they still entertained "...the intention to stick to their own socialism through the laws of the people's economic plans and rejecting the capitalist market economy...". Consequently, there were intensified ideological-orientation programmes in all sectors of North Korean society.[37]

While it was too early to speak of a launch of a new economic development strategy, North Korea had become more active in the international arena since 1999. Besides the economic difficulties, the persistent implementation of the engagement policy on the part of South Korea, including efforts to persuade its major allies the United States and Japan to befriend North Korea, had also contributed to this change. Thus North Korea, during 1999, actively participated in the conferences of international economic organizations. In January 2000, North Korea established diplomatic relations with Italy. Later during the year it also restored relations with Australia and established new ones with the Philippines and the United Kingdom.

North Korea has, from that point, been holding, or planning, negotiations with major Western countries and nations belonging to the non-aligned movement and has, further, sought membership of various international organizations and regional groups. The North Korean Foreign Minister, Paek Nam-sun, visited China, where he held talks with Chinese leaders in mid-March 2000, shortly after Kim Jong Il visited the Chinese Embassy in P'yôngyang in order to strengthen relations with China. The purpose of the Foreign Minister's visit was to re-new cooperative ties with China in order to gain advantages in North Korea's dealings with its two major capitalist foes, the US and Japan, with which it lacked normal relations.[38]

---

37 Ahn, "The Kim Il Sung Constitution and the Change of the Kim Jong-il System in North Korea", *International Journal of Korean Unification Studies* 8 (1999), pp. 179, 191-92, 195-97; Chung and Jeon, "The Farmers' Market in North Korea: The Seed of Capitalism?", *East Asian Review* 12 (2000), no. 1, pp. 101-102; KINU, ibid., 2000a, pp. 66-7, 78. "State supervision" is quoted from Ahn, ibid., p. 191. The quotation is from KINU (ibid., p. 66).

38 Choi, "White Cloak Diplomacy: North Korea emerges from isolation, forging ties abroad", *Korea Now*, 8 April, 2000, pp. 8-9; Harrison, ibid., 3 April, 1999, p. 8; Kim, ibid., 2000, pp. 20-21; KINU, ibid., 2000a, p. 164: 2000b, pp. 75, 130; *Korea Now*, ibid., 25 March, 2000, pp. 12-13.

3.8 Historic North-South summit and its aftermath

While North Korea was becoming more active internationally, a major breakthrough in official contacts was achieved on 10 April, 2000. Following the Berlin Declaration, and secret talks held in China between representatives of the two Koreas, an agreement was announced with regard to the first-ever meeting between the leaders of North and South Korea, to be held in P'yôngyang between 12-14 June, 2000. According to Samuel S. Kim (2001), the summit became possible since "More than anything else, the offer of substantial if unspecified governmental aid to rebuild North Korea's decrepit infrastructure was implicitly the main causal force behind Kim Jong Il's decision to agree to an inter-Korean summit". In fact, a special prosecutor concluded in 2003, that the Hyundai Group, which helped to arrange the summit, had paid the North about $ 500 million just before President Kim's visit. This illegal funding was cited as the reason why the Hyundai Group chairman Chung Mong Jun committed suicide.[39] The scandal implies that North Korea entered dialogue to seek economic aid rather than to engage in an open dialogue that perhaps could have had the potential to transform relations in the long run.

The summit took place in P'yôngyang, during 13-15 June; the supposed reason for the delay was that North Korea wanted to make sure that the money was in one of its overseas bank accounts. The signing of the first document ever issued by the two Korean heads of state, the historic five-point Joint Declaration, took place on 15 June. This document included the points that the reunification of Korea was to be through their own efforts. While reunification was to be achieved, the different unification formulas were to be acknowledged, and from some time around 15 August the exchange of divided families was to be carried out, balanced economic development, together with exchanges in such fields as sport and culture, were to be pursued, and, finally, dialogue was to be established between cross-border governmental authorities. President Kim also invited Kim Jong Il to visit Seoul, which he agreed to do "at an appropriate time". However the Joint Declaration, due to North Korea's strong opposition had nothing to say about military and security matters, not even in general terms about working together for tension-reduction and confidence-building which caused some disappointment in South Korea. In fact, since the core of inter-Korean confrontation is military rivalry, a general perception at this time was that, without solving military issues, it would be impossible to achieve improvements in contacts in other fields, sustaining exchanges and cooperation.[40]

The summit initiated more active contacts than ever between the two Koreas, which was a development entirely in line with the writings of journalists Shim Jae Hoon and Adrian Edwards: "President Kim's trip to P'yôngyang has opened the

---

39 Kim, ibid., 2001, pp. 13-15; KINU, 2000b, p. 86; Lee, "South Korea in 2003: A Question of Leadership?", *Asian Survey* 44 (2004), no. 1, pp. 134-35.

40 Choi et al., ibid., pp. 165, 167-68; Kim, ibid., 2001, p. 17; KINU, 2000b, pp. 90-92, 98; *Korea Now*, "Text of the N-S Accord", 17 June, 2000, pp. 4-5; Lintner, *Great Leader, Dear Leader: Demystifying North Korea under the Kim Clan* (Chiang Mai: Silkworm Books, 2005), p. 20. Author's quotation marks.

door on new possibilities for dialogue and détente".⁴¹ North Korea now ceased to defame South Korea and a South Korean fishing boat, having unintentionally strayed into the North's territorial waters, was immediately returned. More significantly, in the spirit of the Joint Declaration, at the meeting of the North and South Korean Red Cross Societies, held in late June, an agreement was signed on the reunion of 100 members of divided families, from both sides, between 15-18 August, in Seoul and P'yôngyang.

The whereabouts and status of relatives were to be ascertained before finalization of lists of divided family members were to be chosen for the reunions. This was to avoid the pain and disappointment caused in 1985 to those family members who could not meet their relatives. Each first-generation divided family member would be allowed to meet with up to four relatives.

After exchanges of lists, in August 2000, those ordinary people in South Korea who were members of divided families and who had been selected through a computer lottery, were allowed to meet others, in North Korea, who had been hand-picked for their loyalty to the government in the first family re-unions since 1985. *The Economist* wrote that the re-union was "...an important step in dismantling one of the last frontiers of the Cold War". But the actual number of members of divided families who were able to meet was extremely low, an estimated 7.7 million South Koreans, including 1.2 million who fled from the North during the Korean War, still had relatives in North Korea.⁴² Mutual distrust had apparently not diminished significantly in spite of the summit.

While the first round of family reunions were relatively trouble-free, the second round of reunions of 100 members of divided families, from both sides, from 30 November-2 December were delayed by two months for unexplained internal reasons in the North. Prior to the meeting, North Korea had denounced the South Korean National Red Cross President in charge of family reunions for saying in an interview with a local magazine that the North is poor and lacks freedom. In spite of his apologies, the attacks continued which made him withdraw from his position as host to the visiting divided families.

Simultaneously, South Koreans from divided families were subjected to heavy doses of political propaganda and the personality cult of the leader while they were in North Korea. A reporter from the daily, *Chosun Ilbo*, was detained for three hours while his equipment was searched and some 230 images from his digital camera were deleted. The North also demanded an apology for one of the newspaper's

---

41 Shim and Edwards, ibid., 22 June, 2000, p. 19.
42 *The Economist*, "Hugs for Koreans: But not yet for the North Korean leader", 19 August, 2000, p. 12; Foley, ibid., pp. 117-118, 143; Kim, ibid., 2001, pp. 18-19; KINU, ibid., 2000b, pp. 68, 87, 89, 115-116. According to KINU (ibid., 2000b, p. 115), the number of cases where the divided families confirmed the fate of their relatives during 2000 was 1,239 while the number of reunions taking place in third countries was 148 (cf. p. 67: fn. 30). It is unclear how and when the reunions took place. The figures of divided families that are from Kim (ibid.) differ from those on p. 55 but why is unclear. For a review of the contested numbers of divided families see Foley (ibid., pp. 47-60).

articles. Considering this incident, it is not surprising that North Korea, even after the summit, remained hesitant concerning confirmations of family whereabouts, exchanges of letters and the establishment of a permanent meeting place. Yet, in September 2000, North and South Korea agreed to allow a group of 300 members of divided families, from each state, to exchange letters with relatives on the other side of the border. However, South Korea wanted family reunions to be speeded up and expanded.[43]

On 2 September, 63 former agents from North Korea were repatriated to the North, through P'anmunjôm. In the view of the South Korean magazine *Korea Now*, "The repatriation of 63 former North Korean spies and guerrillas is another big step toward thawing relations of animosity and confrontation between the two Koreas". In spite of this positive evaluation there were, however, protests voiced against this repatriation, where some South Koreans demanded reciprocal action on the part of North Korea, which did not return a single prisoner of war or detainee. Such protests should be seen against the fact that, as of late 2000, 351 South Korean prisoners of war and some 487 abductees, mainly fishermen, were believed to be living under difficult circumstances in the North.

After the summit, the opposition party also protested at what it regarded as the South Korean government's obsession with its policy towards North Korea. This was beginning to place a burden on the economy. Conservatives and the opposition party were strongly critical of the government's one-sided policy of giving without receiving, claiming there was a lack of reciprocity. But the government and the progressives argued that the South's support to North Korea, gradually would make the North open up and change its society.[44]

Significant political measures were taken after the summit in terms of official meetings that included inter-Korean ministerial talks, economic talks and discussions on military matters. The foreign ministers met for the first time in late July, when they were participating in the meeting held by the Association of Southeast Asian Nations Regional Forum (ARF) in Bangkok. They agreed on joint diplomatic efforts to promote inter-Korean reconciliation and cooperation, on the basis of the 15 June Declaration. The ARF Forum, in its turn, reached a decision to approve the North Korean application to join the 22-member Regional Security Dialogue Conference; this was yet another sign of opening up to the world.

The first inter-Korean ministerial talks were held in Seoul 29-31 July. The two states agreed to reopen their border liaison offices in P'anmunjôm, which had been temporarily closed, in November 1996; they actually were opened. They agreed

---

43 *The Economist*, "The Koreas start a slow march, not yet in lockstep", 30 September, 2000, p. 75; Kim, ibid., 2001, pp. 18-19; KINU, ibid., 2000b, pp. 87, 89, 116, 140.

44 Chanda and Shim, "Trouble on the Tracks", *FEER*, 28 September, 2000, p. 14; Ha, "South Korea in 2000: A Summit and the Search for New Institutional Identity", *Asian Survey* 41 (2001), no. 1, p. 31; Kim, ibid., 2001, p. 19; KINU, ibid., 2000b, pp. 117, 136; *Korea Now*, "To Smooth Over Ideological Friction: Seoul repatriates 63 imprisoned North Korean spies in goodwill gesture", 9 September, 2000, pp. 10-12.

to rebuild the rail link Seoul-Sinûiju. On 18 September, a historic groundbreaking ceremony was held on the southern side. The removal of mines began. They also agreed to hold ceremonies on 15 August to support and welcome the 15 June Declaration and to allow pro-North Korean residents in Japan to also visit South Korea for the first time. Visits took place in September and November, respectively.[45]

In a second round of talks, held in P'yôngyang 29 August-1 September, it was decided that economic cooperation would be expanded by introducing four supportive legislative measures on investment guarantees, settlement of commercial disputes, clearance of accounts and avoidance of double taxation. At the third round of talks held on Cheju Island 27-30 September, it was decided that the two states would actively cooperate to solve the issue of divided families and to soon introduce the legislative measures. "The inter-Korean Economic Cooperation Committee" (KECC) would be established to expand economic exchanges and cooperation.

At the fourth round of talks held in P'yôngyang 12-16 December, it was agreed how the KECC would be organized and how it would work. When the KECC held its first meeting in 28-30 December in P'yôngyang, besides discussions on how it would work, concrete issues like in the areas of electricity and the building of the Seoul-Sinûiju railway were raised. At the fourth round of ministerial talks, the agreements on the legislative measures were formerly signed, but they awaited ratification by the parliaments so as to enter into force. Previously, the measures had been discussed at the first round of economic talks (since 1985) held between 25-26 September in Seoul and agreement had been reached at the second round of talks held 8-11 November in P'yôngyang.

The two states held, at South Korea's request, the first round of talks on military matters between defence ministers on Cheju Island, 25-26 September. They agreed to cooperate to solve the military issues between them on the basis of the Joint Declaration. They also agreed to work together to remove the risk of war and to solve issues related to the building of the Seoul-Sinûiju railway through the DMZ, in accordance with the 1953 Armistice Agreement. As in the case of family reunions, the proposals of the South Koreans at these talks included measures that were more radical than the proposals of the North Koreans, which were generally limited to suggestions on clearing mines in readiness for the railway project. South Korea pressed for agreement on such confidence-building measures as the establishment of a military hotline, advanced notification of military manoeuvres and exchange of military observers. A second meeting on military questions would be held in the North in November but due to North Korea's delays, the talks were not held.[46]

---

45 Kim, ibid., 2001, pp. 17, 18, 21; KINU, ibid., 2000b, pp. 72, 87, 93-4, 107-108, 138, 139; *Korea Now*, "Welcoming N.K. into the Fold: Two Koreas enter unprecedented diplomatic heights as foreign ministers step up contacts", 29 July, 2000, pp. 5-6.

46 Chanda and Shim, ibid., 28 September, 2000, p. 16; Choi et al., ibid., p. 50; *The Economist*, ibid., 30 September, 2000, p. 75; Kim, ibid., 2001, pp. 18, 19-20; KINU, ibid., 2000b, pp. 87-8, 94, 95-100, 106, 107-108.

Beside these political contacts, trade expanded and South Korea continued to provide economic aid to North Korea. Trade volume reached a record level of US$ 425m in the year 2000 with a new trade surplus for South Korea (cf. p. 62). This trade volume made South Korea the second largest trading partner of North Korea after China. However, it should be noted that non-commercial trade in the form of mainly humanitarian aid but also equipment for the Mt. Kûmgang tourism project and the building of light-water reactors comprised 44.4 per cent of total trade.

Processing-on-commission trade comprised another 30.4 per cent, as of November 2000. Textiles remained by far the main sector involved but its share fell while the proportions of high-value added electrical and electronic products rose. The main reason for this rise was that Samsung Electronics and other manufacturers of such products moved production facilities to North Korea. It should also be noted that the Korea Institute for National Unification (2001) records that South Korean commodities were traded openly and publically after the summit and the following reunions of divided families [but no examples are recorded here].

In the case of economic aid, South Korea provided altogether US$ 114m to North Korea during 2000, while total foreign economic assistance was US$ 220m (cf. p. 66). 75 per cent of the South's aid was aimed to restore agriculture through deliveries of, for instance, fertilizers and seeds. Other aid areas included health and clothing and "general relief". The government accounted for two-thirds of aid and civilian organizations stood for one-third.[47]

The number of visitors to each Korea rose further and socio-cultural exchanges expanded (cf. pp. 64-6). The number of North Korean visitors to South Korea grew to 706 persons during 2000, compared to just 62 in 1999. The number of South Korean visitors to North Korea was 7,280 persons, against 5,599 in 1999 and 3,317 in 1998. Large-scale events were a major part of the socio-cultural exchanges. The P'yôngyang Student and Youth Art Troupe performed in Seoul 24-27 May. Their visit was followed by performances of the P'yôngyang Circus Troupe from 29 May 29-11 June. Between 18-24 August, a North Korean symphony orchestra held concerts in Seoul. In October, a National Unification Concert was held in P'yôngyang.[48]

In sports, an auto rally took place at Mt. Kûmgang in July. Also in July, the two Koreas played table-tennis matches in P'yôngyang in the first sports event ever broadcast in TV by both Koreas simultaneously for three hours. The 1990 football matches and the 1999 basketball games had been edited and broadcast in South Korea only on the basis of the North's restrictive broadcasting policy. In a highly symbolic event, at the opening and closing ceremony of the Sydney Olympics in

---

47 KINU, ibid., 2000b, pp. 103-106, 119, 122, 123; T'ongil yôn'guwôn, *T'ongil hwangyông-mith Nambukhan kwangye: 2001~2002* (Seoul: KINU, 2001), p. 49. Author's quotation marks. KINU (ibid., 2001, p. 98: table 3-4) records the figure of total economic aid to North Korea during the year 2000 as being US$ 296m due to a non-explained higher figure of aid from other countries.

48 Cho, ibid., 2002a, pp. 3-4; Kim, "Nambuk sahoe munhwa kyoryu-ûi sônggwa-wa munjechôm", *Pukhan* (April 2001), p. 68; KINU, ibid., 2000b, pp. 110-112, 134.

September-October, North and South Korea entered the stadium together holding a flag of the Korean Peninsula. The athletes decided to encourage and support each other throughout the games. In September, 109 South Korean tourists visited Mt. Paektu and P'yôngyang. In October, the sacred fire for the National Athletic Games was for the first time put on at Mt. Kûmgang and transported to Pusan by an excursion ship.

In publishing, meetings were held and the North-South meetings as well as family reunions were reported. Although publishing, due to North Korea's fears of the after-effects from making the actual conditions of the land known, as well as of exchanging information, had been regarded as the most difficult area for exchanges and cooperation, a delegation of more than 40 leaders of South Korean media organizations visited North Korea from 5-12 August and signed an agreement on cooperation in media spheres. The documentary "From Mt. Paektu to Mt. Halla" was shown on Korean Broadcasting System (KBS) TV in September. But, more significant, it was the first joint production and broadcast simultaneously, from Mt. Paektu, Mt. Halla and Seoul with film-makers, and experts participating on the two mountains as well as with ordinary citizens from both states.

In October, the first ever Southern live broadcast from P'yôngyang was made by SBS, which covered the festivities celebrating, the foundation of the Korean Workers' Party (KWP). Forty-two South Koreans, among them representatives of eleven citizen groups, subsequently went to the North. Finally, in religion, a joint mass was held in Seoul and P'yôngyang simultaneously in April during the Easter celebrations. Seven South Korean priests participated in two masses held in P'yôngyang. On 15 August, Buddhists in North and South Korea simultaneously held joint prayers in each state praying for unification. It should be noted that in contrast to meetings previously held abroad, these events now largely took place on the Korean Peninsula.[49]

Besides the above developments, the Korean question was debated at a number of international conferences. The Asia-Europe Meeting held in Seoul in October declared its support for peace on the Korean Peninsula. The resolution was welcomed by North Korea; a reference to the curbing of weapons of mass destruction was deleted thanks to China's intervention. On 31 October, the UN General Assembly adopted without a vote the first-ever inter-Korean joint resolution on Peace, Security and Reunification of the Korean Peninsula. The resolution was, however, more important for its symbolism than for its substance since, although initiated by the South, it had been worked out and submitted by both Koreas.

But in spite of the manifold signs of improved relations after the summit meeting there were, as we have seen, ominous signs that the established pattern of warming relations followed by set backs was to be repeated. *The Economist* wrote in June:

---

49 Cho, ibid., 2002a, pp. 4-6; Cho, ibid., 2002b, pp. 113, 114, 115; Ch'oe, "Nambukhan sahoe munhwa kyoryu-ûi ôje-wa onûl", *Pukhan* (October 2000), p. 46; Harrison, ibid., 2002, p. 95; Kim, ibid., April 2001, pp. 63, 65; KINU, ibid., 2000b, pp. 110-113, 129, 136; Lee et al., ibid., p. 118.

"It is hard to exaggerate the problems the two will face even if they are sincerely bent on reconciliation", implying that it would be advisable not to exaggerate the importance of those conciliatory actions described above. Caution is also advisable because of a number of serious issues that have not been addressed during, or after, the summit, such as North Korean missiles, other weapons of mass destruction and the negotiation of a peace treaty.

A concrete issue that caused North Korean irritation in December, soon after the incidents during the second family reunions, was the view expressed in South Korea's *Defence White Paper 2000*. In this, the Ministry of Defence emphasized the need for continuous security awareness while identifying North Korea as the prime enemy. North Korea regarded this view as "antagonistic" and began threatening to scuttle the rapprochement process. The purpose of the North's criticism was to extract more aid from South Korea in the form of electricity. To avoid total breakdown, the issue was adjudicated by the KECC.[50]

The paper claims that North Korea, despite the inter-Korean thawing, was strengthening its military power by the early 1990s. Estimates by the US Government indicated military spending at about 20-25 per cent of GNP and by the CIA to 22.9 per cent of GDP in 2003 alone. Its basic policy of "communizing" South Korea, that until recently was spending six per cent of its incomparably larger GNP on defence, remained. According to Harrison (2002), as of 1999, North Korea had 1.08 million regular conventional forces against 672,000 in South Korea, and a numerical advantage in many important categories of weaponry and equipment. But the numerical advantage was offset in most categories by South Korean and US technological superiority. According to the South Korean scholar Suh Jae-Jung (2004), South Korea has, despite the official position of the South Korean and US governments that the South is inferior in terms of aggregate military power, sufficient capacity to stop and defeat a North Korean blitzkrieg attempt without US support. It outstrips the North in important categories of military power. North Korea has a numerical advantage in every type of weapon, but its military is basically of 1950s vintage whereas South Korea's military has the latest equipment. Other disadvantages for North Korea are the smaller population and economy.

The reunification of Korea on its own terms has always been North Korea's overriding policy objective: the preamble to the charter of the KWP declares that "the present task of the KWP is to ensure the complete victory of socialism in the Democratic People's Republic of Korea and the accomplishment of the revolutionary goals of national liberation and the people's democracy in the entire area of the country". In addition, North Korean law, as well as South Korean, claims authority over Koreans

---

50 *The Economist*, "Encounter in Pyongyang", 17 June, 2000, p. 15; Foster-Carter, "The Koreas: Peace in our time?", September 2000; Kim, ibid., 2001, pp. 20, 21; KINU, 2000b, pp. 101-102, 126-27. Original quotation is from Kim (ibid., p. 20).

in the whole peninsula.⁵¹ The remaining difficulties involved in the rapprochement process should not be underestimated.

3.9 Inter-Korean relations, 2001-2002

The P'yôngyang summit was a breakthrough in North-South relations, but the signs of a return to worsened relations during the fall of 2000, were reinforced during 2001, when contacts became less active. Kim Jong Il made no return visit to South Korea. The third round of family reunions of 100 members of divided families from each Korea took place simultaneously in Seoul and P'yôngyang 26-28 February (cf. p. 73-4). It included the release of a few South Koreans who had been abducted to the North and some prisoners of war. In March, letters were, for the first time, exchanged between 300 members of divided families from each state at P'anmunjôm, through the auspices of the National Red Crosses. South Korea's Ministry of Unification estimated one year after the summit that more than 10,000 people from divided families had had confirmation of the fate of their family members.

In accordance with the sunshine policy, several socio-cultural exchanges took place but they were somewhat less active than they had been during 2000; they were not free from the prevailing North-South Cold War atmosphere and mentality. As previously, far more South Koreans visited North Korea than vice-versa. The latter figure reduced dramatically to just 172 persons and included only one North Korean football player living in Japan in the socio-cultural field.

From 22-24 February, another conference in the series "Computerization of the Korean Language" referred to previously was held in China, with participants from the two Koreas and China who exchanged research materials. In March, "The North-South Joint Exhibition and Scientific Debate Forum on the Illegal Integration of Korea into the Japanese Empire" took place from 1-6 March in P'yôngyang. Twenty-one South Korean scholars participated in this first meeting between historians. Significantly, the exhibition opened on the 82nd anniversary of the 1919 March First Independence Movement. Scholars were united in their condemnation of the Japanese occupation: a joint statement against the Japanese revision of history textbooks was adopted, on the North's initiative. North and South Korean scholars presented papers on such topics as literature, *Sirhak* ("Practical Learning") and archaeology at "The 20th Conference of the Association of Korean Studies in Europe" held in London 4-8 April.⁵²

---

51 Ash, ibid., *2005*, p. 505; Eberstadt, ibid., 25-6, 47, 121; Harrison, ibid., 2002, p. 126; Kim, ibid., 2001, p. 20; KINU, 2000b, p. 101; Song, *The Rise*, p. 49; Suh, ibid., pp. 64-5, 67. Original quotations are from Eberstadt (ibid., p. 26) and Kim (ibid., p. 20).

52 Ahn, "North Korea in 2001: At a Crossroads", *Asian Survey* 42 (2002), no. 1, pp. 46, 48; Association of Korean Studies in Europe, *Conference Programme* (London: University of London), 2001; Cho, ibid., 2002a, pp. 6, 7; KINU, ibid., 2001, pp. 67, 70, 87-8, 90-91, 95, 104, 105; Lee et al., ibid., p. 119; Sin, "Ilche-ûi chosôn kangjôm pulpôpsông-e taehan Nambuk kongdong charyo chônsihoe: Nambuk kongdong taech'ô-ro wanjônhan ilche

In arts, a joint performance as well as separate ones of the national lyric drama *Ch'unhyang* (*Fragrance of Spring*) took place in P'yôngyang 1-2 February.[53] It should be noted that the South Korean scholar O Ki-sông (1999) writes that North and South Koreans can look at Ch'unhyang without much different views. According to his compatriot Ko Yong-gwôn (2002), on this occasion national homogeneity was reconfirmed and mutual understanding was enhanced. Remarkably, the first joint 3D animation film "The lazy cat Dingka" was under production; the first part was presented on Children's Day, 5 May, in South Korea. From 2-5 June, "The Traditional Clothes Exhibition" was opened in P'yôngyang by a South Korean delegation, with more than 50 representatives. The joint photo exhibition "From Mt. Paektu to Mt. Halla", with 50 photos each, was held in P'yôngyang 14-24 June and in Seoul 14-23 August but, whereas eight South Korean officials visited P'yôngyang, no North Koreans went to Seoul.

In the field of religion, seven South Korean religious officials, including the chair-man of the Christian Friendship Association for the Unification of Korea, Chin Yo-han, participated in a joint mass held during Easter at Mt. Kûmgang. In April, a delegation of 31 people from the Korean Council of Religionists for Peace, including Secretary-General Pyôn Chin-hûng, visited the North.

They discussed holding joint activities. In sports, a unification rally took place at Mt. Kûmgang in July. It was followed by "The International Mt. Kûmgang Motorcycle Touring" in August. Previously, a short-run marathon race had been held at Mt. Kûmgang in February.

With regard to the media, two journalists from Munhwa Broadcasting Corporation (MBC) went to North Korea in March to report on the changes in North Korea regarding peoples' lives and the atmosphere after the summit meeting. "The Joint Holding of Labour Day" by labour unions on 1 May at Mt. Kûmgang with altogether 597 participants was shown on South Korean TV. According to Ko (2002), this event also confirmed the extent of national homogeneity. A plan for mutual exchanges was discussed. In May, eight South Korean journalists visited North Korea to cover the visit of the Swedish Prime Minister, Göran Persson, who led a EU delegation that aimed to contribute to the reconciliation process in Korea and also visited South Korea. A 32-member KBS team went to North Korea for an extended visit at the occasion of the first anniversary of the June 2000 summit and made broadcasts on nature, scenery and local culture.

Another joint ceremony extensively broadcast was "The National Unification Debate Forum" held at Mt. Kûmgang 14-16 June with altogether 422 participants on the anniversary of the 15 June Declaration. South Korean civilian organizations

---

ch'ôngsan-ûl", *Minjok 21* (2001.4), pp. 30, 31, 34; Yi, "Pundan ihu ch'oech'o, Nambuk yôksa hakcha P'yôngyang sangbong", *Minjok* 21 (2001.4), p. 35. For a survey on the March First Independence Movement see Lee, *A New History of Korea* (Seoul: Ilchokak Publishers, 1984), pp. 338-45.

53 See Sim, *Fragrance of Spring: The Story of Choon Hyang* (Seoul: Pojinchae Ltd., 1992).

in such fields as unification, labour and womens' issues took part in the event that, according to Cho Han Bum (2002), reconfirmed the Declarations' significance. Plans to expand exchanges and were discussed. From 18-19 July, "The North-South Peasants' Meeting for National Unification" with altogether 664 participants was held at Mt. Kûmgang to discuss exchanges between peasants to implement the 15 June Declaration. From 15-21 August, "The Grand National Festival for Unification" was held in P'yôngyang in which 337 South Korean civilians participated. The event was broadcast in South Korea. As the largest North-South civilian exchange, it was symbolically significant.[54]

Trade continued, although trade volume as of October had fallen, partly due to the state of lull in relations, by 10 per cent to $ 330m compared to levels a year before (cf. p. 76). South Korea's exports were worth $ 197m, while imports amounted to $ 133m. As before, South Korea's surplus derived from economic aid. Commercial trade comprised 55.9 per cent of total trade. Altogether, 351 South Korean companies were trading with North Korea, a trade that involved 623 products. South Korea still exported manufacturing products such as chemical products and North Korea, agricultural and fishery products.

South Korea delivered prior to December $ 127m to the North in economic aid (cf. p. 76). Civilian organizations became more important in terms of the volume of aid and the significantly increasing number of visitors to the North. Aid from other countries to North Korea amounted to $ 245m, thus bringing total aid to $ 372m. The main purposes of South Korean aid were restoration of agriculture followed by "general relief" and health and clothing. Deliveries still included fertilizer, food and medicine.[55]

While socio-cultural exchanges, family reunions and trade took place and economic aid was delivered political relations remained tense. Following the US-South Korea summit held in March, dialogue was stalled due to the new hard-line US policy and President George Bush's expressed distrust of Kim Jong Il. In March, North Korea cancelled the fifth round of ministerial talks scheduled to be held in Seoul and was unwilling to form a joint Korean team for the world table-tennis championships to be held in March, as had been previously agreed upon.

However, after failed attempts by South Korea to reopen dialogue, in early September, North Korea proposed resumption of the ministerial level meetings. This policy change came after the controversial incidents when some radical members of the South Korean delegation to the 15 August Liberation Day celebrations in P'yôngyang had visited Mangyôngdae, the birthplace of the late Kim Il Sung, as well

---

54 Chang, "Nambuk hapchak 3D aenimaisiôn 'keûrûn koyangi Dingka', Hananet-esô chigûm sangyông chung", *Minjok 21* (2002.1), p. 138; Cho, ibid., 2002a, pp. 6-7; Jonsson, "Betydelsen av Göran Perssons besök i Nord- och Sydkorea", *Yoboseyo* 41 (2001), no. 3, pp. 3-4; Kang, "Nambukhan-ûi munhwa yesul chôngch'aeg-ûi t'uksông pigyo-wa kyoryu silt'ae-e kwanhan yôn'gu", *Pukhan hakbo* 28 (2003), pp. 17, 19; KINU, ibid., 2001, pp. 70-71, 88-9; Ko, *Nambuk sahoe munhwa*, pp. 55, 56-7, 58-9; Lee et al., ibid., p. 119; O, ibid., 1999, p. 260.

55 KINU, ibid., 2001, pp. 80-83, 96-8.

as the opening and closing ceremonies of the Three Revolutions Commemorative Tower. Some members were reported to have praised Kim Il Sung and Kim Jong Il in violation of the National Security Law; Professor Kang Jeong-gu of Dongguk University signed the guestbook at Mangyôngdae. Sixteen of the 337 participants received arrest warrants. The incidents, which were widely considered a breach of protocol, greatly undermined the event's significance as an extension of the 15 June Declaration and provoked the dismissal of the South Korean Unification Minister, Lim Dong Won.

The fifth round of ministerial talks were held in Seoul 15-18 September (cf. pp. 74-5). A joint press release was issued but the reunion of divided families mentioned and later agreed upon did not take place. North Korea asserted in October that South Korea's augmented security measures after the 11 September terrorist attacks on the United States were not conducive to safe visits by divided family members, nor to dialogue. With this background, it is not surprising that the sixth round of ministerial talks, held in Mt. Kûmgang 9-14 November, ended with no agreement on the divided families issue or other major issues. To make matters worse, North Korean patrol boats and vessels had crossed the Northern Limit Line and commercial ships passed through, without due pre-notice, South Korea's territorial waters during the year. Armed forces even exchanged fire within the DMZ on 27 November, but there were no casualties.[56] In brief, there were no signs that the Cold War conditions on the Korean Peninsula had come to an end, despite President Kim Dae Jung's expressed hopes in March 2000.

In January 2002, President Bush, in his annual State of the Union Message, defined North Korea, along with Iran and Iraq, as "the axis of evil". The US strongly urged the North not to develop weapons of mass destruction. In February, Bush visited Seoul and expressed his full support for the South's sunshine policy but also declared his great disappointment with North Korea's response. Due to the tense relations, President Kim Dae Jung in April dispatched his Foreign Policy Advisor, Lim Dong Won to P'yôngyang to meet Kim Jong Il. The meeting ended with a joint communiqué; the partners agreed to open railway and road connections near the west and east coasts of the Korean Peninsula, to promote dialogue and cooperation and to reopen military talks. Subsequently, the fourth round of family reunions took place 28 April-3 May followed by the fifth round 13-18 September (cf. p. 79). Both reunions took place at Mt. Kûmgang.

But Lim's visit marked only a temporary improvement in relations: a naval clash occurred in the West Sea on 29 June when North Korean patrol boats clashed at the demarcation line and fired on South Korean naval ships. One high-speed patrol boat was sunk and five of the crew were killed in the first incident suffering casualties since the June 1999 Western Sea battle. In late July, North Korea expressed apologies

---

56 Ahn, ibid., 2002, pp. 48-9; Cho, ibid., 2002a, p. 7; Cho, ibid., 2002b, p. 115: fn. 21; Ha, South Korea in 2001: Frustration and Continuing Uncertainty", *Asian Survey* 42 (2002), no. 1, pp. 57-8, 61; KINU, ibid., 2001, pp. 67-9, 71, 76-80, 89, 91-2, 109, 110; Ko, ibid., pp. 55, 59; Lee et al., ibid., p. 119.

about the incident, the origins of which may have stemmed, according to the South Korean scholar Yinhay Ahn (2003), from different opinions by the North and the US on the drawing of the Northern Limit Line. North Korea aimed to strengthen its position at the negotiation table, primarily. For the first time North Korea now directly expressed its regret to South Korean authorities and indicated a willingness to prevent a recurrence.

The North also proposed ministerial talks, the seventh round of which were held 12-14 August in Seoul and the eighth 19-22 October in P'yôngyang. In Seoul, issues such as connecting cross-border railways and constructing the Kaesông special economic zone were also discussed. When the KECC held its second meeting in Seoul 27-30 August, it was agreed that a railway connection ceremony would be held in September (cf. p. 75). In a symbol of both Koreas' will to implement the project, the ceremony was held as scheduled. At the P'yôngyang ministerial talks, issues on the agenda included the construction of coastal railways and roads and the groundbreaking Kaesông Industrial Complex. From 26 October-3 November, an 18-member North Korean delegation visited industries and research institutes in South Korea, thus showing its interest in economic cooperation. When the KECC met for the third time in P'yôngyang 6-9 November, it agreed on a concrete schedule to reconnect railways and roads and to begin building the Kaesông Industrial Complex during December 2002.[57]

While political tensions remained, several socio-cultural contacts took place (cf. pp. 79-81). As of late October, 1,097 people had visited North Korea in this field, the majority in arts and culture (502), sports (238) and religion (156). The number of North Koreans visiting South Korea rose dramatically to 874 people. The main reason was that 673 North Korean athletes and cheerleaders were dispatched to the Asian Games held in Pusan 29 September-14 October. The "Unification Soccer Game" held in Seoul in September and a North Korean T'aekwôndo team's performance in Seoul 23-26 October brought 49 and 41 visitors south, respectively. Previously, from 14-17 September, a South Korean T'aekwôndo team had performed, in P'yôngyang. Most meetings between North and South Koreans took place in the contexts of academics and education (224), religion (143) and sports (139).

Cheju Island residents visited the North 10-15 May and 25 November-2 December; the island had sent oranges in aid. In May, there were 255 tourists to the North. "The North-South Prayers Meeting for Peaceful Unification of the Fatherland in Mt. Kûmgang" took place 16-18 May and "The North South Peace Arts Exhibition" was held in Seoul 15-25 May. "The National Festival for Unification on

---

57 Ahn, "North Korea in 2002: A Survival Game", *Asian Survey* 43 (2003), no. 1, pp. 49-50, 53-4; Cho, "Chôngch'i punya", in T'ongil yôn'guwôn, *T'ongil hwangyông-mith Nambukhan kwangye chônmang: 2002-2003* (Seoul: T'ongil yôn'guwôn, 2002), pp. 79-80; Chon, "Taenam tonghyang", in ibid., pp. 71-2; Lim, "Kyôngje punya", in ibid., pp. 82-3, 84-7; Kim, "Han-mi kwangye", in ibid., pp. 24-5; Lee, "South Korea in 2002: Multiple Political Dramas", *Asian Survey* 43 (2003), no. 1, pp. 72-3; T'ongil yôn'guwôn, "Purok: 2002 nyôndo chuyo sakôn ilchi", in ibid., pp. 129, 132, 133, 134, 135, 136.

the Commemoration of the Second Anniversary of the 15 June Declaration" was held 14-15 June at Mt. Kûmgang with 208 South Koreans participating. In June, the inauguration ceremony and the South Korean team's matches during the Soccer World Cup were televised on North Korean TV, as was the September soccer game in Seoul. In July-August, the South's Hanyang University conducted courses in information technology in P'yôngyang. This was, in fact, a new form of academic exchange.[58]

In August, "The Joint Conference on Standardizing Linguistic Information" was held in Beijing. From 14-17 August, "The National Festival for Unification" was held in Seoul with 116 North Koreans participating. In September, "The Students and Youth Arts Troupe of Koreans in Japan" performed twice in South Korea. During their visit 16-22 September, the KBS symphony orchestra made one solo and one joint performance with its North Korean counterpart in P'yôngyang, in a return visit to the latter's concert in Seoul, in August 2000. Altogether 200 South Koreans then went to the North. Significantly the performance was simultaneously broadcast on a cross-border basis. In September, popular South Korean singers such as the Yun To-hyôn band took part in "The 2002 MBC, Special Concert in P'yôngyang" that was broadcast live on the North's TV. On this occasion, 181 South Koreans visited the North. Cho (2002) writes that the broadcast was regarded as having contributed to overcoming cultural heterogeneity between the two Koreas: the open concert gave North Koreans a cultural shock and by strongly reflecting national emotions it confirmed the homogeneity of both North and South Koreans.

In September, MBC and KBS reported a few days directly from P'yôngyang shortly before the Asian Games opened, in a follow-up to the August 2000 agreement on media cooperation. Interviews with athletes, streets in P'yôngyang and North-South joint industrial plants were shown. National Foundation Day, 3 October, was for the first time jointly celebrated in "The Joint National Foundation Day Commemoration Event" held at Tan'gun's tomb in P'yôngyang.[59]

In October, scholars from both Koreas participated in "The International Scientific Conference on Modern Illumination of Traditional Korean Culture" and "The Scientific Conference on New Conditions and Plans for Creating Peace on the Korean Peninsula in the 21st Century" in China. In October, the South Korean silent film "Arirang" was shown in P'yôngyang. "The North-South Youth and Students' Meeting" with altogether 225 participants was held 12-14 October and the first "South-North Womens' Unification Meeting" with 352 South Korean participants, took place between 15-17 October. Both events were held at Mt. Kûmgang.

---

58 Cho, "Sahoe munhwa punya", in T'ongil yôn'guwôn, ibid., pp. 101-105; Chon, ibid., p. 72; Foster-Carter, ibid., *2005* (London: Europa Publications Ltd., 2004), pp. 495, 496; Kang, ibid., p. 20; Ryu, "Nambuk ch'eyuk kyoryu-ûi ôje-wa onûl: Nambuk, 'son e son-chapko' At'ene kanda", *T'ongil Han'guk* (2004), 8, p. 69; T'ongil yôn'guwôn, in ibid., pp. 130, 131, 134, 135.

59 Tan'gun is the believed divine progenitor of the Korean race. From Lee (ibid., 1984, p. 335).

In economics, the most significant development was that the trade volume rose dramatically to, as of 30 November, a value of $ 568m (cf. p. 81). Commercial trade comprised 55.1 per cent of total trade. Again, South Korea had a trade surplus deriving from non-commercial trade dominated by economic aid. Also equipment for light-water reactors was delivered. 426 South Korean companies were involved in trade, promoting 550 products, of which 303 comprised processing-on-commision trade. South Korea still exported chemical products and textiles whereas North Korea sold agricultural and fishery products and, of course, textiles.

South Korea provided $ 131m of economic aid until December, of which $ 89m came from the government (cf. p. 81). Aid from other countries amounted to $ 255m. The number of visiting aid workers from civilian organizations rose dramatically from 384 to 1,814. Restoration of agriculture was still the main purpose of aid, followed by "general relief" as well as health and clothing. Deliveries included fertilizers, food and medicines.[60]

3.10 The North Korean nuclear crisis re-emerges in 2002

The year's most shocking event occurred when North Korea in October admitted to the US envoy, James Kelley, that it had been engaged in developing a program of highly-enriched uranium for nuclear weapons. While not in violation of the 1994 Geneva Agreed Framework referred to previously, it violated the 1991 Joint Declaration on the Denuclearization of the Korean Peninsula which the Agreed Framework had pledged to uphold. One explanation could have been that the North wanted to use the program as leverage to push the US into negotiations. North Korea charged the US with not implementing its obligations under the 1994 Agreed Framework since it had stalled the construction of light-water reactors. Tensions had previously been raised by the inclusion of North Korea in the above "axis of evil". North Korea viewed this as "a clear declaration of war" and repeatedly urged to be removed from it.

The confession made the US, Japan and South Korea seek a peaceful solution of the nuclear issue through North Korea's dismantlement of uranium enrichment facilities in a prompt and verifiable way. China, which plays an important role in maintaining regional peace and security in terms of both Koreas, was concerned that North Korea's nuclear program could cause a possible nuclear-armament and arms race in Northeast Asia. At the 19-22 October eighth inter-Korean ministerial meeting held in P'yôngyang soon after the confession had been made, it was agreed that the nuclear issue would be resolved through dialogue while, as before, exchanges and cooperation would be treated as a separate issue (cf. p. 83).

---

60 Cho, ibid., pp. 102-105; Choi, "Kyôngje punya", in T'ongil yôn'guwôn, ibid., pp. 94-6; Chon, ibid., p. 72; Kang, ibid., pp. 20-21; Lee, "Taebuk chiwôn", in ibid., 2002, pp. 117-120; T'ongil yôn'guwôn, in ibid., pp. 133, 134, 135. Author's quotation marks. Cho (ibid., pp. 103-104) does not give the dates for the conferences held in October 2002 in China.

But North Korea's position was that the nuclear issue should be solved through the signing of a non-aggression treaty with the US, which the US refused to accept. In December, the US cut off its heavy fuel oil supplies to North Korea. The North responded by reactivating its Yôngbyôn nuclear reactor, removing the monitoring devices of the International Atomic Energy Agency (IAEA) and telling its inspectors to leave.[61] The hopes created by the above December 1999 agreement between KEDO and Korea Electric Power Corporation had thus failed to materialize.

The nuclear issue escalated in 2003 to its most dangerous level since 1994. The South Korean government made "a peaceful solution of the North's nuclear issue through dialogue" the major target of its "policy for peace and prosperity" the aim of which was to establish a peace mechanism on the Korean Peninsula and to promote mutual prosperity in line with the sunshine policy. On 10 January, North Korea declared its withdrawal from the Non-Proliferation Treaty (NPT) in response to the US refusal to hold bilateral talks and to the IAEA resolution that demanded that the North should comply with its obligations under the NPT. In April, it formally withdrew from the process.

In February, North Korea announced the resumption of a five-megawatt nuclear reactor in Yôngbyôn and launched a missile test that was timed for the inauguration of South Korea's new president, Roh Moo-hyun. Another missile was launched in March. Such actions were taken on the grounds of self-defence against US policies towards the North but also reflected security concerns that were reinforced by the American invasion of Iraq. Also joint US-South Korea military exercises held in March and the wish for bilateral talks explained to some extent these sabre rattling actions. In May, North Korea declared null and void the North-South agreement on a nuclear-free Korea, signed in December 1991.

However, as a result of shuttle diplomacy beginning in January, involving the US, South Korea, China, Japan and Russia, US-North Korean talks became multilateral, as America had originally wished. The nuclear issue was regarded as a regional matter that all concerned countries should have an input on. To achieve a peaceful solution, three-way talks took place in Beijing 23-25 April, which China played a key role in bringing about. China was the largest supplier of food and energy to North Korea and was concerned that a fall of the Kim Jong Il government would lead to an increased inflow of refugees and that a nuclear North could lead to a regional arms race. But no agreement was reached at the meeting, during which North Korea even announced that it already possessed nuclear weapons. Later, in October 2003, the North Korean ambassador in Stockholm in a little noticed interview with a small leftist Swedish weekly stated quite clearly that the North already had nuclear weapons: "Our defence includes a nuclear deterrent" but whether it was true or not is hard to say.

---

61 Ahn, ibid., pp. 49, 51, 54, 57, 58-62; Beal, *North Korea: The Struggle Against American Power* (London: Pluto Press, 2005), pp. 111, 255; Cho, ibid., p. 80; Kim, ibid., p. 25; Lee, ibid., 2002, pp. 73-4; T'ongil yôn'guwôn, in ibid., pp. 135, 136, 137. "A clear declaration of war" is quoted from Ahn (ibid., p. 59).

Thanks to China's shuttle diplomacy, six-party talks with North Korea, South Korea, the US, China, Japan and Russia were held in Beijing 27-29 August. However, these talks also ended with no tangible progress. A symbolic six-point consensus was agreed that called for continued dialogue, a nuclear-free Korean Peninsula, consideration of the North's security concerns and avoidance of actions that could aggravate the situation, but tensions over the unresolved nuclear issue remained even after the meeting.[62]

Military tensions included North Korean ships crossing the Northern Limit Line 23 times. Most crossings involved fishing boats blue crab fishing to earn foreign currency, but they could have been used for military purposes. In June, South Korea responded by firing warning shots. On 17 July, North Korea initiated a shooting incident in the DMZ that was met by South Korean fire, but there were no casualties.

In spite of such tensions, North-South meetings took place regularly. Through the four ministerial talks held in Seoul 21-24 January, in P'yôngyang 27-29 April, in Seoul 9-12 July and in P'yôngyang 14-17 October, South Korea stressed the need for a peaceful solution to the nuclear issue and emphasized the need for multilateral talks (cf. pp. 82, 83).

The KECC held meetings in Seoul 11-14 February, in P'yôngyang 19-23 May, in Seoul 26-28 August and in P'yôngyang 5-8 November (cf. pp. 83). Economic cooperation improved: on 14 June, railways were ceremonially joined in the DMZ, but since gaps remained on both lines on the Northern side this was only a symbolic gesture. A ground-breaking ceremony of the Kaesông Industrial Zone was held on 30 June. On 22 August, the agreements on investment guarantees, double-taxation avoidance, procedures for settling business disputes and the settlement of accounts were enacted. This was necessary to promote South Korean investments in the North. Business was brisk in spite of political tensions: in late November, trade volume had risen to a value of $ 671m (cf. p. 85). South Korea's trade surplus continued. Commercial trade comprised a value of $ 377m, that is 56.2 per cent of North Korean economic activity.

Humanitarian aid, such as materials for projects, rice and fertilizers amounting to $ 252.2m were, as of October, 85.9 per cent of non-commercial trade. South Korea was for the first time North Korea's main export market surpassing China and Japan. This trade was far more important for North than for South Korea: total trade volumes were in 2003 less than $ 2.4bn against $ 372.6bn, respectively. Trading patterns remained: South Korea exported industrial products to North Korea who

---

62 Ash, ibid., *2005*, p. 514; Cheon, "Pukhan haengmunje", in ibid., pp. 8-9; Cho, "Chôngch'i punya", in T'ongil yôn'guwôn, *T'ongil hwangyông-mith Nambukhan kwangye chônmang: 2003-2004* (Seoul: T'ongil yôn'guwôn, 2003), p. 72; Foster-Carter, ibid., *2005*, pp. 496, 502; Huh, "Taenam tonghyang", in ibid., p. 70; Lintner, ibid., p. 125; MoU, *P'yônghwa pônyông chôngch'aek haesôl charyo* (http://www.unikorea.go.kr/kr/uninews/ uninews_policyfocus.php, 10 March, 2003), pp. 1-2, 4, 8; Park, "North Korea in 2003: Pendulum Swing between Crisis and Diplomacy", *Asian Survey* 44 (2004), no. 1, pp. 139-43. The quotations are from Cho and Lintner.

sold agricultural, forestry and fishery products and textiles. Four Southern companies received permits for business: for tourism in Kaesông, sightseeing in P'yôngyang and joint exploration of graphite and food manufacturing. The latter two cases were intended as exports to South Korea.

As of late November, South Korea had provided $ 124.8m in humanitarian aid to North Korea which was almost equally divided between the government and civilian organizations (cf. p. 85). Overall aid amounted to $ 278.6m making South Korea's share 44.8 per cent. Most of the South's aid went to "general relief" (44 per cent) and restoration of agriculture (42 per cent), whereas the remainder went to health and medicines. Fertilizers, rice, clothing and medicines continued to be delivered.

Interestingly, Choi and his associates (2003) write that without foreign economic aid, the North's system could not be maintained. Equally significant, as of 2002, the US had, partly due to national security concerns, contributed about 62 per cent of food aid allocated via the UN, that is 34 per cent of total humanitarian aid, to North Korea. This made the US the largest donor of multilateral food aid between 1995 and 2002, amounting to a value of about $ 600m. As of 2004, North Korea had become the largest recipient of US aid in Asia. In comparison, China's estimated food aid during the same years exceeded $ 800m. Japan had been a large food donor; as of 2001, it accounted for almost 50 per cent of total food aid provided through the UN.[63] Such a dependence on the outside world, including South Korea, Japan and the United States, entirely contradicts the juche idea. The situation reflects the fact that maintaining North Korea as it is, in spite of its pursuit of nuclear brinkmanship while letting its citizens starve, is a far more urgent goal for these nations than Korean unification.

The sixth round of family reunions took place between 20-25 February, the seventh reunion between 27 June-2 July and the eighth between 20-25 September; each time at Mt. Kûmgang to which land travel was initiated in February (cf. p. 82). In that month, 99 members of divided families from the South met 191 relatives from the North. Then 99 members of divided families in the North met 461 relatives from the South, that is altogether 850 people. The corresponding numbers at the seventh reunions were 110 and 217 versus 100 and 472, respectively, that is altogether 899 people. At the eighth round, there were 143 and 246 versus 100 and 453, thus in total

---

63 Ash, ibid., 2005, p. 507; Cho, ibid., pp. 72-3; Choi et al., ibid., p. 172; *Chosun Ilbo*, NKchosun.com (http://nk.chosun.com/schedule/schedule.html?ACT=year&year=1=2000&year2=2003), accessed 28 January, 2005; Foster-Carter, ibid., *2005,* p. 496; Harrison, ibid., 2002, p. 312; Huh, ibid., pp. 68, 70; Jeong, "Kunsa tonghyang", in T'ongil yôn'guwôn, ibid., pp. 46-8; Kim, "Kyôngje punya", in ibid., pp. 85-92; Lee, "Taebuk chiwôn", in ibid., 2003, pp. 107-110; Park, ibid., 2004, p. 146; Schloms, *North Korea and the Timeless Dilemma of Aid* (Münster: LIT Verlag, 2004), pp. 134-35, 145-46; T'ongil yôn'guwôn, "Purok: 2003nyôn Nambuk kwangye ilchi", in ibid., pp. 119, 120, 121, 122. Author's quotation marks. The different figures of humanitarian aid recorded are explained by the lower one only including aid and grants whereas the higher include aid to cooperative projects, Mt. Kûmgang tourism, light-water reactors and oil. From Lee (e-mail, 19 May, 2004).

942 people. Altogether, 2,691 members of divided families met each other through these rounds of the program.

Socio-cultural contacts remained rather active also after the introduction of the policy for peace and prosperity (cf. pp. 83-4). North and South Korea marched together at the opening and ending ceremony of "The 5th Asian Winter Games" held in Japan between 1-8 February. On 1-2 March, a North Korean delegation with 105 participants took part in "The March First Joint National Unification Event" in Seoul.

"The North-South Youth Red Cross Friendship Tree Planting Event" was held between 21-23 March and "The North-South Harmony Prayers Meeting" between 23-25 March, both at Mt Kûmgang. "The Sixth North-South and Foreign Scholars Unification Conference" took place in P'yôngyang, 26-27 March. Some 48 South Korean scholars took part in this conference, which notably became the first televised scientific conference held.[64]

In April, a joint prayer event was announced by Christian churches at "The Conference on Exchanges between Christian Churches" held between 29 March-2 April in P'yôngyang. On 5-9 April, "The Mass of the Groundbreaking Ceremony of the P'yôngyang Theological School" was held. "The 1 May North-South Workers' Unification Meeting" was jointly held in P'yôngyang. On the same day on the occasion of Buddha's birthday, Buddhists announced a joint prayer ceremony. It should be noted that on 29 July-2 August, 130 teachers from the Teachers' Trade Union became the first South Korean teachers to conduct a study tour to P'yôngyang, which included visits to two schools, one children's care home and one kindergarten. Significantly, educational materials had been delivered to the North since 2001, including 250 tons of paper for schoolbooks, sent in 2002. On 11 August, "The KBS Amateurs Song Contest" took place in P'yôngyang. As with the unification conference, the KBS made a televised program of the contest. By attracting 24 per cent of the audience rating, it exceeded that of other programs. A third program made was "The Spots of North-South Economic Cooperation – P'yôngyang, Namp'o and Kaesông". Then "The 15 August National Meeting for Peace and Unification" was held in P'yôngyang and drew more than 880 participants from the two Koreas, of which 330 came from the South and abroad.

When "The Scientific Forum on the Name of Korea in English" was held in P'yôngyang 18-26 August, 57 South Korean scholars went there. In spite of some South Korean organizations' opposition to the North's participation, 520 North Koreans took part in "The Summer Universiad Contest" held in Taegu, between 21-31 August. Participation was secured after President Roh Moo-hyun had apologized for the burning of the North Korean flag at a conservative rally in Seoul. This was the largest visit since the 2002 Asian Games. Significantly the two Koreas marched together holding a flag of the Korean Peninsula at the opening and ending ceremonies

---

64 Cho, "Sahoe munhwa punya", in T'ongil yôn'guwôn, ibid., pp. 94-5, 96, 97; Huh, ibid., pp. 68-9; Lim, "Isan kajongmunje", in T'ongil yôn'guwôn, ibid., p. 98; T'ongil yôn'guwôn, "Purok", in ibid., pp. 119, 120, 121.

for the fourth time, following on the 2000 Summer Olympics, the 2002 Asian Games and the 5th Asian Winter Games. In addition, 256 Cheju Islanders visited the North, between 25-30 August.[65]

From 1-3 September, "The North-South Young Students Representatives Meeting" in which 33 South Koreans took part, was held in the North. Remarkably, on 15 September, 114 South Korean tourists were for the first time, allowed to fly by the North's Air Koryô from Seoul to P'yôngyang, in a joint tour project with a South Korean company. Between 22-26 September, "The Youth Relics Exploration" was held, with 179 South Korean students participating, in North Korea. On 29 September, "The Scientific Conference to Examine the Truth of the Ukisima Incident" was held in P'yôngyang with five South Korean participants. An exhibition on the sinking by explosion of this ship was also held. Between 30 September-5 October, "The Joint North-South Foundation Day Event" was held in the North, with 296 South Koreans taking part, in contrast to just 100 in 2002. The event included scientific discussions on Tan'gun, visits to his grave and other related monuments as well as cultural and arts performances by both Koreas; only North Korea had performed in 2002.

In October, "The Ryugyông Chung Ju Yung Sports Stadium" was inaugurated in P'yôngyang. 1,072 South Koreans attended the events between 6-9 October, in which North and South Korean artists performed. The SBS relayed "The Unification Concert" and "The Unification Basketball Games". Between 6-7 October, the first international conference "Study on Popular Korean Songs Before Liberation", was held in China. "The Medical Science Discussion Forum" was held in P'yôngyang on 14 October and was followed by "The North-South Media Committee", held in the North between 15-19 October. In this first North-South media meeting, 138 South Koreans participated in discussions. A conference on "The Sense of Joint National Community in Korean History" was held in P'yôngyang, between 20-27 October.

"The Cheju Island National Peace and Unification Athletic and Culture Festival" was held on the island between 23-27 October under the slogan "The Korean People Meets". 190 North Koreans took part in the third joint event held in South Korea during the year after "The March First Joint National Unification Event" and "The Summer Universiad Contest". It included mens' and womens' soccer and table-tennis games, but also a marathon as well as folk games such as swinging, see sawing, tug-of-war, wrestling and T'aekwôndo. North Korea displayed more than 100 pieces of handicrafts. The sacred fire had, prior to the games, for the first time by virtue of joint efforts, been transported from Mt. Paektu. But it should be noted that the Northern team arrived late and at the end refused to leave unless they were paid more. North and South Korean scholars participated in "The Scientific Meeting on the Unified Development of the Korean Language and Investigation of Dialects"

---

65 Cho, ibid., pp. 95-7; fax, 16 March, 2005; Foster-Carter, ibid., *2005,* p. 496; Huh, ibid., p. 69; Kim, "Kyoyuk ch'amgwandan-ûro P'yôngyang-e tanyô wa sô", *Minjok hwahae* (2003), 09/10, pp. 51-2; Kim, "58 nyôn man-ûi pungnyôk tongp'o pangmun-ûro t'ongil yôlgi kadûkhan Taegu", *Minjok hwahae* (2003), 09/10, pp. 56-7; Ryu, ibid., pp. 67, 69; T'ongil yôn'guwôn, "Purok", in ibid., pp. 119, 120, 121.

held in Beijing 6-9 November. Finally, "The Mt. Kûmgang Tourism 5th Anniversary Event" was held at Mt. Kûmgang on 19 November.[66]

During 2004, the second and third rounds of six-party talks on the North Korean nuclear program were held in Beijing between 25-28 February and between 23-26 June (cf. pp. 78-79). In February, North Korea's position was that it would only give up its nuclear program if the US abandoned its hostile policy. Due to this policy, North Korea repeatedly announced its will to maintain and strengthen its nuclear deterrent force. It now declared that a freeze of nuclear activities would be the first step towards denuclearization, but demanded compensation to do so. On the other hand, the US demanded a complete, verifiable and irreversible dismantlement of the nuclear program; no compensation could be provided before that. The US maintained its position in the June talks, which also failed to reach a solution.

The issue became more complicated in September when it became known that South Korean scientists had, in violation of the 1991 North-South Joint Declaration on Denuclearization of the Korean Peninsula and the NPT, conducted three uranium-enrichment experiments in January 2000, without the government's knowledge until June 2004. North Korea refused to enter new talks before the actual conditions were explained. On 10 February, 2005 North Korea claimed that it possessed a nuclear bomb and said that it would no longer participate in the six-party talks; this was the third time it had made such a claim. Nuclear weapons were necessary due to the US government's "ever-more undisguised policy to isolate and stifle" North Korea. Previously, Condoleeza Rice had, in her confirmation hearings as US Secretary of State, included North Korea as being among six "outposts of tyranny", which to the North must have sounded no less menacing than being described as part of an "axis of evil".[67]

Nonetheless, a fourth round of six-party talks was held between 26 July-7 August as well as between 13-19 September in Beijing. Finally, an agreement was reached

---

66 Cho, ibid., pp. 95-7; Chông, "Nambuk yôksahak kyoryu hyônhwang-gwa palchôn-ûl wihan cheôn", *Yôksa pip'yông* 65 (Winter 2003), p. 225: fn. 5; Foster-Carter, ibid., *2005*, p. 496; *God dei sinmun*, "Cheje, enôji pojangsi Pungmi chôngsanghwa" (http://news.hot.co.kr/2003/08/24/200308241614374113.shtml); Huh, ibid., p. 69; *The Internet Hankyoreh*, "Nambuk kongdong haksul hoeûi 20il put'ô P'yôngyang sô kaech'oe" (http://www.hani.co.kr/section-009000000/2003/09/009000000200309151426706.html); Kang, ibid., pp. 21-2; Kim, "T'ongir-ûi hanûr-ûl yôlda – 2003 kaech'ônjôl minjok kongdong haengsa", *Minjok hwahae* (2003), 11/12, pp. 30, 32-3; Park, ibid., p. 146; Song, "Cheju, 'p'yônghwa-wa t'ongir-ûi sôm'-ûro - Cheju minjok t'ongil p'yônghwa ch'eyuk munhwa ch'ukchôn mak olla", *Minjok hwahae* (2003), 11/12, pp. 34, 35; T'ongil yôn'guwôn, "Purok", in ibid., p. 121.

67 Beal, ibid., p. 259; Cheon, "Pukhan haengmunje", in T'ongil yôn'guwôn, *T'ongil hwangyông-mith Nambukhan kwangye chônmang: 2004-2005* (Seoul: T'ongil yôn'guwôn, 2004), pp. 10, 11; *The Economist*, "China and North Korea: Managing Chaos", 19 February, 2005; Greenlees & Hiebert, "Nuclear No-No", *FEER*, 16 September, 2004, p. 22; Lee, "Taenam tonghyang", in ibid., p. 79; McCormack, "Pyongyang Waiting for the Spring" (http://www.nationinstitute.org/tomdispatch/, 24 February, 2005), pp. 2, 3; T'ongil yôn'guwôn, "Purok: 2004 nyôn chuyo sakôn ilchi", in ibid., pp. 123, 124.

which stipulated that North Korea was to abandon its nuclear weapons and existing nuclear program, re-enter the NPT talks and permit IAEA inspections of facilities. In reciprocation, the US undertook not to conduct offensive operations against North Korea or stockpile nuclear weapons on the Korean peninsula. North Korea received promises of assistance regarding energy supplies and technical aid. Both the US and Japan further agreed to normalize relations with North Korea and further diplomatic talks were pencilled in for November of that year. Tensions remained, however; already on 20 September, North Korea's Foreign Ministry declared that "The US 'should not even dream' that North Korea would dismantle its arms before receiving a light-water nuclear reactor mentioned in the accord".

At the first session of the fifth round of six-party talks held in Beijing 9-11 November, it was decided to comprehensively implement the September agreement through confidence-building measures. A chairman's statement was issued in which the parties reaffirmed that they would fully implement the agreement in accordance with the principle "commitment-for-commitment, action-for-action" in order to soon accomplish a verifiable denuclearization of the Korean peninsula and lasting peace and stability in the region. An agreement was reached to hold talks between the US and North Korea outside the six-party framework to deal with financial and economic issues.[68] The agreement did of course hold some promise however only time will tell if it will in fact contribute to a lasting solution to this ongoing controversy.

In 2004, ministerial talks were held twice (cf. p. 87). In Seoul, between 3-6 February, South Korea declared that without a solution on the nuclear issue large-scale economic cooperation would be impossible. At the talks held in P'yôngyang between 4-7 May, it was agreed that relations must improve through reconciliation and cooperation. Official military talks were held for the first time since September 2000 on 26 May at Mt. Kûmgang and during 3-4 June at Mt. Sôrak. These first general talks resulted in an agreement to prevent incidental military clashes along the Northern Limit Line in the Western Sea and forbade propaganda and defamation along the military demarcation line. In spite of this conciliatory step, in July, November and December, North Korean naval vessels crossed the line which the North does not recognize.[69]

Tensions escalated when the South Korean government refused to allow a delegation to make a call of condolence on the 10th anniversary of Kim Il Sung's death and when 468 North Korean defectors arrived during 27-28 July from Vietnam. North Korea now declared that the South Korean government had committed a

---

68 Crock et al., "The 'Wrong Signal' on Containing Nukes", *BusinessWeek*, 3 October, 2005, p. 35; Lee, "Latest Round of Six-Party Talks", *Vantage Point* 28 (December 2005), no. 12, p. 24; Lintner, "Nordkorea ger upp kärnvapen: Kompromiss nådd i förhandlingarna – men flera frågetecken kvarstår", *Svenska Dagbladet*, 20 September, 2005; Yonhap news, "Pukhaek t'agyôl 6kaehang kongdong sôngmyông chônmun" (http://bbs.yonhapnews.co.kr/ynaweb/printpage/News_Content.asp), 19 September, 2005. Original quotation marks.

69 Hong, "Nambuk changsônggûp hoedam", in T'ongil yôn'guwôn, ibid., pp. 85-7; Lee, ibid., in ibid., pp. 75, 77; Son, "Changgwangûp hoedam", in ibid., pp. 83-4; T'ongil yôn'guwôn, "Purok: 2004 nyôn chuyo sakôn ilchi", in ibid., pp. 129, 131, 132.

terrorist act by encouraging the defections. Consequently, the scheduled fifteenth ministerial talks were cancelled.

Political tensions affected economic contacts negatively. The KECC met in Seoul, between 2-5 March and in P'yôngyang, between 2-5 June (cf. p. 87). Agreement was reached on the schedule for constructing the Kaesông Industrial Zone, but the scheduled tenth round of KECC talks failed to materialize. 13 South Korean companies received permission to enter the zone; the first products were made in December. In October 2004, trade volume reached $ 548 m, compared with $ 591m a year before (cf. p. 87). Imports of agricultural products, textiles, steel and metal goods amounted to $ 207m. Exports were valued at $ 341m and were dominated by fertilizers and agricultural products as aid, but also materials for processing-on-commission trade that comprised 26.4 per cent of total trade.

Again, the South's trade surplus was due to non-commercial trade that comprised 48.7 per cent of total inter-Korean trade; only 24.9 per cent of trade was purely commercial. Otherwise, the North had a surplus of $ 133m. 420 South Korean companies were involved in trade that included 580 products. South Korea's humanitarian aid to North Korea amounted to $ 165.5m, whereas total foreign aid reached $ 331.3m (cf. p. 87). Of total aid donated, $57.3m was from the government and $ 108.2m from civilian organizations. Restoration of agriculture was the largest portion of aid, followed by "general relief" and food, fertilizers and medicine which were still being delivered.

The ninth round of family reunions took place at Mt. Kûmgang, between 29 March-3 April, where the tenth round was also held between 11-16 July (cf. p. 88-9). In March-April, 147 members of divided families from the South met 235 relatives from the North. Then 101 members of divided families in the North met 486 relatives from the South, that is a total of 969 people. The corresponding numbers at the tenth reunions were 100 from the North and 471 from the South versus 149 from the South and 237 from the North, that is a total of 957 people.[70] Altogether, 1,926 members of separated families thus met each other (the figure was 2,691 in 2003).

Socio-cultural contacts continued but became less active from July onwards (cf. pp. 89-91). Between 24-28 February, "The Joint Scientific Conference on the Return of Cultural Assets Plundered by the Japanese Imperialists" was held in P'yôngyang where also "The North-South Workers' 1 May, 2004 Unification Meeting" was held, between 30 April-3 May and "The Sixth Medical Science Discussion Forum" on 3 May. Twenty-seven South Koreans took part in the conference. "The North-South Foreign Youth Students' Representative Meeting" was held in China, between 20-23 March. Between 4-6 April, 28 members of the South Korean Youth Red Cross visited Mt. Kûmgang and participated in "The Friendship Tree Planting Event".

Significantly more events were held in South Korea with North Koreans taking part. From 20-24 May, "The Seoul Meeting of the International Solidarity Association

---

70 Choi, "Kyôngje punya hoedam", in T'ongil yôn'guwôn, ibid., pp. 88-91; Kim, "Kyôngje punya", in ibid., pp. 92-5; Lee, ibid., pp. 77-8; Lee, "Taebuk chiwôn", in ibid., pp. 104-105, 106; Lim, "Isan kajongmunje", in ibid., pp. 108-109; Lintner, ibid., 2005, p. 221.

To Urge A Cleansing of Japan's Past" was held with nine North Korean participants. It was followed, between 2-5 June, by "The Joint North-South Scientific Conference on the Modern Nationalist Movement" and "The Symposium on the Iron Silk Road" held during 17-18 June, both in Seoul. Significantly, the nine North Korean participants in the former event that dealt with the anti-Japanese movement became the first human and social scientists to visit South Korea ever. There were seven participants in the latter event. "The 15 June National Meeting" held in Inch'ôn 14-17 June drew altogether 1,353 Koreans from the North (103), from the South (1200) and abroad (50). "The National Declaration on Unity" expressing the wish for North-South harmony and a proposal for national unification was adopted. From 14-20 June, "The Joint North-South Photo Exhibition" was held in P'yôngyang. "The North-South Peasants Unification Meeting" was held between 26-28 June at Mt. Kûmgang.

Remarkably, educators from the two Koreas held their first joint event ever, between 18-20 July through "The North-South Educators' Meeting for the Implementation of the 15 June Joint North-South Declaration" at Mt. Kûmgang. North and South Koreans marched together at the opening and ending ceremony of the Olympic Games held in Athens 13-29 August: this was the fifth such experience (cf. p. 89-90).

From 11-12 September, "The Joint Commemorative Photo Exhibition and Scientific Conference on the Registration of Koguryô [37 B.C.-668] Relics as World Cultural Heritage" was held at Mt. Kûmgang. The two Koreas agreed in a joint announcement that "to defend Koguryô history is an important issue related to national dignity...". Cooperation to reach this target would later be strengthened.

In November, religionists took part in the inauguration ceremony of the jointly restored Singyesa temple at Mt. Kûmgang. Finally, "The Mt. Kûmgang Tourism 6th Anniversary Event" was held at Mt. Kûmgang from 19-20 November. Nonetheless, it should be noted that, as of 2004, telephone, fax and e-mail contact with the North remained technically illegal in the South under the National Security Law.[71] While the nuclear crisis constituted a clear deterioration of inter-Korean relations during Roh Moo-hyun's Presidency, it is again a striking and recurring feature, that socio-cultural events continued while political tensions remained. The functionalist approach to relations had further consolidated the development towards an activation and also increasing regularization of contacts in the socio-cultural field, politics, economic and in the delivery of aid.

3.11 Conclusions

Relations between Northern and South Korea have been characterized by mutual distrust. Contacts have been limited and irregular. In these two respects, Korea differs

---

71 Cho, "Sahoe punya", in T'ongil yôn'guwôn, ibid., pp. 99-102; Foster-Carter, ibid., *2005*, pp. 497-98; Lee, ibid., pp. 76-7; T'ongil yôn'guwôn, "Purok", in ibid., pp. 127, 130, 131, 132. Original quotation marks.

greatly from Germany and Yemen. Unification policies have been diametrically opposed. North Korea has promoted a direct model for unification through a confederation and South Korea an indirect one, beginning with contact promotion in the hope of achieving eventual unity. Unification proposals have consistently been rejected by the other side. During the 1990s, South Korea's unification policies were influenced by the enormous costs of German unity and the estimated huge costs of Korean unification, which created a perceived need for a gradual approach towards unification.

Although tensions have dominated inter-Korean relations, there have been periods of local détente, notably during 1971-1972, 1984-1985, 1990-1991 and since 1998. These thaws were followed by periods when contacts were largely broken, but this pattern changed from 1998 onwards. Due in particular to the North's nuclear program, inter-Korean relations were severely strained during the 1990s. Yet limited trade, involving manufactured goods from the South and primary products from the North, continued. South Korea also provided economic aid. In this way, North Korea has, in spite of its pursuit of juche ("self-reliance"), become increasingly dependent on South Korea.

A significant policy break occurred in 1998 when Kim Dae Jung became president. His sunshine policy, which was based on functionalism and showed clear similarities with previous administrations' policies, aimed to promote cooperation to improve relations and attain peaceful coexistence and not only to unify Korea. Given the long state of confrontation, short-term unification was considered unrealistic. In addition, the estimated cost of unity was enormous and the economic gap between the two Koreas by far exceeded those between the two Germanys and Yemens prior to their respective unifications in 1990.

The sunshine policy separates economic cooperation from politics. The policy has been consistently implemented: contacts were maintained even during periods when armed incidents occurred. Besides such positive signs as an expansion of economic contacts and the previously far more limited socio-cultural exchanges, contacts were diversified also into tourism but the significance of these exchanges should not be over exaggerated. Tensions remained and official contacts developed slowly.

The most dramatic example of improved relations was the first inter-Korean summit in June 2000, in P'yôngyang. The 15 June Declaration, was the first inter-Korean agreement adopted and signed between two Korean leaders. Although the summit initiated an activation of official talks as well as socio-cultural contacts, the declaration's noteworthy targets have, with the exception of regular family reunions, not been fulfilled. Military issues in particular have hardly ever been discussed. While South Korea has pushed for an activation of exchanges and cooperation, North Korea has been reluctant to respond; mutual distrust has not been overcome. The new hard-line US policy towards North Korea under President George Bush since 2001 has further contributed to raise tensions on the Korean Peninsula. The recurrence of the North Korean nuclear issue in 2002 has worsened the situation, but it has not ended economic and socio-cultural contacts which, on the contrary, have continued to expand. In fact, President Roo Moo-hyun's "policy for peace and prosperity" basically follows the guidelines of the sunshine policy.

Nonetheless, it is hard to say that inter-Korean relations have dramatically improved since 1998. Indisputably, Korea is still far from developing relations that would resemble those that existed previously between East and West Germany as well as North and South Yemen prior to their respective unification processes in 1989-1990.

Chapter 4

Inter-Korean Socio-cultural Exchanges and Cooperation

4.1 Introduction

As we saw in Chapter 3, relations between North and South Korea have always been tense. Following on President Kim Dae Jung (1998-2003) launch of the sunshine policy, one noticeable consequence has been an increase in cross-border contacts. These socio-cultural exchanges and multi-level cooperation developments are the theme of this chapter with particular focus on developments during the 1990s. In this way, the extent of contacts prior to 1998 will be examined in an effort to present an overview of North-South socio-cultural contacts.

Crucially, in the case of socio-cultural contacts, developments during the leadership of the Kim Dae Jung administration cannot be properly understood without a review of his predecessors' policies. To begin with, legislation in this field is also investigated. Whether the South Korean government's new legislation enacted in 1989-1990 brought concrete results is also examined through a review of the development of subsequent socio-cultural exchanges and which refers here to academia, education, culture and sports. The review begins after the end of the Korean War in 1953 and ends round about the year 2000.

While the development of socio-cultural contacts is referred to through a more chronological approach, the following section follows a more thematic one. Exchanges here refer to academia and education, environmental issues, film, literature, sports, religion and women's conferences in order to give as complete and fair a view of the extent of socio-cultural contacts as possible. As seen earlier, locations of meetings are carefully noted. As was the case in the previous section, the review ends with the author's evaluation of these contacts.

Characteristics of socio-cultural contacts are subsequently investigated in some detail. Scholars' opinions on them are presented, compared and evaluated. The review includes both general characteristics and opinions of developments since the June 2000 summit. In addition, the author's estimation of the diffusion effects of socio-cultural events on the basis of their duration and the number of participants, which, to the extent they have been available, have been duly recorded in some detail throughout the chapter. The diffusion effects are hardly discussed in the literature but they give nonetheless, an indication of the impact of socio-cultural contacts in terms of restoring national homogeneity and spreading knowledge on a cross-border basis. Because of the opinion that non-governmental organizations

(NGOs) should actively participate in socio-cultural exchanges and cooperation, the subsequent section investigates NGO involvement in these fields, with particular focus on developments since 1998.

The final section provides a review of the impact of socio-cultural contacts on North Korea. From the functionalist viewpoint, what kinds of South Korean influences have reached North Korea? Has access to knowledge which, as we have seen, was an important feature in the case of pre-unity Germany, affected the society in any meaningful way through the creation of "value integration"? The North Korean government's policies to combat such influences are analyzed. North and South Koreans perceptions of each other's cultures are also examined and compared. The review concludes in 2005.

4.2 Legal foundations of inter-Korean socio-cultural exchanges and cooperation

The Cold War conditions on the Korean Peninsula had long made socio-cultural exchanges and cooperation virtually impossible. Such contacts were not significantly improved until the 1980s, when government talks began with any degree of frequency. The South Korean government expressed in the 1988 7 July Declaration "its willingness to pursue North-South exchanges in every field". More precisely, "mutual exchanges of politicians, economic officials, media people, religious, culture and arts personalities, athletes, scholars and students, etc. should be actively promoted and the door should be opened for compatriots abroad to freely visit North and South Korea". Consequently, mutual confidence would be created, tensions would come to be mitigated and relations improved and a peace settlement achieved.[1]

As a follow-up measure to the Declaration, in June 1989, the Roh Tae Woo government forged the Guidelines for Inter-Korean Exchanges and Cooperation. Earlier, in March 1989, the Council to Promote Inter-Korean Exchanges and Cooperation had been founded. In February 1990, the government announced the Five Basic Principles for Inter-Korean Cultural Exchanges. These were: first to exchange pre-partition traditional culture, to reject areas of contest and competition, to refrain from transforming and defaming traditional culture, to begin with easy and minor issues and, finally, over time, to make efforts to jointly implement improvements. The government subsequently enacted and promulgated the Inter-Korean Exchanges and Cooperation Act in August 1990.

Consequently, inter-Korean dialogue established a legal foundation and anyone in South Korea could officially exchange and cooperate with North Korea when in conformity with the legislative procedures administered by the Ministry of Unification. A Fund for Inter-Korean Cooperation was set up involving both human and economic exchanges. As of 1998, funds had been used mainly for humanitarian

---

1 Cho, *NGOs-rûl t'onghan*, 1998, p. 22; Cho, *Chôngsang hoedam*, 2002a, p. 8; Cho, *NGOs and Inter-Korean Socio-Cultural Exchanges and Cooperation*, 2002b, p. 109; Ch'oe, *Nambukhan sahoe munhwa*, October 2000, p. 40. Original quotation marks.

aid to North Korea and for economic cooperation. In 1998, the Korean Photographers' Association became the first civilian organization to benefit in the socio-cultural field. Support was also given to the formation of joint table-tennis and soccer teams in 1991, preparations for family reunions during 1992 and building as well as operating an information centre for divided families in 1998-1999.[2]

When the 1991 Basic Agreement was negotiated, South Korea suggested mutual opening of media and publications as well as exchanges and cooperation in the fields of culture, arts and religion, etc. Since North Korea showed a comparatively cooperative attitude towards exchanging and displaying art works and cultural relics as well as cooperating and advancing together internationally, agreement was reached jointly on a clause, that is Article 16, on socio-cultural exchanges.

According to this Article, "North and South Korea should implement exchanges and cooperation in science, technology, education, culture, arts, health, athletics, environment and in the fields of publishing and news, including newspapers, radio and TV broadcasting as well as publications". In the annexed agreements on socio-cultural exchanges and cooperation, specific measures to implement these targets were defined. Article 9 deals with exchanges and cooperation, Article 11 with mutual and joint advances on the international stage, Article 12 with support guarantees and Article 13 with setting up an organization to implement exchanges and cooperation through a joint committee. Finally, Article 14 dealt with making decisions on the implementation of socio-cultural exchanges through a joint committee.

More specifically, Article 9 advocates "mutual visits by students, teaching staff, authors, cultural personalities, scientists, experts and professionals as well as other personnel involved in socio-cultural exchanges through national study tours, friendship visits and news gathering and so forth". But North Korea insisted on "connections and exchanges between institutions, organizations and personnel in various fields". In other words, North Korea opposed identifying actual exchange partners and urged limiting these to its own rather abstract description.[3]

North Korea objected to South Korea's proposal to exchange cultural and arts troupes on joint commemorative days and national holidays, due to the term "arts troupe" and the spelling out of time schedules for exchanges of these. Instead, North Korea favoured the expression "diverse cooperation in the fields of culture and arts". But North Korea responded rather affirmatively to the proposal to open mutual exchange exhibitions of arts works, cultural relics and publications, etc. The positive response was because such exchanges would involve less personnel than in other fields of culture, thereby reducing pressures on the North. In fact, South Korea proposed, when the first round of sub-committee meetings was held in March 1992, that Article 13 in the annexed agreements, "the establishment and management in P'anmunjôm of an exchange room of materials for smooth North-South exchanges of materials in the socio-cultural field", be implemented.

---

2   Cho, ibid., 1998, pp. 22-3, 24, 47-8; Cho, *Nambuk sahoe munhwa kyoryu*, 1999, pp. 60-61; Cho, ibid., 2002b, p. 109.
3   Ko, *Nambuk sahoe munhwa*, pp. 48, 55-6. Original quotation marks.

North Korea did not find this suggestion desirable but accepted it in the seventh round of meetings held by the North-South Joint Committee for Exchanges and Cooperation in September 1992. At this time, the annexed agreement for Inter-Korean Exchanges and Cooperation was adopted that included parts of the South's proposals (the committee had been founded in May). North Korea also expressed its willingness to discuss the establishment of organizations to handle socio-cultural exchanges through the joint committee.

South Korea proposed in relation to the above Article 9 "the protection of rights of the two partners' publications, dramas, music, fine arts, architecture, photos, TV as well as literary works and so forth". After a while, North Korea reacted by not specifying each kind of culture and arts and expressed the opinion that "literary works should be protected in accordance with decisions made by the two partners". North Korea's negative opinion on protection of rights was due to its non-recognition of private property. On the other hand, North Korea expressed a positive attitude towards cooperation in the socio-cultural field in the international arena and joint participation in world events. This attitude was considered to have derived from North Korea gaining confidence from participating in "The North-South Film Festival" held in New York 10-14 October, 1990. A preview of seven films each from the two Koreas then took place in this first North-South contact in film. Eight North Koreans and 31 South Koreans took part in this event.[4]

After the 1990 Inter-Korean Exchanges and Cooperation Act had been enacted, the first new legislation came in June 1997 when the Regulations on Management of North-South Socio-Cultural Cooperation Projects were established. This was followed in 1998 by the 18 March "Measures to Activate Civilian Assistance to North Korea". Civilian organizations' participation would be expanded by allowing them to take part in deliveries of relief goods from the South Korean Red Cross and to visit North Korea for the purpose of discussing and monitoring aid. Regulations on fundraising were eased, which permitted civilian organizations to arrange such activities as fundraising concerts and bazaars. They could also give approval to fundraising by the media and enterprises and accept unanimous depositions. Finally, they could, on the basis of cooperation projects, set an example in terms of assistance to the North.[5]

4.3 Development of inter-Korean socio-cultural exchanges and cooperation

As we have seen, North Korea had proposed cultural contacts at the end of the Korean War in 1953 at a time when cultural heterogeneity had begun to develop in earnest in the fields of literature, arts, religion, language and speech. In reality, those proposals were insignificant attempts to present socio-cultural exchanges and cooperation or at least to use these contacts as political propaganda in line with the

---

4   Cho, *Nambuk sahoe munhwa kyoryu*, 1999, p. 33; Kang et al., *Nambukhan p'yônghwa kongjon-gwa*, 2001, p. 141; Ko, ibid., pp. 48, 49, 56. Original quotation marks.

5   Cho, ibid., 1998, pp. 6, 23, 29.

North's unification policies. In 1957, exchanges of media people were suggested at the Second National Journalists' Meeting. Ch'oe Yong-gôn proposed in 1960 in the Supreme People's Assembly that North and South Korea should establish a joint publishing institute that would report on a wide variety of issues. A new proposal for media exchanges was suggested in a joint statement in 1961 by the Central Committee of the Democratic Front for National Unification and the Inaugural General Meeting for a Peaceful Unification of Korea. Also the Park Chung Hee government proposed media exchanges.

In 1958, North Korea proposed the formation of a united Korean team for the upcoming 17th Olympic Games. Following the 1962 resolution by the International Olympic Committee's General Meeting on the formation of a joint Korean team for the 1964 Tokyo Olympics which the two Koreas agreed to, meetings were held in Switzerland and Hong Kong in 1963. In 1965, the North Korean actor Pak Yông-sin proposed joint film production and the holding of a joint theatre contest. Finally, in 1966, the linguist Hong Ki-mun suggested exchanges of journalists while ornithologist Wôn Hong-gu proposed an exchange of scientists, but all of these proposals for open contacts failed. Instead, the joint holding in 1961 by pro-North and pro-South Koreans of "The Cultural Festival For Peaceful Unification Through the Promotion of North-South Cultural Exchanges", in Tokyo, became the first successful attempt to pursue inter-Korean cultural contacts.[6]

In the Joint Communiqué of 4 July, 1972, North and South Korea agreed to pursue manifold contacts. Cultural exchanges were subsequently discussed in the South-North Co-ordinating Committee but the talks, while outlining the general principles for such exchanges, did not bring any concrete results. Neither did proposals from the South Korean government in April 1976 to exchange and jointly exhibit old arts objects and archaeological materials, in November 1981 to arrange an exchange exhibition of ancient relics, and in November 1984 to promote [non-exemplified] cultural exchanges bring any results.

Talks took place on forming a joint Korean team for the 1979 World Table Tennis Championships in P'yôngyang as well as the 1980 Moscow Olympics and the 1984 Los Angeles Olympics but they also failed; South Korea did not take part in the 1979 World Table Tennis Championships.[7] Later, North Korea proposed the formation of

---

6 Cho, ibid., 1998, p. 20; Ch'oe, ibid., pp. 38-9; Hwang, "Nambuk sûp'och'û kyoryu", *T'ongil Han'guk* (1989), 2, p. 40; Lee, "Nambuk munhwa kyoryu-ûi hyônhwang-gwa munjejôm", in Minjok t'ongil yôn'guwôn, *T'ongil munhwa-wa minjok kongdongch'e kônsôl* (Seoul: Minjok t'ongil yôn'guwôn, 1994), pp. 55-6. Lee does not say how cultural heterogeneity was manifested and when South Korea proposed media exchanges. Ch'oe Yong-gôn is not identified. North Korea had until 1989 on 117 occasions suggested 265 cases of exchanges in arts and culture whereas South Korea then had made only ten proposals (ibid., pp. 55, 56, 58: fn. 2).

7 Since opinions differed in the International Olympic Committee (IOC) on what part of Germany should take part in the Olympic Games, Germany participated after the 1956 Winter Olympics until the 1964 Summer Olympics with a joint team and flag. In 1968, East Germany was admitted into the IOC. From the 1972 Summer Olympics, East and West Germany

a joint team for the 1990 Asian Games, as they had done prior to the 1980 Moscow Olympics, but again no agreement was reached.

Consequently, the first reunions of divided families from 20-23 September, 1985 and the simultaneous performances of traditional songs and dances by the accompanying arts troupes with 50 members each in Seoul and P'yôngyang, respectively, marked the beginning of the first substantial socio-cultural exchanges since the days of national liberation in 1945. These exchanges, which took place at a time when human exchanges were handled under the National Security Law, were achieved after three rounds of Red Cross sponsored talks in 1984-1985. They materialized since the mutual agreement that the exchanges of arts troupes would exclude politicization and that states would not slander, nor incite each other, was respected. But the exchanges that occurred, according to the South Korean journalist Ch'oe Hak-chu (2000), were an occasion to confirm heterogeneity in culture and arts between the two Koreas, and were a one-time event since relations soon worsened, as we have seen in Chapter 3.

In June 1988, South Korea proposed at high-level official talks exchanges of cultural and arts personalities, but North Korea ignored the proposal. Following the 1988 7 July Declaration, the Roh Tae Woo government began in October of the same year to open to the public many previously forbidden materials on North Korea and communist countries at some public institutions. The ban on works by defectors to North or South Korea was partially lifted and some North Korean literary works became available in the South. Both Kim Il Sung and Kim Jong Il could now be shown on TV. While these steps were taken, an additionally sensitive issue was the illegal visits in 1989 to North Korea, by Reverend Mun Ik-hwan and student representative Im Su-kyông, as described previously in Chapter 3.[8]

The first socio-cultural visits to North Korea after The Inter-Korean Exchanges and Cooperation Act had been enacted, took place between 14-24 October, 1990, conducted by the 17-member Seoul Traditional Musical Band. They had been invited by the North Korean Musicians' Federation to participate in "The Pan-National Unification Concert", performed at eight different locations. The P'yôngyang Music Troupe and Korean music groups from the United States, Japan, Canada, China, Germany and the Soviet Union took part in the concerts. Additionally, as a result of government agreement, during a visit from 8-13 December, 1990 the equally symbolic "Year-end National Unification Concert" took place in Seoul.

---

participated separately. The dispatch of a joint Olympic team while political relations were tense is a good example of the possibilities for inter-German cooperation. From Kim (*Tong sôdok injôk*, 1996, pp. 79-80).

8 Cho, *T'ongil kwajông-esô mingan tanch'e-ûi yôkhal* (Seoul: Minjok t'ongil yôn'guwôn, 1996), pp. 36-7, 48: fn. 16; Cho, ibid., 1998, pp. 22, 23: fn. 35; Cho et al., *Pichôngbu kigu(NGO)-rûl t'onghan Nambukhan kyoryu hyômnyôk chûngjin pangan yôn'gu* (Seoul: T'ongil yôn'guwôn, 2000), p. 21: fn. 8; Ch'oe, ibid., pp. 39-40; Hwang, ibid., (1989), 2, pp. 40, 41; Ko, ibid., p. 49; Lee, ibid., 1994, pp. 59-60. Lee (ibid., p. 59) does not say why North Korea ignored the South Korean proposal on 3 June, 1988 for cultural exchanges.

The 33-member P'yôngyang National Music Band performed, in addition to its own repertoire, traditional music alongside its South Korean counterparts in this return visit. This was the last socio-cultural exchange in arts on the Korean Peninsula before the tour of the above "Little Angels" in P'yôngyang in May 1998 who consisted of a troupe of 66 members. The only exceptions were the performances in Seoul of traditional music and dance by North and South Korean arts troupes on the occasions of four rounds of North-South Prime Minister talks held in Seoul in September 1990, December 1990, December 1991 and May 1992.

But contacts continued abroad and in March 1991, the first permit for partnership was issued for the formation of a unified Korean team for the World Table Tennis Championships held in Japan supported by the Fund for Inter-Korean Cooperation. In May of that year, permission was given for a united Korean team to participate in the 1991 World Junior Soccer Championships in Portugal. Permits were given, since the required criteria – the representative activities, the legal procedures and contributions to improve inter-Korean relations – were fulfilled.[9]

Cultural exchanges abroad were quite frequent in the early 1990s when, as we have seen, inter-Korean relations had entered a third period of dialogue. In March 1991, a successful joint event took place of the music series "Echo of One Nation". It was held in Japan over six parts: the two Koreas refrained from irritating and criticizing each other as well as not pointing out negative issues related to their respective societies. According to Ko (2002), the event reflected the existing good will in terms of national homogeneity and national harmony, in spite of different ideologies. It also manifested the extent of unity among Korean residents in Japan and their wishes for unification domestically, as well as internationally. From 2-5 May, 1991, 60 North and 52 South Korean artists took part in "The International Arts Exhibition" held in Japan. The South Korean Central National Music String Instruments Troupe and the P'yôngyang Music and Dance Troupe made joint performances. From 27-29 May, 1991, ten artists from North and 28 from South Korea participated in "The North-South Paintings and Writings Exhibition" held in Beijing in the first exchange of arts.

From 17-18 August, 1991, "The Unified North-South Traditional Dance, Customs and Arts Festival" was held on Sakhalin Island. Traditional arts such as farmers' music and the Chindo drum dance were jointly performed. There was an attendance of 80 participants from North and 120 from South Korea. In August 1992, "The Unification Arts Festival" took place on Sakhalin with 42 participants from North and 78 from South Korea. South Korean popular songs and North Korean traditional songs and dances were jointly performed as well as "The Echo of One Nation" concert.[10]

---

9 Cho, ibid., 1998, pp. 6, 23: fn. 36; Cho, ibid., 1999, pp. 31-2; Cho et al., ibid., 2000, p. 44; Hwang, "Direction of Inter-Korean Musical Exchanges", *Korea Focus* 9 (2001), no. 4, pp. 138-39; Kang et al., ibid., 2001, p. 140; Ko, ibid., pp. 50, 56; Lee, ibid., 1994, p. 61.

10 Hwang, ibid., 2001, p. 139; Kang et al., ibid., 2001, p. 141; Ko, ibid., p. 61; O, ibid., *Nambuk kyoryu*, December 1999, p. 93: fn. 136.

In April 1993, "The Korean People's Music Concert" was held in Japan, where "The Unified Korea Arts Exhibition" was also held 12-24 October, the same year with three participants from North and 16 from South Korea. According to the South Korean scholar O Ki-sông (1999) it was, in spite of the long division, possible to feel a common denominator of homogeneity reflected in the artistic work. But in terms of style, the art works differed markedly: the North Korean works were like photo pictures since Kim Il Sung had established these techniques for national arts in the 1960s and had continued that policy determinedly.

The event was followed 8-13 February, 1996 by "The Korean Peace Arts Exhibition" and from 28 October-1 November, 1997 by "The North-South Peace Arts Exhibition" both of which were held in Japan. In 1997, there were six Northern and 25 South Korean participants in all.

In 1991, the first contact in theatre took place in Beijing at "The Symposium on Traditional Theatre in Asia" but afterwards no distinct results were recorded in this field. From 23 August-3 September, 1992 both Koreas participated in "The Celebrations of the 40th Anniversary of the Establishment of Self-government of Koreans in Yônbyôn". In September 1992, they took part in "The Echo of One Nation Music Festival" held in New York.[11]

Besides pursuing such various contacts, South Korea tried in the early 1990s to open media contacts. The media had played an important role in German unification, South Korean media people and high-level North Korean officials met abroad to discuss media cooperation that included joint production, opening of other broadcasting materials and joint training of staff. Although North Korea feared the negative effects of broadcasting on its society, it showed interest in some of the South's techniques. Publishers' contacts and meetings abroad resulted in indirect imports of 5,032 North Korean scientific books (in 193,372 copies) in the fields of philosophy, social sciences, pure sciences, science and technology, arts, linguistics, literature and history between 1990 and 1992. In 1993, imports of non-political and non-ideological publications from North Korea for sale and exports of such South Korean works were permitted. As of 1994, 1,107 North Korean works (in 64,161 copies) had been imported to South Korea.

Student contacts were initiated and photo exhibitions were held during the 1990s. From 21-26 June, 1994, 19 North and 26 South Korean students took part in "The Second World Student Leaders' Science and Peace Conference" in Beijing drawing 170 delegates who focused on the Korean Peninsula. The death of Kim Il Sung in

---

11 Cho, ibid., 1999, pp. 33-4; Hwang, ibid., 2001, p. 139; Kang et al., ibid., 2001, p. 141; Lee, ibid., 1994, pp. 62, 66; Minjok t'ongil yôn'guwôn, *T'ongil hwangyông-gwa Nambukhan kwangye: 1996~1997* (Seoul: Minjok t'ongil yôn'guwôn, 1996), p. 94: ibid., *1997~1998*, 1997, p. 76; O, *Nambukhan munhwa t'onghamnon*, 1999, pp. 237-8; T'ongilbu, *T'ongilbu 30nyônsa* (Seoul: T'ongilbu, 1999), p. 287. Cho (ibid, pp. 33-4) does not say when in 1991 "The Symposium on Traditional Theater in Asia" was held. The evaluation of "The Unified Korea Arts Exhibition" was made by [non-identified] Wôn Tong-sôk in the first number of *Minjok yesul* [*National Arts*] in 1994 (quoted in O, ibid.). "The Echo of One Nation Music Festival" is quoted from Hwang, ibid.

July 1994 as well as the 1996 submarine incident led to a decrease in cross-border Korean meetings. Yet "The North-South Korea-China Photo Exhibition" was held in China 26-30 September, 1994 with three participants from North and five from South Korea.

From 5-9 February, 1995, 53 North Korean and 177 South Korean university students participated in "The Third World University Students' Peace Seminar" in Beijing. Opinions were exchanged on the topic "New Civilisation of the 21st Century and the Role of the Youth". Students participated particularly in discussions on "The Influence of Korean Unification on World Peace". From 8-11 October, 1995 leaders of the student groups from both Koreas met informally to discuss exchanges and cooperation at the "The Northeast Asia Youth Leaders' Conference", held in Beijing, but, as of 2000, no concrete results were achieved.

The September 1994 photo exhibition was followed in July 1997 by "The International Korean People's Photo Seminar and Exhibition" that was also held in China. As we have seen, it was followed up from 29 May-11 June 1998, by a photo exhibition that was held in Seoul and Pusan. The photo book *Paektu-esô Halla kkaji – lensû-ro pon choguk [From Mt. Paektu to Mt. Halla – The Fatherland Seen from the Lens]* that was printed in 2,000 copies, was the result of two years of joint work, including two rounds of meetings in China and three rounds of exchanging revisions. 20 South and 46 North Korean writers took part in this project.[12]

Although socio-cultural exchanges expanded during the 1990s, they were less frequent than economic contacts. However, as we have seen, socio-cultural exchanges and cooperation have increased significantly since Kim Dae Jung became president in 1998, both in qualitative and quantitative terms, albeit at a low level. Between March 1991 and July 2001, 24 South Korean organizations received permits for partnerships with North Korean counterparts in socio-cultural areas, including 21 since 1998. As of September 2003, the number had risen to 40. The projects often had a budget of less than $ 1m due to their small scale. Fields of cooperation were sports, academia, education, environment, mass communications and health. Besides the joint photo exhibitions and music concerts referred to, CDs, films and music videos were also manufactured or were earmarked for manufacture.

The first permit received after the two issued in 1991, was issued in December 1997 when the Unification Culture Research Centre of the South Korean daily *Joong Ang Ilbo* received permission for a project to visit North Korea. The purpose was to collect data on historic relics and to present them in South Korea. The first permit issued after the new June 1997 legislation on socio-cultural cooperation had been

---

12 Cho, ibid., 1999, p. 34; Cho et al., ibid., 2000, p. 23; Ham et al., *NGO-rûl t'onghan Nambukhan ch'ôngsonyôn kyoryu hyômnyôk pangan yôn'gu* (Seoul: T'ongil yôn'guwôn, 2000), pp. 96-7; Kang et al., ibid., 2001, pp. 137, 140, 141, 142; Ko, ibid., p. 50; Lee, ibid., 1994, pp. 63-4, 67, 87. Cho et al. (ibid., p. 23) do not give any statistics of the fall in Koreans meeting each other and South Koreans visiting North Korea in 1994 but records that visits in 1996 fell by almost half.

enacted, was issued. During 1998, three visits to the North by staff from the Centre marked the beginning of a program in the fields of media and publishing. Among the 21 organizations that received permits between 1998 and 2001, were the Sports Art, the Korean Welfare Foundation, Hyundai Asan, the SN 21 Enterprise, the Korean Cultural Network Research Centre and the Korean Culture Foundation. The Korean Cultural Network Research Centre visited the North in 1998.[13]

Those organizations made broadcasts on North Korean historic relics and scenery, establishing a factory for making medicine and managing a hospital, as well as building an indoor stadium and pursuing cooperation in sports. In addition to coverage of the National Unification Concert in the North, processing North-South culture and, finally, holding the 1998 cross-border, joint photo exhibition.

In another sign of expanding exchanges, 62 North Koreans, including media people, visited Seoul in December 1999 when the second "Unification Basketball Games" were played (cf. p. 65). But, it was noted that South Korean opinion expressed the view that the games were allowed by North Korea for political propaganda purposes, thereby reducing the event's significance. Yet only 1,534 North Koreans, among a total population of 22.5 million in 2002, visited South Korea between 1989 and April 2002. During the same period, 30,248 South Koreans of, in 2003, 48 million inhabitants actually visited North Korea.

It should also be noted that 27,843 South Koreans had travelled across from 1998 onwards, that is 92 per cent of the visitor total. No less than 56 per cent of mutual visits were accomplished after the June 2000 summit. As of July 2003, the figure of visitors had risen to 49,408, among them 46,611 South Koreans to the North, but there were, in spite of a marked rise, only 2,797 North Korean visitors to the South.

The total number of Koreans meeting each other in socio-cultural fields amounted to 4,601 visitors between June 1989 and October 1999, whereas the total number of people meeting each other was 10,705. As a comparison, economic exchanges and divided families were the largest categories with 2,801 and 2,112 people, respectively. Visitors in the socio-cultural areas were divided into education and academia (1,941), religion (867), culture and arts (702), athletics (518), science and environment (282), media and publishing (146) and tourism (145; Mt. Kûmgang visitors excluded). That the number of South Koreans visiting North Korea in the socio-cultural field amounted to 2,197 people between June 1989 and late December 2001 reconfirms the fact that most meetings occurred in third countries.[14]

---

13 Cho, ibid., 1998, pp. 6, 24, 25, 27, 30-31; Cho, ibid., 2002b, pp. 110-111, 113-114, 115; Ko, ibid., pp. 50-51, 58; Yi, "Indojôk chiwôn, kyoryu hyômnyôg-ûl t'onghan Nambuk kwangye-ûi palchônchôk chônmang", in Uri minjok sôro topki undong p'yônghwa nanum sent'ô, *Taebuk indojôk chiwôn, kyoryu hyômnyôg saôp-gwa Pukhan-ûi pyônhwa* (Seoul: Uri minjok sôro topki undong p'yônghwa nanum sent'ô, 2003), pp. 66-8.

14 Cho, ibid., 1999, pp. 20-21, 36, 52; Cho, ibid., 2002a, pp. 3-4; Cho, ibid., 2002b, pp. 114, 115; Kang, *Nambukhan-ûi*, p. 16; Ko, ibid., pp. 50-51; World Bank, *World Development Report 2004: Making Services Work for Poor People* (New York: Oxford University Press, 2003), pp. 252, 263.

Statistics of visitors however, omit the, as of June 2002; more than 500,000 South Korean tourists who visited Mt. Kûmgang – that is one per cent of the population – clearly reflecting the fact that while South Korea pushes for increasing contacts and exchanges, North Korea was reluctant to open up its society as was previously described (in December 2004, there were some 822,000 visitors to Mt. Kûmgang). Besides the marked increase of visitors, a notable change is that unlike the previous pattern of meetings mainly being achieved in a third country, human exchanges now also increasingly began to take place on the Korean Peninsula.

During 2000, all 706 North Koreans who had applied for visiting permits to South Korea did get to go. Altogether 336 persons visited South Korea for socio-cultural purposes during the performances of the P'yôngyang Student and Youth Art Troupe (102) from 24-27 May, the P'yôngyang Circus Troupe (102) from 27 May-11 June and the North Korean National Symphony Orchestra (132) from 18-24 August.

The Arts Troupe was invited by "the Peace Motor" and gave five public performances in Seoul to celebrate the upcoming June inter-Korean summit. The Circus Troupe, which made eleven public performances in Seoul drawing more than 130,000 people, was invited by the performing art program organizer, SN21, as main sponsor. The North Korean National Symphony Orchestra, which made two ordinary performances and two joint performances, visited Seoul to celebrate the 55th anniversary of national liberation and the 15 June Declaration. The performances, which took place did so thanks to the work, primarily, of the South Korean government. The event was significant because they represented the first visits to Seoul by North Korean artists since a traditional music concert for unification was held in late 1990. It should be noted that all 125 members of the Symphony Orchestra went to Seoul and that the final joint concert was broadcast live across South Korea.[15]

Although most socio-cultural exchanges have consisted of South Koreans visiting the North, North Korea has not entirely rejected mutual exchanges. This becomes clear from the fact that besides the visits in socio-cultural spheres by 336 North Koreans, altogether 287 persons visited South Korea during 2000 for family reunions. Another 83 North Koreans participated in various North-South talks that were being held. Consequently, among 768 North Korean visitors to South Korea between 1999-2000, 685 persons, that is almost 90 per cent, were engaged in socio-cultural exchanges.

In addition, 82 members of the Kûmgangsan Opera Troupe of the pro-North Korean organization *Chochongryun* (The General Association of Korean Residents in Japan) were invited by the Korean Culture Foundation and made four public performances at the Little Angels Arts Centre from 15-17 December. Previously, 50 Chochongryun members in Japan had made a six-day visit to South Korea in

---

15 Cho, ibid., 2002a, pp. 1, 3-4; Cho, ibid., 2002b, pp. 110-112, 115; Hwang, ibid., 2001, p. 143; Kim, "Geumgang: mountain of one's dreams", *Korea Now*, 11 December, 2004, p. 28; KINU, ibid., 2000a, p. 137; Lee, *Pukhan munhwa-ûi*, 2001, p. 45. Kim (ibid., p. 28) spells Mt. Kûmgang according to the Ministry of Education transliteration system.

September and 119 stayed six days during November 2000. Another 80 members visited for six days in April 2001. A notable feature was that among the 7,280 South Koreans who visited North Korea during 2000, the number of visitors in the socio-cultural field more than doubled from 329 persons in 1999 to 674 (9.3 per cent); the number had been only 238 in 1998. On the other hand, what this clearly shows is that socio-cultural exchanges are sensitive to the development of inter-Korean relations in that the number of North Korean visitors to South Korea fell dramatically to just 191 persons during 2001. No less than 140 of those visited on the occasion of the third round of family reunions. Meanwhile, the number of South Korean visitors to North Korea in socio-cultural exchanges rose to 701, compared with 668 visitors in the field of economics. The stagnation of people to people exchanges remained during the first months of 2002 but, as we have seen, 874 North Koreans had visited South Korea by the end of October.[16]

This figure exceeded the 706 visitors in 2000 but since the vast majority came on the occasion of the Asian Games, it does not offer proof that visits had become more frequent: indeed if that had been the case, it would have been most remarkable. The significance of the Asian Games visitors and the resulting goodwill was also undermined by the subsequent re-emergence of the nuclear crisis on the Korean Peninsula.

4.4 Types of socio-cultural exchanges and cooperation

Besides these examples, socio-cultural contacts had taken place in the fields of academia and education, environment, film, literature, sports, religion and through participation in women conferences. Scientific exchanges through participation in international conferences had also been relatively frequent. Economics and the unification issue had become the most active of fields: North Korea sought to guarantee some practical benefits as well as alleviating its economic crisis, attracting foreign investment and improving its image world-wide through utilizing an opportunity to proclaim its stand on unification.

Academic contacts took place throughout history, which was comparatively easy to achieve since this field was not influenced by the different social systems and developments apparent in post-war inter-Korean relations. From 15-18 March, 1990 two scholars from North Korea and three from South Korea participated in "The Foundation Meeting of the Association of Asian History" in Japan. In "The Second Asian History Meeting" held 20-28 May, 1991 in China, two North and 16 South Korean scholars participated. The meeting included joint surveys of Koguryô relics.

---

16 Cho, ibid., 1999, p. 15; Cho, ibid., 2002a, pp. 3-4, 6, 7; Cho, ibid., 2002b, p. 112; Cho, *Sahoe munhwa punya*, 2002c, p. 102; KINU, *T'ongil hwangyông-mith*, 2000b, p. 111; Lee et al., *Nambukhan p'yônghwa*, pp. 118, 119. KINU (ibid., 2001) records on p. 87 that during the year there were 172 visitors to South Korea. It is unclear why the figure is different from Cho (ibid., 2002a, p. 4).

From 2-5 August, 1990 at "The Third International Scientific Conference on Korean Studies" held in Japan, 11 North Korean and 145 South Korean scholars took part. In the fourth conference held in Beijing in 20-22 August, 1992, there were 29 North and 90 South Korean scholars present. Both Koreas took part in the fifth conference that was also held in Beijing 20-22 February, 1994.[17]

In 1991, three North Korean and 15 South Korean scholars participated in "The 15th Conference of the Association of Korean Studies in Europe" in France from 22-26 March. The North had taken part, since the 13th 1989 London conference. The author participated in the London conference and noted that North and South Korean scholars socialized well. From 29-31 July, North Korea participated with 12 scholars and South Korea with 75 in "The Young Scholars' Conference in Korean Studies" in China. A North-South "Scientific Discussion Forum for Peace in and Unification of Korea" was proposed. From 19-22 August, North and South Korean technicians took part in "The Korean People's Scientific Forum of Scientists and Technicians" held in China in the first such exchange. North Korea participated in "The International Scientific Conference on Korean Studies" in China 12-14 August with three scholars and South Korea with 45. Inter-Korean exchanges in linguistics and literature and research on the independence movement were proposed. In 1992, the two Koreas participated in "The Asia-Pacific Education Forum" in Tokyo from 3-6 March.

Also in 1993 both Koreas participated in international conferences. From 15-17 April, four North and 11 South Korean scholars took part in the conference "Inheritance and Development of Korean Culture in Northeast Asia" held in China that discussed subjects such as language and customs. Notably, Kyônghûi University's Asia-Pacific Regional Research Institute in South Korea was coorganizer with the Yônbyôn University Northeast Asia Political Research Institute. From 27 May-13 June, five North and three South Korean scholars participated in "The Excavations of Parhae [668-926] Relics in the Maritime Provinces of Siberia" in Russia. From 11-14 August, five North and seven South Korean scholars participated in "The International Scientific Conference on Koguryô Culture" in China. Joint surveys of relics were made. Both Koreas also took part in "The Third International Scientific Conference on Koguryô" 20-21 July, 1997 in Tokyo; North Korea with nine scholars through the Chochongryun and South Korea with 12.

From 14-17 February, 1994, four North and more than 40 South Korean scholars participated in "The International University Students Peace Seminar" in Moscow. From 1-5 August, 1994, five Northern and ten South Korean scholars took part in "The International Scientific Conference on Northeast Asian Historical Research" in China. The juridical foundation Ch'ônwôn Korea Theological Research Institute was coorganizer with the Shanghai College of Education. From 4-6 August, 1995, four North and ten South Korean scholars participated in the conference "Reappraisal of

---

17 Cho, ibid., 1999, pp. 22, 25; Kang et al., ibid., 2001, pp. 132, 133; Ko, ibid., p. 53.

the Primitive and Old Civilisations in Northeast Asia" in Japan. Presentations on old Korean history were made.[18]

In 19-20 August, 1996, 12 scholars from each Korea met at "The Scientific Conference on the Present Conditions of and Prospects for Korean Studies" in Beijing. It was coarranged by the Sungsil University's Social Science Research Institute and the Asian section of the International Koryô Society. For the third time, South Korea was thus coorganizer. Topics on the conference agenda included language, literature, law, philosophy, history, economics, social welfare and regional development. In 22-23 August, 1996, scholars including those of Air and Correspondence Colleges, held a scientific conference in China on life-time education and education through correspondence. Finally, in November 2000, scholars held "The Ancient History Symposium on the 100th Anniversary of the Korean Society for the Promotion of Learning" in Tokyo. Besides those organized exchanges, during 2000 there were a few South Korean scholars who were invited to North Korea or who made visits on an individual basis.

More significantly, in June 2000, Seoul National University (SNU) Press bought the copyright for the pictorial book on Korean relics and antiquities published in 20 volumes in North Korea as a state-led project during the years 1988-1996 and published *Pukhan-ûi munhwajae-wa munhwa yujôk* [*North Korea's Cultural Treasures and Cultural Remains*]. The volumes on Koguryô, Koryô (918-1392) and anthropology were reorganized in the first five volumes published. Copyright was transferred thanks to an agreement on scholarly exchanges with Yônbyôn University in China. Yônbyôn University then transferred the copyright from its North Korean counterpart to SNU in an official way.[19] Academic cooperation led to a third publication after the photo book *From Mt. Paektu to Mt. Halla – The Fatherland Seen from the Lens* had been published in 1998 and the inter-Korean common dictionary of computer terminologies in 1999. Given the tense relations, these were remarkable achievements.

In *economics*, there were, during the early 1990s, more exchanges between North and South Korea than in other fields. From 9-12 October, 1990, three North and five South Korean scholars took part in "The Third International Symposium on a North-east Asian Joint Economic Community" in Beijing. In 1991, the two states participated in five conferences. From 28 January-1 February, eight North and 13 South Korean scholars participated in "The Conference on Economic Development and Cooperation in the Northeast Asian Region" held in China. They agreed to pursue joint research and to share research results to promote economic

---

18 Cho, ibid., 1999, p. 25; Kang et al., ibid., 2001, pp. 132, 133; Ko, ibid., pp. 53-4; Minjok t'ongil yôn'guwôn, *T'ongil hwangyông-gwa Nambukhan kwangye: 1991~1992* (Seoul: Minjok t'ongil yôn'guwôn, 1991), p. 114: ibid., *1992~1993,* 1992, p. 103: ibid., *1994~1995*, 1994, p. 114; T'ongilbu, ibid., p. 276.

19 Cho, ibid., 1996, p. 46: fn. 13; Cho, *Nambukhan haksul kyoryu hyômnyôk chûngjin pangan yôn'gu* (Seoul: T'ongil yônguwôn, 2000), pp. 33-4; Kang et al., ibid., 2001, p. 132; Kim, *Nambuk sahoe munhwa*, April 2001, pp. 62-3.

development in the region. In 17-19 July, two North Korean scholars and one South Korean scholar took part in "The Foundation Meeting of the Civilian Association for Economic Development and Cooperation in the Northeast Asian Region" held in Beijing. From 27 August-1 September, four North and 21 South Korean scholars participated in "The Seminar on Northeast Asian International Cooperation" in China. From 29-31 August, three North and 19 South Korean scholars participated in "The International Scientific Conference on Northeast Asia's Economic and Technological Development" in China. At this time, the development of the Tumen River Basin was discussed. Finally, in November, two scholars from the North and one scholar from the South took part in "The International Symposium on a Northeast Asian Economic Bloc" held in Japan.

In 1992, North and South Korea participated in four conferences. From 3-5 February, two scholars from each Korea participated in "The International Scientific Conference on Economic Cooperation in Northeast Asia" held in Japan. North Korea had allowed 18 South Korean experts to attend the conference "Northeast Asia Economic Forum" held in P'yôngyang 28 April-4 May on the plan to establish a free trade zone in the Najin-Sônbong area that was coorganized by North Korea, the United States and Japan [Sônbong is situated north of Najin]. 47 North Korean scholars participated in the conference. From 10-12 July, five North and 21 South Korean scholars participated in "The International Scientific Conference on Comparative Research on Development in the Northeast Asian Region" held in China. Finally, from 25-28 August, four North and ten South Korean scholars took part in "The Forum on Economic Cooperation in the Northeast Asian Region" held in Russia.[20]

In 1993-1994, North and South Korea participated in three conferences. From 18-20 April, 1993, three scholars from each Korea participated in "The Second General Directors' Meeting of the Civilian Association for Economic Development and Cooperation in the Northeast Asian Region" held in China. Due to the Tumen River Basin Development Program pursued by the United Nations' Development Program (UNDP), both Koreas took part in "The Third Meeting of the Planning and Management Committee" in Seoul 9-10 May and in "The Second Expert Meeting on Resources, Industry and Environment" in P'yôngyang 8-11 November.

From 16-25 July, 1994, four North and six South Korean scholars took part in "The International Scientific Conference on Economic Development and Cooperation in the Northeast Asian Region" held in China. In 18-19 August, five North and eight South Korean scholars participated in "The Scientific Conference on the Prospects for Cooperation Among the Northeast Asian Countries in the 21st Century" held in China. Nonetheless, academic exchanges were somewhat dull between 1992 and 1994 due to the nuclear issue. North Korea also feared external influences and restricted intellectuals' contacts with the outside world. Given these circumstances, it is remarkable that socio-cultural contacts continued, especially those on the Korean Peninsula.

---

20 Cho, ibid., 1999, p. 24; Kang et al., ibid., 2001, pp. 131, 134; Ko, ibid., p. 54.

From 18-21 July, 1995, five Northern and seven South Korean scholars participated in "The International Scientific Conference on Northeast Asia in the 21st Century" held in China. Participation became more active in 1996. In 18-19 January, both Koreas participated in "The Sixth Northeast Asia Economic Forum" in the US, where they also took part in "The Seminar on the North Korean Economy" held 22-23 April. Previously, from 7-9 February, five North and 10 South Korean scholars had participated in "The Niigata Northeast Asian Economic Conference". From 8-12 May, five North and six South Korean scholars participated in "The Scientific Conference on the Prospects for Economic Cooperation at the Gulf of Pohai" held in China. In June, both Koreas took part in "The Scientific Conference on Peace and Economic Cooperation in Northeast Asia" in China. Both Koreas participated in "The Scientific Conference on Northeast Asia in the 21st Century" held 1-4 August in China. From 17-21 August, 1997, they participated in "The Seventh Northeast Asia Economic Forum" in Mongolia. From 17-19 February, 1998, five North and six South Korean scholars participated in "The Niigata Northeast Asian Economic Conference" and in 28-29 July, four North and 31 South Korean scholars took part in "The Eighth Northeast Asian Economic Forum" in Japan.[21]

The *unification issue* was initially debated at conferences on international politics arranged by the United States, Japan, China and Russia. Peace on and unification of the Korean Peninsula were discussed in a Northeast Asian regional context with participants from the neighbouring countries and invited scholars from both Koreas. The first such conference was "The Second International Scientific Conference on Dialogue, Peace and Cooperation in the Asia-Pacific Region". Five North and three South Korean scholars took part in the conference that was held 4-6 September, 1990 in the Soviet Union.

It was followed by four conferences in 1991. From 23-25 March, three scholars from each Korea participated in "The Northeast Asia Security Conference" held in Beijing. Arms reduction was the theme of the other conferences. From 27-29 May, four North and three South Korean scholars participated in "The Northeast Asian International Conference" held in Tokyo. From 31 May-2 June, four North and three South Korean scholars participated in "The Seventh International Scientific Symposium on Unification of the Korean Peninsula" in Tokyo. Finally, three scholars from each Korea took part in "The First North Korea-United States Scientific Conference" held 3-7 June, in the United States.

The two Koreas participated in four conferences also in 1992. In 17-18 May, three North and 11 South Korean scholars participated in "The Eighth International Scientific Symposium on Unification of the Korean Peninsula" held in Tokyo. Two scholars from each state participated in "The Conference on North Pacific Security and Cooperation" held in Canada 22-23 May that dealt with arms reduction and confidence-building measures. From 23-25 June, three North and two South Korean scholars participated in "The Hawaii Six Nations International Scientific

---

21 Ch'oe, ibid., p. 44; Kang et al., ibid., 2001, p. 135; Minjok t'ongil yôn'guwôn, ibid., *1993~1994*, 1994a, pp. 114-115: ibid., *1996~1997*, 1996, p. 93: *1997~1998*, 1997, p. 75.

Conference" on Korean unification. Finally, from 17-19 August, two North and three South Korean scholars participated in "The 1992 UN Arms Reduction Conference" held in China.[22]

In 16-17 April, 1993 North and South Korea participated in "The Second Symposium on the Unification of the Korean Peninsula" arranged by the Korean Students' Association at Berkeley University in the United States. They also took part when "The Fifth Symposium on the Unification of the Korean Peninsula" was arranged there 19-22 April, 1996. At the first conference, there were four North and five South Korean scholars whereas three from each state took part in the second one, in which students also participated thanks to the first formal permissions from the Korean governments. Restoration of national homogeneity was on the agenda.

From 28-31 August, 1993, "The Scientific Conference on Language and Philosophy Towards Unification" was held in Beijing with seven North and ten South Korean scholars. South Korean participants reportedly did not consider North Korea's position on language policies and were pretty offensive by one-sidedly blaming linguistic differences on the absence of contacts during 50 years of division. Although, to the author's knowledge, it was unrelated to the unification issue, from 3-8 August, 1994, four Northern and seven South Korean scholars participated in "The First Conference on the Next Generation of Politicians in East Asia" held in Malaysia. Three North and four South Korean scholars participated in "The '96 International Scientific Conference for the Unification of the Fatherland" held in London 5-6 May, 1996.[23]

From 31 July-1 August, 1995, the first in a series of annual conferences abroad on peace on the Korean Peninsula and North-South reconciliation, were held in China with six North Korean, 16 South Korean and six expatriate Korean scholars participating. Academic exchanges thus became more frequent while relations remained tense. Since 1996, the conferences have been arranged by South Korea's Academic Unification Forum and the North Korean Academy for Society and Politics, not least thanks to the bridge-building role of Korean scholars abroad. In the 13-15 September, 1996 conference, nine Northern and 21 South Korean scholars participated. The theme was "The Prospects for and Tasks of National Unification". Since the third conference was held 29-30 August, 1997 with 11 North and 15 South Korean scholars taking part, such issues as economic cooperation, establishing trust in political and military affairs, improving the North's agriculture and the Mt. Kûmgang tourist project were discussed. The fourth conference took place 20-21 February, 1998 and was attended by seven North and 17 South Korean scholars.

After the fifth conference had been held 26-27 October, 1999, the keynote speeches, papers and discussions from the conferences with more than 150 participants held since 1995 were published together in September 2000 by Kôn'guk University Press

---

22 Cho, ibid., 1999, p. 23; Kang et al., ibid., 2001, p. 136.
23 Cho, ibid., 1999, p. 23; Kang et al., ibid., 2001, pp. 136-7, 139; Kim, "Nambuk haksaeng mannam-ûn sunsuhae ya handa", *T'ongil Han'guk* (1996), 6, p. 80; Lee, ibid., 1994, p. 87.

in the volume *Pundan-ûl nômô t'ongir-ûl hyanghae* [*Beyond Division Towards Unification*]. Again, academic exchanges resulted in the publication from joint events following on previous ones in 1998, 1999 and June 2000. Also the conference "Germany and Korea: Meeting Within Division, the 1945-1995 Cold War and Afterwards" held in Germany dealt with unification issues. Two scholars from each Korean state participated.

On 30 June-1 July, 1997, the "Joint Conference for Peace and Harmony on the Korean Peninsula" arranged by the Council for Restoring Mutual Trust between North and South Korea and the North Korea Research Institute of National Issues was held in Beijing, with eight North and 13 South Korean participants. From 13-17 September, 1997, "The Fourth Seminar of World Youth Students for Peace" was held in Beijing. 85 university students from Northern and 167 from South Korea participated, thus comprising the majority of the more than 330 participants who attended in total. The students discussed unification but also held cultural and sport events and sang Korean songs, including the folk song "Arirang", together, it was reported.[24]

From 16-20 February, 1998 North and South Korea participated in "The Scientific Conference on Security in Northeast Asia" held in the United Kingdom. They also took part from 16-18 February at "The UN Conference on Arms Reduction in Southeast Asia" in Indonesia and 20-24 February at "The Tenth Conference on Peace and Arms Reduction in the Asia-Pacific Region" in Nepal. At these meetings, North Korea raised its confederative proposal along with the withdrawal of American troops from South Korea arguing that it would contribute to security in the region. But since they avoided discussions on their own nuclear, missile and weapons of mass destruction program, participants from the two Koreas did not fall into dispute.

When the fifth joint seminar "North-South Youth and Students' Seminar on Unification" with the theme "The Role of Youth In Establishing A Unified Fatherland" was held in China 25-29 July, 1999, 203 students, professors and officials from both Koreas participated, of which 60 came from the North and 143 from the South. From 22-24 July, 1999, eight Northern and 17 South Korean scholars as well as Korean scholars from the Yônbyôn region took part in the conference "Situation and Future of the Korean People Towards the New Millennium" held on the occasion of the 50th anniversary of the foundation of the Yônbyôn University. The conference was coorganized by the Yônbyôn University Research Institute of Racial Issues and the [South] Korean Future Policies' Research Institute and was supported by the

---

24 Cho, ibid., 1996, p. 46: fn. 13; Cho, ibid., 1999, pp. 23-4; Cho, ibid., 2000, pp. 30-31, 42: fn. 49; Cho, ibid., 2002a, p. 14; Ham et al., ibid., p. 98; Kang et al., ibid., 2001, p. 137; Kim, ibid., April 2001, p. 62; Minjok t'ongil yôn'guwôn, ibid., *1995~1996*, 1995, pp. 94, 95; *1997~1998*, 1997, p. 75; T'ongilbu, ibid., p. 281. Kang et al., (ibid.) records that Seoul National University's Korean Politics Research Institute was coarranger of the 1995 unification conference. Minjok t'ongil yôn'guwôn (ibid., 1995, p. 95) does not say when the 1995 conference in Germany was held.

Korea Institute for National Unification covering history, the humanities, the social sciences and the arts.

Scientific technology has attracted interest as an area for exchange but with rather more North Korean participants: 45 specialists from North Korea and 87 from South Korea took part in "The 1991 International Science and Technology Contest" held 19-24 August in China. From 21-23 August, 1991, ten Northern and 44 South Korean scholars participated in "The '91 International Scientific Conference on Electronics, Intelligence and Telecommunications", held in China. Finally, from 7-12 August, 1995, at "The '95 International Scientific Conference on Electronics, Intelligence and Telecommunications" held in China, 10 Northern and 72 South Korean scholars participated. Scientific papers were presented. The [South] Korean Association for Electronical Engineering was coorganizer along with the Yônbyôn Council for Science and Technology.[25]

Environmental issues are another area where contacts have taken place through conferences. The South Korean scholar Son Gi-Woong and his associates (2002) express the opinion that exchanges and cooperation in the cross-border environment may gradually restore national homogeneity by creating contacts with North Korean citizens as well as specialists in the field and policy officials, thereby advancing unification.

Whether a correct evaluation or not only time will tell, but contacts began at "The Northeast Asia Environment Conference" held by the UNDP in Mongolia, in July 1991. The two Koreas, along with China, Japan and Russia, then took part in the preparatory meetings of the United Nations' Environment Program's (UNEP) "Northwest Asia Pacific Action Plan" in October 1991 in Russia, as well as in October 1992 in China and in November 1993 in Thailand. This was significant, as it was the first time North Korea participated in a regional environmental organization, but participation ended in September 1994 when the meeting was held in South Korea and the Action Plan was formally adopted.

In 1994-1995, environment specialists from both Koreas, along with other scholars from China, Japan, Russia and Mongolia, took part in founding "The East Asian Biosphere Preservation Network" at the United Nations' Educational, Scientific and Cultural Organization (UNESCO)-sponsored conferences on the East Asian Biosphere held in China and South Korea. "The UNESCO Comparative Research Seminar on the Preservation of the Northeast Asian Biological Sphere" was held in China 13-23 March, 1994, with three South Korean scholars participating. From 14-21 August, "The Second UNESCO Research Seminar on the Preservation of the Biological Sphere in the Northeast Asian Region" was held in South Korea. Such

---

25 Cho, ibid., 1999, pp. 24: fn. 22, 25-6; Cho, ibid., 2000, p. 31; Kang et al., ibid., 2001, p. 138; KINU, *The Unification Environment*, 2000a, pp. 138, 163; Minjok t'ongil yôn'guwôn, ibid., ibid., *1998~1999*, 1998a, p. 96.

seminars were held altogether seven times between August 1994 and September 2001.[26]

In 1995, North and South Korean scholars met at "The East Asian Conference on the Protection of National Parks and Nature" in Beijing in May and in September at "The Fourth Northeast Asia and Pacific Environmental Forum" held in Japan. On the latter occasion, scholars agreed to exchange research materials and implement joint investigations on natural resources.

In October 1995, five North Korean and nine South Korean scholars participated, along with scholars from the US, Thailand, Phillipines, Singapore, Indonesia and UNDP in "The Scholars Conference of Environment and Development in East Asia" held in Bangkok. Debates were held on such issues as Asia's economic development and environmental problems and environmental cooperation with Asia-Pacific Economic Cooperation (APEC). Notable is that the first case of indirect exchanges and cooperation was accomplished in April 1995 through the UNDP-supported project "Tumen River Area Development Program" that involved both North and South Korea, as well as China, Russia and Mongolia. They both undersigned its implementation in the comprehensive "Memorandum of Understanding on Environmental Principles". North Korea's main task was to investigate the status of pollution in the Tumen River Area whereas South Korea would set up a strategic action plan.[27]

In *linguistics,* scholars' main focus has been to alleviate the growing heterogeneity of the Korean language caused by the division. The South Korean Professor Yi Hyôn-bok of SNU and his North Korean colleague Roh Kil-yong from the Hyesan College of Education worked from June 1991 to June 1992 at Warsaw University on the study *Nambukhan ônô pigyo yôn'gu* [*A Comparative Study of Language in North and South Korea*] in the first joint language research project. They made extracts of linguistic differences between North and South Korean text books, newspapers and magazines, etc. and did reviews and comparisons in order to unify language. After the time in Poland, joint research was continued through correspondence but after Professor Roh Kil-yong had returned to North Korea contact was lost. Consequently, Professor Yi Hyôn-bok completed the study that deals with pronunciation, spelling, vocabulary, grammar and expressions in 2002. Nonetheless, this became the second joint research publication, after the 1999 computer dictionary and the fifth joint publication in total.

Joint activities continued afterwards. In 27-31 May, 1991, officials from both Koreas held the meeting "Simplification of the Romanization of Han'gûl for Mechanization" in Denmark and reached agreements on some points. The two

---

26 Minjok t'ongil yôn'guwôn, ibid., *1994~1995*, 1994b, pp. 114, 115: Son, *Nambukhan hwangyông punya kyoryu hyômnyôk pangan yôn'gu: tajachôk yangjachôk chôpkûn* (Seoul: Minjok t'ongil yôn'guwôn, 1996), pp. 31, 62, 64; Son et al., *Nambuk hwangyông enôji hyômnyôk hwalsônghwa chôllyak yôn'gu* (Seoul: T'ongil yôn'guwôn, 2002), pp. 21, 120, 134, 138: table 4-4.

27 Minjok t'ongil yôn'guwôn, ibid., *1995~1996*, 1995, pp. 101, 118; Son, ibid., pp. 31-2, 33-4; Son et al., ibid., pp. 131, 135-136, 138: table 4-4.

states then met in 16-17 June, 1992, in France at "The North-South Conference on the Spelling of Han'gûl in Roman Letters" under the auspices of the International Standardization Organization. Significantly, they agreed on a single proposal that accommodated the North's proposal for the consonants and the South's for the vowels as well as meeting the international society's requirements for standardization of Korean in Roman letters.[28]

In May 1994, at "The International Conference for Establishing a Standard Spelling of Han'gûl in Roman Letters", held in Stockholm, representatives from the two Koreas met and agreed to publish a technical report on proposals for pre-standards. On 3-4 August, 1995 "The International Scientific Conference on Korean Language Standards" was held in China with four scholars from the North and ten from the South participating. From 5-9 August, 1996, "The International Scientific Conference for Korean Language Scholars" was jointly organized by the North Korean National Language Committee, the South Korean National Language Research Institute and the Chinese Korean Language Assessment Committee in China, and drew six North and five South Korean scholars. In this first meeting between representatives of national language institutes, participants basically agreed on language standards and were united on not wishing to widen the existing linguistic differences. From 11-13 August, 2000, "The International Scientific Conference on the Position of the Korean Language in the World", was held in Beijing.

Beginning in 1994, the Korean Language Research Society, the North Korean General Federation of Science and Technology and the Yônbyôn Science and Technology Association organized four joint annual conferences in China on how to computerize Korean. Some 25 North Korean specialists and 24 from South Korea participated in "The International Scientific Conference on Computerization of the Korean Language" held 5-10 August, 1994. As was the case with the above 1991 science and technology contest, the number of North Koreans dispatched thus exceeded the numbers in other fields (but the above 1997 and 1999 peace seminars in fact attracted more participants). At the second conference held 14-16 September, 1995, there were 20 North and 35 South Korean participants. From 12-14 August, 1996, ten North and 28 South Korean scholars participated in the third conference when a joint proposal on necessary technical dimensions was selected and announced as a joint agreement. As we have seen, the fourth conference held 12-14 August, 1999 resulted in a joint dictionary of computer terminologies.[29]

---

28 Cho, ibid., 1999, pp. 26-7; Kang et al., ibid., 2001, p. 139; Kim, "Chôt Nambuk hakcha kongdong yôn'gusô palgan", http://www.hani.co.kr/section-005000000/2002/02/005000000 200202182246032.html, 18 February, 2002; Ko, ibid., p. 54; Lee, ibid., 1994, pp. 64-5; Paek, *Kukje kigu-rûl t'onghan Nambukhan kyoryu hyômnyôk chûngdae pangan yôn'gu* (Seoul: Minjok t'ongil yônguwôn, 1994), p. 53. Lee (ibid.) does not say on what points agreement was reached in May 1991 in Denmark.

29 Cho, ibid., 1996, p. 46: fn. 13; Cho, ibid., 1999, pp. 26, 27; Kang et al., 2001, ibid., pp. 138, 139; Kim, ibid., April 2001, p. 63; Minjok t'ongil yôn'guwôn, ibid., *1994~1995*, 1994b, pp. 114-115.

Exchanges between universities through the establishment of associational ties and setting up branch schools in North Korea, have been discussed both on an academic and at governmental level, for instance, in the third ministerial talks held in September 2000. Previously, one-day student contacts had taken place at P'anmunjôm in August and September, 1991. The first collegial ties were established in May 1998 between the Sônggyungwan University in Seoul and the Koryô Sônggyungwan University in Kaesông during the visit by the president of the former to North Korea 28 April-5 May.

In January 1998, the Yônbyôn Scientific Technical College Supporters' Association received the first permit for academic cooperation to establish and manage a Scientific and Technical College in the Najin-Sônbong region. Partners were the Committee for Pursuing Foreign Economic Cooperation and the Administrative and Economic Committee of Najin-Sônbong city. The project involved $ 5m and would last for some 15 years. Yônbyôn University would build facilities for teaching, administration, lodging as well as restaurants whereas North Korea would provide land, roads, electricity and labour. Later on, at the occasion of the June 2000 summit, the presidents of 192 South Korean universities decided at a joint meeting of the Korean Council of University Education to pursue scientific exchanges with North Korea. But the general trend is that, in spite of diverse exchanges and cooperation in education and academia, the level of these is as yet only voluntary. Hardly any concrete forms of cooperation exist in practice.

However, a project agreed upon in June 2001 by the Northeast Asian Foundation for Cooperation in Education and Culture and the North Korean Ministry of Education was the plan to establish and manage an Information Technology Scientific College in P'yôngyang and open it in September 2003. Construction began in June 2002. Altogether, North and South Korea between 1989 and May 2002 pursued more than 190 cases of civilian exchanges in education and academia. In total, they involved more than 2,100 specialists from the South and 400 from the North.[30] There was clearly a severe imbalance in the number of people meeting each other also in this field on a North versus South axis, which seems to contradict the suggestion that North Korea has dispatched a larger number of participants to joint events in the fields of science and technology than in most other areas.

Contacts in *film and literature* have been far more limited than academic exchanges, not least since the National Security Law has been enacted hindering free contacts with North Korean culture. Nonetheless, North Korean films have been shown at the Ministry of Unification's North Korea Resources Centre which, as of 2001, was the only place where it was possible to watch them freely, and on TV. In 1998, TV companies had even competed to show films from North Korea. Previously, a few carefully selected radio and TV broadcasts from North Korea such as *North-South Window* and *Observatory of Unification* had been aired in South

---

30 Cho, ibid., 1998, p. 25; Cho, ibid., 2000, pp. 37-9; Cho, ibid., 2002c, p. 103; Ham et al., ibid., p. 99; Ko, ibid., pp. 50, 51, 54; Minjok t'ongil yôn'guwôn, ibid., *1991~1992*, 1991, p. 114: ibid., *1998~1999*, 1998a, p. 82.

Korea providing opportunities for South Koreans to glimpse some of the official images of North Korean citizens, as shown by the North's state-run media.

The first film shown on TV was *An Chung-gûn Shoots Hirobumi Itoh* in September 1998. The first cinema movie was *Pulgasari* in July 2000. However, the films failed to gain popularity and, due to copyright and quality problems, viewings were not extended. Five North Korean films were shown in 16-18 June, 2000 at "The Fifth Hwanghae Arts Festival" held in Inch'ôn. Three films from each Korea were shown at "The 23rd Moscow International Film Festival" in June 2001 for the first time since the October 1990 North-South Film Festival in New York.

The KBS (the Korean Broadcasting Service) received, in 1997, the first permit from the South Korean government to make a documentary on life in the North as well as on Mt. Paektu. KBS did the planning whereas filming was made by Koreans residing in China in this three parties cooperative project which was completed in September 1997. In 1998, the Sports Art made the documentary *P'yôngyang Report* that was shown on SBS (Seoul Broadcasting Station). In 1999, the SBS made and showed the program *The Homecoming of Dr Cho Kyông-ch'ôl after 52 years*. But also documentaries on North Korea such as the joint *From Seoul to P'yôngyang* made after the June 2000 summit have been seen by very few people, in this case at most 8 per cent. It should also be noted that only three per cent of the South Korean TV audience watched the September 1999 "Unification Basketball Games" in the afternoon and only 4.7 per cent at noon.

In *literature*, South Korea's Culture and Arts Foundation was working in fall 2000 on publishing *The Grand Collection of Unified Literature*. It was to contain altogether 100 representative works, half from each Korea, published between 1945 and 1995 in the following genres: novels (70), poems (10), dramas (10) and literary reviews (10). In 1998-1999, Nuri Media had, through China, introduced a few historical works from the North and published them on CD-Rom. In 1999, the North Korean Export-Import Publishing Company began to sell publications from the North through the Internet.[31]

In *sports*, the first contact after the October 1990 Unification Soccer Games was, as we have seen, the formation of a unified Korean team with 56 members (28 each) for the 24 April-6 May, 1991 World Table Tennis Championships and another with 62 members (31 each) for the 14-30 June, 1991 World Junior Soccer Championships. Cooperation took place between the national table tennis associations and the respective Olympic committees. The Soccer Games resulted from joint support at the 1990 Beijing Asian Games and the contacts sports officials had built up. The Soccer Games and the 1991 joint participation was rather a result of government

---

31 Cho, ibid., 1999, pp. 35-6; Ch'oe, ibid., October 2000, pp. 41, 42, 43-4; Grinker, *Korea and its Futures*, p. 28; Han'guk munhwa yesul chinhûngwôn, "2000nyôn kukak kwallyôn haengsa-mith minsok yesulche" (http://www.kcaf.or.kr/yearbook/2001/kukak/umak-kukak22.htm), p. 3; Kang, ibid., p. 16; Kang et al., *Nambukhan chigôp kyoyuk hullyôn punya-ûi kyoryu-mith hyômnyôk pangan yôn'gu* (Seoul: T'ongil yônguwôn, 2000), p. 95; Kang et al., ibid., 2001, pp. 93-4; Lee, ibid., 2001, pp. 83-4; Lee et al., ibid., p. 73, 116.

contacts than purely civilian exchanges. 76 South Koreans went to the North when the first game was played whereas 78 North Koreans travelled to the South later in October. Re-broadcast tryout games were played in Seoul and P'yôngyang and in May 1991, before the World Junior Soccer Championships, in which the team participated under the name "Korea". It was decided the team would be represented by a flag showing the Korean Peninsula and which had the 1920s version of Arirang as the official song. As of October 1991, 46 South Korean athletes had had contacts with their North Korean counterparts.

However, North Korea became unwilling to cooperate after a judo athlete had defected in August 1991. The economic difficulties also contributed to make sports exchanges dull. Yet, from 24-25 October, 1993 the Director Emeritus of the South Korean Olympic Committee and five other officials participated in "The Seventh General Meeting of the East Asian Athletic Council" in P'yôngyang. From 27-28 June, 1994, three high-level sports officials from the South met eight colleagues from the North at "The Association of East Asian Athletic Meeting" held on Taiwan. Athletes had contacts in third countries. From 24 April-5 May, 1997, contacts took place between the Korean women's teams at "The World Table Tennis Championships" held in the United Kingdom. In 1998, contacts took place during "The Asian Table Tennis Championships" in September in Japan and "The Asian Games" in December in Thailand. There, supporters united and three representatives of South Korea's Koryô University met sports officials from North Korean universities to discuss sports exchanges as the first South Korean university to have done so. At the December 1999 "Unification Basketball Games" in Seoul, the P'yôngyang Circus Troupe performed in the interval along with the players. This suggests that sports, combined with other socio-cultural exchanges, is a fruitful contact to develop.[32]

According to the South Korean scholar Cho (2002), the most significant event in sports during 2002 was when a North Korean delegation of 312 athletes and 361 supporting party members attended the 14th Asian Games held in Pusan from 29 September-14 October. In his words, the North's participation "created a symbolic opportunity for reconciliation and cooperation between South and North Korea". In fact, such a large delegation had never been dispatched before or been allowed to stay for such a long period. He regards it as especially significant that watching the games provided repeated one on one contacts between North and South Koreans making them an important opportunity to dissolve the Cold War popular culture.

The symbolic significance of this event becomes clear also from the following writing by the South Korean scholar Lee Hong Yung (2003): "What attracted South Korean public attention was the North Korean cheerleading teams, composed of

---

32 Cho, ibid., 1999, pp. 37-9; Ham et al., ibid., pp. 99-100; Kang et al., ibid., 2000, p. 76; Kang et al., ibid., 2001, pp. 152-53, 156; Ko, ibid., pp. 50, 55; Lee et al., ibid., p. 114; Minjok t'ongil yôn'guwôn, ibid., *1991~1992*, 1991, pp. 111, 112, 114: ibid., *1994~1995*, 1994b, p. 115; T'ongilbu, ibid., p. 291. North Korea won the soccer game by 2-1 in P'yôngyang and South Korea by 1-0 in Seoul (Kang et al., ibid., 2001, p. 156). Cho (ibid., p. 38) does not exemplify the April-May 1997 and September 1998 contacts.

250 North Korean women, whose beauty and disciplined performances earned enthusiastic applause from the South Korean public and thereby raised hopes for reconciliation and eventual unification". In addition, the North Korean flag was hung up and its anthem played. Cheerleaders cheered together for Korean athletes. They even shouted "Unification of the Fatherland" jointly. Curious citizens visited the boat where the North Koreans lived.

In contrast to the positive evaluations of the impact of the Pusan Asian Games, the South Korean scholar Yi Chu-ch'ôl writes (2002) that whereas socio-cultural contacts have expanded radically after the June 2000 summit, these accomplished contacts had not reached a sufficient level to help create harmony between citizens of North and South Korea on multiple levels. It is to be noted that, according to the South Korean scholar Chông Un-jong (2003), the women supporter groups reportedly received "political education" through "brain washing" directly after having returned to North Korea for one month in order to eradicate the capitalist "virus". The central message was "that we have occupied and returned from Pusan that we could not occupy during the national liberation war".[33] These evaluations may all be regarded as correct: whereas Cho's and Lee's evaluations imply that North and South Koreans can get well along together at one short-time event, Yi's view indicates that socio-cultural contacts had not yet developed to a stage capable of transforming inter-Korean relations. Chông's view implies that the experiences from the Asian Games should be regarded with some degree of scepticism.

Regarding *religion*, the South Korean scholar Kim Pyông-no and his associates (2002) argue that religion may contribute far more to national harmony and to the restoration of homogeneity in the unification process than other contacts. Historically, Buddhism coexisted well together with traditional beliefs and became deeply rooted in Koreans' lives. Traditionally, Buddhism fulfilled a mission as defender of the country. In addition, the North Korean government has a more positive attitude towards such religions as the domestic *Ch'ôndogyo* (*Religion of the Heavenly Way*), than other ones. If such points of advantages are well utilized, religion is expected to significantly contribute to create harmony and to restore national homogeneity. On the other hand, they express the opinion that North Korea, as a closed society limiting religion, fears that religious contacts, by collating knowledge about the actual conditions in South Korea and the outside world, may contribute to an atmosphere of opening up in the North towards the outside world. Capitalist and democratic ideas from South Korea may even cause a disintegration of the socialist system.[34]

---

33 Chang, "Asian Geimsû Puk ch'amga, simnijôk naengjôn kujo haech'e ch'ôt pal", *T'ongil Han'guk* (2002), 11, p. 39; Cho, ibid., 2002c, p. 103; Chông,"Sisa nondan - Taegu U taehoe-ga namgin munjejôm: simgakhan Nambukhan munhwa ijilhwa hyônsang", *Pukhan* (October 2003), p. 58, Lee, "South Korea in 2002", 2003, p. 73; Yi, "'Haeppyôt' chôngch'aek 5nyôn-ûl p'yônggahanda: sahoe munhwa kyoryu, ije hyônsil alge twae", *T'ongil Han'guk* (2002), 12, p. 18.

34 Kim et al., *Nambukhan t'onghab-ûl wihan chonggyo kyoryu hyômnyôg-ûi chedohwa pangan* (Seoul: T'ongil yôn'guwôn, 2002), pp. 87, 89; Lee, *A New History*, 1984, p. 335.

Yet, also relatively active contacts in religion have taken place in third countries. But since North-South religious exchanges have been strongly related to humanitarian aid that began in 1995, they have also often gone through direct contacts in the North. Such contacts have brought economic benefits to the North and improved its international image: North Korea has preferred religious exchanges combined with economic benefits rather than purely religious ones. South Korean protestant organizations have played a very important role in pursuing religious exchanges and cooperation.

In the 1980s, contacts began between Christian churches due to help from Korean Christians abroad. In November 1981, two Korean Christian scholars residing abroad met with three North Koreans for the first time in Austria at "The Dialogue between North Korean and Foreign Christians Abroad for the Fatherland's Unification". North Korea's 1980 proposal for a confederation was discussed. Follow-up meetings were held in December 1982 in Finland and in December 1984.

In June 1986, the heads of the Korean National Council of Churches (KNCC) and the North Korean Christian Federation (NKCF) met for the first time at the "North-South Council on Peace and Unification" in Switzerland thanks to the mediation of the World Council of Churches (WCC). Five North Korean and six South Korean officials participated in this meeting that became the starting point for the southern churches' work for national unification.

The second meeting in November 1988 and the third in December 1990 were also held in Switzerland. In November 1988, North-South churches declared the 50th anniversary of liberation in 1995 as a holy year and decided to lead the way towards peaceful unification. Thanks to indirect contacts between Catholic Churches through the Vatican, in March 1984, Reverend Matheo visited North Korea. During the visit in 1988 by Fathers Chang Ik and Chông Ûi-ch'ôl, they dedicated the evening mass on 30 October on the occasion of the consecration of the Changch'ung Cathedral and a commemorative mass on All Saint's Day, 1 November. Another visit took place 17-22 February, 1989 when Reverends Pak Ch'ang-tûk, Nam Hae-gûn and Cho Yông-hûi, along with nine Korean Catholics living in the United States, went to the North and celebrated mass together with more than 100 North Korean Catholics. From 29 July-12 August, 1989 Reverend Yi Tae-gyông, a Korean resident in Japan, went to the North and was followed, 24 September-1 October, 1991, by Reverend Kwak Sôn-hûi and, from 7-13 January, 1992, by the KNCC Director Reverend Kwôn Ho-gyông. Peace on and unification of the Korean Peninsula were discussed on each occasion.[35]

The two Koreas participated in February 1991 in "The Seventh WCC General Meeting" in Australia. In March 1991, "The North-South Church Scholars' Symposium" was held in the United States. In April 1993, a North Korean Catholic delegation with four members met Korean priests residing in Japan.

---

35 Cho, ibid., 1999, pp. 27-8; Kang et al., ibid., 2001, p. 146; Kim et al., ibid., 2002, pp. 49, 58, 68-70, 75; Ko, ibid., p. 57; Lee, ibid., 1994, pp. 60, 61; Lee et al., ibid., p. 112. Kim et al. (ibid., p. 69) do not say where the December 1984 meeting was held.

It is to be noted that as a regular exchange North and South Korea participated in the "The Christians' Tokyo Conference on Peaceful Reunification of the Fatherland and Missionary Work" held first 10-13 July, 1990 and then 9-12 July, 1991, 20-22 October, 1992 and 31 May-2 June, 1994. Five North Korean priests participated on each occasion, but the number of South Koreans were far higher, varying between 35, 24, 36 and 63, in total, per year. The two Koreas then participated in the fifth conference held 5-7 June, 1996, the sixth held 8-10 October, 1998 in Osaka, the seventh in December 2000 in Fukuoka and the eighth 22-25 July, 2002 in Tokyo. At the fifth conference there were five participants from the North and 67 from South Korea, whereas the numbers for the sixth were four and 80, respectively. At these conferences, peaceful unification was for the first time discussed at an official North-South Church level. The participants agreed on the church's missionary task and that peace and unification are Christians' duties.

From 28-31 March, 1995, five North and 31 South Koreans participated in "The Fourth International Christian Conference for Peace on and Unification of the Korean Peninsula" held in Japan. From 26-29 June, 1995, Korean Christians met at "The Fourth General Meeting of the Council of American Korean Churches Peaceful Unification 70 Year" and 19-24 July at "The 50th Anniversary of Liberation Meeting", both of which were held in the US. In June, there were seven participants from the North and nine from South Korea whereas in July, nine hailed from the North and 35 from the South took part in total. From 9-11 October, 1995, North and South Korean Christians participated in "The General Meeting of Korean Christians in Japan" and then from 27 October-2 November in "The Foreign North-South Catholics' Seminar" in New York. In the latter seminar, five North and seven South Koreans, as well as five Koreans from the American church, took part.

The two Koreas participated in "The International Ecumenical Conference for Peace and Solidarity in Northeast Asia" held in 29 January-2 February, 1996 in Macao and "The North-South Religionists' Conference for the Unification of the Fatherland" held in Beijing in 26-29 February, the same year. On the latter occasion, there were eight participants from the North and 19 from South Korea.[36]

From 17-19 March, 1997, North and South Korea participated in "The North-South American Church Conference" held in New York with five and 25 representatives, respectively. In 30-31 May, "The North-South Religious Leaders' Conference" was held in Beijing on the North's initiative. Strengthening of cooperation and food aid were on the agenda. In Beijing, they also participated in "The North-South Catholics' Seminar", 4-7 June, at the second meeting of Catholics. From 16-18 March, 1998, both Koreas took part in "The North-South Churches' Conference on Unification and Sharing" held in Australia with 54 participants from the North and 17 from South Korea. Humanitarian aid to the North was on the agenda.

---

36 Cho, ibid., 2002c, p. 103; Kang et al., ibid., 2001, pp. 149-151; Kim et al., ibid., 2002, pp. 75-6, 81; Lee, ibid., 1994, p. 61; Minjok t'ongil yôn'guwôn, ibid., *1995~1996*, 1995, p. 95.

In March, they also took part in the third Catholic meeting held in Beijing. On this occasion, agreement was reached on deliveries of maize and fertilizers and to simultaneously hold a joint mass in the two Koreas as well as abroad for peace and unification during Easter. From 13-15 July, 1998 the fourth Catholic meeting was held and the fifth took place 14-18 September. A new agreement was then reached on maize deliveries to the North up until the year 2000 and the attendant monitoring procedures. The sixth, seventh and eighth meetings were held in China 5-7 April, 1999, 2-3 May, 1999 and 27-29 March, 2000.

From 28-30 May, 1995, the first visit to the North by a Catholic priest since January 1992 took place. Kim Sang-jin and three priests were invited to discuss the establishment of a hospital with 200 sickbeds in the Najin-Sônbong area. During his second visit, 25-29 November, 1997 (together with three priests), the medical services' mission was discussed and he attended the groundbreaking ceremony of the hospital. Previously, from 22-28 August, 1995, Reverend Kwak Sôn-hûi had visited North Korea for the second time (after 1991) to discuss missionary work and cooperation.[37]

A few contacts took place in 1997. When KNCC Director Kim Tong-wan visited North Korea September 23-30th, exchanges and cooperation were discussed. From 25-26 September, the chairman of the General Federation of Korean Churches (GFKC) Chi Tôk met with representatives of North Korea in Beijing to discuss the restoration of the North's Mt. Kûmgang Church. Other contacts were established at "The North-South-American Churches Conference" held in New York 17-19 June and "The World Reformist Churches' Federation General Meeting" held in Hungary 8-20 August.

Religious contacts have expanded since 1998, through the KNCC and the GFKC who have had contacts with their North Korean counterparts. In 1998, the number of visits by Protestant Churches to the North for purely religious exchanges rose. Bishop Ch'oe Ch'ang-mu and six priests from the National Committee of Reconciliation were from 15-22 May invited by the North Korean Catholics' Association. During the visit, he became the first South Korean Bishop to ever celebrate mass in the Changch'ung Cathedral in P'yôngyang, in which North Korean Catholics took part, also discussing cooperation. From 26 May-2 June, KNCC Director Kim Tong-wan visited the North for a second time to discuss the establishment of a church in the Najin-Sônbong region.

During the visit by a six-member delegation to North Korea 18-25 May, 1999 that included ministers Kim Myung-gi and Eun Hi-kon from the Korean Methodist Church Association to meet representatives of the NKCF, the establishment of a

---

37 Cho, ibid., 1999, pp. 28-9; Kang et al., ibid., 2001, pp. 146, 150-151; Kim, "Pukhan chumin-ûi chonggyo saenghwal: Nambukhan chonggyo chôngch'aek-gwa kidokkyo-rûl chungsim-ûro", in Minjok hwahae hyômnyôk pômkungmin hyôbûihoe, *Pukhan chumin-ûi ilsang saenghwal-gwa taejung munhwa* (Seoul: Orûm, 2003), p. 212; Kim et al., ibid., 2002, p. 81; Lee et al., ibid., p. 115; Minjok t'ongil yôn'guwôn, ibid., *1997~1998*, 1997, p. 75. Kim et al. do not record the place of meetings between Catholics after March 1998.

third church and support to build the P'yôngyang Seminary were discussed. In October 1999, a noodle factory project which had received support was visited. The whereabouts of South Korean Christian families in North Korea and support for building of the P'yôngyang Seminary were discussed.

In October 1999, Reverend Chu Pong-t'aek from the Methodist-affiliated Korean Missionary Association for National Unification and his delegation visited the North to discuss family reunions and support to establishing a hospital in P'yôngyang. A few joint events took place in 2001. In January, the Korean Methodist Church received government permission for a cooperation project to provide support for management costs of the P'yôngyang Seminary which it also did. On 28 March, 2001 the South Korean Council of Religionists for Peace and the North Korean Council of Religionists announced a joint statement opposing the distortion of Japanese history. The KNCC and the NKCF jointly participated in the German Churches' Day held in Frankfurt from 11-17 June and held a mass to commemorate the first anniversary of the inter-Korean summit (they had previously participated 17-22 June, 1997). From 27 November-4 December, 2001, Catholic churches held a joint Holy Communion and a seminar on An Chung-gûn in P'yôngyang.

Finally, it is worth noting that, as of January 1995, it was confirmed that there were more than 25,000 religious books published in South Korea at the Kim Il Sung University Library.[38] But it is unclear whether these books were widely available and thereby could have any impact on inter-Korean relations.

Exchanges between Buddhists have also been relatively active. In July 1988, the monk Taewôn, who lived in the United States, visited North Korea and laid foundations for North-South exchanges. In November 1988, "The Committee for Exchanges between Buddhists in North and South Korea" was formed. In June and October 1989, the monks Sin Pôpt'a and Taewôn visited North Korea to find out the actual conditions of Buddhism as well as to discuss contacts. In April 1991, Sin Pôpt'a and the monk Toan from the US visited the North and had a formal meeting with the North Korean Federation of Buddhists (NKFB) to discuss exchanges. In July 1991, officials from the Korean Buddhists Youth Association and the NKFB met at the celebrations of the 250th anniversary of the introduction of Buddhism to the Soviet Union.

The next contact took place 28 October-4 November, 1991 when, during "The North-South Buddhists' Joint Meeting" held in Los Angeles, "The Joint Buddhist Mass Praying for Unification of the Fatherland" took place. In this first joint Buddhist event ever held, four Northern and 22 South Koreans who had been invited took part (as well as Korean residents living abroad).

From 23 April-1 May, 1995, a delegation of Korean Buddhists in the United States from the Buddhist Association for a Peaceful Unification of the Fatherland (BAPUF) met in the North with representatives of the North Korean Association

---

38 Cho, ibid., 1996, pp. 49-50: fn. 19; Cho, ibid., 1999, pp. 28, 29; Kang et al., ibid., 2001, pp. 146, 147; Kim, ibid., 2003, p. 212; Kim et al., ibid., 2002, p. 49; KINU, ibid., 2000a, p. 136; Ko, ibid., p. 58; Minjok t'ongil yôn'guwôn, ibid., *1998~1999*, 1998a, pp. 82-3.

of Buddhists to discuss exchanges. The meeting failed: the North Koreans wanted the South's Buddhists to take part in its struggle for unification. In May 1995, Song Wôl-chu, director of the Chogye sect in South Korea, met the head of the NKFB Pak T'ae-ho in Beijing and agreed to hold "The Joint Mass Praying for Unification" in P'yôngyang.[39]

In August 1995, the monk Toan went to North Korea as a member of the American section of the BAPUF to celebrate Liberation Day, 15 August. In February 1996, at "The North-South's Religionists' Conference" held in Beijing, the missionary chief of the Chogye sect, monk Sôngt'a, also participated. In April 1996, the vice-Director of the Chogye sect, monk Sin Pômt'a, was invited to participate by the NKFB. The state of Buddhism in the two Koreas and the plan to support flood victims in the North were discussed. In April 1997, working-level talks on food aid to North Korea were held between North and South Korean Buddhists; the Chogye sect delivered maize to the North. An agreement on North-South Buddhist exchanges were reached in June.

In March 1998, cooperation between Buddhists was discussed in Beijing. The meeting agreed on a common prayer for Buddha's birthday and to restore Buddhist temples in the North. In April 1999, the BAPUF and the NKFB held a meeting on exchanges in Beijing. From 25 May-1 June, 1999 two officials of the Korean Buddhist Fraternities Association were invited by the NKFB in the first official visit by representatives of the association.

In June 1999, the American section of the BAPUF held a welcome dinner for the North Korean women's team in the World Soccer Women Championships. In October 1999, representatives of the Chingak sect were invited to the North. They visited Buddhist temples and welfare facilities and held a joint prayer for peaceful unification. They reportedly also got positive responses for the proposals to found an international federation for the Buddhist clergy and to jointly translate the Complete Collection of Buddhist Sutras from the Koryô dynasty. In November, a meeting between the BAPUF and the NKFB was held in Beijing. Finally, in May 2002, famous North Korean painters' Buddhist paintings, one of them depicting the founder of the Chingak sect, were displayed in Seoul at "The North-South Arts Peace Exhibition".[40]

Exchanges and cooperation in *Ch'ôndogyo* have been more limited than in other religions. The first contact took place in 1988 when sacred books were sent to the North. The first meeting took place at "The Fourth Asian Religionists' Peace Conference" held 28 October-2 November, 1991 in Nepal. Two North and 11 South Koreans took part. When a meeting between Ch'ôndogyo directors to discuss exchanges was held in Beijing in October 1993, a joint agreement on exchanges was announced. In August 1998, nine representatives of Ch'ôndogyo visited North

---

39 Ch'oe, ibid., October 2000, pp. 45-6; Kang et al., ibid., 2001, p. 149; Kim et al., ibid., 2002, pp. 64-5; Ko, ibid., p. 57; Lee, ibid., 1994, p. 60; Lee et al., ibid., p. 113.

40 Cho, ibid., 1999, pp. 29-30; Kim et al., ibid., 2002, pp. 65-6; KINU, ibid., 2000a, p. 136.

Korea to discuss participation in the 15 August Grand Unification Festival, which attracted criticism. From 24-26 August, 1999, the "North-South Ch'ôndogyo Leaders' Meeting" was held in Beijing. It was decided that a standing consultation organization would be set up to discuss joint investigations of the battlefields during the 1894 Tonghak Rebellion and other joint projects.

Representatives of Ch'ôndogyo held working-level talks in 1-2 May, 2000 in Beijing on the unification issue. They agreed to strengthen wills to create an atmosphere of harmony and peace for an independent and democratic unification. Another meeting took place in North Korea 9-13 October to discuss exchanges. Representatives met 20-22 June, 2001 in P'yôngyang to discuss such exchanges as joint investigations of places related to the Tonghak Rebellion and joint activities on the National Foundation Day. Contacts took place during the August Grand National Festival in P'yôngyang. In September 2001, a high-level delegation visited North Korea. They met high-level officials to discuss the pursuit of exchanges and joint events. Finally, meetings took place through *Taejonggyo* in Beijing in April 1994 and then illegally in North Korea in April 1995, through their main officials An Ho-sang and Kim Sôn-jôk who visited Tan'gun's grave. The only concrete result was the agreement reached in 1994 to hold a joint event on National Foundation Day.

Altogether, between June 1989 and December 2001, 1,079 Koreans met each other in a religious context, among which 232 people met in North Korea; no religious visits took place in the South. 223 of a total of 502 South Korean visitors went to the North from 1998 onwards, indicating a shift of meeting locations.[41] It is indisputable that there have been many contacts in religion, but unlike exchanges in academia and education, they are normally one-off contacts between senior officials. Humanitarian aid may thus be regarded as the most important subject matter stemming from these contacts.

Women of North and South Korea have met at conferences frequently and declarations on a few occasions have been adopted. Following the above 7 July, 1988 Declaration, South Korean women proposed to meet their North Korean sisters. A preparatory meeting was held in 1991 between the North's Korean Democratic Women's Federation and the South's Korean Women's Association and the Korean Women Team Union, aimed at holding a joint contest on local food and a joint exhibition of crafts. But the plans failed since the North raised the issue of releasing imprisoned political activists in the South. Thanks to the mediation of Japanese women organizations they could, however, meet for the first time at the first conference in the series "Peace in Asia and the Role of Women" in Japan 28 May-4 June, 1991 at a time of, as we have seen, improving relations.

---

41 Cho, ibid., 1999, p. 30; Kang et al., ibid., 2001, p. 149; Kim et al., ibid., 2002, pp. 5-6, 58-9, 85-6, 91; KINU, ibid., 2000a, p. 136; Lee, ibid., 1994, p. 60; Lee et al., ibid., p. 116; T'ongilbu, ibid., p. 290. Taejonggyo is a religion seeking to revive ancient belief in Tan'gun as the divine progenitor of the Korean race. From Lee, ibid., 1984, p. 335. For a survey of the Tonghak Rebellion see Lee, ibid., 1984, pp. 283-88.

At this conference, there were three participants from each Korea among more than 100 people altogether. The suggestion for this and the following conference came from the South Korean Women Association's director, Yi Hyo-jae, to the Supreme People's Assembly vice-speaker, Yô Yôn-gu, who in turn proposed the third conference. At the Tokyo meeting a declaration was adopted that urged compensation for comfort women, denuclearization of the Korean Peninsula and normalization of relations between Japan and North Korea.[42]

That the second and third conferences in the series were organized and held in Seoul, 25-30 November, 1991, and in P'yôngyang, 1-6 September, 1992, was a positive sign by deviating from the pattern of holding conferences abroad. At the Seoul conference the 15-member North Korean delegation became the first women to visit South Korea. However, referring to personal threats and being refused the right to visit Ihwa Womens' University and interview the families of illegal visitors to North Korea, Mun Ik-hwan and Im Su-kyông, they returned the day before the meeting was scheduled to end and, as a result, no declaration was adopted. When the third conference was held in P'yôngyang in 1992, about 250 people from the two Koreas and Japan, among them nine representatives of women's organizations, of altogether 30 participants from South Korea, took part. They became the first South Korean women to visit North Korea. Conference topics were "Grand National Solidarity and the Role of Women" and "the Japanese Imperialist Invasion of Korea and the Post-War Compensation Issue". Significantly, participants agreed to organize solidarity activities on the comfort women issue.

At the fourth conference held in Tokyo-Osaka 24-29 April, 1993 that had been proposed by 10 South Korean parliamentarians, there were 13 North Korean, 11 South Korean and nine Japanese women among the over 1,000 participants. Comfort women were the main issue on the agenda. North Korea wanted an apology and compensation from Japan but South Korea called for a joint investigation. When inter-Korean relations worsened in 1994, conferences ceased to be held.[43]

But contacts through participation in the conferences did not end. From 21-23 October, 1993 the two Koreas participated at South Korea's initiative in "The Second Asia Solidarity Conference on Comfort Women" held in Tokyo. Following a

---

42 Kim and Chang, *Yôsông pichôngbu kigu-rûl t'onghan Nambukhan kyoryu hyômnyôk hwalsônghwa pangan yôn'gu* (Seoul: T'ongil yôn'guwôn, 2000), pp. 54-6, 215; Kim et al., *Nambuk yônhap tangye-esô-ûi yôsông chôngch'aek ch'ujin pangan* (Seoul: T'ongil yôn'guwôn, 2001), pp. 24-5, 30, 48-9. Kim et al. do not say when and where in 1991 North and South Korea held the failed meeting (ibid., p. 24). Author's quotation marks.

43 Kang et al., ibid., 2000, p. 93: table III-16; Kim and Chang, ibid., pp. 54-6; Kim et al., ibid., 2001, pp. 25-6, 48-9; Ko, ibid., p. 54. In 1992, the North Korean Ambassador to Geneva had proposed cooperation on the comfort women issue to his South Korean colleague. The two Koreas took a joint position on the issue at the 2-27 August, 1993 United Nations Commission on Human Rights (UNCHR) session. North Korea emphasized that the Japanese government must conduct a full investigation of the issue and provide appropriate compensation to the victims. South Korea agreed on the proposal to appoint a specialist to investigate the issue. From Paek, ibid., pp. 52, 53-4.

suggestion by the joint representatives of the South Korean Association of Comfort Women, from 6-9 November, 1993, the two Koreas participated in "The Conference on Japan's Management of its Post-War Days" in P'yôngyang with 11 and two women, respectively. The conference that focused on the issue of compensating comfort women drew participants also from Japan, the Philippines and the Netherlands. It is remarkable that this meeting and "The Second Expert Meeting on Resources, Industry and Environment" 8-11 November were held in P'yôngyang at a time of sharp tensions due to the nuclear issue (cf. p. 111). In August 1995, both Koreas participated at "The Fourth World Women's Conference" held in China, in which 14 South Korean women took part, and at South Korea's proposal in "The Third Asian Solidarity Conference on Comfort Women" held 3-5 July in Japan. In 17-23 June, 1997, the two Koreas participated in "The International Women's Peace Symposium".

In 1998, North and South Korean women participated in the international symposium "Women and Sexual Violence" at the South's proposal. From 30 July-1 August, the two Koreas took part in "The Symposium on Forced Arrests by the Japanese in War-time" in Tokyo, South Korea with six women representatives. From 9-11 October, eight women from North Korea, six from South Korea and seven from Japan participated in "The Fifth Asian Solidarity Conference On Comfort Women" in Beijing. A joint appeal to send to the Japanese government and a request to deliver to the UNCHR were adopted. From 11-18 September, 1999 "The Womens' Exchanges in Relation to Assistance to North Korea" was held in the North, thanks to the initiative of the Korean Sharing Movement. Four women from the movement interviewed three women from the North Korean Womens' Association involved in humanitarian aid.

In 19-20 December, 2000 "The International Scientific Conference on Korean Womens' Life in North Korea, South Korea and China" was held in China. "The North-South Women's Unification Meeting" was held 15-17 October, 2002 at Mt. Kûmgang with altogether more than 770 participants from North and South Korea and from abroad. It became an occasion to share warm affection among sisters and to confirm homogeneity as well as the differences caused by division. As a large-scale meeting with women from different occupations, regions and ages, thus differentiating it from the series "Peace in Asia and the Role of Women" and conferences on comfort women, it was highly significant. A wide variety of North Korean women were also represented. Discussions, games and dances at once united North and South Korean women and they became aware of the Korean issue's meaning on a personal level. Prayers for peace were held, arts and handicrafts were exhibited and joint arts performances were held.[44]

---

44 Chôn, "Nambuk yôsông t'ongil taehoe-rûl mach'imyô...: Nambuk yôsông hamkke ch'un p'yônghwa-wa taedong ch'um", *T'ongil Han'guk* (2002), 11, pp. 42-3; Kang et al., ibid., 2000, p. 93: table III-16; Kim and Chang, ibid., pp. 54, 56-7, 215; Kim et al., ibid., 2001, pp. 27, 28-30, 47; Kim, ibid., April 2001, p. 63; Minjok t'ongil yôn'guwôn, ibid., *1995~1996*, 1995, p. 94; Mun, "NGO Ch'onghoe-e tanyô-wa-sô – segye-nûn hanada" (http://www.wfwp.

The account shows that socio-cultural exchanges have been relatively active, even during periods when relations have been tense. In this way, they have contributed to securing peace on the Korean Peninsula, but their relative influence is virtually impossible to objectively determine. However, in the author's opinion, a more remarkable achievement is that five joint publications were issued in 1998, 1999, 2000 and 2002: it implies that North and South Korea can cooperate not only in science but even publish a conference report on the unification issue. Such an experience could contribute to a "can-do" spirit that ideally could be extended into other fields if mutual will is reciprocated.

But since the contacts, so far, have been limited, irregular and involved extremely few people in comparison to the cases of pre-unity Germany and Yemen, it is hard to believe that they have significantly contributed to restoring national homogeneity. This would require far more extensive contacts, which would be difficult given the high level of mutual distrust and the closed nature of North Korean society. The fixation on this target seems inappropriate: recognizing and adjusting to differences is as important a policy factor since partition has changed Korea, even if common cultural characteristics remain.

It might be assumed that socio-cultural contacts have contributed to reaching the targets of the 1988 7 July Declaration, to create mutual confidence, mitigate tensions, improve inter-Korean relations and a peace settlement. But there is still a long way to go towards fulfilling these targets. To establish mutual confidence seems to be the most difficult task considering the continuous ups and downs in relations that are largely a consequence of long term mutual distrust. Expanded contacts on a multi-level basis could well contribute to reaching this goal.

4.5 Characteristics of inter-Korean socio-cultural exchanges and cooperation

In spite of the perceived positive effects of socio-cultural contacts on inter-Korean relations, scholars' evaluations of them differ. The South Korean scholar Pak Sang-bong (2000) writes that they are one-sided, commercialized and offensive.

First, whereas during the visits to Seoul in May, June and August 2000, where North Korean culture was presented to the South Korean public, there were no cases of South Korean culture presented in North Korea. In fact, all 11 accomplished cases of exchanges during the first half of 2000 consisted of North Korean culture presented in South Korea. However, it must be noted here, as we saw in Chapter 3, that in 1998-1999 South Korean culture actually was presented on a few occasions, in North Korea.

---

or.kr/kukjea/ngo8.htm), p. 1; P'yônghwa-rûl mandûnûn yôsônghoe, "Kôrô on kil" (http://www.peacewomen.or.kr/new_wmp/makepeace/ walking_peace.htm), p. 1. Kim et al. do not record the dates for the fourth women's conference in 1995, the place for the women's peace forum in 1997 and date and place for the symposium on sexual violence against women in 1998 (ibid., pp. 28-9).

In addition, political distortions of North Korean culture flowed in partly as a result of KBS staging the concerts of the visiting North Korean symphony orchestra in August 2000 from a private company. Therefore, KBS had to one-sidedly stage them. The [non-exemplified] representative distortions took place during the displays of North Korean art works at the "Grand Arts Exhibition for World Peace" held in Seoul 10-21 February, 2000, the visits of the two art troupes later in May-June and the showing of the film drama *Hong Kildong* on TV.[45]

In broadcasting, the drama *Im Kkôk-chông,* which is based on Kim Il Sung's teaching "where ever there is oppression, resistance is inevitable" and indicts feudal corruption, was shown on KBS in September-October 1998. Two years later, there had been 16 cases of exchanges in this field but all presented North Korean films and songs to South Koreans. The only exception is that the delegation of South Korean media representatives to North Korea in August 2000 reportedly donated four South Korean films to Kim Jong Il but they were given to him personally (cf. p. 77).[46] This tends to present the cultural exchange context in another light entirely.

North Korea has, in addition, consistently demanded payments for cultural exchanges. For instance, the KBS, which had invited the North Korean National Symphony Orchestra to hold concerts in Seoul, had reportedly "decided to, without an official guarantee, deliver 20,000 TV sets to North Korea" but hardly anyone believed this. The orchestra demanded $ 2m for two performances. This is four times more than the performance fee for two performances of the world top-class Berlin Philharmonic Orchestra. Many South Koreans found such a monopoly price exorbitant and worried that under the pretext of cultural exchange substantial amounts of cash would be paid to the North Korean government and thus solidify the dictatorship. However, South Korean daily newspapers' reviews were very favourable and the audience applauded the performances. When the July 2000 Mt. Kûmgang auto-rally took place, a South Korean sports promoter gave North Korea $ 1m to stage the auto-race (cf. p. 76).

Demanding payments applied, as of 1998-1999, also to visits of company and media representatives with sums involved reportedly ranging from some $ 10,000 to above $ 1m. Failing to pay was reportedly the main reason for agreed meetings not taking place. South Korea had to pay $ 600,000 for holding the joint 2000 "Peace and Friendship Concert" in addition to donations of 30,000 Korean-made Nix jeans as well as 5,000 sets of bearable cassette radios and headphones for North Korean youths.

---

45 See *The story of Hong Gil dong* (Seoul: The Korean Classical Literature Institute, 2000). The different spelling is due to South Korea using the Ministry of Education transliteration system.

46 Cho, ibid., 1999, p. 33; Chông, "Pukhan-ûi yesul hyônhwang", in Minjok t'ongil yôn'guwôn, *1997 nyôndo ch'och'ông seminar kyôlgwa pogosô* (Seoul: Minjok t'ongil yôn'guwôn, 1998a), p. 35; Pak, "Nambuk munhwa kyoryu", October 2000, pp. 50-53: Segye p'yônghwa t'ongil kajông yônhap, "Nam-gwa puk, kûrim-ûro mannatchi" (http://www.tongil.or.kr/main2/boardnews/boardcontent.html?&no=794&code=WEB), pp. 1, 2. Original quotation marks.

North Korea tends to use socio-cultural exchanges to make propaganda for its own political system while looking down upon that of South Korea. For instance, the North Korean linguist Ryu Yôl stated without hesitation when family reunions took place in August 2000: "We have put efforts on preserving our national language but why are foreign loanwords overflowing in South Korea?". He added that "our language gets damaged" (cf. p. 73). Such statements challenge common sense while emphasizing cultural superiority and rejecting cultural diversity but, as we have seen, South Korean participants had displayed similar attitudes in August 1993, at "The Scientific Conference on Language and Philosophy Towards Unification".

In addition, it became known that the violin concert "Sahyangga" ("Thoughts of Home") held in August 2000, had been arranged for orchestra on the basis of "The Eternal Revolutionary Songs of Kim Il Sung". Reportedly, Kim Il Sung had written this song to educate the revolutionary fighters and the masses during the anti-Japanese struggle.[47] This concert was performed four times from 20 August to 22 August. But the South Korean Music Professor Hwang Byung-ki writes that the symphony orchestras at the last joint performance played the North Korean version of "Arirang" and then the South Korean nursery rhyme "Spring of My Hometown" as an encore while the performers were joined in song by the audience. After the performance had ended, the orchestras and the audience jointly sang an unaccompanied version of the song "Our Wish" ("Uri-ûi sowôn-ûn t'ongil") expressing the will for unification.

However, Pak points out that the politicization of this visit became clear also from the fact that when a member of the orchestra saw that a large-size poster of President Kim Dae Jung and Chairman Kim Jong Il had got wet from rain he protested by saying "I can by no means see our Great Leader General Kim Jong Il be so exposed to rain", after which the poster was removed. Because of the enumerated characteristics of socio-cultural exchanges, they do not have any particular impact on inter-Korean relations at large and may exert a negative influence on preparing for unification.[48] In the author's opinion, Pak's view is too pessimistic since, as we have seen, a new tendency in recent years has been that socio-cultural exchanges have taken place while overall inter-Korean relations have remained tense.

Another act of politicization took place during the above Taegu Universiade in August 2003: the North Korean supporting group removed the welcoming placards carved in with the photo of Kim Jong Il and even cried! The placards were placed too low and failed to protect the leader from being exposed to rain. As a cheering group the women attracted sympathy from many South Koreans. However, these university

---

47 "Sahyangga" refers to Catholic texts written in 4.4 tunes in Han'gûl created by Father Ch'oe Yang-ôp (Thomas) in 1850. The texts were written to defend and diffuse Catholicism at a time when it was suppressed. "Sahyangga" also advocated opening Korea for foreign culture. No reference is made here to Kim Il Sung. From Kim, "Sahyangga", Han'guk chôngsin munhwa yôn'guwôn, *Han'guk minjok taepaekkwa sajôn* (Sôngnam: Han'guk chôngsin munhwa yôn'guwôn, 1991), pp. 81-2.

48 Cho, ibid., 1999, p. 64: fn. 45; Cho et al., ibid., 2000, p. 40: fn. 27; Harrison, *Korean Endgame*, 2002, p. 92; Hwang, ibid., p. 144; Kim, *Tasi saeroun*, 1998, p. 337; Pak, ibid., October 2000, pp. 51-4, 58. Original quotation marks.

students were chosen for their beauty to attract South Korean men and make them forget about the North's nuclear program and famine. The women also belonged to a politically reliable and privileged group trained for making propaganda.[49] Whether true or not, contradictory developments are, as we have seen, an established pattern in inter-Korean relations.

The South Korean journalist Kim Sang-hwan points out (2001) four problems in socio-cultural exchanges that need to be addressed. Firstly, like Pak, Kim points out that South Korea pays excessive performance fees to North Korea and that transparency is not guaranteed. The above SN21 Enterprise paid $ 3m to invite the P'yôngyang Circus Troupe in May 2000 and delivered 20,000 20-inch colour TV sets.

Samsung Electronics donated, as coorganizer of the July 2000 Unification Table-Tennis Games, 10,000 21-inch colour TV sets (cf. p. 70). Reportedly, KBS delivered 20,000 14-inch colour TV sets on the occasion of broadcasting by satellite directly from Mt. Paekdu at *Ch'usôk* (*Thanksgiving Day*) in September 2000 and SBS delivered another 20,000 14-inch colour TV sets when it broadcast the 55th anniversary of the foundation of the Korean Workers' Party the same year. Finally, SBS and KORECOM who jointly sponsored the "2000 Peace and Friendship Concert" reportedly paid $ 1m for the performance. Since large sums of money have allegedly been paid also for other events, such as more than $ 500,000 for each visit by some media companies, a few parliamentarians from both the government and the opposition have criticized the tendency. A few of them asserted that reasonable prices must be paid if transparency is to be guaranteed.

Secondly, there is excessive competition between South Korean organizations and many events are, as we have seen, "one-offs". Specialists on North Korea explain this by the fact that the communist North demands payments for every single event and thereby avoids such contacts from which they do not earn money from. This behaviour is explained by the excessive competition among South Korean organizations which encourages the North to demand unreasonable performance fees and considerable amounts of money. But it should be remembered that there exists a failure on the part of the South Korean government to prevent excessive competition and thereby they must share responsibility for the high payments demanded.[50]

Thirdly, arts and cultural exchanges have been used for political propaganda purposes, although the two Koreas have agreed to reject politics as part of such contacts. Not only Kim Sang-hwan but also the South Korean scholar Yi Chong-sôk (1998) writes that North Korea has violated such promises and has used academic conferences to make propaganda for its unification policies; Kim adds arts performances to this list of broken promises. However, they record no examples of South Korea having violated the promise to avoid politicization.

According to Yi, at "The Joint Conference for Peace and Harmony on the Korean Peninsula" held in Beijing, 30 June-1 July, 1997, the North Korean participants tried

---

49 Chông, ibid., October 2003, pp. 57-8.
50 Kim, ibid., April 2001, pp. 67-8.

to make their way into a "meeting between North and South Korean civilians" to propagate for its unification policies. Kim Jong Il's sayings were cited as much, if not more, than those of Kim Il Sung at the conference. The 4 July Joint Communiqué was upheld, and it was implicitly critical of South Korean policy.

On the other hand, the South Korean scholar Paek Yông-ch'ôl (1998) presents some unexpected data with regard to the unification conferences held in 1995-1997, with the purpose of confronting national heterogeneity. The themes were "Reconciliation and Cooperation Expressed in the 4 July Joint Communiqué" followed in 1996 by "Sectoral Propulsion of the Basic Agreement" and in 1997 by "Concrete Grouping for Peace and Cooperation between North and South Korea". North Korea demanded the withdrawal of American troops from South Korea and the abolishment of the National Security Law and asserted that it was impossible to pursue a dialogue with the present South Korean government. But Paek also writes that North Korean participants showed lack of confidence and recognized that the South Korean system was superior to their own. Unofficially, they joked several times "Will you take good care of us when unification comes?" and used to speculate that South Korea would at some stage absorb North Korea.[51] While surprising, these statements' impact on inter-Korean relations remains unclear.

Kim Sang-hwan records (2001) that at "The Fifth Unification Conference for Korean Scholars" held in Beijing in October 1999, a North Korean Professor asserted that "to accomplish national unity South Korea must first abolish the National Security Law that hinders reconciliation". A month later, the Korean Central News Agency (KCNA) reported that scholars had agreed that Korean unification must be achieved through the implementation of the three great principles of peaceful unification, transcending ideological differences and removing foreign intervention. KCNA also claimed that the conference was held to discuss the North's proposal for unification based on a confederation. Furthermore, at the October 2000 National Unification Concert the invited singers "Koreana" were not allowed to perform since their song "Hold my Hand" had been the main song of the 1988 Seoul Olympics. Instead, North Korean singers had to sing songs praising Kim Jong Il and the communist system.

Finally, while personal exchanges are increasing, legislation to protect visitors is insufficient. Due to the over 50-year old partition laws, customs and culture have developed differently. This raises the possibility that unexpected things will happen, as in June 1999, when, as we have seen, a South Korean housewife was briefly detained. More effective protection for visitors, insisted upon by the South Korean government, is therefore required.[52]

---

51 Kim, ibid., April 2001, p. 68; Paek, "Hyanghu t'ongil chôngch'aek panghyang IV", in Minjok t'ongil yôn'guwôn, ibid., 1998b, pp. 154-56; Yi, "Pukkyông Nambuk haksulhoeûi kaeyo mith ch'amga sogam", in ibid., 1998b, pp. 87-9. Original quotation marks. On p. 113, the theme "The Prospects for and Tasks of National Unification" from Cho (ibid., 1996, p. 46: fn. 1) is recorded but what explains the differences is unclear.

52 Kim, ibid., April 2001, pp. 68-9.

As we have seen, the South Korean scholars Cho Han Bum and Ko Yong-gwôn argue that socio-cultural exchanges and cooperation exert a positive influence on inter-Korean relations. However, in reality such contacts have not been a focus point for reconciliation and cooperation, on the contrary, they have very often been abused as a propaganda tool by the two competing political systems. In particular, North Korea has used such exchanges as a tool for its unification policies. In South Korea, anti-communism has hampered socio-cultural exchanges and cooperation.

Cho (2002) enumerates five characteristics of inter-Korean socio-cultural exchanges and cooperation. First, those contacts have often been accomplished by the government, even in the case of civilian exchanges. This has made it difficult to pursue those contacts that could have had a positive and lasting impact on the rigid political systems. Consequently, there have hardly been any exchanges and cooperation in politically sensitive fields. On the other hand, non-political academic exchanges and humanitarian aid have been relatively frequent. The government's role in pursuing socio-cultural exchanges and cooperation has remained an important feature, also after the June 2000 summit.[53]

Secondly, socio-cultural exchanges and cooperation have normally been irregular and dependent on the Cold War atmosphere. In 1990, a second round of family reunions (after 1985), did not take place since North Korea wanted to perform the revolutionary opera "The Virgin Selling Flowers". In 1992, "The Old Parents' Delegation Hometown Visit" failed to take place due to the sensitive issues of returning long-term prisoner Yi In-mo to North Korea and holding "The Focus-Lens Exercise".

Following these visits to North Korea by South Korean musicians and the subsequent return visits in 1990, exchanges stagnated during the mid-1990s. This was due to the worsening of relations caused by Kim Il Sung's death in 1994 and the South Korean government's refusal to express its condolences. Consequently, "The Unified Korea Arts Exhibition and Festival" and "The Unified Korea Arts Exhibition" that were scheduled to be held in Japan and Seoul, respectively, were cancelled by the North. That this fixed pattern remains, in spite of the Kim Dae Jung administration's active pursuit of the sunshine policy, is shown by the fact that, as of 2002, no firm basis to pursue socio-cultural exchanges and cooperation had yet been established.[54] The five basic principles referred to in section 4.2 aimed at generating cultural exchanges have hardly been implemented.

Thirdly, as we have seen, many contacts have been one-off events taking place in third countries. In fact, most accomplished contacts have become possible rather thanks to the mediation of institutions in China, Russia, Japan and the United States or of Koreans residing abroad rather than due to the policies of the two Korean governments.

---

53 Cho, ibid., 2002a, p. 8; Lee ibid., 2001, pp. 45, 47. Cho does not elaborate on what "positive impact" and "politically sensitive fields" refer to. He mistakenly writes "negative" in the text.

54 Cho, ibid., 2002a, pp. 8, 12; Foley, *Korea's Divided Families*, p. 80; Ko, ibid., p. 47.

China has been the most important actor in this respect. Many Korean residents in China live in the neighbouring Yônbyôn region which has made it, together with Beijing, the centre for such exchanges. Besides the obvious advantages in terms of geography, the friendship between China and North Korea, as well as the institutions and organizations in Yônbyôn working with Korean Studies, have made it an important meeting place. North Korea's economic difficulties during the 1990s have also contributed to the holding of conferences abroad. In addition, since academic exchanges bring few possibilities for economic assistance, scholarly visits have rarely taken place on the Korean Peninsula.

The formation of ties with foreign institutes and scholars and the ability of those institutes to keep a neutral position have been an advantage in holding conferences in third countries. On the other hand, as North and South Korea have not been the main actors involved in arranging scientific events there have been difficulties in efficiently preparing them. There have also been inefficiencies economically due to holding conferences abroad, which seemingly contradicts North Korea's official policy. The reasonable explanation is that North Korea does not want foreigners to get first-hand experiences of its society although, as previously outlined, humanitarian assistance has contributed to opening it up. A disadvantage with holding cultural exchanges abroad is that they have been confined to just the participants. More popular exchanges on the Korean Peninsula would have enabled far more Koreans to experience their counterpart's culture.[55]

Fourthly, most exchanges have ended with Koreans meeting on a one-off basis without being extended into actual cooperative projects. As we have seen, omitting the projects led by the South Korean government in 1991, no such projects were approved until late 1997. Consequently, in contrast to the steady rise of meetings between Koreans, North-South socio-cultural exchanges have not developed that much in reality. However, that argument has become weakened by increasingly active contacts in recent years, although once-off events have of course tended to dominate.

Fifthly, as we have seen, the number of North Koreans who have visited the South is extremely low compared to the number of visits by South Koreans to the North. In fact, after the visit of six North Koreans to the South in the May of 1993, meeting on the Tumen River Area Development Project, no northerners visited South Korea prior to the visit of the North's basketball team in December 1999. The explanation is that North Korea's government has responded selectively and passively to the South Korean government's proposals for socio-cultural exchanges and cooperation. As of April 2001, according to recent North Korean defectors, a considerable number of citizens asked why they could not travel, whereas South Koreans often visit North Korea.[56] This indicates that there is a strong pent-up demand to go to South Korea.

---

55 Cho, ibid., 1999, pp. 21-2; Cho, ibid., 2000, p. 42; Cho, ibid., 2002a, pp. 8-9; Lee, ibid., 2001, p. 46. Cho (ibid., 2000, p. 42) does not exemplify what he means by "difficulties in efficiently preparing and proceeding conferences" and "economic inefficiencies".

56 Cho, ibid., 1999, pp. 38-9: fn. 30; Cho, ibid., 2002a, p. 9; Kim, ibid., April 2001, p. 69.

Another point worth adding is that, as we have seen, extremely few people have been involved in socio-cultural contacts, which indicates that the diffusion effects have been limited presumably to the disadvantage of restoring national homogeneity. While it is virtually impossible to measure these diffusion effects, they may be indirectly estimated by analyzing the statistics of the number of people actually involved, the size of the audiences and the length of meetings. With some exceptions such as the 2002 Asian Games, the 2003 Taegu Universiade and a few joint events held in North Korea after the June 2000 summit, people-to-people contacts have been limited and brief. In addition, the people involved have all belonged to specific sectors of society such as politicians, publishers, journalists, scholars and cultural personalities, implying that the impressions and knowledge they acquire may not contribute to growth among wider sectors of the populations: a wider diffusion would be desirable to promote mutual understanding and creating peaceful coexistence. It would also raise public awareness of the indisputable fact that the partition of Korea has created cultural diversity, a recognition that is a must for peaceful coexistence as well as reunification. Some joint characteristics remain and others may be restored, but almost 60 years of division have undoubtedly created different societies.

Even if one includes Koreans who have attended cultural performances, people who have experienced both the North's and the South's culture remain few. To the author's knowledge, there are no figures for the number of North Koreans who have attended the socio-cultural events held by visitors from South Korea or the joint events. However, on the basis of TV ownership, the diffusion effect should have been lower in the North than in the South: the ratio of households owning a TV set in South Korea was 97.2 per cent in 1991 and 99.9 per cent in 2001, whereas estimated ownership in North Korea reached around 1.3 million sets in 1999, 2000 and 2002. But it is unclear whether the figure refers to individuals or workplaces.[57] In the latter case, the diffusion effect may have been similar. In any case, this effect should also have been negatively affected by the government's reluctance to import foreign influences.

In addition to the few recorded events that have been broadcast some others have also, to the author's knowledge, been shown on South Korean TV facilitating information exchange. But considering the low ratios of the population who have watched the recorded events it is improbable that they have significantly raised the diffusion effect. It is also worth pointing out that the short duration of meetings' implies that the contacts have been superficial, although they may have led to at least some degree of changed perceptions with each side benefiting through mutual understanding, with the goal of peaceful coexistence.

Ko Yong-gwôn (2002) identifies three factors that have hindered socio-cultural exchanges and cooperation and which largely correspond with those of Cho. First, socio-cultural exchanges have been dependent on competition between the two rival political systems as well as political circumstances.

---

57 Statistics from Song, *The Rise*, p. 210; Yonhap news, *2000 Pukhan yôngam* (Seoul: Yonhap News Ltd., 1999), p. 644; ibid., 2001 (2000), p. 773; ibid., 2003 (2002), p. 322.

Secondly, socio-cultural exchanges have basically been pursued in order to confirm the sovereignty of the two different political systems, in addition to reducing tensions. Actually, when the North's political system in the early 1990s was potentially threatened by German unification in 1989-1990, the dissolution of the Soviet Union in 1991 and the collapse of the socialist bloc, exchanges were utilized to actually buffer it. But from around 1993 onwards, North Korea emphasized, as a result of the stabilization of the regional state of affairs and its own attitude "our way of socialism", the unity of its political system and had returned to a more or less status quo position.

Thirdly, North Korea has shown a passive attitude towards such contacts that result in a large influx of people, thus avoiding opening its society to avoid negative after effects from outside influences. Consequently, North Korea has preferred to hold meetings in third countries rather than pursuing cooperation and exchanges based on mutual visits.[58]

Ko also puts socio-cultural exchanges and cooperation in a broader perspective by enumerating four problems in pursuing such contacts. First, exchanges difficult to accomplish in any event have often been pursued without a long-term perspective in mind but rather with the purpose "to hold activities for their own sake". Efforts to broaden and diversify exchanges from the focus on one-off performances and arts events, have already exposed their intrinsic limitations. The large number of brief events supports Ko's view but, as we have seen, there are also a few exceptions to the trend.

Secondly, the content of many events have been inappropriate. One example is [non-exemplified] films implicitly displaying the development of the South's society and its free social atmosphere (but we should recall that no South Korean films had, as of October 2000, been shown in North Korea). In fact, the South Korean scholar O Ki-sông writes (1999) that during the art performances on the occasion of the first family reunions in September 1985, when the song "The Ulsan Girl" was sung; the Ulsan oil refinery was shown in the background. During the finale when "Arirang" was sung, an exhibition site for cars was shown, thus again showing off the more advanced South Korean economy to the audience. Another example is that North Korea has avoided performances of Royal Court Music by labelling such music as possessing class significance. Finally, South Korean exhibitions of experimental art works are difficult for the North Korean public to understand.

Exhibitors have not considered the state of affairs in the North and have thereby provided North Korea with a pretext to break off contacts. Such one-sided reasoning becomes evident by the fact that, while it is estimated that exhibitions of North Korean fine arts have been held more than 20 times in South Korea and that 100,000 fine art works from the North have been brought into the South, no exhibition of South Korean fine arts had, as of May 2002, been held in North Korea. It is also worth noting that North and South Korean artists have held such exhibitions as the

---

58 Ko, ibid., pp. 59-60, 63. Ko records on p. 60 that the Soviet Union was dissolved in 1990 but it is common knowledge that it was in 1991.

above "The Unified Korea Arts Exhibition" in Japan (in 1993 and 1997), not on the Korean Peninsula.

Thirdly, some media have reported schematically, as for example, when the North Korean art troupes performed in 1985 and 1990. Reportedly, the performances lacked artistry while emphasizing popularity and politics. Such reporting overlooked the fact that culture and arts in North Korea implement the aesthetics of the socialistic collective mass culture as dictated by the North Korean leadership.

Fourthly, socio-cultural exchanges and cooperation have, during the past 20 years, been dependent upon political circumstances and thereby lack originality. In addition, most exchanges have been poorly planned one-off events. The problems experienced need to be rectified and a more rational and mature attitude is needed to restore national homogeneity through pursuing exchanges.[59]

Consequently, it is significant that the two Koreas agreed to intensify socio-cultural exchanges and cooperation in the 15 June Declaration. The characteristics of such contacts have, according to Cho (2002), begun to change. First, as we have seen, exchanges and cooperation were intensified after the summit, both in qualitative and quantitative terms, although that trend had begun at an earlier stage.

Secondly, thanks to the Mt. Kûmgang tourist tours and family reunions the previous opportunities for only a small number of people to visit the North have been widened to include ordinary people, even in the context of multiple visits.

Thirdly, as we have seen, projects and approval of such projects in the socio-cultural field have risen. North Korea has become more open to socio-cultural contacts by treating them as a means to acquire economic benefits and to improve its world-wide image: South Korea paid an unspecified sum of money for the holding of the 2000 "Unification Concert" in P'yôngyang that was broadcast by the Cable News Network (CNN). In addition, the 2002 Arirang Festival was a combined multi-purpose large-scale cultural, arts and sports event with a particular emphasis on profitability.

Consequently, tourist souvenirs were made and entrance fees for public performances and sightseeing were in the range between $ 50 and $ 300. Tourist courses and cultural events were arranged within and outside P'yôngyang, mainly for commercial purposes. The festival was also an opportunity to show the world that North Korea is opening its society to improve its poor international image and to reveal, both to a domestic and foreign audience, the stability of its political system. For the same reason, North Korea has recently suggested that the DMZ and P'anmunjôm should be developed as major sightseeing resorts for Japanese and Chinese tourists. In May 2002, the DMZ and P'anmunjôm were for the first time opened for Western journalists, in a symbolic sign of a policy change.

---

59 Ko, ibid., pp. 60, 63; O, ibid., 1999, pp. 231, 310-311; Pak, ibid., October 2000, p. 51. Ch'oe (October 2000, ibid., p. 41) writes that an estimated one million art works were brought into South Korea after imports were permitted in 1998. What explains the huge difference to Ko's figure on p. 63 that is in the text is unclear. Original quotation marks.

Fourthly, North Korea has been careful not to provoke the South's policy towards the North in return for obvious economic benefits. Socio-cultural exchanges and cooperation have therefore, unlike former practice, been continuously pursued regardless of political developments. Two examples are those of the Mt. Kûmgang tours that continued in spite of the June 1999 sea battle in the West Sea and the detention of a South Korean tourist soon afterwards that was solved more quickly than any such past incident (cf. p. 68). In addition, as we have seen, socio-cultural exchanges continued during 2001, albeit less actively, despite deteriorating relations.

Fifthly, as a consequence of the expansion of socio-cultural exchanges and cooperation, problems have been created by the impact of the National Security Law which was a legacy of the cold war on the Korean Peninsula. One example is the incident during the celebration of the 15 August Liberation Day in P'yôngyang in 2001, previously referred to. Also, while academic exchanges have expanded, legal problems have arisen due to disputes concerning the copyrights of scientific materials published in North Korea and demands for compensation for the use of such materials without permission.

Allegedly materials on Korean history, including the Parhae Kingdom (698-926), the Koryô dynasty (918-1392) and chronicles from the Yi dynasty (1392-1910), have repeatedly been reprinted as books and CDs in South Korea for commercial sales. A most serious problem has arisen surrounding the copyright for the Yi dynasty chronicles, which were translated from Chinese into Korean and published in 400 volumes in a state-supported project pursued by the North's Academy of Social Sciences between 1954 and 1990. In 1991, one South Korean publishing company reprinted these volumes without permission and sold them on the market. North Korea responded by sending a written protest and has allegedly continued to demand compensation. In spite of these problems, it is necessary to realize that socio-cultural exchanges and cooperation are the most realistic way of removing Cold War conditions on the Korean Peninsula and enhancing peaceful coexistence. It must also be recognized that socio-cultural exchanges and cooperation creates a basis for social unity that precedes systemic unification.[60] Only time will tell if this aspiration really materializes.

4.6 South Korean NGOs and unification

Considering the expressed need for more active socio-cultural exchanges and cooperation, it is worth paying attention to the opinion of Cho (2002) who advocates active participation of NGOs in cross-border contacts. Since the authoritarian military governments in South Korea prohibited public participation in unification issues, NGOs had, until the late 1980s, minimal involvement in such moves. However, in the 1990s, the number of NGOs working with unification issues rose drastically

---

60 Cho, ibid., 2002a, pp. 9-12, 17-18.

thanks to the end of the Cold War on the international level. South Korea's advancing democratization since July 1987, and North Korea's requests for international aid and, in particular, the promotion of the sunshine policy since 1998, advanced this state of affairs.

In late 2001, 95 NGOs were registered by the Ministry of Unification, which is a big rise from 50 in June 1998 and 82 in November 2000. Their work was divided into the fields of non-specified unification activities (37), in academia and research (19), in exchanges and cooperation and humanitarian aid (13). South Korean NGOs, including religious organizations, have, in recent years, been active in delivering humanitarian aid to North Korea where all NGOs are bureaucratic organizations controlled by the government.[61] While this creates asymmetry in NGO contacts, they are, due to Cho's opinion, still worthy of investigation.

After new policy measures had been enacted in March 1998, representatives of six civilian organizations took part in Red Cross assistance as deliverers of relief materials, whereas representatives of four NGOs visited North Korea to discuss aid. In June 1998, the Korean Welfare Foundation became the first NGO to pursue cooperation with North Korean counterparts in the building of a medicine factory. In September, the Korea Neighbour-Loving Association delivered milk cows to North Korea. Also in September, the Korean Sharing Movement launched a campaign for North-South book exchanges. The Korean Sharing Movement had been founded in June 1996 to help alleviate starvation in North Korea, to promote national well being, and to prepare the foundations for unification. Its activities embrace fundraising and assistance, investigation and research, citizens' education, enlarging membership and pursuing projects needed to implement its targets. In approving the NGO projects, the government established three standards: respect for the law, professionalism and the capacity to ensure transparency of distribution, in the actual aid operations.

The book campaign, which focused on books on medicine and scientific technology wanted by North Korea, was launched in cooperation with the Korean Publishers' Cooperative Association, the Kyôngin Womens' University and the Korea Economic Daily. The North Korean counterpart was the Asia-Pacific Committee. As of November 1998, more than 30,000 books, that is above the original target, had been requisitioned. The books would be sent by boat from Inch'ôn to Namp'o in January 1999. In return, North Korea would send its books. South Korea's requests, amongst other subject areas, included primarily scientific books.[62] To the author's knowledge, the book campaign was comprehensively implemented.

---

61 Cho, ibid., 1998, pp. 15-17, 24; Cho et al., ibid., 2000, pp. 86-7; Cho, ibid., 2002b, pp. 102-103, 106, 107, 108, 116-117. Cho et al. (ibid., 2000, pp. 86-7) record the 82 NGOs that were active in unification issues in November 2000.

62 Cho, ibid., 1998, pp. 17-18, 29; Cho, ibid., 1999, p. 37; Cho et al., ibid., 2000, pp. 88-90; Chung, "The Role of South Korea's NGOs: The Political Context", in *Paved with Good Intentions: The NGO Experience in North Korea* (eds L. Gordon Flake & Scott Snyder, Westport, Connecticut: Praeger Publishers, 2003), p. 90; O, ibid., December 1999, p. 85.

In October 1998, a Northeast Asian Forestry Forum was initiated through NGO cooperation. The purpose was to form an international front to prevent deforestation in North Korea, China and Mongolia. The meeting, in which environmental activists, professors, officials from the forestry industry and media people participated, announced that it would launch an international tree planting campaign together with the UN Development Program, the Environment Research Institute at Beijing University, as well as forest planting institutes in Hong Kong, Taiwan and Japan. The above meeting on the comfort women issue, held 9-11 October, 1998 in Beijing, was organised by NGOs. The proposal came from North Korea's Committee for Comfort Women and for Compensation to the Victims of the Pacific War. South Korea's Association for Comfort Women and the Japanese Womens' Association for Solidarity with Korean Women took part in the meeting, which resulted in a written protest to the Japanese government demanding recognition for and an apology to the victims. The crimes were a violation of international law and compensation to the victims is an ongoing source of tension between the two Koreas and Japan.

The account does not give a complete view of NGO activities in the unification issue but they give credit to the opinions expressed by the South Korean scholar Lee Woo-Young (2004), who, to the author's knowledge, has made the most recent evaluation in this field. The activation of NGOs in unification issues has contributed to raise public interest, broaden the participation of the civil society in unification matters and widen the scope of interest in North Korea and unification. Interest was previously exclusively focused on Kim Il Sung and Kim Jong Il but it now also includes socio-cultural contacts.[63] In spite of the asymmetry in this field, the enumerated activities show that NGOs supplement the government by providing expertise on specific issues re-confirming that there is an important role for them to fulfill in North-South relations.

4.7 The impact of socio-cultural exchanges and cooperation on North Korea

Given the perception of the beneficial impact of socio-cultural exchanges and cooperation on inter-Korean relations, a relevant question is how such contacts affect North Korea. In 2002, North Korea tried to minimize the impact on its society of improved relations with South Korea and the inflow of external trends of thought. This was done through ideological and cultural control but in more flexible and indirect ways than previously. Through diversification of broadcasting from openly agitating political programs, to dramas and films with less political content, citizens' education and social stability were simultaneously promoted. Although political

---

63 Cho, ibid., 1998, p. 18; Lee, "Simin sahoe-esô pon ch'amyô chôngbu-ûi taebuk chôngch'aek", in Uri minjok sôro topki undong p'yônghwa nanum sent'ô, *Ch'amyô chôngbu Inyôn, Nambuk kwangye chindan-gwa palchôn panghyang* (Seoul: Uri minjok sôro topki undong p'yônghwa nanum sent'ô, 2004), p. 34.

themes continued to dominate in broadcasts and literature, dramas with little political content have, nonetheless, recently become popular.[64]

Nonetheless, inter-Korean socio-cultural exchanges and cooperation have made North Koreans who have come into contact with South Korean culture more aware of it. During the first family reunions in September 1985 in P'yôngyang, the South Korean arts troupe made performances of "Arirang" and other folk songs as well as traditional and newly created dances. The evaluations of North Korean culture and arts personalities who came into contact with musical performances by South Koreans for the first time were highly critical. Comments included "blasphemy of folk music", "music being a mixture of reactionary and serving-the-great attitude" and "Can arts be discoloured and rotten in such a way?". South Koreans were critical of North Korea's music and musical instruments for distorting tradition and betraying Korean nationality!

But the North Korean audience showed an entirely different attitude towards the performance of the Seoul Traditional Music Band, which participated in "The National Unification Concert" held in P'yôngyang in October 1990. Sông Tong-ch'un, vice chairman of the Federation of North Korean Musicians, even said: "Traditional folk music is indeed, as the term says, a nation's treasure comprised of intelligence and wisdom inherited from generation to generation. In this respect, there can be no difference between North and South or foreign countries". North Korean dailies reported that "the stage was flooded with enthusiasm for unification".

At the return visit to Seoul in December, South Korea was far more receptive to the P'yôngyang National Music Band's performances at "The Year-End Unification Concert". South Korean dailies' reports were generally favourable whilst pointing out that musical styles had diverged in the two states and predicting that regaining national homogeneity would be difficult. In sharp contrast, the P'yôngyang Beacon Publishing House wrote in a review: "Through the concert, our fellow musicians confirmed that despite 45 years of national division, our beautiful and fertile musical tradition and national spirit have remained alive, demonstrating that Koreans are still one though living in separation". Musical exchanges had confirmed the Korean people's united identity.

Later, in November 1998, when the Yoon Yi-sang Unification Music Band performed during "The Yoon Yi-sang Unification Concert" in P'yôngyang the audience repeatedly demanded a second performance. South Korean culture was no longer regarded by North Koreans as "rotten art" but even received "ovations" showing that they had become more familiar with that culture. However, this should not be surprising considering their common language and their common culture. In fact, the present cultural differences derive from non-cultural factors such as the political systems.[65] That the impact of the common cultural legacy both in 1990 and 1998 offset the ideological differences implies that the dissimilarities between North

---

64 Cho, ibid., 2002a, pp. 13-14.
65 Cho, ibid., 2002a, pp. 14-15; Hwang, ibid., 2001, pp. 138-140; Lee, ibid., 2001, p. 23. Original quotation marks.

and South Korea perhaps should not be exaggerated. This indicates that restoring national homogeneity, while acknowledging diversity, would, at least to some extent, be possible.

That South Korean music has become popular in North Korea and, above all, that South Korean products have become popular in the North seems to the author to be the major outcome of inter-Korean socio-cultural exchanges and cooperation in terms of having a potential for transforming relations by providing increased knowledge about the South.[66] This data also contradicts the view of the scholar Pak Sang-bong (2000) on the one-sided nature of North-South cultural exchanges.

Reportedly, South Korean popular songs and disco began to come into fashion in the late 1980s. Especially when the 13th World Youth and Students' Festival was held in P'yôngyang in 1989, South Korean songs reached North Korea through the Yônbyôn region. But they had also begun to come in as the 1988 Seoul Olympics were approaching, in spite of heavy punishments on listening to South Korean songs. At the same time, secret listening to radio broadcasts raised awareness of South Korean culture and society. The reportedly widely popular songs became known as "Yônbyôn songs", where many of the performers hailed from.

The introduction of South Korean songs exerted influence on song-making in North Korea manifested by the rapid tempo of greatly popular songs among young people. In 2001, the favourite songs amongst the youth were, while not discussed publically, South Korean songs that, unlike North Korean ones, did not emphasize ideology. South Korean songs reached North Korea through trade with China as well as other foreign transactions but, in spite of fixed radio channels, some people reportedly even listened to them on radio. In 2002, lists of songs at studios in South Korea recorded which ones were popular in North Korea.

Even more surprisingly, due to the recent more direct cultural influences from South Korea, even the opinion that "children who cannot sing South Korean songs are one decade behind" was, in the fall of 2001, reported officially from North Korea. Previously, when singer Kim Yôn-ja had performed 5-12 April, in P'yôngyang as the first South Korean solo singer in North Korea following on an invitation to "The April Friendship and Arts Festival" in 2001 that was held on the 89th anniversary of Kim Il Sung's birthday, Kim Jong Il told citizens that they were allowed to sing 20 South Korean songs.

The concert was sent on Korean Central TV (KCT) and later recorded on South Korean TV, albeit slightly edited. The visit included an unplanned concert in Hamhûng and was extensively reported in *Rodong Sinmun* [*Workers' Daily*] and after the visit in periodical publications. Kim Yôn-ja was received by Kim Jong Il, who also gave a banquet for her. South Korean songs were reportedly still spreading in North Korea as of 2003.[67]

---

66 Grinker (ibid., p. 251) records that South Koreans, as of 1996, knew no North Korean songs.

67 Cho, ibid., 2002a, pp. 2, 15; Ch'oe & Yi, "Pukhan-ûi taehak saenghwal-gwa sae sedae-ûi kach'igwan", in Minjok hwahae hyômnyôk pômkungmin hyôbûihoe, ibid., pp. 312-

That the "capitalistic singer" Kim Yôn-ja was regarded by the North's media as "a famous singer with deep national characteristics and advanced skills and techniques" is a clear sign of change in cultural policies; criticism was even more positive than in the South. Reportedly, the performance, which included a few previously forbidden songs as well as old ones, was warmly received by the audience. Some of them were in North Korea titled "songs of the enlightenment period" and had, as late as in the early 1990s, been forbidden since they were regarded as decadent songs promoting "national nihilism". It was reported that due to her visit and the removal of the prohibition the demand for such songs rapidly expanded in North Korea.

As of 2002, most North Koreans knew about such events as the inter-Korean exchanges and the South Korean delegation's visit on 15 August Liberation Day, in 2001, family reunions as well as the fact that the South is well off economically; along with the North's poor economy and general curiosity, this should explain why North Koreans complained that they could not go to South Korea. Knowledge about China's economic development has become wide-spread, which is forcing North Koreans into comparing their own system with that of China. Such knowledge has percolated through society in a North Korea already weakened by economic crisis and underlined by incoming media reports.

In addition, a rising number of people have reportedly secretly listened late at night to South Korean radio: North Korea's broadcasting is controlled by the Party and its function is largely to preserve the Kim Jong Il administration. According to a survey made by KBS in February 2003 that included 103 North Korean defectors, 69 of those (67 per cent) had listened to the KBS Education Broadcast in the North, mainly since 1996 onwards. 56 of them (81.1 per cent) had listened more than once a week. The high figures reflect that the interviewees are defectors but due to social control and the low radio ownership ratio, it is hard to know the figures for the whole North Korean population. The most preferred news was about South Korea followed by those describing events in North Korea. On North Korea, criticism of the Kim Jong Il administration raised most interest followed by news about the economy and the society which could reflect both defectors' positions and general discontent.[68]

Knowledge about the outside world has also been received through North Korean loggers working in Siberia, North Koreans seeking food in China, traders conducting

---

313, 317-318; Kil et al., *Nambukhan p'yônghwa kongjon-ûl wihan ch'ôngsonyôn-ûi sahoe munhwajôk tongjilsông chûngjin pangan yôn'gu* (Seoul: T'ongil yôn'guwôn, 2001), p. 84; Lim, *Pukhan-ûi taejung munhwa: silt'ae-wa pyônhwa chônmang* (Seoul: T'ongil yôn'guwôn, 2000), p. 83; Pak, "Han'guk kasu-ro-sô-nûn ch'ôûm-ûro Kim Chông Il wiwônjang mannago on Kim Yôn-ja", *Yôsông Chosôn* (April 2001), p. 1; Lee et al., ibid., p. 74; Lee, ibid., 2001, pp. 19, 43. Original quotations marks. "Yônbyôn songs" is quoted from Choe & Yi, ibid., p. 312.

68 Cho, ibid., 2002a, p. 15; Lee, ibid., 2001, p. 43; Lee et al., ibid., pp. 74-5; Suh et al., *White Paper on Human Rights in North Korea 2003* (Seoul: Korea Institute for National Unification, 2003), pp. 208-209; Yi, "Pukhan chumin-ûi Namhan pangsong suyong silt'ae-wa ûisik pyônhwa", *T'ongil munje yôn'gu* 40 (2003), pp. 315-319, 320, 324, 325. It is unclear what Cho refers to by "national nihilism" on p. 15. Original quotation marks.

illegal trade along the Korean-Chinese border, people who have worked abroad such as diplomats, businessmen and students, Korean businessmen in China crossing the border, foreign citizens of Korean heritage who have visited the North and foreign correspondents. Since the North Korean government strictly blocks news about the outside world, it has, in recent years, tried to stop information gathered in China from reaching the general public by discouraging North Koreans from spreading it.

Consequently, while the impact on the society of the inflow of information is hard to evaluate, it is indisputable that North Korea differs greatly from East Germany where foreign influences had significantly affected citizens' values long before the 1990 unification. In such a way, "value integration" may have been created also in North Korea by stimulating a desire to live in peace, freedom and prosperity, although Chapter 3 showed that "structural integration" prior to 1993 had been the core of the two Korea's unification policies. However, such effects do not show up immediately and the sense of being of one race as one aspect, of value integration, is still a strong factor.

Unlike what would previously have been the case, North Korea showed the opening of the 2002 Soccer World Cup from Seoul that vividly displayed the South's enhanced national power. At a time when a majority of North Koreans were aware of the expansion of inter-Korean exchanges and cooperation and economic aid from the South, they could thereby get a realistic view of the propaganda which claims that North Korea is better off economically than South Korea. This would tend to reduce their shock through realizing the extent of this distortion of facts in advance. However, the knowledge that North Korea received economic aid from South Korea was not new: as of 1997, in contrast to 1996, many people knew that they were receiving food assistance from the South.

It was reported that on the occasion of the June 2000 summit and the following family reunions the ban on the use of South Korean products was unofficially lifted. North Koreans who used South Korean products were previously regarded as political criminals and received heavy penalties; people working abroad could only buy such South Korean products as clothes on the condition that they would remove the trademarks.[69] To the author's knowledge, it is unknown how widely the South's products are spread amongst the North Korean population.

Information about the outside world, the diffusion of South Korean songs and products and the South's provision of economic assistance raises the question what impact such contacts have on inter-Korean relations and North Korean domestic politics. The South Korean scholar O (1999) records that the influx of such South Korean (and Japanese) consumer goods as home electronic products through the border with China stimulated a consumerist desire there. On the other hand, that the political impact may have been limited is indicated, by the following quotation from

---

69 Cho, ibid., 2002a, pp. 15-16; Lim, ibid., p. 102; Quinones, "Ch'oegûn Pukhan-ûi silsang", in Minjok t'ongil yôn'guwôn, ibid., 1998a, p. 95; Suh et al., ibid., pp. 208-209; Yi, ibid., p. 320.

defector Hong X-hee's testimony at the Korea Institute for National Unification on 20 December, 2002:

> North Korea is exercising ideological control over its people, first, to minimize the adverse effect on its populace of its pragmatic foreign policy for economic assistance and promoting external support for the Kim Jong Il regime, and second, to reduce the impact of the increasing inter-Korean exchanges on its political system. In an effort to forestall any ideological demise in the face of increasing exchanges with the outside world, the North Korean authorities are further reinforcing the ideology education on its inhabitants and repeatedly reminding them that capitalism and liberalism should be rooted out even before they begin to bud. The main focus of recent ideological education is to plant fears in the people's mind by stressing that the world of capitalism is a world of survival of the fittest and to emphasize the merits of protection culture under socialism.[70]

Nonetheless, South Korean products owned by returnees were, after the summit, not retrieved at border stations. It was reported that people returning from abroad could buy South Korean products publicly and then use them freely in North Korea. Some South Korean products were sold at a few markets in the North with the trademarks actually on the products. North Koreans, although it is unclear how many, preferred such South Korean products as medicinal and clothing and are reported as saying that they knew that their quality was superior to products available normally in the North. If sales of South Korean products were publicized, they were confiscated but, due to the demand for them, they were continuously sold on the market.

According to North Korean defectors, South Korean and American products were, as of 2001, considered to be the best ones. Although second-hand South Korean and American products were more expensive than new ones hailing from North Korea and China, they sold well nonetheless. As of 2005, a growing number of people were reportedly watching South Korean TV and CDs containing South Korean TV programs were widely traded among the people. Notably, at the same time, the expansion of exchanges with South Korea had led to changes in education in North Korea. Students were occasionally taught with South Korean economic textbooks and were educated about the South's development models.

Besides the influx of South Korean songs, products and influences on education, it is worth pointing out that the family reunions have changed the perception of how defectors' families are dealt with. In February 2001, prior to the third round of family reunions (after the summit), KCT showed the ten-part drama "Horizon" about a maritime engineer who, in spite of his outstanding skills, could not find employment: the defection of the father to South Korea had made the person a victim of contempt and discrimination by people. But thanks to the Party's non-discriminatory concerns he finally overcame his difficulties.

In April 2002, before the fourth round of family reunions, KCT showed the film drama "The Woman in the Well House" which emphasizes that discrimination against defectors' families takes place because some people are narrow-minded

---

70 O, ibid., 1999, p. 220; Suh et al., ibid., p. 6.

by not following the Party's policies and that, in fact, discrimination is not the Party's official policy. Such films were previously taboo but were later shown for the purpose of promoting adaptation to changes in inter-Korean relations.[71] Clearly, North Korea was influenced by South Korea's functionalist approach through the sunshine policy but it was rather a question of adapting to changes than to pursuing policies to reinforce them. However, the impact of Southern influences on the North should not be underestimated.

4.8 Conclusions

Although inter-Korean socio-cultural exchanges and cooperation are important for the goal of restoring national homogeneity, it is, considering that such contacts have been few, irregular and, with only a few exceptions, involved few ordinary people during short periods of time, difficult, therefore, to imagine that they so far contributed in any meaningful way to reaching this target. Regardless of criteria, diffusion effects have been limited. Socio-cultural contacts between North and South Korea have been incomparably more limited than they were in the cases of pre-unity Germany and Yemen.

The development of North-South socio-cultural contacts has continuously been affected by politics, which long made it impossible to implement the proposals made by both states from 1953 onwards. Although a joint cultural festival had been held by Korean residents in Japan in 1961, the art troupes' performances during the first family reunions in September 1985 marked the beginning of socio-cultural exchanges.

A legal framework for pursuing socio-cultural exchanges and cooperation was established in 1989-1990 and was later expanded. Nonetheless, tense North-South relations largely prevented active contacts from developing until Kim Dae Jung became president in 1998. During the mandate period of his government, they expanded both quantitatively and qualitatively. However, contacts had begun to expand during the 1990s; indeed many took place in academia and education, unrelated to political trends. But more significant was that a few meetings were held on the Korean Peninsula while the North's nuclear policy caused severe tensions. Yet, this did not change the general trend towards socio-cultural contacts which took place in third countries. However, in recent years an increasing number of exchanges have taken place on the peninsula, facilitating contacts.

Socio-cultural exchanges have taken place in academia and education, film, literature, sports, religion and through women's conferences and NGOs involved in humanitarian aid. Contacts have been most active in academia and education, as we have seen, dealing with unification issues, economics, environment and linguistics, sports and religion. Whereas the larger number of contacts have been one-time

---

71 Cho, ibid., 2002a, pp. 2, 16-17; Lee et al., *White Paper on Human Rights in North Korea 2005* (Seoul: KINU, 2005), p. 268; Suh, *North Korea's Market Economy Society from Below* (Seoul: KINU, 2005), pp. 35, 55.

events, it is remarkable that five joint academic publications have been published between 1998 and 2002, including one on the unification issue. Joint declarations have been adopted a few times. Socio-cultural contacts have also contributed to securing peace on the Korean Peninsula by taking place even during periods of high tension.

Scholars' opinion on the impact of socio-cultural exchanges and cooperation on inter-Korean relations differ. Criticism has been directed towards them being commercialized, politicized and one-sided. The first two points are hard to reject but, although there are far more South Korean visitors to North Korea than vice-versa, contacts have not been merely a one-sided communication. Positive results noted include the fact that since 1998 contacts have continued in spite of political tensions and that more Koreans have been able to meet each other recently.

The recent influx of South Korean products and songs into North Korea, as well as improved knowledge of the South largely as a consequence of the North's economic crisis from the mid-1990s onwards, have the potential to transform inter-Korean relations in the long-run. The sunshine policy's functionalist approach has thus contributed to creating "value integration", as was the case in East Germany. North Korea fears the impact of socio-cultural contacts and cooperation on its social system but has not rejected those contacts which bring economic benefits. There is an opinion that contacts benefit the North Korean government thereby consolidating the status quo rather than contributing to improving relations. North Korea has implemented policies to minimize the impact of foreign influences on its society, including influences emanating from South Korea.

Chapter 5

Case Studies of Inter-Korean Socio-cultural Exchanges and Cooperation

5.1 Introduction

As we have seen in Chapter 4, North and South Korea expanded their socio-cultural contacts in scope, especially from 1998 onwards. That these contacts have been maintained at a time when inter-Korean relations have been tense and brought some concrete results in the form of five joint publications and exposure to South Korean influences through popular music and southern products in North Korea should not be underestimated, although it will take some time until the full impact becomes clear.

Three kinds of contact spheres – the position of North Korean defectors in South Korea, South Korean humanitarian aid to North Korea and reunions of divided families – are the focus of this chapter. The purpose is to give a more complete overview of how socio-cultural contacts affect inter-Korean relations.

Unlike the contacts that were described in Chapter 4, defectors have had to adapt to a new life style on a daily basis. Consequently, their experiences say more about the impact of national division on an individual level and provide a better standpoint to judge how Koreans who have long been separated from each other can live together, regardless of whether they previously have experienced socio-cultural contacts or not. Defectors' experiences of life in South Korea are analyzed in view of the opinion that socio-cultural contacts are important to restore national homogeneity and, ultimately, for the future prospects for a united Korea.

To arrive at an overview of the defectors issue and government policies to handle it, this chapter begins by investigating what is characteristic for defectors and what policies successive South Korean governments have pursued following the end of the Korean War in 1953. But more emphasis is put on investigating policy outcomes by analyzing the situation of defectors in South Korea on the basis of question surveys made in 1996, 1998 and 2003. These surveys consist of both statistics and defectors' statements about their new lives.

Humanitarian aid from South to North Korea since 1995 onwards is then analyzed, to give an overview of what policies lie behind aid, through what channels it has been distributed and its extent and composition. That, as we saw in Chapter 3, humanitarian aid has been continuously provided to the North also places the aid issue in a different context from the kind of contacts presented in Chapter 4. A most important issue to analyze in this section is whether humanitarian aid has affected inter-Korean relations and North and South Koreans' notions of each other. Consequently, the number of people involved in aid work, under what conditions they have conducted their work and the outcome of the aid itself are analyzed. How aid affects relations is also investigated by analyzing and comparing scholars' evaluations. In this way, the impact of humanitarian aid compared to other forms of socio-cultural contacts is assessed.

Exchange of divided families is, as we saw in Chapter 1, an issue of the utmost humanitarian importance but differs from the other types of contacts by being less regular. Nonetheless, by investigating family reunions that began to be regularly held in 2000 it is possible to get a sense of how divided families' notions of "the other Korea" have been affected by separation. Due to limited empirical materials only a few interviews with divided family members who took part in the first post-June 2000 summit family reunions are included, but they still give some sense of this issue. By analyzing the numbers of people involved in family reunions, whether there have been any diffusion side-effects provoked by the reunions is discussed.

5.2 North Korean defectors to South Korea

In late 1995, there were 561 North Korean defectors living in South Korea. The number had risen to 616 in August 1996, to 1,033 in August 1999 and to 1,187 in December 2000. At the end of 2002, a total of 3,131 North Korean defectors had arrived in South Korea, of which 2,886 still remained. A year later, the figure was 4,410, of which 4,147 were still resident in South Korea. At the end of 2004, the number had risen to 6,304. Defectors' numbers have fluctuated: in 1949-1950 they were only 18 but the number rose to 223 between 1951 and 1960. In the 1960s and 1970s, the numbers were 146 and 31, respectively. However, from then the figures rose due to the North's economic hardship and food shortages: whereas only 64 North Koreans had defected during the 1980s, there were 487 defectors during the 1990s. The number of defectors fleeing to the South during the years between 2000 and 2004, were 312, 583, 1,139, 1,281 and 1,894, respectively.[1]

---

1 Han, "T'alpuk ijuja-ûi namhan sahoe chôgûng munje-wa chaesahoehwa pangan," *T'ongil yôngu nonch'ong* 5 (1996), no. 2, p. 216; Lee, *T'alpukcha munje haegyôl pangan* (Seoul: T'ongil yôn'guwôn, 1999), pp. 5, 52-3; Lee et al., *Pukhan it'al chumin munje-ûi chonghapchôk chôngch'aek pangan yôn'gu* (Seoul: T'ongil yôn'guwôn, 2000), pp. 29-30, 41; Lee et al., *White Paper on Human Rights in North Korea 2004* (Seoul: KINU, 2004), pp. 255, 257; Lee et al., ibid., *2005,* p. 331; Park et al., *Pukhan it'al chumin-ûi sahoe chôgûng-e kwanhan yôn'gu: Silt'ae chosa mith kaesôn pangan* (Seoul: Minjok t'ongil yôn'guwôn, 1996), p. 6; Suh et al., *White Paper*, p. 207. Lee (ibid., p. 53: table 4-1) records 607 defectors until 1989, which exceeds the figure of Han (ibid., p. 216) for 1995. It is unclear what explains the different figures. Lee's figure also exceeds the 482 defectors recorded by Park et al. (ibid., p. 6) for the whole period 1949-1990 but what explains the different figures is unclear.

According to research made public by the Ministry of Unification in 1994, reasons for defections had changed depending on the time period. On the basis of interviews with 209 people who had defected after the 1960s, ideological reasons such as comparisons with South Korea and dissatisfaction with the North Korean system explained 72 per cent of defections. After the 1980s, common reasons were dissatisfaction with social treatment, inferior social positions, accompanied defections and fear of punishment. Defections rose from 1994 due to such reasons as people seeking guarantees for the right of life, escaping from human rights violations, evading crimes committed and the state of the economy. That North Koreans, due to the economic crisis, received increased information from the outside world accelerated defections.[2] However, numbers were extremely low compared to defections from East Germany regardless of time period.

The ways of escape have changed also. In the 1960s, 50 per cent of defectors escaped through the DMZ or by sea. In fact, many defectors either lived close to the border or had overseas experience. After the 1980s, defections through third countries such as China and Russia rose markedly. The border to China was, in spite of security reinforcements, impossible to control.

Defectors' social background had also changed. Among the 209 defectors investgated in 1994, 46 were soldiers, 35 party members, 25 each students and loggers and 23 technicians (data is lacking for 55 defectors). In the 1990s, the number of party members, students and loggers among defectors, who came from all parts of the nation and sometimes even consisted of whole families, grew. Also the number of defecting children, whose parents had died of starvation, rose markedly. Many recent defectors belong to the society's upper strata such as researchers at the Agricultural Science Academy, family members of people who have been repatriated to the North, senior officers in the People's Army and foreign exchange dealers residing in Europe.

Statistics from August 1999 show that in terms of occupation, there were 199 woodcutters, workers and farmers amongst the 416 defectors (48 per cent) investigated by the Ministry of Unification. Students and people without work were 110 (26.4 per cent). Government officials and teachers (50 people), people working overseas including businessmen, diplomats and foreign exchange dealers (28) and soldiers (27) comprised only 12.3 per cent, 6.7 per cent and 6.5 per cent, respectively of the total (two persons were self-surrendering spies). According to data from 1998, the vast majority of defectors were men in their late teens or twenties but the number of women and children defecting was rising at this time. As of 2003, most defectors were women workers and farmers from the north-eastern region.[3]

---

2 Grinker, *Korea and,* p. 232; Lee, ibid., 1999, pp. 5-6; Lee et al., ibid., *2004*, pp. 255, 257; Lee et al., ibid., *2005*, pp., 333-34; Park et al., ibid., pp. 6-7; Suh et al., ibid., pp. 208-209.

3 Grinker, ibid., p. 232; Lee, ibid., 1999, pp. 6, 53-4; Lee et al., ibid., 2000, pp. 29-30, 41; Park et al., ibid., pp. 7-8.

Support for North Korean defectors has changed depending on period of time. Although defectors after the end of the Korean War in 1953 were used for South Korea's propaganda purposes and were treated well, there was no special legislation on defectors and no systematic government policies to protect and support them.[4] However, since, according to the Third Article of the South Korean constitution, "The territory of the Republic of Korea shall consist of the Korean Peninsula and its adjacent islands", North Koreans, as well as defectors, are legally citizens of South Korea, while in practice and from the point of view of international law they are citizens of North Korea. In contrast, the current North Korean constitution contains no such paragraph.

In practice, military authorities took care of defectors after 1953. In April 1962, "The Special Law to Support Men of National Merit and Defectors to the South" was enacted. Consequently, after one year of investigations through the Agency for Relief that belonged to the Ministry of Defence, defectors received resettlement allowances whose sums varied with their rank. Work was arranged for them as well as vocational training. They were given favoured status in receiving houses and received support for old age welfare as well as child supports. Education was free up until high-school.

With the enactment of "The Special Law to Compensate Brave Defectors to the South" in December 1978, the support was systemized. The law was enforced from January 1979. The Ministry of Defence's Agency for Patriots and Veterans' Affairs took care of the defector issue from 1984.

Defectors got different amounts of allowances and personal equipment depending on their position and supply of information. They could also be especially nominated as soldiers and public officials and received large apartments freely. They received social support and help to get work, along with their families. Education was still free for their children until high-school. Companies were required to employ 5-10 per cent of the fixed numbers of patriots, including defectors.

Regardless of defectors' qualifications, almost all of them got employed at companies they had hoped to work for. The same rules applied to their children making the defectors rather well off economically, but due to their particular status in South Korean society they were still not being given equal treatment. As may be expected, the aim of the policies undertaken to benefit defectors is considered to have been to prove for North Koreans the superiority of South Korea.[5]

When North Korean defectors arrived in South Korea they had, until 1996, first been transferred to the Agency for National Security Planning for interrogation,

---

4   East German defectors to West Germany first stayed at urgent repatriation centres where they received financial support and were consulted on such issues as region, work and studies for their resettlements. After resettlements, they received support with such issues as residence, work and social welfare services. From Kim (*Tong sôdok injôk*, 1996, p. 72).

5   Grinker, op. cit. p. 233; Lee, ibid., 1999, pp. 19-20, 56, 58-60, 61: fn. 107; Park et al., ibid., pp. 8-10; *South Korea – Constitution* (http://www.oefre.unibe.ch/law/icl/ks00000.html), p. 1; Suh, ibid., 2004, p. 70; Suh et al., ibid., p. 204.

including police clearance. During the 7-10 days of interrogation, the defector's identity, motives for and way of defection and their achievements in North Korea were investigated. Afterwards most defectors conducted interviews and were admitted to the settlement facility *Taesông kongsa* run by the Ministry of Defence. Since 1993, most defectors have stayed there for six months (previously ten) but defecting soldiers were investigated longer and by several agencies to acquire information about North Korea. Not surprisingly, defectors felt reluctance about being investigated, especially by American military authorities.

Defectors could receive news at Taesông kongsa. They learnt about life in Seoul by visiting, for instance, department stores during weekends and about South Korea via films and videos as well as from invited lawyers. Inspections of South Korean industry took place. Education also included learning about such essential things as personal relations, ceremonial occasions and reading genealogies. Teaching took place seven hours a day.

Defectors waited after finishing settlement training to undergo administrative and legal procedures to become South Korean citizens. The Ministry of Health and Welfare has been responsible for supporting them in settling down since December 1993, in accordance with the then enacted "Law to Protect North Korean Defectors". Defectors received financial support in proportion to family size.[6]

Civilian defectors were, after leaving Taesông kongsa, protected and supervised by the police during a two year period, since their adaptation to life in South Korea was viewed as a function of maintaining public security. Two policemen were responsible for one defector and helped them with basic matters to get along with their new life. Defectors had to report their comings and goings to the police daily. Policemen had to follow defectors when they attended lectures. The police in this way heavily influenced defectors' social adaptation, a work that tended to be a trial-and-error process.

When defectors got a residence permission and an identity card, they formally became South Korean citizens. There then followed procedures such as accessing housing, arrangements for work and applying for medical insurance. Getting work was the most difficult problem to solve. Until 1993, employment was not a particular problem thanks to the requirement for companies to employ North Korean defectors. But since they have had to seek work at companies within the police district they were resident at, the number of rejections grew: most defectors lacked the necessary skills and knowledge about South Korean society. Although a survey of 41 North Korean defectors conducted in 1996 showed that vocational training and recommendations of work were what the defectors wanted most (57.5 per cent of 38 replies) from the South Korean government, there was no systematic vocational education for them. When they could get work at companies where they wanted to work regardless of their experiences or skills, vocational education was not necessary.

But when loggers defected in 1994, vocational education partially stemmed from the difficulties they had in getting work. Since 1994 there is a vocational education

---

6 Lee, ibid., 1999, p. 56; Park et al., ibid., pp. 10, 11, 17-19.

training centre dedicated to the group. Defectors received one year of basic technical skills which was divided into ten months of training and two months of practical work. Reportedly, due to the differences in the education systems of the two Koreas, loggers had, as of 1994, difficulties in acquiring vitally needed skills.

They were dissatisfied with being under constant surveillance while living at the training centre and having to receive the same training regardless of their skills. It was difficult for the centre personnel to teach them; training was concluded in 1994. Yet all but one of the 18 defectors got work at such companies as Samsung and Daewoo, etc.[7]

Also the Evangelical Church implemented vocational training, but in 1996 only ten defectors applied for the one-year program which required severe restrictions on personal freedom. Technical skills taught in repairing cars, woodworking and computers were basic ones, a situation which caused great dissatisfaction.

There are two friendship organizations for defectors: the *Sungûi Tongjihoe* (Loyalty Friendship Foundation) and the *T'ongilhoe* (Unification Foundation). The former was founded in 1981 and consisted, as of 1996, of about 510 defectors. It holds its general meeting every second year and previously arranged visits to industrial facilities. The Foundation received financial support from the North Korean Defectors' Support Association. The latter had, as of 1998, about 40 members, among them many former soldiers, and was administered under the Public Security Department. There were also a few private organizations for defectors.

As of 1999, defectors were still first questioned by military authorities after arrival. It was necessary to find out whether there were some false defectors as well as to gather and confirm information provided by them. But since most defectors arrived after a long stay in China or other countries they did not know much about recent events in North Korea. Thus, the period of questioning was, as a principle, minimized to one month while emphasis was put on education and training in an effort to raise defectors' ability to manage on their own.[8]

Legislation at this time stipulated a period of one year of protection at the Ministry of Unification run institute *Hanawôn* ("One institute") but with the exception of defectors being somewhat suspect from the point of national security; there could be individuals masquerading as defectors. Hanawôn replaced Taesông kongsa, which, as a military-run institute, was unsuitable for contacts with civilians who needed another form of reception. The rapidly rising number of defectors also made it inevitable that a new institute, Hanawôn, be established which catered for some 500 people.

At Hanawôn, defectors received education for social adaptation within three months, which was then followed by 6-8 months of vocational training at nearby training centres, schools and companies. Education aimed at covering such broad and complex issues as mental adaptation, understanding of South Korean society, information on daily life, vocational training and visits to workplaces and, finally,

---

7   Park et al., ibid., pp. 20-22, 105.
8   Grinker, ibid., pp. 239-241; Lee, ibid., 1999, pp. 65-6; Park et al., ibid., pp. 22-3.

such practical knowledge as Chinese characters, English, current vocabulary, computers and driving. It was necessary to conclude three months of education, which was conducted in circulating groups of about ten people, to qualify for settlement support.

Consideration was taken to defectors' academic merits, qualifications, career and hopes in order to find employment suitable for their capacity and talents while they received training on commission at vocational training institutes, schools and companies but this was no easy task. Hanawôn also worked to solve each defector's troubles through consultations on such issues as their psychological state and health status and established a room for religious activities to promote defectors' mental stability. Settlement funds were provided as well as support for education and employment.[9]

The targets of Hanawôn do appear to have been ambitious but the institute did not lack obstacles that derived from defectors' backgrounds as well as the fact that it had to take care of defectors' lives in general. First, it was difficult to conduct efficient training since the tasks of taking care of a rising number of defectors and protecting them was not successfully implemented. There was a lack of people in charge and those available had insufficient specialist knowledge. Only teaching of basic skills such as driving training was properly implemented.

Secondly, education for social adaptation, as well as vocational training, were inefficient. There was a lack of funds and personnel to conduct the diverse curriculum. That the age of defectors and their educational background differed provided additional problems, along with defectors' poor health due to the North's economic crisis and concerns for their families. Lectures as a basis for teaching did not work well for everyone and many people did not attend the lectures. Defectors had problems in absorbing many classes as a result of, for instance, having wandered around in China for a long time, a lack of experience of life in South Korea and poor knowledge of English and foreign loanwords. They also found some teaching repetitive which reduced their interest spans. Defectors were most satisfied with teaching of practical skills such as driving and computers. Also visits to workplaces and "cultivation of emotions" were highly appreciated courses. As of December 2000, 80 per cent of the defectors at Hanawôn thought that the training was helpful in understanding and adapting to the South Korean society but they wanted training focused on examples related to real life.

Thirdly, there were many occasions when defectors, due to concerns for their families, wanted a shorter period of protection. This was the case both for defectors who had their families in China and those who already had their families in South Korea. Some of the latter even regarded education for social adaptation as being unnecessary.

Fourthly, instructors had had bad working conditions and experienced difficulties in leading and administering defectors. Instructors had to stay away from home for

---

9 Lee, ibid., 1999, pp. 65-70; Lee et al., ibid., 2000, pp. 105-109.

ten days and had to follow defectors during days off, which gave rise to excessive work burdens.[10]

After the one-year stay at Hanawôn, defectors got support for housing as well as employment and received personal protection from the police for two years; tense inter-Korean relations whipped up fears that they may have been disguised spies. Support embraced not only personal protection but also administrative and legal matters. In August 1999, a responsibility system for protecting places of residence nationwide that also covered a wide range of basic daily issues for defectors such as medical protection, education, employment, housing, social welfare, etc. was enforced. Previously, in May 1999, a centre for consultation on daily issues of defectors had been set up within the Support Committee for North Korean defectors.

The centre identified all kinds of problems defectors had and consulted with the government, support organizations and specialist institutes to help to solve these problems. The centre also aimed to, along with specialists and civilian organizations, create employment as well as programs for social adaptation. In 1999, the centre carried out investigations on defectors' living conditions, made a program for improving defectors' capacity for employment and gave lectures on legislation and how to set up companies. There were also such social activities as music concerts, North Korean food festivals and meetings of defectors for their benefit. In addition, the centre had a volunteer corps of university students, offered the provision of employment information for these people with which it had established contact as well as supplementary classes for students.

The Support Committee for North Korean defectors consisted of religious and civilian organizations as well as special institutes. Consequently, to promote equity among and efficiency for civilian organizations' support, in November 1999, The Civilian Organizations' Council to Support North Korean Defectors was inaugurated. The Council consisted of domestic as well as overseas organizations, supporting defectors through their self-regulatory participation and cooperation. In this way, defectors would get help to settle and their survival would be guaranteed.[11]

The Council aimed to support defectors by building up an equal and efficient support system based on mutual exchanges of information, promoting research of civilian organizations, raising the general public's interest in the defectors issue through the holding of research seminars and working to get the accumulated experiences to be reflected in the government's policies of support for defectors. The Council could receive support from the government budget for its diverse activities but had difficulties in implementing its targets since the participating organizations lacked special support programs for defectors. Instead, they often made one-time financial contributions. In fact, support from civilian organizations was, in 1999-2000, still in its initial stage.

---

10 Lee, ibid., 1999, pp. 67, 70-74, Lee et al., ibid., 2000, pp. 107, 109-111, 115-116.
11 Lee, ibid., 1999, pp. 78-81, 83; Lee et al., ibid., 2000, pp. 121-3, 127.

It is obvious that defectors had become an urgent issue during the 1990s which had to be tackled. The rising number of North Korean defectors during the 1990s had also become a financial burden for the South Korean government and raised concerns about their capacity to handle the issue if the number continued to rise.

Critics argued that the government did too much for them. Consequently, "The Law to Protect North Korean Defectors" was enacted in December 1993. The law drastically reduced the material benefits hitherto provided to defectors, as well as their social welfare provisions. The defectors were no longer regarded as men of national merit but as people who needed help for living in South Korea. Thus, responsibility for them was shifted from the Ministry of Defence to the Ministry of Health and Welfare.[12]

The law had four characteristics. First, resettlement allowances and additional dues were reduced. The level of support differed depending on the number of defectors.

Secondly, support for housing was provided. Houses smaller than 50 square metres were provided freely and rent support was promised.

Thirdly, the defectors became responsible for seeking employment themselves. But the minister of the Ministry of Health and Welfare that set up the Committee to Support North Korean Defectors with a broad mandate could request employment at schools, as well as private and public companies and organizations which, if requested, had to give priority to defectors in selecting people within the scope of their technical services if they had more than 16 employees.

Fourthly, defectors became responsible for seeking support for education. Defectors and their families could also receive beneficial medical protection.[13]

In December 1996, "The Law on the Protection and Resettlement of North Korean Defectors" was enacted. The law was promulgated in January 1997, and was enforced from July of the same year. A consequence of the South Korean government reducing its support to defectors was reflected in the fact that they could neither receive education to adapt to life in South Korea nor vocational education. Instead, they had to manage on their own economically.

Thus, it became necessary to establish a new policy for the settlement of North Korean defectors in South Korea. But the law excluded people suspected to be disguised defectors and people who had committed crimes against international law such as the hijacking of aeroplanes, dealing in the narcotics trade and terrorist acts or mass killings. Also, people who had committed major non-political crimes and crimes over which their temporary country of residence had signed extradition agreements with North Korea were exempt from the legislation. Finally, people who had stayed for a long time in their new country of residence and people who were suspected of causing South Korea major political and diplomatic damage were

---

12 Grinker, ibid., p. 233; Lee, ibid., 1999, pp. 56, 58-60, 81-4; Lee et al., ibid., 2000, pp. 98-100, 123-25, 127; Park et al., ibid., pp. 10-11.

13 Park et al., ibid., pp. 11-13. Lee (ibid., 1999, p. 59) and Lee et al. (ibid., 2000, p. 98) record the size of houses as 15 square metres. It is unclear what explains the difference.

also excluded. Still, South Korea had, according to the 1997 law on defectors, an obligation on humanitarian grounds to give special protection to North Koreans who had not acquired foreign citizenship and who had sought refugee protection at South Korean diplomatic and consular offices abroad.

With the enumerated exceptions, in the new law emphasis was put on programs for social adaptation and vocational training to enable defectors to independently survive in South Korea instead of, as previously, relying on benefits. The programs included deciding a period for defectors to receive protection and supervision, education for social adaptation, vocational training, recognition of career records and special employment. The new law differed from previous laws in several respects.[14]

First, the Ministry of Unification became the sole agency responsible for the defectors. "The Council for Countermeasures Towards North Korean Defectors" was established under the influence of the Ministry. The Council became responsible for such issues as providing protection of defectors and support for settlements.

Secondly, a concrete plan for defectors' social adaptation was set up by arranging facilities for the settlement of defectors and deciding the period of protection and supervision. Defectors would receive support for one year at their place of education and for two years at their place of residence. Large investments were planned to reach these targets.

Thirdly, an important part of the law was that defectors would undergo education for social adaptation to learn basic rules of South Korean society and receive vocational training. The period of learning was set at six months. Within one year of their stay, defectors could receive vocational training supported by the Ministry of Labour.

Fourthly, for the sake of defectors' settlement in South Korea, their educational background as well as their qualifications would be recognized. Considering their positions, fields of responsibility and career special appointments would be given to defectors who were officials or soldiers in North Korea.[15]

Fifthly, the defectors would, while attending facilities for settlements, receive cash and other possessions but in other respects social benefits did not differ much. There was to be no high school fees and fees for university studies were to be reduced.

Sixthly, a plan for providing defectors with secure work to make them adapt to life in South Korea was drawn up. This made it possible, if the Minister of Unification so demanded, to give priority to defectors in employing people among the fixed number of officials at state agencies, local organizations and at state and public schools. Companies employing defectors could also receive reduced taxes within the scope of the law as a measure to encourage them to employ North Koreans.

Seventhly, the heads of local self-governing agencies would solve the problems for defectors associated with moving from initial settlement facilities to their places

---

14 Grinker, ibid., p. 228; Lee, ibid., 1999, pp. 35-6: fn. 67, 56-7, 58-60; Lee et al., ibid., 2000, pp. 86-7; Park et al., ibid., p. 13.

15 Park et al., ibid., pp. 14-15.

of residence. The agency heads would report every six months to the Minister of Unification.

Eighthly, the state would provide all protection and costs for support of settlements and hand over them to local self-governing bodies every year. Deficits would be supplemented or normalized afterwards. Finally, "The Aid Association for North Korean Defectors" was established to support defectors.[16]

Although the new law seems to have been highly ambitious, due to defectors' economic difficulties it was supplemented in October 1998 by "The Enforcement Ordinance of the New Legislation on the Settlement of and Support for North Korean Defectors". Settlement funds were raised four times, support for residence became more generous and allowances for vocational education were elevated. Minimal living costs were provided for families with severe economic difficulties and it became possible to apply for support for further education.

But to support defectors' social adaptation it was necessary to guarantee them a basic standard of living. In fact, in spite of South Korea recognizing their academic merits and qualifications, the difficulties of finding employment were reinforced by the economic crisis South Korea went through at that time. The government introduced a revised proposal to support defectors in 1999 which was adopted in November and was enforced from 1 January, 2000. The proposal consisted of five principles.

First, the period of support for defectors' employment would be over two years. The period would apply for all defectors having arrived since December 1993 due to the high level of unemployment amongst these.

Secondly, consideration was taken to the rising number of old people among the defectors by applying the National Pensions Law to guarantee them a basic living standard. Defectors between 50 and 60 years of age who had joined the terms of the National Pensions Law for more than five years would receive a certain amount of pension rights.

Thirdly, to create employment, the government, local authorities and other public organizations would give priority to employing defectors with economic problems when public building projects were undertaken.

Fourthly, The Support Committee for North Korean Defectors' tasks were given clear expression through the legislation in supporting defectors to achieve a stable life in adapting to South Korean life.

Fifthly, the period of protecting the place of residence would be extended from two to five years to strengthen support for defectors (police protection would still be maintained over a period of two years).[17]

---

16 Park et al., ibid., pp. 15-17.
17 Lee, ibid., 1999, pp. 57-8, 61-5.

5.3 Adaptation of North Korean defectors to life in South Korea

Successive South Korean governments have obviously made great efforts to help North Korean defectors adapt to their new lives. However well intended, the outcome of the supportive measures were, as of 1995, discouraging. The study of defectors' adaptation to South Korean society published in 1996 by the scholar Park Jung Chul and his associates at the Research Institute for National Unification (now Korea Institute for National Unification) showed that among 561 defectors, 19 worked as officials, 13 at public companies, 24 at banks, four as doctors, one as a soldier, 203 as company employees and 44 in commerce. But the balance of some 253 defectors either ended up in some form of physical labour or were unemployed. They belonged to the poorest section of society.

A common hope for the defectors was to be well treated, to be well off materially and to live a comfortable life in South Korea but this was clearly a forlorn hope for many people. One example is Kim Hyông-dôk who defected in February 1996 but had not got a secure job. Instead, he worked as a newspaper delivery man or at a luggage centre for people moving. His difficulties even made him try to re-defect to China but he failed in this and was sentenced to prison.[18]

The South Korean scholar Han Man-gil records (1996) that other symptoms of difficulties experienced by defectors came in the form of loneliness, self-identity issues, feelings of guilt and stubborn and negative thoughts. Loneliness was their major difficulty. It was caused by the lack of opportunities to form personal relationships with South Koreans, problems with accepting the individualistic South Korean culture, a sense of economic inferiority, exclusiveness and unyielding negativity. Defectors received cultural shocks in South Korea due to the collectivistic, vertical and standardized way of life in North Korea that disabled them in adapting to change. Besides being a personal problem, defectors' difficulties had in the mid-1990s become both a social and national one. While recognizing defectors' difficulties, the South Korean scholar Lee Keumsoon (1999) even argues that most of them, while adapting themselves to society, are neither North nor South Koreans but what she refers to as "marginal men".

Her view is supported by the South Korean scholar Chôn U-t'aek (1999) writing that his research from 1997 showed that most defectors regarded themselves not as being from North or South Korea but as Koreans. Further evidence of their uncertainty is that 45 of 68 defectors investigated during the period 1994-1996 replied that they would support both North and South Korea if they would play each other in soccer games. A negative evaluation of ethnicity is made by the American scholar Grinker (1998), who writes that South Koreans, in spite of being constantly taught that their Northern brethren are of the same blood and ancestry as themselves, see North Korea as another nation and North Koreans as immigrants.[19] Such an opinion may be

---

18 Grinker, ibid., p. 242; Han, ibid., p. 216; Park et al., ibid., p. 8.
19 Chôn, "Namhan-e innûn t'alpukja-dûr-ûi simnijôk kaltûng-mith kû-e taehan haegyôl pangan", in T'ongil yôn'guwôn, *T'alpukja-ûi poho-mith kungnae chôgûng kaesôn pangan*

exaggerated but the opinion of defectors being people classed as being "in between" clearly resembles the division between first and second-class citizens in Germany and Yemen in the aftermaths of their 1990 unification processes.

Han Man-gil in 1996 analyzed defectors' adaptation to life in South Korea in terms of politics, the economy, socio-cultural life and the work place. The study was based on in-depth interviews with 20 defectors, of whom most had defected during the 1990s, but the total number of people involved was forty two. Defectors experienced difficulties in adapting to democratic politics. First, they were used to being passive in the face of the authoritarian political system in North Korea. Secondly, they had insufficient understanding of their individual rights and responsibilities, since the collectivistic system regarded individualism as immoral. Thirdly, they had insufficient understanding of the South's pluralistic democracy.

The following words relate succinctly to the first point: "Since North Koreans only have done things ordered by the monolithic system, the sense of independence and creativity is insufficient. While living in South Korea, I have noticed that having an independent attitude is especially important".

An equally succinct comment on the second point is: "Since you do as you are told to do in North Korea, it is possible to shift responsibility on another's shoulders. However, whether possible or not, in South Korea everyone has to be responsible on her own causing many inconvenient occasions. Sometimes I am even frightened".

Concerning the third point, it is obvious that defectors' opinions entirely differ from that of South Koreans: "In South Korea, people make their own assertions too much and take care only of their own matters making it difficult to establish the norm of evaluation". In addition, "South Korean politics move, like a sailing boat, in accordance with the wind. With one word, it is the same thing as markets being busy in the morning".

Characteristics of defectors' experience of the market economy was reflected in their passivity generated by the omnipotent role of the state in the planned economy. They suffered from insufficient understanding of such features of a market economy as the role of money and advance recognition of the greater economic gap between the two Koreas. Such knowledge created expectations of a better life in South Korea that were not easily delivered on which thus caused a great degree of frustration. Defectors expressed the view that South Korea was an egoistic society with a cruel market economy. They also anticipated that the economic gap will cause economic inequalities and social tensions in a reunified Korea. In other words, South Koreans will look down on inferior North Koreans and feel themselves superior, as is already often the case.[20]

Han also records that it was difficult for defectors to adapt to their new life because of differences in culture and values as well as psychological difficulties.

(Seoul: T'ongil yôn'guwôn, 1999), p. 53; Grinker, ibid., p. 250; Han, ibid., pp. 216, 221-2; Lee, ibid., 1999, pp. 52-3.

20 Han, ibid., pp. 224-8. The defectors' social background is not recorded. All quotations in this section were made by anonymous defectors.

Two remarks vividly describe their experiences: "South Koreans have a strong personality and their subjectivity is distinct. In particular, it is my impression that whatever they do they do not look for others' reactions but give their own beliefs". Also, "North Koreans have affection and a sense of duty between neighbours. But it seems that affection and the sense of duty is insufficient in South Korea due to excessive individualism".

Not only the individualistic life-style but also living alone in South Korea caused psychological troubles for defectors. One defector expressed this view:

> There were no troubles in North Korea since you only did as the ideological and political control told you to do. But since in South Korea you have to live among numerous complicated temptations there are many times when it is difficult to live only by your own will. There should be something to believe and follow mentally. Sometimes I have irresolute thoughts and even think sceptically about having come to South Korea. When I think about my suffering parents and brothers in North Korea, I feel pain.

Various concerns are expressed in the following account: "I am concerned how my marriage partner or parents will face me. I am also concerned that I may not adapt at work and get fired. Finally, if Korea reunifies, I am concerned how the issue of me and other defectors will be dealt with". The sense of loneliness becomes clear from this account: "I go around during the day and when entering the apartment at night in the dark the feeling of loneliness touches my bones at once".

Loneliness made some people become religious while others remarried or became homeless. In spite of common cultural characteristics, defectors had difficulties because of some cultural differences created by the division. In family life, defectors reacted at the importance of money in keeping the household and maintaining the position of women at home. They were also worried whether they could take care of their families and thought that parents generally showed an excessively laissez-faire attitude towards childrens' education and thereby neglected teaching them disciplined practices.

Defectors experienced difficulties in such fields as language, recognition of history and acquiring information. Specifically foreign loanwords, Chinese characters and work terminology caused problems. Defectors were not used to quickly acquiring information on their own so as to get on in society. They had problems with facing such popular phenomena as sexual issues, pop music and films.

The enthusiasm for education in South Korea caused problems, it was hard for the defectors and their children to adapt to competitiveness. The opinion was that school teachers possessed insufficient sincerity, neglected their pupils and made too little preparations for class. However, student defectors reportedly did not have any particular problems but parents and teachers had difficulties. This was noted particularly in courses such as English, history, economics and Chinese characters which were difficult. University students in particular felt alienated when studying in a different culture. The older defectors were also affected by the age difference which was a considerable obstacle for them.[21]

Defectors also had difficulties at work due to their attitude towards work and working culture, including the concept of efficiency. They expected that the state would underwrite work and people with high education expected to get work but that of course was often not the case. In addition, defectors had more work to do than they had had in North Korea, the hierarchy of the work place was more distinct and it was hard to adapt to the authoritarian and competitive atmosphere at work. The sense of personal responsibility was much stronger in South Korea and the division of labour far more distinct. As defectors, they suffered from a lack of social contacts which caused alienation. One defector said:

> This society is such in every respect but also companies are ruled by blood, school and regional ties. Yet, my company is a secure place to work at, but other places would be worse from this point of view. To distinguish such complicated human relations is the most difficult thing while living here.

Defectors lacked skills applicable in South Korea which caused them serious problems. One defector said:

> I majored in electrical engineering in North Korea. But since I learned skills equivalent to the level of the 1960s of South Korea, they are hardly useful. The basic skills should be useful but on the whole it can be said that the level of knowledge and techniques in North Korea are those of South Korea 20 to 30 years ago.

Another opinion was: "There are hardly any North Koreans who can work properly in South Korea. The only choice may be to work in physical labour or in service industry". However, it should be noted that North Korean workers reportedly were very diligent. They also had a sincere attitude and the quality was considered to be good thanks to, for instance, their high level of education. Defectors themselves asserted that their level of life power and diligence was worth world-wide recognition. Evidence for this assertion was that North Koreans at large-scale construction projects worked with their bodies due to the lack of capital and technology. In addition, North Korean logging workers endured working in the bitter cold in Siberia.

Considering defectors' experiences, North Koreans are expected to face confusion and troubles in a reunified Korea. Assuming that South Korea's democratic system will come to rule a unified country, North Koreans will experience the same difficulties as defectors so far have done, but to a degree that will possibly exceed all forecasts. Consequently, preparations for unification should be made by discovering the strengths and characteristics of defectors encouraging them to contribute to national development, generally.

It should be noted that in the socio-cultural field, the common culture, traditions, language, life style and the numerous family bands should be a catalyst for North

---

21 Han, ibid., pp. 228-230.

Koreans to adapt to the new conditions pertaining in a unified Korea.[22] Clearly, there are good sides of defectors that should be utilized for the greater national benefit. But it is unclear to what extent that will help in the light of the expected difficulties, from unity as well as due to such issues as competition over jobs between North and South Koreans.

The above study on defectors from 1996 was based on interviews through a questionnaire with 41 defectors followed by in-depth interviews. This number comprised around five per cent of the more than 800 defectors of that time. Due to their special position it was impossible to make a scientific selection among the whole group. Consequently, it is hard to say whether the selected defectors were representative. For instance, their educational level was higher than that of the 209 defectors in the investigation made by the Ministry of Unification in 1994.

Thirty-four of these 41 defectors had arrived during the 1990s. Seventeen of them were party members and 19 had family members who were party members; five were non-party-members. 35 defectors had completed university or high school studies and the majority were in their twenties and thirties. In North Korea, more than half of them had been workers (12), soldiers (11) or public officials (6). In South Korea, 20 defectors had office or technical skills but as many as 16 people were unemployed (two were students, two were self-employees and one was a soldier).[23]

The study investigated defectors' recognition and evaluation of South Korean society. The level of recognition was high. Based on ten variables of main characteristics in the fields of politics, economics and society including, for instance, the presidential system, the Board of Audit and Inspection, bargain sales, stock investments, singing rooms and HIV/aids, the average levels of recognition were 82.4, 83.2 and 75.6 per cent, respectively.

Voting, membership in social and voluntary organizations and donation were investigated to find out defectors' sense of belonging to South Korea. 68.3 per cent of them voted; the remainder did not vote or were not eligible for voting at the time of elections. In this respect, they proportionally exceeded most ordinary voters: their will to participate in politics was strong. On the other hand, 63.4 per cent of them did not take part in any social organization at all whereas only 9.8 per cent were members in more than three organizations. 46.3 per cent of them had not made donations and 29.3 per cent of the others had only made donations once or twice. Clearly, defectors were relatively passive in terms of social participation.

Concerning defectors' expectations of South Korea, 44.7 per cent of them had desired freedom and 18.4 per cent opportunities to display their own skills. These figures indicate defectors' positive view of these particular characteristics of South Korea. However, the two Koreas' different social systems made it difficult for

---

22 Han, ibid., pp. 230-232, 237-38. "Common culture" refers to traditional culture which means that it does not contradict the above data on cultural differences generated by national division.

23 Park et al., ibid., pp. 59-60. This study records on p. 6 the number of defectors as 616, as of August 1996. It is unclear what explains the inconsistencies.

defectors to adapt to life in South Korea. Yet, 85.4 per cent of them supported the principle that you are paid according to the level of work. But 70.7 per cent of defectors thought that the gap between the rich and poor in South Korea was a serious issue. Defectors thus recognized the South's capitalist system but were critical of social inequality (which is also a controversial issue amongst South Koreans).

In the case of life attitudes, defectors believed that South Koreans in terms of diligence, creativity, educational policy and satisfaction about work exceeded conditions in North Korea. On the other hand, North Koreans were better than South Koreans when concepts such as patriotism, family ties and cooperative spirit were concerned.

When the strengths and defects of the two states were compared, freedom (41.5 per cent) and being paid according to level of work (26.8 per cent) were regarded as the best features of South Korea. The sense of community (34.1 per cent) was seen as at its best in North Korea. Egoism and individualism (34.1 per cent) were regarded as the primary defects of South Korea.

Conformity and political control (43.9 per cent) was the main defect in North Korea. Defectors regarded mutual support and the restoration of a sense of community (35.9 per cent) as the most important task for South Korea in preparing for unification. Thereafter came economic development and the desire for unification (both 15.4 per cent).[24] In spite of division, homogeneity was thus important also for these defectors but the data does not explain whether this is a general view amongst the North Korean population.

Defectors did not get the feeling that South Koreans welcomed them. They thought that South Koreans' main attitudes towards them were cold-heartedness (33.3 per cent) and antagonism (25.6 per cent). The study evaluated defectors' integration on the basis of self-esteem and life satisfaction. In this respect, the outcome was positive. 70 per cent of the respondents expressed confidence with their own abilities. 51.3 per cent responded that they felt confident with their lives while 30.8 per cent felt some degree of confidence. 79.5 per cent of the defectors had plans for the future whereas 72.5 per cent were satisfied with their present lives.

Nonetheless, defectors were dissatisfied in other respects. From an economic point of view, 56.1 per cent responded that life had become better in South Korea but as many as 31.7 per cent thought that it had become worse than in North Korea. More significantly, in terms of social treatment, 48.7 per cent thought that they were worse off in South Korea than they had been in North Korea, in contrast to 31.8 per cent who thought that life had improved in this respect.

Like the study by the scholar Han Man-gil, the study showed that defectors faced difficulties at work and in social life. 63.4 per cent of the defectors responded that marriage was the major difficulty, against only 19.5 per cent not regarding it as a special problem. It was followed by language, which 53.6 per cent regarded as a difficulty but as many as 41.4 per cent did not. Opinions on getting employment and working life were roughly equally divided: 43.9 per cent found the latter hard

---

24 Park et al., ibid., pp. 61-71.

against 46.3 per cent not regarding it as a special difficulty. With regard to working life, the figures were 36.6 per cent versus 34.4 per cent. 65.8 per cent of defectors found harmonizing with South Koreans easy, against only 16.9 per cent having the opposite opinion. Whereas these figures give a somewhat mixed picture of defectors' integration with life in South Korea, they found life difficult in particular due to South Koreans' lack of interest in and inhospitality towards them (36.8 per cent). This, allied with a sense of guilt towards their families in the North (26.3 per cent), their lack of relatives and friends (23.7 per cent) and their inability to find relevant jobs (15.8 per cent), represented a not inconsiderable burden for the group.

Most of the defectors who had got work (61 per cent) still worked at their first job. This may seem positive, but characteristics of work (38.5 per cent) and personal relations (23.1 per cent) in particular caused difficulties (26 respondents). Defectors considered earning money as the most important factor (24 per cent) in terms of adapting to life in South Korea, followed by accumulating knowledge and forming deep human relations (each 20 per cent). Defectors had the closest ties with their family and acquaintances (29.3 per cent), followed by officials from the government and social organizations (22.2 per cent) and other defectors (19.4 per cent). They (36 respondents) were thereby heavily influenced by such people.

Due to the differences in ideology and social systems North and South Korea have developed linguistic differences, in spite of previous linguistic and ethnic homogeneity. Fifty-nine per cent of the defectors had experienced difficulties in speaking with South Koreans. Linguistic differences was given as the main reason (52.4 per cent) followed by different ways of thinking (28.6 per cent; 20 respondents).[25] Cultural and linguistic homogeneity had clearly been undermined by national division.

The study analyzed defectors' integration with the social system and life style as well as how they were mentally affected by their new lives in South Korea. The above data implies that defectors adapted rather well to South Korea's social system. But the statements, "I reject people speaking ill of Kim Il Sung or North Koreans" and, "I do not feel well when people speak ill of North Koreans. As usually, my feelings towards Americans are not good" show that their internalized Kim Il Sungism and anti-Americanism were deep-rooted and hard to shake off.

In adapting to life style, there were several problems for defectors due to social rather than political or economic circumstances. The use of English loanwords in South Korea caused defectors some difficulty. Defectors' deficient knowledge of Chinese characters made it difficult to read newspapers and absorb other information media. The national heterogeneity caused problems with daily things, in particular the relationship between the sexes which had changed due to the division: North Korea has remained a patriarchy whereas women's positions are relatively stronger in South Korea. The differences become clear in the statements, "The difficulty in

---

25 Park et al., ibid., pp. 72-83. Multiple choices were apparently permitted for reasons of difficulties of living in South Korea since percentages exceed 100 (p. 78). What "linguistic differences" refer to is not explained on p. 83.

family life is that relations between men and women are different. In North Korea, men decide everything and women are obedient. In South Korea, the wife has the economic power and interferes in husband's doings" and, "The house-holder exercises all authority in North Korea". That defectors said that they had many difficulties at work also showed how difficult they found it generally in adapting to southern society.

The main reason for their enumerated difficulties was the heterogeneity caused by national division. Also the different school curricula and differences in basic knowledge made integration with life in South Korea difficult. This becomes clear from the following statement:

> I entered university but quit after only one year. As in the case of English and Chinese characters, there were also during history classes many people I heard about for the first time. For instance, I had never learnt about such persons as Sin Ch'ae-ho during history lectures in North Korea.[26]

Another supportive statement is, "I do not know even elementary school's problems. I lack confidence since education is computerized and mechanized. My knowledge is insufficient". Finally:

> I receive vocational education. I am repairing cars but it was far more difficult to understand the terminology than to learn the skills. I could understand the lectures only after two months had passed. Consequently, it is hard to finish education within the same time as South Koreans and take the qualification test.

This lack of basic knowledge not only causes difficulties in daily conversations but makes it hard to associate with South Koreans and also renders defectors unable to use their special knowledge or techniques acquired in North Korea.[27]

Whereas the above data to some extent shows that defectors adapted rather well to life in South Korea, in reality they faced psychological troubles, as this statement shows:

> I had never fought in North Korea after drinking liquors. I was gentle. But after my defection, I have become sensitive. When I drink liquors, I quarrel pointlessly with people besides me and I have even gone to the police station. But there have, of course, not been great problems for me on such occasions.

In addition, "When the police accompanied me, everyone treated me well and I began expecting that everything would go well. But when the period of protection ended, I was completely deserted. Afterwards, no one treated me. I felt really lonely". Finally, "It is hard to take part in activities by school groups. There are differences in age and great differences in ways of thinking".

---

26 Sin Ch'ae-ho was a scholar of Korean history active in the early 20th century. From Lee (ibid., 1984, pp. 336-37, 370).
27 Park et al., ibid., pp. 85-8.

Besides these opinions, one defector said in 1996 that, although he/she had arrived in 1989, he/she felt like being a South Korean only to 50 per cent, a view strikingly similar to the South Korean scholar Lee Keumsoon's reference to "marginal men". Many defectors said that in areas where large numbers of them lived, they drank liquour and resorted to outrageous acts and thereby experienced problems with the authorities.

In contrast to other aspects of integration, the extent to which defectors were mentally affected varied depending on their background. Not surprisingly, defectors who had got work were more confident and content with life than those who were unemployed, although many of the former lacked confidence in their qualifications. The main reason why defectors felt alienated was South Koreans' critical views of them. Defectors thought that, "South Koreans treat defectors as second-class or inferior citizens" and said that South Koreans' attitudes towards them changed when they told them their birthplaces.

Such attitudes affect several areas of life. In the case of marriage, one opinion was, "When I was to marry, I experienced many difficulties due to resistance from the parents of my wife's home". Another example is the statement:

> There is one person I now mix with. I am thinking about marriage but have not yet been able to say that I am from North Korea. This is because of my experience of having to separate from a girl I got acquainted with because of her family's resistance towards marriage with a North Korean.

Defectors sometimes got upset:

> When communist guerillas came to Kangnûng, work colleagues asked, "Will you not go to meet your friends". That person must have joked but I felt enormous frustration. Every time an incident related to North Korea takes place, the business firm uses to call and ask me. I feel that I am, as usually, treated as a North Korean.

The sense of inferiority becomes clear also from this statement: "When saying that I am from North Korea people looked strangely at me. I disliked this and said that I just was from China. Then they showed an attitude of contempt".

Other examples of difficulties encountered are: "South Koreans say that 'I have left my family' and reject me. How difficult would it have been to come abandoning your family?" and, "When I got employed, people were critical and said 'a person who has betrayed once betrays often'". It is worth adding what the American scholar Grinker (1998) writes about defectors that, "Many are distressed by what they perceive to be a general South Korean view that nothing in the north is worth preserving".[28] Whether true or not, such cynical contempt only reinforces antagonism and distrust between the two Koreas.

Given the above statements, it is hardly surprising that the main obstacle for defectors to settle in South Korea was the contempt and discrimination shown

---

28 Grinker, ibid., p. 227; Park et al., ibid., pp. 89-91.

towards them by South Koreans. Such attitudes undermined the impact of successive government's support for defectors and their own will to adapt to South Korean society.

Due to the different levels of compensation provided to defectors depending on their time of arrival, a sense of psychological deprivation has been created amongst them. But what has caused even more general dissatisfaction is that, depending on their background and social position, defectors got different payments and were differently treated in society. The best paid defectors were those who had belonged to the vested interest rights groups in North Korea and supported the oppressive political system.

An illustration is this statement by a defector:

> Those people who were well-off in North Korea get good treatment also in South Korea. There are also people who brought with them foreign exchange when they arrived, which is the same thing as having stolen money from the North Korean people. High-ranking North Korean officials have all exploited the people, but the South Korean government's treatment of them is much better. If Korea reunifies, there may be North Koreans who will retaliate against high-ranking defectors.

This view concurs with the data on fears for retaliation in Chapter 3. There were few people or organizations supporting defectors to help them to mentally adapt to South Korean society, which reinforced some of these difficulties. The importance of such support is clear from this statement: "The house-owner where I live has taken good care of me, which has been of great help. I think it is necessary that one important person understands and takes care well rather than that many people are doing well". The consequences of the lack of social contacts are expressed through this statement: "Lacking bonds and connections is the greatest problem in social life". Finally, it should be noted that Park and his associates record that some defectors on Liberation Day 15 August, 1996 performed the play "Father's Land" in an attempt to let South Koreans know about the full extent of their mental adaptation to their new lives and their internalized mental conditions in South Korea. To make their problems known through theatre and thus seeking to solve them in this way was regarded as an act of particular significance.[29]

The Ministry of Unification (MoU) published in December 1998 a report on defectors' living conditions. The criteria for successful social settlements were employment rate, monthly average income, presently owned property and the level of satisfaction with settlement support and life in South Korea. The survey involved defectors who had arrived since 1990, of which 188 responded. The report showed that 97 people (51.6 per cent) had found employment and that 28 people (14.9 per cent) were attending schools above junior college level. The other 63 people (29.4 per cent) were unemployed. Most of the unemployed received their living costs from settlement funds (41.1 per cent), day work (24.2 per cent) or support funds from

---

29 Park et al., ibid., pp. 91-3, 116; Lee et al., ibid., 2000, p. 53.

religious organizations (14.2 per cent), etc. As in the 1996 study referred to earlier, this study showed too that defectors belonged to the low-income classes.

Most defectors were badly off both in terms of income and property but still 61.3 per cent expressed the view that they were satisfied with their new life in South Korea. In the author's view, this apparent paradox could be explained by defectors' dissatisfaction with life in North Korea rather than with their newly won satisfaction with life in South Korea.

The main reasons of discontent were indicated as being the lack of support funds (64.7 per cent) and difficulties finding employment (35.3 per cent). In settling in South Korea, defectors' main obstacles were earning money (30.9 per cent), finding employment (24.2 per cent) and feelings of loneliness (18.3 per cent). Establishing contacts with South Koreans gained a lower score with "only" 14.3 per cent, whereas language and life style only received 5.5 per cent and 3.6 per cent, respectively.[30]

Also a study on woman defectors by the Women's Association for Peace, published in March 1999, showed that economic difficulties were the main obstacle for successful integration. The main reasons for these difficulties were unemployment (44.1 per cent) or deficient skills (17.6 per cent). In fact, unemployment was a major problem at this time: a survey made in fall 1998 by a South Korean parliamentarian showed that, among 168 defectors who had arrived during the 1990s, 39.2 per cent were unemployed whereas only 19.6 per cent were company employees. The total number of defectors who had secure jobs such as company employees and public officials was just 23 per cent. A survey conducted by the MoU in the same year did not differ very much: the unemployment ratio among defectors was only slightly lower at 34 per cent. The recorded figures are only marginally lower than the 1996 statistics.

Unemployment had risen substantially as of 30 July, 2000: 360 (66.1 per cent) of the 545 defectors between 18 and 65 years of age who responded (of 603 people included) in the investigation made by The Association of Support for North Korean Defectors were unemployed. Only 10 people (1.8 per cent) had professional jobs while 100 people (18.3 per cent) worked as clerical staff or soldiers. Another 51 people (9.4 per cent) worked in commerce or were self-employed (23 were students). This figure could include a few defectors who were successful entertainers or ran popular restaurants. Unsurprisingly, most defectors still belonged to the lower-income classes.

As of December 2000, among the more than 200 members of The Association of Support for North Korean Defectors only around 70 had a job. But since defectors who had a job did not join the association, these statistics do not give a complete overview. In any event, lacking employment was the main reason for defectors' psychological tensions which even made some people long after the more secure life they had enjoyed in the North.

Data from this time confirms the recorded difficulties of defectors. Their first experience of South Korea was that they had arrived in an entirely different society.

---

30 Lee, ibid., 1999, pp. 54-5; Lee et al., ibid., 2000, p. 38.

Such a situation disabled them during their first two years making them feel that they were living with a different type of people albeit of the same race. To overcome such new experiences as the loud noise made by itinerant traders in the mornings took around two years. During these years, defectors were reluctant to go out and meet other people. Only after four or five years had passed could they mix well enough with South Koreans to go out to drink alcohol or to sing. After five or six years, defectors felt that they had become more like South Koreans and began to enjoy emotional stability.[31]

It caused much stress for defectors who had lived in a monolithical political system to integrate into a pluralistic South Korean society. They felt confusion when confronting such things as political strife, collective egoism and numerous social organizations with opposing opinions. Tensions and struggles between politicians, in particular, created uncertainty. Defectors even feared that they as a group could be used for political purposes. To face numerous foreign loanwords and a decadent culture caused confusion and shock. The rising gap between rich and poor people made defectors acutely feel a sense of social disharmony.

Together with finding work, marriage was one of defectors' main problems. Not least since it was hard to marry with South Koreans, less than 10 per cent of those who had arrived after 1995 had married; women preferred men with stable jobs and men, refined women. Defectors could hardly meet these requirements resulting in a trend whereby they tended to marry each other. Through not being married, defectors felt a considerable sense of stress. They also became lonely through living alone and could not live a stable life, often wasting money.

Defectors often had a guilty conscience by feeling that they had left their families behind in North Korea and thereby causing them political damage. This was the most annoying thing for defectors, making them want to bring their families into South Korea. There were also many occasions when expectations of life in South Korea were not fulfilled, which made defectors regret their defections and suffer even more psychologically.

The difficulties in adapting to life in the South were reinforced by South Koreans' prejudices towards North Korean defectors. Firstly, many South Koreans thought that the defectors were criminals, although defectors explained their reasons for defecting. This was a great obstacle for defectors generally, in terms of establishing trust among South Koreans.

Secondly, many South Koreans believed that defectors were different from themselves since they had lived in a socialist state and had taken orders from above. This made them think that defectors were lazy. There was also an opinion that defectors could not support themselves and that they showed an egoistic attitude. Such prejudices made it difficult for The Association of Support for North Korean Defectors to acquire an office.

---

31 Lee, ibid., 1999, pp. 55; Lee et al., ibid., 2000, pp. 38-41, 46-7, 54-5; Pak, *Nambuk munhwa kyoryu*, October 2000, p. 58.

Defectors also faced unequal social treatment since their careers and qualifications were not recognized in the South. Unlike South Koreans, they could not benefit from the number of years of service and instead got lower positions at work places. Defectors who were office workers, administrators or specialists in North Korea often ended up in work below their educational level. Such discrimination was hard for them to endure and made them lose their sense of self-identity and self-respect. This loss applied also to defectors such as party members and university graduates. In South Korea, self-identity at work was instead affected by such negative notions as being a defector or not being able to speak good English.

Unsurprisingly, there were defectors who could not adapt to life in South Korea due to their inability to psychologically overcome the structural obstacles. These people suffered from difficulties such as the feeling of being helpless and meaningless. The feeling of being helpless was, generally speaking, caused by defectors jumping from being employed to unemployed during their second year in South Korea, that is after the protection period had ended. In such cases, defectors generally became dependent on charity organizations. The general sense of life being meaningless resulted from regretting defections and feeling that adapting to life in South Korea would be a meaningless exercise. In addition to such feelings, defectors could lay the blame for their inability to adapt on the South Korean government's failures or on South Korean's improper treatment of them and prejudices towards them. In fact, many defectors had a bad image of South Koreans, whom they regarded as manipulative and arrogant.[32] Such impressions could only have reinforced defectors' difficulties.

Korea Institute for National Unification (KINU) published, in 2003, a comprehensive study on North Korean defectors' adaptation to life in South Korea. 778 of 2,510 selected defectors replied. Roughly 70 per cent of them had lived less than two years in South Korea. 469 of 775 respondents (60.5 per cent) were satisfied with life in South Korea but only 52 (6.7 per cent) were dissatisfied. 116 of 276 respondents (42 per cent) were satisfied with their work and only 55 (19.9 per cent) dissatisfied (others were "usual" in both cases). The low number of respondents was due to the high unemployment among defectors.

Defectors' health status tells a somewhat different story of their new lives: 335 of 773 respondents (43.3 per cent) replied that they suffered bad health in contrast to only 169 (21.9 per cent) who said it was good (34.8 per cent were "usual or average"). The largest number of defectors, that is 301 of 682 respondents (44.1 per cent), had expected a free life before their arrival.

While in South Korea, 201 of 697 respondents (28.8 per cent) replied that material affluence was what they most needed, whereas before arrival only 95 (13.9 per cent) had expected such affluence.[33] The different values are almost certainly explained by defectors' economic difficulties in the South.

---

32 Lee et al., ibid., 2000, pp. 48-52, 55-6.
33 Lee et al., *Pukhan it'al chumin chôgûng silt'ae yôn'gu* (Seoul: T'ongil yôn'guwôn, 2003), pp. 158-160, 164-7.

Also this survey confirmed defectors' economic difficulties: 458 of 737 respondents (62.1 per cent) had no regular job (138 were students). 432 of 740 respondents (58.4 per cent) replied that their income was insufficient against only 96 (13 per cent) who thought that it was sufficient (28.6 per cent "usual"). Among those who did have a job, only 88 of 244 respondents (36.1 per cent) worked regularly as against 136 (55.7 per cent) working irregularly. The main reason why 61 of 191 respondents (31.9 per cent) had irregular jobs was their lack of skills. Lack of skills was also a main problem at work for 61 of 250 respondents (24.4 per cent), followed by personal relations (35; 14 per cent). On the other hand, 72 respondents (28.8 per cent) had no problems. 114 of 252 respondents (45.3 per cent) replied that vocational education had been helpful in getting employment and 69 (27.4 per cent) not helpful (69; 27.4 per cent "usual").

More men (41.4 per cent) had a regular job than women (26.8 per cent). In the case of irregular jobs, the figure for women was 68 per cent against 48.3 per cent for men. More defectors below 30 had irregular jobs than those above 40, among which regular and irregular jobs were equally divided. As many as 141 of 264 defectors (53.4 per cent) replied that they got their present job through their own efforts and 39 (14.8 per cent) through people they knew individually. Only 68 people (25.7 per cent) got work through institutes and organizations that worked to provide employment ("others" 16; 6.1 per cent), However, by basing the survey on present work these statistics neglect the fact that defectors' first work experience probably was obtained through public support. 363 of 756 respondents (48.1 per cent) replied that they mixed well with neighbours and work colleagues against 95 (12.6 per cent) who did not mix well (298; 39.4 per cent "usual"). In particular, youth and people in their twenties replied that they mixed well.

The picture was different in terms of adapting to South Korean society: 350 of 769 respondents (45.5 per cent) were negative against 123 (16 per cent) being positive. On the other hand, 296 people (38.5 per cent) responded "usual" which, along with those who replied affirmatively, gives a far more favourable view of how defectors adapted. Youth and people in their twenties and sixties adapted better than those in their forties and fifties. Defectors who had stayed less than a year were, along with those residing 3-5 years, largely positive whereas people staying 7-8 years were the most negative.

230 of 708 respondents (32.5 per cent) replied that it took more than three years to adapt to South Korean society, whereas 139 (19.6 per cent) replied around three years. On the other hand, 228 respondents (32.2 per cent) gave the required time period as six months to one year. Individual characteristics and inclination clearly affected the ability to adapt.

The main reasons for not adapting were that they had great expectations without making their own efforts (257 of 682 respondents; 37.7 per cent), uncertain targets for quality of life (154; 22.6 per cent) and insufficient education for adaptation (103; 15.1 per cent). Among factors making social adaptation difficult, the main reasons were defectors' own passive attitudes and lack of skills (266 of 689; 38.6 per cent),

South Koreans' inhospitality and prejudice towards them (157; 22.8 per cent) and economic difficulties (106; 15.4 per cent).

It is worth pointing out here that the South Korean scholar Kim Soo Am (2004) notes that for defectors' successful integration into the South's society, South Koreans must above all abandon their prejudice towards them and help them with an open mind.[34]

In spite of the perception of lack of skills, 426 of 666 respondents (63.9 per cent) replied that the required time period of vocational education for employment was six months or one year, which indicates either an underestimation of themselves or a reasonable ability to acquire new skills. In spite of the common language, 355 of 679 respondents (52.3 per cent) replied that it took three years or more before speaking without inconveniences. In sharp contrast, only 173 (25.4 per cent) replied six months or a year. The required periods for forming personal relations without inconveniencies were similar: 343 of 664 respondents (51.7 per cent) replied three years or more against 193 (29.1 per cent) six months or a year. It was more difficult to overcome alienation, frustration and loneliness: for 360 of 671 respondents (53.7 per cent) it took three years or more against 203 (30.2 per cent) who needed six months or a year to integrate into society.

387 of 753 respondents (51.4 per cent) replied that South Koreans showed lack of interest towards defectors but 309 (41 per cent) replied that they were friendly; 57 (7.5 per cent) said that they were hostile. On the other hand, views were divided on South Koreans' lack of interest in defectors; 248 of 754 respondents (32.8 per cent) answered affirmatively and 231 (30.6 per cent) negatively (275; 36.5 per cent "usual"). According to 232 of 759 respondents (30.6 per cent), South Koreans' attitudes contributed positively towards social integration, to be compared with negative replies from 177 people (23.4 per cent) and "usual" 350 (46.1 per cent).

In the case of reasons for prejudice towards defectors, 263 of 656 respondents (40.1 per cent) replied it was because they were from North Korea whereas 181 (27.6 per cent) said it was due to different ways of thinking. Contrary to what one would expect from the investigated issues, only 65 (9.9 per cent) pointed out different ways of talking and 38 (5.8 per cent) deficient skills. While the opinion among defectors was that marriage with South Korean men was beneficial for social integration, the divorce rate among North Korean women marrying South Korean men was high. In fact, there was an opinion that cultural differences could make marriages difficult.

Getting employment was the main difficulty for defectors in terms of social integration, which made them wish for better employment protection. Among 737 respondents, 306 (41.5 per cent) replied that they were unemployed whereas the number of employed was 293 (39.8 per cent); 138 (18.7 per cent) were students. Most of the 141 working defectors were either company employees (87) or self-employed (38). It should be noted that employed defectors include 152 (17.3 per

---

34 Kim, "T'alpukja munje-ûi taeûng-gwa chôngch'aek taean: choyonghan wegyo t'onghan ch'egyejôk poho sigûphada", *T'ongil Han'guk* (2004), 9, p. 44; Lee et al., ibid., 2003, pp. 167-171, 177-79, 182-83, 193-98. Kim does not elaborate on how to implement his view.

cent) unspecified "others". Unemployment was 35.8 per cent among male defectors but 47.6 per cent among women defectors.

A major reason for unemployment was reported as being due to deficient skills: 122 of 510 respondents (23.9 per cent) replied in this way whereas high or low age received 84 replies (16.5 per cent). 60 respondents (11.8 per cent) pointed out deficiencies in government arrangement of jobs. Since non-specified "others" received 173 replies (33.9 per cent), it was apparently difficult for defectors to point to a single reason indicating that there were probably several reasons contributing to their situations.

334 of 760 respondents (43.9 per cent) thought that the curricula in North Korea was not helpful in adapting to life in South Korea whereas 248 (32.6 per cent) thought that it was (178; 23.4 per cent "usual"). Among those who had studied at university level, 55.9 per cent said that the curriculum was beneficial in contrast to only 26.8 per cent who said it was not.

The longer the period of stay the more positive defectors became about their own curriculum. 313 of 732 respondents (42.7 per cent) expressed the view that their work experiences from the North did not benefit social integration in contrast to 230 (31.4 per cent) saying that they did (189; 25.8 per cent "usual"). However, many defectors who had stayed more than two years replied affirmatively.[35] Similarities at work may also facilitate development of closer human contacts.

701 of 775 respondents had received training at Hanawôn. 438 of 695 respondents (63 per cent) made a positive evaluation of the training's contribution to social integration but only 68 (9.8 per cent) a negative one (189; 27.2 per cent "normal"). In particular, 198 of 629 respondents (31.5 per cent) appreciated the provision of information on South Korean society and 163 (25.9 per cent) work information and skills training. However, 228 of 649 respondents (35.1 per cent) pointed out the organization of training as Hanawôn's main weakness followed by 151 (23.3 per cent) pointing out insufficient training on desired techniques and skills.

School education is a problem for most youths due to the different school systems. The disruption caused by the food crisis to schools in the North and the period of time spent in China before defecting is a key aspect here. Consequently, educational levels do not match up with their South Korean counterparts, more often than not resulting in North Korean youths have to attend lower classes than their age would indicate. The following anonymous account by a defector illustrates some of the difficulties encountered:

> I don't even know how to deal with English, history and social problems, in particular English. It is impossible for me without having taken the middle qualification examination to go directly to the university qualification examination. To pass, it is insufficient with only what you have learnt at educational institutes. Only if you have an extra teacher can you easily understand to a certain degree. The second problem is history which I am unfamiliar with. I did not study Korean history in North Korea and do not know it yet, in spite of having studied it for more than one year. I don't know about Tan'gun and Kyebaek

---

35 Lee et al., ibid., 2003, pp. 183-88, 190-193, 205-207, 209, 267.

> so when the question who Kyebaek was was asked at the educational institute the other students used to stare at me.[36] Although the teacher used expressions common in South Korea and I did not know, the reaction was, "Don't you know even that?".
>
> Since I do not even know easy things which the other students know, there are many times when I feel depressed. I do not know the names of tea sorts and names of old cakes. For instance, when the teacher spoke about Thikho I did not know while the other students laughed. When I asked what it is, the teacher said in front of the other students in a way as, "You don't have to know that". I felt offended by not knowing, while the other students just laughed. Consequently, due to such experiences I lose self-confidence and often stay quiet during classes. Somehow I feel alienated and think that the situation should not be like this. For fear of becoming a focus for laughter, I stay quiet.

Both Korean and world history are difficult for youth defectors. Students learn basic things about continents, but not the history of different countries. They do not study it until the fifth class of high-school. The consequences of this are revealed in this account: "Such subjects as society are the most difficult. When the teacher mentions some region, students roughly know but I do not. It is most difficult to understand when the teacher mentions a region".

In the case of students attending the Educational Institute for Qualification Examinations they have to pay school fees themselves making studies difficult. This is clear from the following account:

> I was tired from work and did not come to school often. Since I often was late, students got a somewhat bad impression of North Korean students. To be honest, North Korean children on the contrary, are pure and the best at the Educational Institute for Qualification Examinations. In contrast to South Korean children, they do not smoke either. The recognition of North Korean students at the institute is rather better than for the South Korean students.[37]

The accounts show that defectors faced difficulties at school but they also possessed qualities that should facilitate social integration.

While the overall position of North Korean defectors in South Korea from these general characteristics and the comparatively few accounts should not be generalized; it is indisputable that the vast majority of them have experienced difficulties. On the other hand, it cannot be denied that the 2003 study shows that defectors are receptive and that differences caused by national division can be overcome with time, although the low response ratio raises the question of how representative the survey is of defectors' opinions.

The empirical material does not tell us whether any defectors had had socio-cultural contacts or had met South Koreans in advance, but the possibility that such meetings took place in China cannot be excluded. Yet, the defectors' position in South

---

36 Kyebaek is an officer from the Paekche Kingdom (18 B.C.-660). From Lee (*A New History*, 1984, p. 66).

37 Lee et al., ibid., 2003, pp. 211-213, 234-37.

Korean society clearly shows that the perceived positive impact of socio-cultural contacts on inter-Korean relations is undermined, albeit it is unclear to what degree, by the two Koreas' different political and economic systems. In fact, such systems affect Koreans' daily lives more than any other contacts do and will continue to do so prior to unification. On the other hand, it is impossible to develop closer contacts without expanding human exchanges: as we have seen, German unification was facilitated by "value integration" that was created thanks to the expansion of human exchanges. Thus, there is no alternative to continue receiving and taking good care of North Korean defectors in South Korea in an effort to improve relations.

The most desirable change in the defectors' issue is to transform Koreans' attitudes: they must learn more about each other through contacts and realize that both sides have to give and take and live peacefully together. But this is easier said than done: many South Koreans may think that the South already has enough problems to take care of and do not have to also take care of North Koreans. For North Koreans, improved advance knowledge of South Korea may facilitate social integration. But as long as the situation in North Korea does not significantly improve, hopes for a better life will motivate further defections. Defectors' situations in South Korea imply that the difficulties in achieving "human unity" in Korea are at least as big as those experienced in Germany following on unification.

5.4 Humanitarian aid from South to North Korea

As we saw in Chapter 3, South Korea has, since the mid-1990s, provided significant amounts of humanitarian aid to North Korea. The appropriateness of such aid appears in the 1991 Basic Agreement's "Supplementary Agreement on Implementation and Observance of Exchanges and Cooperation between North and South Korea" of September 1992 that contains the clause "Solving humanitarian issues". It says, among other things:

> North and South Korea should, on the basis of humanitarianism and common-fellowship, help each other when natural calamities and other misfortunes take place in either state. They should provide for convenient transfer of the remains of and the disposal of the articles left by the deceased among dispersed families and relatives.

In fact, already in 1995 the South Korean government provided 150,000 tons of domestic rice in direct aid to North Korea which had requested food aid. After an agreement on deliveries had been reached through inter-governmental talks held in June in Beijing, the rice was delivered by boat in, notably, unmarked bags from South to North Korea between June and October. The cost of the delivery amounted to US$ 232m which was financed through The Fund for Inter-Korean Cooperation.[38]

---

38 Cho, ibid., 1996, p. 18; Choi et al., *Nambukhan nongôp kyoryu hyômnyôk pangan yôn'gu* (Seoul: T'ongil yôn'guwôn, 2000), pp. 52, 53; Chung, *The Role of South Korea's NGOs*, 2003, p. 83. The quotation is from Cho.

International organizations involved in providing humanitarian assistance to North Korea included, as of 1996, the International Federation of the Red Cross (IFRC), the United Nations Childrens' Emergency Fund (UNICEF), the Food and Agricultural Organization (FAO) and the World Food Programme (WFP). Through their aid to flood victims they exerted considerable influence on the South Korean government's policies towards North Korea by making it more difficult to provide aid as a way of improving relations. Nonetheless, in 1996, 3,409 tons of mixed grains and 203 tons of powdered milk for children were provided as South Korean government aid to the North through the WFP and UNICEF, to a value of US$ 3m.

In 1997, South Korean food aid rose dramatically in scale to an amount of US$ 26.7m. An additional delivery of 18,241 tons of mixed grains, 50,000 tons of maize and 10.8 million tons of powdered milk were also delivered via the WFP and UNICEF. The South Korean government also provided financial support for deliveries of the UNDP and the FAO. In 1998, food aid consisting of 30,000 tons of maize and 10,000 tons of wheat flour reached a value of US$ 11m and was delivered via the WFP. In 1999, aid to a sum of US$ 28.3m was delivered directly by the South Korean government for the first time since 1995: direct aid was considered a better way to improve relations. 155,000 tons of fertilizer was the main product involved in the aid package. Deliveries of fertilizers rose to a value of US$ 80m, as of September 2000, and the total quantity to 300,000 tons. The total value of government aid thus reached US$ 381m for the years 1995-2000 (cf. p. 66). Meanwhile, aid changed character from food stuffs to fertilizers to help in raising agricultural productivity.

At the second inter-Korean ministerial talks held in September 2000, South Korea agreed to provide 300,000 tons of foreign rice and 200,000 tons of maize to a value of US$ 90m as loans to be financed through The Fund for Inter-Korean Cooperation according to the first commercial government transaction (statistics for 2000 end in September). It was also decided that 100,000 tons of maize would be delivered freely through the WFP.[39]

The Korean National Red Cross (KNRC) became in September 1995, the first and, in practice, the only civilian organization to provide humanitarian aid to North Korea; all other non-governmental organizations (NGOs) had to work through the KNRC. One reason for this was that direct assistance had been delayed by such incidents as the hoisting of the North Korean flag on a South Korean ship transporting food to the North, the detention of the crew on the South Korean ship *Samson Venus* on the basis of crew members having taken pictures of Ch'ôngjin port and the repatriation issue of the crew of the kidnapped South Korean ship *Woosung*. However, more important was that the South Korean authorities wanted to prevent contacts with North Korea and outside competition in providing aid.

Consequently, antagonism and conflict between the government and the NGOs, of which most were closely related to religious organizations, were created. A problem was that since the KNRC had delivered aid through the IFRC who had only one official for monitoring food aid, it could not be confirmed whether it was

---

39 Cho, ibid., 1996, p. 32; Choi et al., ibid., pp. 52-5, 67-8.

appropriately distributed to North Korean citizens. In addition, since the North Korean government controlled most of the food aid, it often happened that famine-stricken regions did not receive any food causing suspicions that it was diverted for military use. Finally, criticism was directed towards the North Korean government when it built the extravagant Kumsusan Memorial Palace to commemorate Kim Il Sung after his death in 1994. Resources were directed away from alleviation of the suffering people, creating difficulties for the then Kim Young Sam government who wished to send aid to the North.[40]

At this time, aid consisted mainly of food stuffs and daily necessities. Civilian aid was interrupted by the September 1996 North Korean submarine incident, but as a way of showing flexibility the South Korean government allowed aid via the WFP and UNICEF to go through. However, relief aid through the KNRC was resumed after the North's official apology in December. Due to the aggravating food crisis, the South Korean government, in March 1997, following conflicts between the government and the civilian organizations on the distribution of humanitarian aid, permitted organizations to deliver rice and other products in order to increase aid to North Korea. Government support for civilian organizations, which often used China as an indirect channel to North Korea, expanded.

Following North-South Red Cross talks in Beijing, an agreement was reached in May 1997 on direct deliveries of relief goods instead of as hitherto working through the IFRC. In fact, since 1997 the North and South Korean Red Cross Societies have been able to maintain direct contact. Deliveries of mainly wheat flour (3,664 tons), powdered milk (94 tons), ramyôn (noodles; 100,000 bags), potatoes (1,900 tons), seeds (11,200 tons) and maize (4,980 tons) had amounted to roughly US$ 5m for the period September 1995-May 1997.

In June-July 1997 the KNRC delivered US$ 8.5m of maize (41,511 tons), wheat flour (2,000 tons), ramyôn (150,000 boxes) and fertilizers (2,000 tons). Deliveries of maize (17,000 tons), millet (14,576 tons), wheat flour (5,501 tons), potatoes (1,300 tons), baby food (97 tons) and powdered milk (100 tons) to a value of US$ 8.9m took place in August-October 1997. In March 1998, 800 tons of fertilizers to a value of US$ 170,000 was delivered. From April to June, a third round of aid worth US$ 9.4m of maize (16,585 tons), wheat flour (13,500 tons), powdered milk (111 tons), fertilizers (2,500 tons), salt (1,000 tons), rice (57 tons) as well as medicine was delivered. The 500 cows delivered in June 1998 were included (cf. p. 61). In supplementary deliveries between September and December 1998, maize (4,010 tons), wheat flour (2,000 tons), white rice (60 tons), powdered milk (128 tons) and sugar (34 tons) worth US$ 11.3m were transferred. The 501 cows delivered in October 1998 were included.[41]

---

40 Choi et al., ibid., p. 55; Chung, ibid., pp. 83-4, 86-7; Lee, "Assisting North Korea by Inter-governmental Agencies and Non-Governmental Organizations: Current State and Implications", in Korea Institute for National Unification, *International Organizations' Assistance to North Korea and Inter-Korean Cooperation* (Seoul: KINU, 2001), p. 15.

41 Choi et al., ibid., pp. 55-7; Chung, ibid., pp. 84-5, 86; Lee, ibid., 2001, p. 15.

From March to June 1999, 40,000 tons of fertilizers to a value of US$ 10.3m collected by fund raisings by the KNRC were delivered to North Korea. In 1999, 24 NGOs delivered an additional US$ 2.8m value of food stuffs, fertilizers and medicine through the KNRC. In addition, ten organizations, including the Korean Sharing Movement, the Christian Support Association for North Korean Compatriots, the Catholic Committee for National Reconciliation and the Yujin Bell, delivered in 1999, through their own channels food stuffs, fertilizers, medicine, medical equipment, agricultural tools and daily necessities worth US$ 5.5m.

Deliveries by NGOs, including the KNRC, the Korean Sharing Movement and the Korea Neighbour-Loving Association, of food stuffs, fertilizers, agriculture chemicals, medicine, clothes, agricultural tools and daily necessities continued during 2000 and amounted to US$ 20.9m, as of 30 September. Altogether, growing aid through civilian organizations reached a value of US$ 82.8m for the period September 1995-September 2000, or about one-fifth of government aid during the same period. The figure rose to US$ 122.2m in 2001. Government material assistance since 1995 then reached US$ 391.3m; the sum was US$ 513.5m, this to to be compared with more than $1.6 bn total from all aid sources together (cf. pp. 66, 180).

Following the June 2000 summit, there was an influx of South Korean NGO projects into North Korea in humanitarian aid, but the level of financial aid from NGOs declined while government involvement expanded. In fact, after the summit North Korea shifted focus to official relations to the disadvantage of NGOs. North Korea preferred government aid instead of NGO assistance since there was no monitoring by any international organization when it arrived and no requirement to submit follow-up data on the distribution or use of the significant amounts of aid.[42]

The Asia-Pacific Committee or the Committee for Overseas Compatriots hosted South Korean visitors in specialized areas. The objective was to contain their influence and interaction with specific sectors due to a lack of confidence in the South's economic and political system. In the words of the American scholar Scott Snyder (2003), "If anything, South Korean NGOs found that they were even more constrained in their actions than other international NGOs". South Korean NGOs were unable to establish a permanent presence and could not monitor a site without prior notification. North Korea invited large numbers of supporters of Southern aid organizations to visit aid projects rather than expert personnel who could monitor the projects' technical aspects. Unrelated sightseeing in P'yôngyang and to Mt. Myohyang tended to reinforce scepticism about the visits.

Unsurprisingly, the NGOs had little contact with ordinary North Korean citizens. In fact, while South Korean donors in many cases were more generous to and aware of North Korea's needs and cultural sensitivities than were their European or American counterparts, North Korea was even more reluctant to provide anything other than a

---

42 Choi et al., ibid., pp. 56, 58-60, 67; Chung, ibid., pp. 87, 90-91; Lee, ibid., 2001, pp. 15, 22; Snyder, "The NGO Experience in North Korea", in Flake & Snyder, *Paved with Good Intentions*, 2003, pp. 9, 11.

minimal standard of monitoring and access for them, causing considerable frustration. Other differences were that South Korean NGOs observed internal dynamism and possibilities for change in North Korea more optimistically; they tended to put more emphasis on confidence-building through frequent contacts than on closely following humanitarian principles. Nationalism, unification and reconciliation were the main motivations for relief activities which extended beyond pure humanitarianism. However, North Korean authorities were not primarily interested in widening cooperation, but in regime survival. Nonetheless, South Korean NGOs have served as a buffer by playing a complementary role in reducing tensions and in increasingly having an impact on a compromised North Korean society (cf. pp. 140-42).[43]

As intended, humanitarian aid delivered by South to North Korea has, together with international aid, contributed considerably to alleviating the food shortages. Fertilizers and seeds have been especially important in terms of raising production. One opinion on aid delivery is expressed by the scholar Lee Keumsoon (2001): "As the government permitted various direct channels of aid to the North in 1999 and supported NGOs through the South-North Cooperation Fund in 2000, the cooperation between the government and NGOs has made for more effective delivery of humanitarian aid to the North". She writes on the impact on inter-Korean relations: "Most importantly, it has undermined central government propaganda concerning South Korea and the US, and to some extent it has eased tensions on the Korean peninsula". In 2003, she wrote that the evaluation was that North Korean antagonism towards South Korea had eased greatly as a result of citizens' direct experiences of the quality of aid and the marking of the origin of country and organization from which the aid stemmed.

The South Korean scholar Chung Oknim (2003) expresses a similar opinion by writing that South Korean NGOs "...have contributed to lowering existing tensions between the two Koreas" by maintaining contacts while relations have been tense due to, for example, the Yellow Sea battles in June 1999 and 2002 (cf. pp. 68, 82). In the opinion of her compatriot scholar Yi Ki-bôm (2003), aid and exchanges have created a foundation for North and South Korean residents to recognize each other's existence. Since the number of South Koreans involved in aid has risen dramatically, they have learnt to distinguish between the North Korean people and the political system. In fact, 6,175 South Koreans visited North Korea in relation to humanitarian aid between 1991 and 2003, of which 5,621 visited during the Kim Dae Jung administration (1998-2003). Meanwhile, North Korean residents, in spite of the authorities' control, have gained knowledge about South Korean aid workers and their work, which reportedly has had a positive effect on the image of South Korea, generally.

Yi also writes that aid and exchanges have created opportunities for South Korean citizens to take part in the process and provided a basis for the expansion of the capacity of civil society. In fact, 3,580 of the South Koreans involved in aid work

---

43 Chung, ibid., pp. 82, 103, 104, 105; Lee, *Taebuk indojôk chiwôn-ûi yônghyangnyôk punsôk* (Seoul: T'ongil yôn'guwôn, 2003), pp. 100, 101-102; Snyder, in ibid., pp. 9-10, 11.

between 1998 and 2003 came from civilian organizations. Opportunities for human and material exchanges have been created. Humanitarian aid leads the way towards creating confidence and a cooperative relationship between the two Koreas. It is the first kind of continuous contact since national partition that has not been shaken by recent political and military developments such as cancelled official meetings, the West Sea battle in 2002 and the North's nuclear issue. Both states have agreed at least about the importance of aid. Consequently, a considerable level of confidence has been created in continuously pursuing aid projects, although cooperation was not free from friction caused by the restrictions on work.[44] The confidence created through the provision of humanitarian aid to North Korea suggests that the impact of those contacts on inter-Korean relations should not be underestimated. Although involving very few people directly and probably many more indirectly, the continuous contacts and the positive side-effects generated from these are, in the author's opinion, the most important socio-cultural exchanges heretofore. In contrast, as we have seen, most other contacts have normally been irregular and have brought few other results than the exchanges themselves.

5.5 Divided families

The historic origin of divided families is the Kisa famine that was a result of a series of disastrous crop failures in northern Korea between 1869 and 1875. Consequently, large-scale emigration to Manchuria and the Maritime Provinces of Siberia led to the establishment of Korean communities there. Among those communities, the Manchurian one has continuously provided a vital channel of contact for many divided family members to their relatives in North Korea: after South Korea and China established diplomatic relations in 1992, 90 per cent of family reunions in third countries have taken place in China via relatives living there, inviting North and South Koreans to meet at the same time. Most of the two million Korean residents in China in 2003 were living in the border regions.

When people such as collaborators, landowners and religious groups who opposed the northern government's policies in creating a communist state after the Japanese surrender on 15 August, 1945 were allowed to go to the South, the first groups of divided families within Korea were created. Most people did not expect partition to become so permanent and therefore left behind their relatives in the North. This opinion was predominant also among opponents to the policies of the US Army Military Government in Korea in creating an anti-communist state in the South by supporting the social forces who had served and profited from the Japanese occupation 1910-1945. An unknown number of people thus fled to the North to seek political asylum and left behind many family members. An estimated 25-35 per cent of the total number of divided families experienced their trauma during the post-

---

44 Chung, ibid., p. 106; Lee, ibid., 2001, pp. 15, 25; Lee, ibid., 2003, pp. 79-80, 82, 100, 101, 103, 105; Yi, ibid., pp. 60-61. Lee records all 20 South Korean NGOs involved in humanitarian aid to North Korea since 1994 (ibid., 2001, pp. 18-20).

liberation years. During the first year after the outbreak of the Korean War in 1950, the majority of divided family members caused by warfare were separated from their relatives. An estimated 65-75 per cent of divided families derive from the war. Most Koreans believed that some sort of resolution from national division would result from the war and thought that their separation from relatives would be temporary.[45]

As we saw in Chapter 3, very few family reunions have taken place and the issue has been abused politically. According to the South Korean scholar Suh Jae Jean (2002), "The main reason for the delay in resolving the separated family issue has been the evasiveness of North Korea leaders. North Korea perceives this issue as a political matter, whereas South Korea regards it as a humanitarian one".[46]

Whether true or not, such a situation is indeed a great human tragedy: "The International Conference on Humanitarian Laws" held in Geneva in 1976 established the "right of family" as a fundamental human right. Furthermore, in a survey of 60 North Korean refugees in South Korea made in 1997, most respondents were between 60 and 79 years of age. Consequently, the first generation of divided family members who had living memories of their families in the North was fast disappearing and little time remained if a solution to the infringement of their basic human rights was to be found before they died. Evidence of this fact is that, as of 28 June, 2001, 12,664 of the 116,640 original applicants (10.9 per cent) for the three rounds of reunions in 2000-2001 had died. Two people who were scheduled to meet their relatives had died before the meetings.

While the human tragedy is indisputable, the divided families issue has been involved in many North-South contacts. Consequently, in the absence of direct diplomatic links between the two Koreas the issue has provided an invaluable avenue of contact via the national Red Cross Societies. A solution to the divided families issue requires, according to the British scholar James A. Foley (2003), "... the renewal of natural human contacts, links beyond the control of either government, among ordinary Koreans across the unnatural border...". However, both Koreas have avoided such contacts "with the utmost care". An obstacle noted by Suh is that North Korea fears negative influences on its system from the inflow of foreign information from the outside world.[47] As we have repeatedly seen, such fears are regarded as a significant obstacle to closer inter-Korean relations. Apparently, the fact that in East Germany the impact of foreign influences, in particular West German TV, was immense by creating notions of an alternative to their own social system eventually facilitating unification makes the North Korean leaders fear such a worst case scenario.

The main criticism directed against the family reunions in 2000-2001 concerned the limited numbers of divided family members involved (cf. pp. 73, 79). The total

---

45 Foley, *Korea's Divided Families*, pp. 7-9, 23, 30-34, 42, 43, 56, 58, 59: table 2.3, 64, 65, 70; Suh, "The Reunion of Separated Families under the Kim Dae-Jung Government", 2002, p. 356. *Kisa* literally means "to starve to death" (Foley, ibid., p. 7: fn. 3).

46 Suh, ibid., 2002, p. 353.

47 Foley, ibid., pp. 62-3, 83-4, 90; Suh, ibid., 2002, p. 353.

number of people who, then and at the subsequent two reunions in 2002, could meet their family members was only 5,087. At the first family reunions, 100 people from South Korea met 218 family members in P'yôngyang, whereas 100 from North Korea met 750 family members in Seoul, that is altogether 1,168 people. The corresponding figures for the second reunions were 100 and 254 people in P'yôngyang, against 100 and 770 in Seoul (1,224). At the third reunions, 100 people from the South met 497 family members in P'yôngyang, while 100 from the North met 243 family members in Seoul (940). At the fourth reunions, 565 people from South Korea and 283 from North Korea met (848). Finally, at the fifth reunions, 554 people from South Korea and 353 from North Korea met; in 2003 and 2004, 2,691 and 1,926 people, respectively, met making the total figure 9,704. That the fourth and fifth rounds of family reunions were held at Mt. Kûmgang can, in the words of Suh "...be seen as a move by North Korean officials not to allow North Korean citizens to visit South Korea".

Another strong point of criticism concerned the fact that no effective and durable mechanism had been put in place to ensure that the reunions would continue. It should also be noted that the divided family members who benefited from the reunions, after 50 years of division, could only meet their relatives for six hours and dine together twice during the first round of reunions in August 2000.[48]

The ongoing ideological competition between the two Koreas was inevitably reflected in the seven interviews Foley made in 2001. Divided family members from the North invariably praised the state, its system and leader, Kim Jong Il, on every occasion in public and in private. Questions on economic conditions and whether separation from their relatives had caused suffering were usually answered in similar ways: "Thanks to the Great General (Kim Jong Il) we have all lived well and without hardships". Only one interviewee admitted that life was difficult in North Korea. On the contrary, the North's socio-political system was considered to be superior to that of the capitalist South.

Divided family members who lived in the South were more careful when such issues as ideology, standards of living and personal freedom were discussed by asking more general questions about how life in the North was. But ideology affected all interviewees, in some cases by making them careful about what to say or not to say.

Unsurprisingly, interviewees' stories were also affected by the common cultural legacy. In fact, the most commonly reported sentiments among divided family members from both states were feelings of guilt and recrimination for perceived failure to fulfil their familial obligations and duties. This way of blaming the tragedy of their separation from their family members on themselves was particularly true in the case of eldest sons separated from their families, parents separated from their

---

48 Foley, ibid., pp. 120, 121; Suh, ibid., 2002, pp. 371-73. Suh writes (ibid., p. 371) that a total number of 5,477 people were able to meet but subsequent figures do not match this sum. The figures given on p. 372 of people meeting each other at each family reunion are followed in the text.

children and sons separated from their mothers. While being universal feelings, they were reinforced by the influence of Confucianism and its emphasis on familial duty and, in particular, the obligation of filial piety. Eldest sons in Korea are expected to become the head of the family, look after their parents in life, ensure that the proper Confucian rituals are performed for them in death and shoulder the burden of taking care of their younger siblings to give them the best possible start in life.[49]

Although opinions expressed by a small number of interviewees hardly can be regarded as the predominant ones among divided family members, the above views show that the two Koreas had radically different social systems reconfirming the opinion that division has created national heterogeneity. On the other hand, opinions also reflected the joint cultural legacy, which indicates that the degree of national heterogeneity perhaps should not be exaggerated. The main impact on the two Koreas from family reunions appears to be spreading knowledge about each other. However, considering the advanced age of the extremely few divided family members involved and the fact that reunions have been short and abused for political purposes, the positive effects on society must have been far less significant than those created by the provision of humanitarian aid.

5.6 Conclusions

The numbers of North Korean defectors was low prior to the 1990s, when it rose dramatically due to, in particular, the economic crisis. Since the year 2000, the number has risen incrementally, each year. However, the number is extremely low compared to what it was in preunification East Germany. The South Korean government enacted legislation on defectors in 1962, 1979, 1993, 1997 and 1998 to support defectors' integration into life in South Korea by providing education, capital, housing and work. Institutes for social integration were also created.

However good the general intentions were, studies from 1996, 1998 and 2003 clearly show, that it had become increasingly difficult for defectors to integrate, into South Korean society. Defectors' new lives often differed from their own expectations causing a considerable degree of frustration. The political and economic differences caused by national division have led to national heterogeneity. Such differences undermine the impact of socio-cultural contacts on restoring national homogeneity, regardless of whether defectors have had experiences of such contacts or not. Defectors are regarded as "marginal men" indicating that their position in South Korea resembles that of the division between first and second-class citizens in Germany and Yemen after their unification in 1990. However, although economic and political realities now are more important for South Koreans in their daily lives than contacts with their Northern compatriots, there are also indications of common cultural characteristics remaining. Such a situation could facilitate development of closer relations and eventual unification.

---

49 Foley, ibid., pp. 123-28. Translations of the interviews appear on pp. 159-203.

Unemployment has continuously been high among defectors but there are also a successful few. Defectors' difficulties to get work have derived from their lack of skills required in South Korea and knowledge of the society. Marriage has been another major difficulty. They also face discrimination and contempt from South Koreans, who have to change their superior attitudes to facilitate defectors' social integration. In spite of the common language, even language causes difficulties for defectors. Defectors' present difficulties imply that creating "human union" is a most difficult task. Yet, human exchanges have to expand to bring the two Koreas closer to each other.

South Korea has provided large amounts of humanitarian aid such as foodstuffs and fertilizers to North Korea since 1995 through international organizations as well as through domestic public and civilian channels. Although humanitarian aid has been affected by political tensions, it has, besides contributing to alleviating food shortages, in spite of severe restrictions imposed upon South Korean NGOs, been important in terms of contributing to the creation of mutual confidence and reducing tensions on the Korean Peninsula. Humanitarian aid has been the most important socio-cultural contact since it has provided regular and largely positive developments in inter-Korean relations, which distinguishes it from other forms of contacts. Through aid, human exchanges have taken place promoting mutual knowledge and understanding. South Koreans have learnt to distinguish between the North Korean government and the North's citizens. The impact of improved notions about each other should not be underestimated.

Reunions of divided family members are of the utmost importance from a humanitarian point of view. While reconfirming the notion of national heterogeneity, family reunions in other ways show that a joint cultural legacy remains intact and that the degree of heterogeneity should not be exaggerated. Yet, family reunions have been less important than humanitarian aid in terms of confidence building measures as they have been less regular and have involved only a few people of, more often than not, advanced ages.

Chapter 6

Views of North Korea, Unification and the Great Powers

6.1 Introduction

As we saw in Chapter 5, South Koreans' negative opinions on North Korean defectors is a serious obstacle to bringing Koreans closer together, in addition to many of the practical difficulties referred to in Chapters 3 and 4. On the other hand, humanitarian aid has had a major positive impact in terms of creating mutual confidence and reminding ourselves of the importance of family reunions should not be underestimated.

Since not only people-to-people contacts but also opinions of each other affect the opportunities for Koreans to live together whether in a state of peaceful coexistence or in a unified country, the main purpose of this chapter is to investigate South Koreans' opinions of North Korea and unification. This is done on the basis of recently published opinion surveys. A few results of these extensive surveys are presented and their relevance is discussed to evaluate the impact of socio-cultural contacts on relations. Issues to be investigated include perceptions of North Korean society and culture, interest in the unification issue, opinions on the likely time of unification, how to achieve unity and what the perceived obstacles in this process may be. The same issues will appear more than once in order to compare the survey results and thereby find out how representative the results indeed are. Since basing a study on surveys that include only a limited number of people may not give a fair and representative view of South Koreans' opinions on such complex issues, consideration is taken to the low number of interviewees.

Eight opinion surveys are referred to. Firstly, views of North Korea are investigated on the basis of a survey from 1996. Secondly, a survey from 2001 of South Koreans' accommodation of North Korean culture is analyzed. Thirdly, in the following section views on unification among South Korean high-school students are investigated based on an opinion survey made in 2000. Fourthly, a follow-up study of high-school students from 2001 on the views of North Korea and unification is presented. Surveys on North Korean defectors' opinions on South Korea are included. Fifthly, an opinion survey from 2000 on North Korean defectors' consciousness of unification is analyzed. As in the 2001 survey, comparisons are made with opinions about South Koreans. In order to give a more comprehensive view of Koreans' views of each other, the discussion also includes a number of other studies. In the next section an opinion survey from 2002 that is a second follow-up study on youths views on the process of North-South unity is presented.

Additionally, scholars' opinions of unification and North Korea are investigated on the basis of a survey made in 2002. Finally, a survey from 2003 of the same issues among the general public is analyzed. Since, as we saw in Chapter 1, Korean reunification is an international issue, the last two surveys include Koreans' perceptions on the views on Korean unification held by the United States, Japan, China and Russia to complete the survey.

In the final section, key characteristics of these countries' policies towards the two Koreas during recent years are investigated. The main purpose is to find out whether South Koreans' perceptions of their views of Korean unity match with their actual policies. However, since the two Koreas in the 1972 4 July Communiqué referred to in Chapter 3 agreed to unify without foreign intervention, the impact of these countries' policies towards Korea is given far less attention than Koreans' views of each other. In analyzing the great powers' policies towards Korea, particular emphasis is put on the United States and China since they are the main regional powers. Political as well as scholarly perspectives on a unified Korea are included in the discussion.

6.2 Views of North Korea and accommodation of North Korean culture

As we saw in Chapter 3, mutual distrust is a major obstacle in improving inter-Korean relations. That the perceived positive impact of socio-cultural exchanges and on relations may be offset by images of North Korea is clear from a study made by the South Korean scholar Lee Woo-Young (1996). He analyzed the views expressed on North Korea and the unification issue through the 283 editorials in the daily *Hankook Ilbo* published in this field, mainly on political and military issues, between January 1993 and July 1996. Hankook Ilbo was selected since it was considered to hold a relatively neutral position among major national newspapers.

Cognitions of North Korea in 251 editorials are shown in Table 6.1.

Not surprisingly, the cognitions were highly negative. This was especially the case when Kim Il Sung died in July 1994. There was no sense of trust towards North Korea and the images of the political system were, without exception, negative. The dominating opinion was that North Korea had not changed, but the view that the North had transformed was expressed during the third quarter of 1994, since changes were expected in the aftermath of Kim Il Sung's death.[1]

Besides these negative images, the dominating view was that changes in North Korea were a pre-requisite for unification. That his data showed that reports on the North failed to reduce the sense of heterogeneity between the two Koreas can only further have contributed to weaken the impact of socio-cultural contacts on relations. Such a situation contrasted diametrically with the media's own opinion that their most important task was to report the events in order to restore national homogeneity.

---

1 Lee, ibid., 1996, pp. 3-4, 41-2, 44-7.

Table 6.1   Cognitions of North Korea, 1996

Division	Number	%
Rival	140	55.8
Hostile state	97	38.6
Same ethnical identity	14	5.6

Source: Reproduced from Lee, T'ongil kwajông-esô maesû midiô-ûi yôkhal *(Seoul: Minjok t'ongil yôn'guwôn, 1996), pp. 44-5 with kind permission of Korea Institute for National Unification. Permission for reproduction is acknowledged for all the following tables.*

Regarding attitudes towards unification, 93 of 118 editorials expressed views on desirable changes in North Korea. These were divided between opening and reform (46), system changes (29) and reduction of military expenditure (18). Only 17 views were domestically oriented, of which 12 stressed the need for domestic stability and five wanted a strengthening of the military. The other views expressed the need for diplomatic recognition of North Korea. Virtually all editorials argued for a leading role for the government in the unification process. All editorials supported a gradual unification, as a contrast to unification by absorption.[2] North Korea was clearly considered to be the main obstacle to unification, whereas international factors hardly mattered, apparently. It is, given the content in Chapter 3, hard to believe that a larger sample of editorials would have changed this picture.

An important question to ask regarding the impact of socio-cultural exchanges and on inter-Korean relations is to what extent South Koreans are capable of accommodating North Korean culture. This issue was investigated by Lee Woo-Young in 2001 on the basis of questionnaires and interviews with 670 people. They were divided as follows: elementary school students (194), high-school students (90), university students (244), teachers (41) and visitors to arts exhibitions (101).[3]

Experiences of North Korean culture appear in Table 6.2.

Table 6.2   Experiences of North Korean culture, 2001

Division	Number	%
No experience	450	67.4
Experience	211	31.6

Source: Reproduced from Lee, Pukhan munhwa-ûi suyong silt'ae chosa, *2001, p. 51: figure 1; p. 52: table 2; p. 53: tables 3, 4. Notes: Seven respondents did not reply. The different categories of interviewees identified are aggregated in this table.*

---

2   Lee, ibid., 1996, pp. 47-9, 56-7, 61, 62.
3   Lee, ibid., 2001, pp. 4-5.

The lack of experience is striking. However, among visitors to arts exhibitions, 51 (50.5 per cent) had previous experiences of North Korean culture reflecting their own interests.

Experience of lectures at school on North Korea are recorded in Table 6.3.

Table 6.3 Experiences of lectures on North Korea, 2001

Division	Number	%
Experience	207	56.0
No experience	163	44.0

Source: Reproduced from Lee, ibid., 2001, p. 54: table 5. High-school students, university students and teachers responded.

Statistics are clearly different in this respect, but only 31 students (8.4 per cent) had attended two to three courses. 60 of 89 high-school students (67.4 per cent) had not attended any lectures on North Korea since they have hardly ever been available. The figure for teachers was even higher with 29 of 37 (78.4 per cent), although most of them had been trained at the Unification Education Institute. On the other hand, 170 university students (69.6 per cent) had attended lectures on North Korea but only 36 per cent of those students had experienced North Korean culture since the subject was not included in their courses.

Types of North Korean culture experienced are shown in Table 6.4.

Table 6.4 Types of North Korean culture experienced, 2001

Division	Number	%
Film	145	38.5
Media	81	21.5
Literature	79	21.0
Music	45	11.9
Arts	23	6.1

Source: Reproduced from Lee, ibid., 2001, p. 56: figure 2; p. 57: table 6. High-school students, university students and teachers replied.

Experiences are varied. It is to be noted that since teachers were educated at a time when there was hardly any teaching on North Korean culture, students had experienced more of it than their teachers![4] Anyhow, the tables show that experiences of North Korean culture were limited.

---

4 Lee, ibid., 2001, pp. 51-7.

Opinions of North Korean films are recorded in Table 6.5.

Table 6.5 Opinions of North Korean films, 2001

Division	Number	%
Somewhat entertaining	198	53.7
Very entertaining	40	10.8
Somewhat boring	93	25.2
Really boring	38	10.3

Source: Reproduced from Lee, ibid., 2001, p. 58: figure 3; p. 59: table 7. High-school students, university students and teachers replied.

At first glance, positive opinions dominate. But since the films seen had little political content, there was little reason to reject them: it is hard to regard the response positively.

Reasons for liking the films are recorded in Table 6.6.

Table 6.6 Reasons for liking North Korean films, 2001

Division	Number	%
Fulfilling curiosity	91	35.5
Sound contents	62	24.2
Forms and techniques	35	13.7
National homogeneity	32	12.5
Others	36	14.1

Source: Reproduced from Lee, ibid., 2001, p. 61: figure 4; p. 63: table 10. High-school students, university students and teachers replied.

Curiosity was a primary reason given, but, for teachers, confirming national homogeneity was a major factor for 20 of 30 respondents (66.7 per cent). The latter fact could reflect the fact that they had relatives in the North or had experienced pre-divided Korea before 1945 or both.

Reasons for disliking the films are recorded in Table 6.7.

Tediousness dominate; it was the main reason for disliking the films among both 44 high-school students (27; 61.4 per cent) and 79 university students (41; 51.9 per cent). But for teachers the main reason was political propaganda (7; 50 per cent).

Table 6.7 Reasons for disliking North Korean films, 2001

Division	Number	%
Tediousness	73	53.3
Forms and techniques	25	18.2
Political propaganda	14	10.2
Hard to understand	11	8.0
Others	14	10.2

Source: Reproduced from Lee, ibid., 2001, p. 62: figure 5; p. 64: table 11. High-school students, university students and teachers replied.

Opinions of North Korean arts are shown in Table 6.8.

Table 6.8 Opinions of North Korean arts, 2001

Division	Number	%
Favourable	95	94.0
Not favourable	6	6.0

Source: Reproduced from Lee, ibid., 2001, pp. 60, 61: table 9. All interviewees are visitors to arts exhibitions.

The highly favourable opinions reflect positive attitudes towards North Korean culture as well as the almost complete lack of political motives for the works that were not significantly different from South Korean works.[5]

Reasons for liking North Korean art works appear in Table 6.9.

Table 6.9 Reasons for liking North Korean arts, 2001

Division	Number	%
National homogeneity	34	35.8
Forms and techniques	24	25.3
Fulfilling curiosity	21	22.1
Sound contents	13	13.7
Others	3	3.2

Source: Reproduced from Lee, ibid., 2001, pp. 66, 67: table 13. All interviewees are visitors to arts exhibitions.

---

5 Lee, ibid., 2001, pp. 58-64. Percentages may not reach 100 per cent due to roundings.

Views of North Korea, Unification and the Great Powers 195

The importance of national homogeneity and satisfying curiosity is striking.

Concerning the appreciation of North Korean culture, it was asked to what extent art and literary works were heterogeneous from their South Korean counterparts. The replies are enumerated in Table 6.10.

Table 6.10   Heterogeneity between North and South Korean art and literary works, 2001

Division	Number	%
Heterogeneity	245	94.6
	85	84.1
No heterogeneity	14	5.4
	15	14.9
Minor linguistic heterogeneity	138	52.9
Big linguistic heterogeneity	103	39.4
Hardly any linguistic heterogeneity	20	7.7

Source: Reproduced from Lee, ibid., 2001, p. 68: figures 6, 7; p. 69: table 14; p. 70: table 15; p. 71: table 16. High-school students, university students, teachers and visitors to arts exhibitions replied. Note: The lower row under "heterogeneity" and "no heterogeneity" refers only to the last category, among which one interviewee did not reply.

Heterogeneity in art works were far larger than linguistic ones which is explained by the great complexity of the cultural sphere.

The impact of watching North Korean art and literary works is shown in Table 6.11.

Table 6.11   The impact of North Korean art and literary works, 2001

Division	Number	%
Closer affinity	122	46.7
No difference	94	36.0
Less affinity	27	10.4
Much closer affinity	18	6.9

Source: Reproduced from Lee, ibid., 2001, p. 73: figure 8; p. 74: table 18. High-school students, university students and teachers replied. Note: 56 of 101 of visitors to arts exhibitions (55.5 per cent) replied that going to exhibitions of North Korean art had reduced the cultural distance (ibid., pp. 74-5).

Since replies vary somewhat, there was no guarantee that cultural exchanges would enhance mutual understanding. However, the works observed had no distinct political content unlike the North's cultural mainstream. Otherwise, the replies would have been more negative.[6]

Although no opinion survey can give an exhaustive view of South Koreans' accommodation of North Korean culture, the respondents' limited experiences clearly gave rise to curiosity. More significantly, only a few respondents expressed difficulties with understanding North Korean films which indicates that the joint historical legacy has not been entirely undermined by the national division. That watching North Korean art and literary works caused greater affinity for most respondents confirms this view. On the other hand, the opinion that the political content makes films boring reconfirms the view that the division has created differences between the two Koreas, that may not be so easy to overcome. The views of visitors to arts exhibitions are unrepresentative of the total South Korean population, but they imply that efforts to learn about North Korea are of the utmost importance for creating closer relations.

6.3 Views of unification in South Korea, 2000-2001

The Korea Youth Development Institute completed, in September 2000, a study of the views on unification among 1,095 South Korean high-school students who attended 12 humanistic and vocational high-schools in the Seoul area. The purpose was to develop a plan for promoting exchanges and cooperation between North and South Korean youths.

The question of how often they spoke about the unification issue with their families, friends and acquaintances is analyzed in Table 6.12.

Table 6.12 Discussion on unification, 2000

Division	Number of respondents	%
Hardly discuss	453	41.3
Discuss slightly	449	40.9
Do not discuss at all	107	9.8
Discuss frequently	83	7.6
Discuss very frequently	5	0.5

Source: Reproduced from Ham et al., NGO-rûl t'onghan Nambukhan ch'ôngsonyôn kyoryu hyômnyôk pangan yôn'gu (Seoul: T'ongil yôn'guwôn, 2000), p. 30: table III-3.

The lack of interest is obvious and reflects the fact that high-school students were not interested in the unification issue and thereby were affected by the absence of

---

6 Lee, ibid., 2001, pp. 66-75, 88, 90. Percentages may not reach 100 due to roundings.

information and education on unification and North Korean issues.[7] Such a situation can only make it more difficult to develop closer relations.

The reasonability of unification is recorded in Table 6.13.

Table 6.13 Reasonability of unification, 2000

Division	Number of respondents	%
Wants reunification	533	48.6
Unification is a must	299	27.3
Maintain division	173	15.8
Not interested	72	6.6
Oppose unification	20	1.8

Source: Reproduced from Ham et al., ibid., p. 32: table III-5.

It is to be noted that 24.2 per cent of the respondents preferred the status quo to a unified Korea, which contradicts the opinion recorded in Chapter 1 that unification is an aspiration. Plausible explanations are mutual distrust, lack of interest and fears for the estimated huge costs of unification recorded in Chapter 3. But in the study, 929 respondents (85.8 per cent) replied that reunification was possible, whereas only 154 (14.2 per cent) said that it was impossible. Unsurprisingly, people with a lower standard of living were more negative towards unification than well-off people.

Opinions on the time-scale of unification appear in Table 6.14.

Table 6.14 Time for unification, 2000

Division	Number of respondents	%
Within 5 years	162	17.5
Within 10 years	405	43.8
Within 20 years	245	26.5
More than 20 years	113	12.2

Source: Reproduced from Ham et al., ibid., p. 35: table III-9.

A surprisingly high number of people replied that Korea would become reunited within five years. Only 113 expressed the in, the author's opinion, more realistic view, that is, given the expected difficulties of unification and the aims of the sunshine policy, that it would take at least more than 20 years. Unlike the opinions on the plausibility of unification, more people with a lower standard of living believed that

---

7 Ham et al., ibid., pp. 31-5. Percentages do not reach 100 per cent due to roundings.

it was possible within five years than well-off people.[8] This could reflect an opinion that the former will be more affected by the estimated higher costs for a long-term unification than the latter group.

Respondents were asked to rank the importance of eleven obstacles to unification on a scale from one to five; one marked "no obstacle" and five "very great obstacle". The average value calculated is shown in Table 6.15.

Table 6.15   Obstacles to unification, 2000

Division	Average
North-South economic gap	4.15
North Korea sticking to communism	4.10
North-South ideological confrontation	3.97
North-South ruling classes' interests	3.92
Deepening of national heterogeneity	3.60
Stationing of US troops in South Korea	3.60
North-South military confrontation	3.55
Different unification formulas	3.43
Lack of mutual efforts	3.30
Interests of the regional powers	3.14
Lack of will	2.98

Source: Reproduced from Ham et al., ibid., p. 39: table III-15. Note: The number of respondents is not recorded.

Arranging the factors by character showed that confrontation and tensions were the most important ones, followed by the interests of the great powers and the general lack of will for unification (national heterogeneity was not included).

The main tasks to prepare for unification are enumerated in Table 6.16.

Clearly, the opinion was that Korea should reunify through its own efforts via contacts and dialogue and that systemic reform of North rather than South Korea was a prerequisite for unification.[9]

In spite of the low number of respondents, it is, based on previous accounts in this book, hard to believe that a larger sample would have given a significantly different outcome. Given the estimated huge costs of unification, it is not surprising that the economic gap is regarded as the main obstacle. To point out North Korea's adherence to communism is primarily to say that the North should change but opinions on other obstacles show that both Korean states have to change their present policies considerably.

---

8   Ham et al., ibid., pp. 26-7, 29-31, 77, 179. The number of respondents to each question differs slightly from the number recorded on p. 27. Percentages do not reach 100 per cent due to roundings.

9   Ham et al., ibid., pp. 37-41. Percentages do not reach 100 per cent due to roundings.

Table 6.16 Main tasks for unification, 2000

Division	Number of respondents	%
Creating mutual understanding and trust	379	34.6
Opening and liberalization of North Korea	270	24.7
North-South exchanges and cooperation	261	23.8
Withdrawal of US troops and abolishment of the National Security Law[10]	94	8.6
Conclusion of a North-South Peace Treaty	77	7.0
Requesting support from the great powers	5	0.5
Others	9	0.8

Source: Reproduced from Ham et al., ibid., p. 38: table III-13.

The deficiency in will to unify indicates that unification is a difficult task to undertake and will bring about unpredictable problems for the two Koreas, not least for their respective leaders. That the interests of the great powers are given a lower importance confirms the view that Koreans wish to unify only through their own efforts.

In October 2001, the Korea Youth Development Institute completed a follow-up study on the views of North Korea and unification that focused on the issues of heterogeneity and homogeneity among 1,165 South Korean high-school students, at 15 schools in the greater Seoul region. The purpose was to establish a desirable outline for exchanges and projects between North and South Korean youths.[11]

The desire for unification is illuminated in Table 6.17.

Clearly, the majority for unification was overwhelming, in fact stronger than in 2000. However, as shown in Table 6.18, interest for unification was still much lower.

---

10 To scrap or retain the National Security Law was heatedly debated in fall 2004. The debate focused on how much of a threat North Korea posed to the internal security of South Korea. The ruling Uri party insisted that times have changed and that the law is out of time whereas the conservative Grand National Party still regarded the North as a clear and present danger. The law was considered to be an essential safeguard against North Korea. Also the supreme and constitutional courts have ruled against challenges to the law. From *The Economist*, "Times change, so why not laws?", 6 November, 2004, pp. 62-3.

11 Kil et al., *Nambukhan p'yônghwa kongjon-ûl wihan ch'ôngsonyôn-ûi sahoe munhwajôk tongjilsông chûngjin pangan yôn'gu* (Seoul: T'ongil yôn'guwôn, 2001), pp. 27-9, 130. The number of respondents to each question differed slightly from the number recorded on p. 29. Percentages may not reach 100 per cent due to roundings.

Table 6.17 Reasonability of unification, 2001

Division	Number of respondents	%
Korea must reunify	709	61.0
Korea must absolutely reunify	242	20.8
Korea must not reunify	177	15.2
Korea must absolutely not reunify	34	2.0

Source: Reproduced from Kil et al., ibid., p. 34: table III-7.

Table 6.18 Interest in unification, 2001

Division	Number of respondents	%
Do not care	579	49.8
Interested	313	26.9
Not interested	156	13.4
Not interested at all	67	5.8
Very interested	48	4.1

Source: Reproduced from Kil et al., ibid., 2001, p. 36: table III-10.

The lack of interest may reflect both an opinion that a divided Korea is the natural state of affairs and reflects concerns about the estimated huge costs of unification.

Respondents were asked to rank eleven obstacles to unification from the criteria no obstacle at all, no obstacle, normal, obstacle and great obstacle. The percentages given to "great obstacle" and "obstacle" are calculated in Table 6.19.

Arranging the obstacles by types, "mutual confrontation and tensions" created by the division, were the major ones followed by "interests of the great powers" and "will and efforts for unification". The lower ranking of the will for unification reflect the targets of the sunshine policy, to promote dialogue and cooperation.[12]

That this survey also showed that the main obstacles to unification were domestic rather than international ones reflects the opinion that unification should be achieved by the Koreans themselves. The lower rank of deepening of heterogeneity than political and economic factors reflects the view that national homogeneity could be easier to restore than to build a politically and economically reunified Korea. This in turn implies a belief that the joint historical legacy has not been completely eradicated by the division, thus concurring with the above data on toleration of North Korean culture in the South. Again, North Korea is seen as the main obstacle to unification. But since the following factors also involve South Korea there are, as we saw above, obviously obstacles on both sides.

---

12 Kil et al., ibid., 2001, pp. 37-9.

Table 6.19   Obstacles to unification, 2001

Division	Average
North Korea sticking to communism	76.1
North-South economic gap	73.3
North-South ruling classes' interests	70.0
North-South ideological confrontation	69.7
North-South military confrontation	60.0
Stationing of US troops in South Korea	58.3
Deepening of national heterogeneity	58.0
Different unification formulas	57.2
Lack of mutual efforts	54.7
Interests of the regional powers	52.2
Lack of will	47.2

Source: Reproduced from Kil et al., ibid., 2001, p. 38, table III-12. Note: The number of respondents is not recorded.

In fact, since North-South relations have been characterized by confrontation, both states have struggled for self-survival by presenting proposals beneficial towards itself. Consequently, both Koreas have a responsibility for the division being maintained for almost 60 years: according to the South Korean scholar Hwang In Kwan (2004), "The main enemy to unification is therefore the two sovereign Korean states". His view reconfirms that nationalism is strong in both states and shows that it reinforces division but it could be too pessimistic: Kim Choong-hwan from the Ministry of Unification points out (2004) as his personal opinion that Korea may unify after the Korean War generation dies out since South and North Koreans who remember the war greatly distrust each other. However, while being a logical argument, the fact that, as of 1998, 87 per cent of the North Korean population and 83 per cent of the South Korean were born after the 1945 national division would tend to weaken this argument: the large majority of Koreans may regard division as the natural state of affairs.

It is also worthy to note here that the former North Korean diplomat Hyôn Sông-il in 1998, argued for changes within South Korean politics. North Koreans had long stressed education/propaganda pointing out South Korea as an enemy and distorted public information in an extremely negative campaign against the South's society. Examples include the notions that it is impossible in South Korea to get medical treatment and education without having money, that capitalism is characterized by extreme individualism, greed, mutual distrust and the law of the jungle operates which stimulates crime and corruption and, finally, that successive governments have sold out the nation to the United States and Japan.

To change such perceptions, the most important thing was to make North Koreans understand that the liberal democratic system is a superior political system. Thus,

South Koreans had to revive the fundamentals of liberal democracy while attracting admiration and understanding from North Korean compatriots. In other words, South Koreans had to change themselves in order to actually show why liberal democracy is a better system. It was necessary to show the unity between the government led by a strong leader receiving support from the majority of the people, to develop political pluralism for the sake of national welfare, to create clean politics as well as the rule of law, to secure social unity and stability and, finally, implement a foreign policy that fulfilled national interests. In this way, North Koreans will get a sense of and expectations for liberal democracy.[13] These views seem logical but to implement them is no easy task.

Also in the 2001 study, the 1,165 respondents were asked to rank the importance of tasks to implement and achieve unification on the scale "not at all important" to "very important". The percentages given to "very important" and "important" are shown in Table 6.20.

Table 6.20 Main tasks for unification, 2001

Division	%
Creating mutual understanding and trust	75.8
Opening and liberalization of North Korea	72.0
Correspondence and family reunion	71.6
Reducing heterogeneity and promoting homogeneity	69.1
Socio-cultural exchanges	68.0
Conclusion of a North-South Peace Treaty	66.7
Withdrawal of US troops and the National Security Law	51.8
Reduction of defense budgets and armaments	48.7

Source: Reproduced from Kil et al., ibid., 2001, p. 42: table III-18. Note: The number of respondents is not recorded.

As in Table 6.16, the need to create mutual trust and for North Korea to open up is apparent. Notably, the following three tasks in Table 6.20 concern socio-cultural contacts, thus supporting the views expressed by scholars Cho and Ko (2002) that such contacts are important factors in restoring national homogeneity and creating peaceful coexistence recorded in Chapter 1. Arranging the tasks by type, "opening and expansion of contacts" were more important than "backing down from military confrontation".[14]

---

13 Hwang, "Yôngse chungnip t'ongil pangan-ûi yuyongsông: t'ongil sôngsasik'il hwanggûm-ûi chungganch'i", *T'ongil Han'guk* (2004), 9, pp. 76-7; Hyôn, in Yi (ed.), *T'ongirûl wihae*, pp. 15, 16, 18-20; Kim, "Toward the End of Agony", *Han'guk-Sûweden hyôphoe sosik* (2003), no. 7, p. 16; Yang, "Kim Dae-jung Administration's", 1998, p. 61.

14 Kil et al., ibid., 2001, pp. 42-3.

Since education in South Korea has emphasized negative views of the North, it is of interest to investigate opinions of South Korea's unification education in Table 6.21.

Table 6.21　Opinions on unification education, 2001

Division	Number	%
Inadequate	497	43.0
Very inadequate	352	30.4
Neither bad nor good	231	20.0
Appropriate	61	5.3
Very appropriate	15	1.3

Source: Reproduced from Kil et al., ibid., 2001, p. 46: table III-23.

Since opinions were highly negative, there was an urgent need for improvements of the teaching syllabus on the North. The South Korean scholar Lee Woo-Young and his associates (2001) record that since anti-communism has been the core of unification education during 50 years of hostile division it is a very strong aspect for ordinary people. This has created a negative view of North Koreans and the North's system. In addition, the economic crisis has recently encouraged South Koreans to ignore North Korea.

Respondents were asked how they perceived the level of heterogeneity between the two Koreas by ranking to what extent nine items linked to daily life and consciousness differed on a scale from "entirely different" to "very similar". The percentages given to "very different" and "different" are enumerated in Table 6.22.

Table 6.22　Perceived heterogeneity between the two Koreas, 2001

Division	%
Ways of thinking and values	79.7
Game culture	72.7
Language practices	71.6
School life	69.2
Life styles	62.9
Family life	59.5
Religious activities	55.9
Historical consciousness	46.1
Traditional culture	35.3

Source: Reproduced from Kil et al., ibid., 2001, p. 51: table III-29. Note: The number of respondents is not recorded.

Ranking the socio-cultural differences structurally, "modern life culture" showed greater differences than "historical consciousness and traditional culture". Consequently, as one would expect, the main differences derived from the division.

Students were asked to rank the impact of ten traditional rules and customs on present society. The percentages given to "far more" and "slightly" are shown in Table 6.23.

Table 6.23 Perceived impact of tradition in the two Koreas, 2001

Division	%
Authoritarianism (North)	76.6
Patriarchism (North)	72.5
Predominance of men over women (North)	68.9
The custom of interdependence (North)	64.9
Piety towards parents (North)	63.9
Respect for the elder (North)	60.3
Worship of ancestors (North)	59.8
Academic factionalism (South)	84.9
Regionalism (South)	70.7
Family (blood) ties (South)	67.1

Source: Reproduced from Kil et al., ibid., 2001, p. 54: table III-34. Note: The number of respondents is not recorded.

It is to be noted that in South Korea, only the impact of such distortions of traditional culture as academic factionalism, regionalism and family ties was considered to be stronger in the South than in North Korea.[15] The view of North Korea as a more traditional society may, by implying the existence of conservatism towards change, emerge as an obstacle to developing closer relations as well as to unifying Korea.

Explanations of the deepening of national heterogeneity appear in Table 6.24.

Table 6.24 Explanations of the deepening of heterogeneity, 2001

Division	Number of respondents	%
Ideological differences	414	35.6
Different political systems	191	16.4
Economic imbalances	190	16.4
Different popular cultures	161	13.9
Different life styles	120	10.3
School education	86	7.4

Source: Reproduced from Kil et al., ibid., 2001, p. 58: table III-40.

---

15 Kil et al., ibid., 2001, pp. 45-6, 50-52, 53-5; Lee et al., ibid., 2001, pp. 81-2.

It is obvious that all major explanations derive from national division, thus supporting the view expressed by O (1999) in 1999, that the two Koreas maintain their common traditional values recorded in Chapter 1.

Respondents' perceptions of North and South Korean youths' way of thinking are shown in Table 6.25.

Table 6.25 Perceptions of North and South Korean youths' way of thinking, 2001

Division	Number of respondents	%
Different	549	47.7
Entirely different	377	32.7
Similar	135	11.7
Very similar	91	7.9

Source: Reproduced from Kil et al., ibid., 2001, p. 60: table III-42.

The differences are striking. A main explanation could be the lack of cross-border contacts.

The main tasks for North Korea to implement to promote homogeneity are recorded in Table 6.26.

Table 6.26 North Korea's main tasks to promote homogeneity, 2001

Division	Number of respondents	%
The fall of Kim Jong II	333	28.7
Reform and opening	298	25.7
Expanding North-South exchanges and cooperation	294	25.4
Economic development	135	13.4
Normalization of diplomatic ties with the US and the West	91	6.8

Source: Reproduced from Kil et al., ibid., 2001, p. 62: table III-45.

The same data for South Korea are shown in Table 6.27.

The need for South Korea to expand contacts to promote homogeneity is obvious, which is in line with the arguments presented in Chapter 1. Greater importance is given to a government change in North Korea, but a change of leader is no guarantee of meaningful change: top officers, such as government officials, live in an exclusive area in P'yôngyang known as the Executive Apartments. These apartments are equipped with luxury goods like colour TV sets, refrigerators and imported Japanese air conditioners that are beyond the reach of most ordinary citizens. This is the privileged elite who Kim Jong Il can count on for loyalty and support. They were not affected by the famine. They are also shielded from the sight of other citizens who have no access to the area. Such people belong to the core class in North Korea that comprise about 28 per cent of the population.[16] There can be no doubt that this class concurs with those people who fear the consequences of a unification referred to in Chapter 3.

Table 6.27   South Korea's main tasks to promote homogeneity, 2001

Division	Number of respondents	%
Expanding exchanges and cooperation with North Korea	536	46.3
Improving unification education	206	17.8
Improving media reporting on North Korea	192	16.6
Revising North Korea policies	168	14.5
Increasing economic aid	55	4.8

Source: Reproduced from Kil et al., ibid., 2001, p. 63: table III-47.

The Korea Youth Development Institute also made in-depth interviews with six young North Korean defectors who had fled during 1999 and 2001 since they could not stand life in the North any longer, economically, politically or socially. Too broad conclusions should not be drawn on the basis of such a small group of people, but it turned out that these North Korean youth were very interested in the unification issue. Unification was regarded as a necessity and as the only way to liberate the Korean people. Such attitudes derived from indoctrination under Kim Il Sung's rule and the wish to overcome the economic difficulties. Unification was also regarded as the way to liberate the South Korean people.

The view on obstacles to unification differed entirely from that of the South Korean youth: the reason why unification does not occur was considered to be the roles of the United States and South Korean governments that manipulated the South's population. However, it should be noted that information in North Korea was strictly controlled by the government making defection the only way to learn about life in the South (however, this view is somewhat contradicted by data on South Korean influences in Chapter 4). Unlike the opinions they had held in North Korea, all defectors thought that the most plausible way to unification was through Kim Jong Il's death or the collapse of his system; other [non-specified] ways would

---

16   Lee et al., ibid., 2005, pp. 106-107; Lintner, ibid., pp. 99-100.

hardly work. Perhaps because of such views, both their will for unification and negative feelings against the Kim Jong Il government were strong.

By "homogeneity" North Korean youth most often meant the united Korean people: they regarded feelings and human characteristics as the two Koreas' common points. However, in terms of such daily issues as economics and culture there were, due to partition, striking differences such as the higher degree of competition in South Korean society. They thought, in contrast to the views of South Korean students referred to above, that South Korea had preserved traditional culture better than North Korea had done as a result of Kim Il Sung's unitary thoughts.[17]

In 2000, the Ministry of Unification had made a survey on North Korean defectors' consciousness of unification, generally. Among 453 defectors who had arrived between 1994 and 1999, 383 were randomly selected. 100 of those, 70 men and 30 women due to their distribution, received inquiries but only 33 replied (18 men and 15 women). It is therefore hard to say whether the views are representative of the whole North Korean population. Nonetheless, 75.8 per cent of those expressed that they had a deep interest in unification and 21.2 per cent interest; of the others less so. The figures by far exceeded the average 45.1 per cent expressed by South Koreans in a [non-specified] survey. The main reason for North Koreans' strong wish for unification was that it was regarded as the supreme task of the Korean people (48.5 per cent) followed by the aims of strengthening national competitiveness (24.2 per cent) and achieving social stability (18.2 per cent).

Defectors were asked to give a number of the degree of homogeneity between the two Koreas with ten as the maximum degree and zero the minimum degree. The average figure given was just 5.4; 9.1 per cent replied zero.[18] The low figure implies that North Korean citizens could regard the degree of homogeneity as even lower. 63.6 per cent of the respondents regarded the costs of division as greater than the costs of unification whereas 27.3 per cent expressed the opposite opinion. The costs were thus not regarded as an obstacle to unification; it seems that they expected South Koreans to pay for it!

The North Korean political system was regarded by 72.7 per cent of the respondents as the main stumbling block towards unification, while 15.2 per cent pointed towards the attitudes of the North's leadership. Three per cent each replied the North's economic system, the South Korean government's attitudes and those of the neighbouring countries. Thus, the main obstacles towards unification were, as in the above cases, placed on the shoulders of the North Korean side.[19]

---

17 Kil et al., ibid., 2001, pp. 74, 75, 77-9, 90-92, 97.

18 According to the South Korean scholar Kim Kook Sin (2001), the degree of heterogeneity between citizens of North and South Korea is, considering the period of division and the actual record of exchanges and cooperation, assessed to far exceed that of Germany and Yemen. From Kim, "Togil, Pet'ûnam, Yemen", 2001, p. 35. However, whether the average figure supports this view is hard to say.

19 Ko, "Pukhan naebu-ûi chôngch'i kaltûng kwalli pangan", in Moon et al., *Nambukhan chôngch'i kaltûng-gwa t'ongil* (Seoul: Orûm, 2002), pp. 269-272, 273-74, 276-77, 278. Replies were expressed in percentages, not numbers of people.

Considering the perceived view of the need for the North to change it is worth noting that, according to the South Korean scholar Cho Han Bum (2002), North Korea shows a high degree of unity politically but it has, in recent years, begun to be undermined economically, socially and culturally. The transfer of power from Kim Il Sung to Kim Jong Il went smoothly and it is hard to find divisions and tensions within the core of power. However, by giving priority to P'yôngyang and its surroundings in distribution of aid, social polarization has increased and tensions have been created. Such a policy creates hostility and undermines confidence in the ruling class of any society in the long run.

Due to the economic crisis, few industries operate; the arms industry being the only exception. There is lack of energy and the food ration system has collapsed. This has created serious distrust within the official economy. Whereas central economic planning has begun to disintegrate, an underground and subsistence economy is developing. According to the South Korean scholar Suh Jae Jean (2005), the widespread practice of bribery has led to the proliferation of black markets which are changing the North Korean society. He concludes that, "The practice of money taking is deeply permeating the society and eroding the system".

Social control has been weakened by the food crisis. The crisis has affected the whole population and has made control of people's movement difficult, which was the basis for social control. The society's basis in the family has been weakened by these movements. The crisis has also created such social problems as thefts and robbery of nationalized property and has, as we have seen, led to a rising number of defectors.

Finally, cultural unity has been weakened. The economic difficulties have undermined loyalty to the state and made ideological control more difficult to implement, but to create a civil society and organize opposition is impossible. Yet, such a situation may erode the foundations of the North Korean system in the long run.[20] If this data is correct, there is a strong potential for change in North Korea outside the ability of South Korean influence to affect change through songs and products described in Chapter 4, but only time will tell what the outcome will be.

6.4 Views of unification in South Korea, 2002-2003

The Korea Youth Development Institute carried out in September 2002 another opinion survey to find out youth's views about the process of North-South unity. The study comprised of 1,125 high-school and university students opinions, in the Seoul area.[21]

Also this survey investigated interest in unification, as is shown in Table 6.28.

---

20 Cho, *Nambukhan sahoe munhwa kongdongch'e hyôngsông pangan yôn'gu* (Seoul: T'ongil yôn'guwôn, 2002), pp. 20-23; Suh, *North Korea's Market Economy*, 2005, p. 23.

21 Kil et al., *Nambukhan-ûi silchiljôk t'onghab-ûl wihan ch'ôngsonyôn kyoryu hyômnyôk chedohwa pangan yôn'gu* (Seoul: T'ongil yôn'guwôn, 2002), pp. 73, 74, 77-8, 79, 80, 81-2, 171. Percentages may not reach 100 per cent due to roundings.

Table 6.28   Interest in unification, 2002

Division	Number of respondents	%
Interested	712	63.3
Not interested	262	23.3
Very interested	116	10.3
Not interested at all	35	3.1

Source: Reproduced from Kil et al., ibid., 2002, p. 78: table V-4.

The figure of interest in the unification issue is remarkably higher than it was in the 2001 survey referred to in Table 6.18, but it is unclear why.

Data on the reasonability for unification are shown in Table 6.29.

Table 6.29   Reasonability of unification, 2002

Division	Number of respondents	%
Korea must reunify	621	55.4
Korea must absolutely reunify	287	25.6
Korea must not reunify	195	17.4
Korea must absolutely not reunify	18	1.6

Source: Reproduced from Kil et al., ibid., 2002, p. 79: table V-6.

The overwhelming majority for unification (81 per cent) remains (cf. p. 200: table 6.17).

Opinions on the time for unification are enumerated in Table 6.30.

Table 6.30   Time for unification, 2002

Division	Number of respondents	%
Within 5 years	49	4.4
Within 10 years	303	27.0
Within 20 years	428	38.1
More than 20 years	343	30.5

Source: Reproduced from Kil et al., ibid., 2002, p. 82: table V-10.

Clearly, the opinion was, unlike that in the survey made in September 2000 (see Table 6.14), that unification would take longer time, but why is unclear.

Data on the formula for unification are recorded in Table 6.31.

Table 6.31 Formula for unification, 2002

Division	Number of respondents	%
Peaceful and gradual unification	713	63.7
Inner collapse of North Korea	349	31.2
War through the North's intention	33	2.9
War through accidental collision	24	2.1

Source: Reproduced from Kil et al., ibid., 2002, p. 80: table V-8.

The wish for a "peaceful and gradual unification" that refers to unification through negotiations between North and South Korean authorities is apparent.

"Inner collapse" refers to a failure of the North Korean system followed by unification through absorption.[22] Notable is that the Yemeni way of unification appeared far more acceptable than a German-style unification. This may reflect concerns over the costs of Korean unity and the social consequences of German reunification. That a few respondents regarded unification through war as possible is highly surprising but it is an entirely unrealistic view.

The Korea Institute of National Unification made, in October 2002, an opinion survey on North Korea and unification issues that included 69 academic specialists. The purpose was to find out their opinions in order to develop an appropriate forecasting model for Korean unification. Opinions on time for unification are shown in Table 6.32.

Table 6.32 Time for unification, 2002

Division	Number of respondents	%
Within 5 years	9	13.0
10-15 years	15	21.7
15-20 years	16	23.2
More than 20 years	28	40.6
Unification will not take place	1	1.4

Source: Reproduced from Park et al., T'ongil sinario-wa (Seoul: T'ongil yôn'guwôn, 2002), p. 55: table IV-13.

The results are similar to the above in Table 6.30.

Opinions on obstacles to unification are recorded in Table 6.33.

Again, the obstacles are internal ones but notable is that unification costs are not regarded as a serious obstacle to unification. In fact, since the costs and aftermaths

---

22 Kil et al., ibid., 2002, p. 80.

of German unification were presented in a wrong way in Korea, the general public regarded the costs as excessive which caused a negative view of unification.[23]

Table 6.33   Obstacles to unification, 2002

Division	Number of respondents	%
North Korea difficulties to transfer towards liberalization and pluralism	10	21.7
Different social systems	9	19.6
Vested interest groups	9	19.6
Neighbours' different interests	8	17.4
Difficulties for Korea's leaders to agree	7	15.2
Unification costs	3	6.5

Source: Reproduced from Park et al., ibid., 2002, p. 60: table IV-16.

Since the main obstacle identified is the difficulties for North Korea to transfer towards liberalization and pluralism, it should be noted that economic management improvement measures were unveiled on 1 July, 2002 as preparations to adopt a market economy. The previous collapse of the public economy had served to breed market economic elements that forced the government to implement these measures. Price and income hikes were concurrently implemented, the state managed rationing system was abolished, the foreign exchange rate was adjusted to a realistic level and currency exchange was freed to strengthen the population's consumption capacity. In 2003, the wôn was devalued to close the gap between official and black market rates and to absorb American dollars that circulated on the market. Floating exchange rates were adopted. Consumer and industrial goods, not only agricultural products, were allowed to be traded in the public market in another step of economic liberalization; black markets that were an important part of citizens' livelihood became "general markets".

As of April 2005, such policies that North Korea, since they were introduced officially, has termed "pragmatic socialism", had raised awareness of the market economy. In the words of the above Suh (2005), North Korea is heading toward "market socialism". The criteria for evaluating enterprises had shifted from volumes produced to profits earned enhancing attention to quality. As the rationing system was abolished and a differentiated wage system determining wages according to individual performance introduced, awareness of private ownership and belief in the concept "the more you work, the more you earn" had risen. Productivity in agriculture and light industry had improved and the commercial sector had been revitalized.

---

23   Park et al., ibid., 2002, pp. 21, 22, 23, 59-60.

However, most North Koreans' livelihoods had deteriorated due to price hikes. The poor state of social overhead capital and the lack of investment capital and market economy management expertise hampered reforms. Markets did not function properly due to the economy's poor supply function. In addition, tensions over the nuclear program made it difficult for North Korea to obtain foreign capital and technology needed to pursue reform policies. Given this mixed picture, it is not surprising that Suh (2005) writes: "However, it is too early yet to conclude that North Korea has dissolved its planned economic system and has made the transition to a market economy".[24]

Scholars' views on prerequisites for unification are recorded in Table 6.34.

Table 6.34 Prerequisites for unification, 2002

Division	Number of respondents	%
Peaceful coexistence	32	46.4
Institutionalization of non-political exchanges	14	20.3
Liberalization of North Korea	9	13.0
Reduction of armaments	8	11.6
Recognizing different political systems	3	4.3
Family reunions	1	1.4
Pluralization of North Korean politics	1	1.4
No reply	1	1.4

Source: Reproduced from Park et al., ibid., 2002, p. 58: table IV-15. Note: "Non-political exchanges" refer to economics, culture and academia.

The need for peaceful coexistence and institutionalization of non-political exchanges in a functionalistic approach is obvious. This gives support to the views expressed by scholars Cho and Ko (2002) recorded in Chapter 1 on the need for socio-cultural contacts to create peaceful coexistence.

Unification was expected by scholars to take place on South Korean terms, as shown in Table 6.35.

---

24 Ahn, ibid., pp. 49, 51-2; Kim & Choi, *Understanding North Korea's Economic Reforms* (Seoul: Korea Institute for National Unification, Center for the North Korean Economy, 2005), pp. 44-7; Park, ibid., 2004, pp. 145-46; Suh, ibid., pp. 5, 25, 26, 28, 29, 33. Original quotation marks. "Pragmatic socialism" and "general markets" are quoted from Suh, ibid., pp. 5 and 33.

Table 6.35 Formula for unification, 2002

Division	Number of respondents	%
On South Korean terms	21	30.4
Changing North Korea through aid	20	29.0
Unification through agreement	9	13.0
Unification after eruption in North Korea	8	11.6
Exchanges widen but no unification	4	5.8
Others (non-specified)	3	4.3
North Korean collapse after military collisions	2	2.9
No reply	2	2.9

Source: Reproduced from Park et al., ibid., 2002, p. 57: table IV-14.

The main expectation was that following changes like those that took place in East and Central Europe, the North Korean system would become self-destructive and unify with the South. The most desirable unification would be a peaceful one through agreement.[25]

The Korea Institute of National Unification made, in 2003, a survey of such issues as cognitions of North Korea and policies towards the North. The purpose was to systematically analyze those issues in order to present countermeasures to meet them. The survey was based on the recognition that national consent and international support are the most important factors in pursuing policies towards North Korea. 1,000 persons above 20 years of age from all parts of South Korea, with the exception of Cheju Island, were randomly sampled to participate.[26]

The main cognitions of North Korea are shown in Table 6.36.

Table 6.36 Cognitions of North Korea, 2003

Division	%
A state to cooperate with	38.2
A state to be alert with	28.6
A state to assist	16.2
A hostile land	12.5
A rival	4.5

Source: Reproduced from Choi et al., ibid., p. 62: table III-1-1.

---

25 Park et al., ibid., 2002, pp. 56-8. Percentages do not reach 100 per cent due to roundings.

26 Choi et al., *Nambuk kwangye-ûi*, p. 34. Responses only appear in percentages which may not reach 100 per cent due to roundings. The response rate is not recorded.

Interestingly, after five years of the sunshine policy, positive views comprised 54.4 per cent against negative views 41.1 per cent (neutral view 4.5 per cent). In 1998, the figures had been reversed: 37.2 per cent against 54.4 per cent. However, these figures should be cautiously evaluated against the data on the North's policy of unification through communizing the Korean Peninsula recorded in Table 6.37 (cf. p. 78).

Table 6.37 Communization of South Korea, 2003

Division	%
Remains but lacks power	51.7
No change	33.5
Policy abandoned	14.9

Source: Reproduced from Choi et al., ibid., p. 74: table III-1-7.

Opinions had changed markedly since 1998 when 58.1 per cent had replied that the policy had not changed at all and that North Korea was always watching for an opportunity to communize the South. 30 per cent thought that it remained but that the North lacked power to pursue the policy. Only 7 per cent replied that North Korea had abandoned the policy and wanted coexistence.[27]

Interest in unification is recorded in Table 6.38.

Table 6.38 Discussion on unification, 2003

Division	%
Discuss sometimes	39.4
Hardly discuss	28.6
Discuss almost not at all	23.7
Discuss frequently	8.3

Source: Choi et al., ibid., p. 64: table III-1-2.

The data differ from those of September 2000 (Table 6.12) which may reflect the different composition of respondents.

The main tasks for unification are enumerated in Table 6.39.

---

27 Choi et al., ibid., pp. 61-6, 73-4, 149, 151, 253. Percentages do not reach 100 per cent due to roundings. The authors record (ibid., p. 253: fn. 90) that the 1998 survey included "does not know" as an alternative. This may explain why the 1998 figures on unification through communizing South Korea do not reach 100 per cent.

Table 6.39 Main tasks for unification, 2003

Division	%
Achieving national harmony	41.3
Elevating national power	38.6
Strengthening preparedness for security	12.6
Consolidating democracy	7.6

Source: Reproduced from Choi et al., ibid., p. 108: table III-3-5.

In contrast to data presented in Tables 6.16, 6.20 and 6.34, the overwhelming importance of national harmony and national power is striking. However, the different tasks emphasized may not contradict but supplement each other.

6.5 Implications of the great powers' policies towards Korea

As said in Chapter 3, the two Koreas agreed in the 1972 4 July Communiqué to reunify without foreign interference. However, Korean unification is, as was the case in Germany and Yemen, also affected by the regional context: domestic and international developments must match each other.[28] 68 South Korean scholars' opinions of the attitudes of China, Japan, Russia and the United States on Korean unification are shown in Table 6.40.

Table 6.40 Opinions of great powers' attitudes on Korean unification, 2002, 2003

Division	Wants unification	%
China	4	5.9
		9.3
Japan	1	1.5
		5.5
Russia	5	7.4
		5.8
United States	31	45.6
		29.3
Do not want unification	27	39.7
		50.1

Sources: Reproduced from Choi et al., ibid., p. 88: table III-2-4; Pak et al., ibid., 2002, p. 63: table IV-18. Notes: Lower row for percentages refers to 2003 and are from Choi et al., ibid.

---

28 Hwang, ibid., 2004 (9), p. 78.

The table shows that interest in Korean unification is limited, especially in 2003. Given the Japanese occupation of Korea (1910-1945), it is not surprising that Japan is regarded as being the country most against unification both years. That the United States is seen as being most positive towards unification may reflect a view that its role as the world's sole superpower requires American support in the unification process.

The South Korean scholar Shin Sang-Jin (2000) confirms the opinion that the United States, Japan, China and Russia prefer a divided rather than a unified Korea. One explanation was that the possibilities in the short-run for political changes in North Korea such as those that took place in Eastern Europe in the late 1980s were low. In fact, the American scholar Selig S. Harrison (2002) points out that the Confucian ethos and the traditions of absolute centralized rule that go with it had facilitated totalitarianism which, along with the power of nationalism, made a repetition unlikely. Shin also notes that South Korea at present was incapable of bearing the costs of unification, that military collisions may take place in the process of unification and, finally, that a unified Korea with a total population of 70 million people could appear as a great regional power. The South Korean scholar Suh Jae-Jung (2004) provides the, to the authors's knowledge, most recent confirmation of the four powers' views of unification: "All four powers have a vital stake in peace on the peninsula, but they all prefer a divided Korea that no single power controls to a unified Korea under the lopsided influence of one of them".

Given the standpoint of the United States, Japan, China and Russia, it is not surprising that compatriot scholar Hwang In Kwan (2004) expresses the opinion that for unification to occur it should be agreed upon from a fair and equal standpoint and the unified Korea must not be a security threat to the neighbours. To maintain independence after unity in order to achieve a secure and complete unification, he proposes permanent neutrality, as in Switzerland or Austria, to keep Korea out of international conflicts and tensions.[29]

The United States, China, Japan and Russia have all had their own interests to pursue in their policies towards Korea. As a signatory power of the 1953 armistice agreement, the US has a central role in establishing peace on the Korean Peninsula. The Republic of Korea-United States Mutual Security Treaty signed in 1953 is the main basis of the American force presence in the South. After the end of the Cold War, the US has been determined to maintain a stable world order. Thus, diffusion of weapons of mass destruction must be restricted. To stop the nuclear program and missile development have been the major targets of the policy towards North Korea.

---

29 Harrison, *Korean Endgame*, 2002, p. 21; Hwang, ibid., (2004), 9, p. 78; Shin, "Taebuk p'oyong chôngch'aeg-ûi hyoyulchôk ch'ujin-ûl wihan chubyôn anbo wegyo hwangyông chosông pangan", in T'ongil yônguwôn, *Nambukhan hwahae hyômnyôk ch'okjin pangan* (Seoul: T'ongil yôn'guwôn, 2000), pp. 8-10; Suh, ibid., 2004, p. 83. Percentages do not reach 100 per cent due to roundings.

After the 1994 Agreed Framework that included provisions on a freezing of the North's nuclear programme, replacement of graphite-moderated reactors with light-water reactors and the establishment of liaison offices in the two nations' capitals had been signed, the Clinton Administration in January 1995 slightly eased sanctions against North Korea and provided humanitarian aid. When sanctions were eased further in June 2000, trade with most goods was permitted. The United States has attempted to ease tensions through such channels as high-level talks and missile negotiations with North Korea but, as we have seen, with dubious results.

Four-party talks, involving South Korea, the United States, North Korea and China, have also been held in Geneva. After Kim Dae Jung had become president in 1998, such talks were held in March and October the same year and in January, April and August 1999. The parties agreed, in October 1998, to create two subcommittees, to deal with the easing of tensions and confidence building on the Korean Peninsula. This became a significant step since it established a framework for fully-fledged negotiations on transforming the armistice agreement into a peace treaty. The three subsequent plenum meetings were led by the sub-committees. But no results were forthcoming since the US/South Korean camp wanted mutual confidence to be gradually built up, whereas the North proposed the withdrawal of American military personnel from South Korea and the conclusion of a peace treaty between North Korea and the US. The high-level mutual visits that took place in October 2000 failed to bring North Korea and the United States closer to each other, although in the joint Washington communique of 12 October it was declared that North Korea and the United States would no longer have "hostile intent toward each other".

As of 2002, the US hoped that, if unification occurs, the unified Korea becomes an allied country with a liberal democratic system. If South Koreans so wish, the US would be willing to maintain troops in Korea also after unification. If the troops remain, it would alleviate US concerns that unification might end the special security ties with South Korea that are considered by the US to have helped both to stabilize the entire region and to extend its influence in Asia. In fact, the troops play a dual role by keeping an eye on both China and Russia.[30]

China aimed in 2000 to raise its influence on North Korea by providing economic and political assistance to prevent a collapse, persuading the North to open up to the outside world and restoring the traditionally friendly relations. But China's transition to a socialist market economy has made it impossible to provide free large-scale aid to the North, as it did before. China regarded North Korea's isolation in the world as one reason for the tensions on the Korean Peninsula and therefore intended

---

30 Eberstadt, *The End of North Korea*, p. 126; Bae et al., *Nambukhan siljilchôk t'onghap-gwa chubyônguk hyômnyôk yudo pangan* (Seoul: T'ongil yôn'guwôn, 2002), pp. 22, 23-4, 27, 32, 33, 87, 105; Harrison, ibid., 2002, pp. 165, 171, 228; KINU, *The Unification Environment*, 2000a, pp. 116-18, 167, 171, 177; Ministry of Unification, *Kim Dae-jung's policies,* pp. 40-41; Shin, ibid., pp. 24-6; Tang, "A Neutral Reunified Korea: A Chinese View", *The Journal of East Asian Affairs* 13 (1999), no. 2, p. 466; Yang, ibid., 1998, p. 60. Original quotation marks.

to persuade the North to not only open up its society but also to pursue reform policies.

China also wanted improved relations between North Korea on the one hand and Japan and the US on the other and urged visiting North Korean leaders to go to its open zones. Economically, North Korea had become a burden to China but due to the North's strategical importance as "...a useful buffer zone that contributes to their national security" it was necessary to maintain good relations.

China maintained a military alliance treaty with North Korea formed in 1961 that included a clause on automatic military intervention. High-level visits to China in 1999-2000 showed that North Korea also needed China. Meanwhile, China recognized South Korea and pursued by, for instance, supporting the expansion of North-South contacts, a policy that aimed to create stability and peace on the Korean Peninsula, not least to promote its own economic development that was considered necessary for domestic stability and for enhancing its influence in the region.

Given China's role in the formation of the Cold War structure on the Korean Peninsula and its political and economic position in the region, China did not want to be excluded from a solution of the Korean problem. As of 2002, China wanted a unified Korea to be friendly towards China or at least neutral. China expressed support for a peaceful and gradual Korean unification without foreign interference and was particularly anxious for a rapid unification taking place through intervention by the United States. In fact, a unified Korea with American troops would become a security threat to China given the disappearance of the North as a buffer. On the other hand, by supporting the cause of a neutral reunified Korea and refraining from polling the united country under Chinese influence, China will not damage the interests of the United States only but also of Russia and Japan.[31] China's position on how to achieve unification thus concurred with the two Korean governments' wishes and opinions among the South Korean public as well as scholars. On the other hand, Chinese concerns for the US role in the unification process indicate that it may get even more complicated than is expected.

Japan tried to normalize relations with North Korea in 2000. Negotiations had previously collapsed due to the tensions between the US and North Korea caused by the nuclear issue but were now held for the first time in seven years. The process was affected by the US relations with North Korea, inter-Korean relations and the state of security in Northeast Asia. Consequently, Japan tried to base its North Korea policy on that of South Korea and the United States. The policy was based on dialogue and restraints: there were fears of the North's missile and nuclear programs.

Again, normalization talks failed to bring results due to the different standpoints and only informal contacts took place in third countries. The first North Korea-Japan summit meeting held in September 2002 brought them closer to each other in such outstanding issues as the suspicions of the North for kidnapping Japanese citizens

---

31 Bae et al., ibid., pp. 56-7, 60-61, 111; Eberstadt, ibid., p. 126; Shin, ibid., pp. 23-4, 32; Tang, ibid., pp. 472-73, 478. Original quotation marks.

and compensation by Japan for the colonial occupation and was considered to have laid a foundation for normalizing relations.

At the second summit meeting held in May 2004, North Korea allowed five remaining daughters of kidnapped Japanese citizens who had returned to Japan to travel to Japan but three citizens were not allowed. It also promised to investigate the actual conditions of ten Japanese citizens who had died or disappeared. Japan urged a solution of the nuclear issue. North Korea responded that the target is a denuclearization of the Korean Peninsula and that the issue would be peacefully solved through the six-party talks. But, as we have seen, the situation has since aggravated.

As of 2002, Japan preferred a gradual unification to a sudden one and hoped that a unified Korea would be friendly towards both Japan and the United States. This position is not surprising given that apparently there are apprehensions that a unified Korea might pose greater economic and diplomatic challenges to Japan, partly because of the deep animosity toward Japan among Koreans. In Korean eyes, Japan fears that a reunified Korea could become an economic competitor, although that would not happen immediately.

Russia did not, as of 2000, want unforeseen accidents on the Korean Peninsula to cause unexpected changes of the regional power balance at a time when it was overwhelmed with its own internal troubles that weakened its power. Therefore, Russia tried to maintain friendly relations with both Koreas which contrasts to the tilt towards South Korea during the years 1992-1999. In July 2000, President Vladimir Putin became the first Russian (including the former Soviet Union) head of state to visit North Korea. The summit was followed by Kim Jong Il's visit to Russia in August 2001. In between, President Putin had visited South Korea in February 2001. While pursuing a two-Korea policy aiming to strengthen its influence on the Korean Peninsula, Russia opposed North Korean nuclear arms for the sake of regional stability. Russia also attempted to attract labour from North Korea for its development of Siberia and to promote economic ties. As of 2002, Russia wished a peaceful unification of Korea in which Russia participates.[32]

That the US, China, Japan and Russia want to maintain the status quo on the Korean Peninsula does hardly bode well for unification, but the joint wish for peace may benefit the ongoing development towards peaceful coexistence by restraining the two Koreas from using military force towards each other. While US-Chinese rivalry could become an obstacle to Korean unification, a lesson from German and Yemeni unity is that if a process towards unity begins no one can stop it. That rivalry over the influence on the Korean Peninsula may continue also after unification supports the opinion that permanent neutrality is the best way for Korea to maintain independence.

---

32 Bae et al., ibid., pp. 39-42, 77-80; Eberstadt, ibid., p. 126; Harrison, op. cit. 2002, p. 301; Kim, "Puk-il kwangye", in T'ongil yôn'guwôn, ibid., 2004, pp. 64-5; Shin, ibid., pp. 26-8; Tang, ibid., p. 468.

6.6 Conclusions

North and South Koreans have negative views of each other. The South Korean daily *Hankook Ilbo* expressed negative views of North Korea between 1993 and 1996 and changes in North Korea were regarded as a prerequisite for unification. A survey from 2000 shows that North Korean defectors have negative views of South Koreans as a result of educational policies; this also applies for South Koreans since anti-communism has been the core of unification education. However, according to a survey from 2003, images had improved thanks to the sunshine policy pursued since 1998.

A survey from 2001 shows that few respondents had previous experiences of North Korean culture but they were curious to get them. Since most respondents could understand North Korean films, the influence of the joint historical legacy remains: watching North Korean art and literary works caused greater affinity. On the other hand, that the political content made films boring confirms that the division has created differences between the two Koreas. Although unrepresentative of the whole population, the positive views of South Korean visitors to arts exhibitions imply that learning about North Korea is of the utmost importance to create closer relations.

Surveys made in 2000-2002 of South Korean students' views of North Korea and unification issues show that most respondents wanted a gradual unification, but interest was limited since division was regarded as the natural state of affairs. In contrast, the survey of North Korean defectors shows that they both wanted unification and were more interested. The dominating opinion was that North Korea had to change to achieve unification, a view that was shared among the few defectors surveyed. North Korea shows a high degree of unity politically but it has been undermined economically, socially and culturally indicating that there is a potential for change. A notable development is that North Korea introduced the 1 July, 2002 economic management improvement measures. A market economy ("pragmatic socialism") has since begun to develop.

The main obstacles to unification were North Korea adhering to communism and the economic gap in the South's favour, but the views of other factors imply that also South Korea has to change. Among defectors, the opinion was that the United States and South Korean governments were the main obstacles. The lower rank of the great powers reflects the view that Korea must unify through its own efforts.

The lower rank of deepening of heterogeneity than political and economic factors deriving from the national division may reflect a view that national homogeneity could be easier to restore than to build a politically and economically unified Korea. For South Korea, the most important task to promote homogeneity was to expand contacts. For North Korea, it was the fall of the Kim Jong Il Government. North Korean defectors supported this view, although the consequences are unclear. A survey of scholars made in 2002 confirmed that the main obstacles to unification were domestic ones. A peaceful and gradual unification was considered desirable.

Whereas Korean unification is affected by international developments, opinion surveys from 2002 and 2003 show that the United States, China, Japan and Russia all prefer a divided rather than a unified Korea. In fact, Korean unification could affect the regional political situation to their disadvantage. Their actual policies confirm scholars' views, but positive signs are the joint wish to maintain peace and for a peaceful and gradual unification. The wish for peace can contribute to secure peaceful coexistence on the Korean Peninsula. As the major regional powers, China and the United States exert most influence on Korean unification but they may become rivals in the process, making it more complex.

Chapter 7

General Conclusions

7.1 Inter-Korean socio-cultural exchanges and cooperation

It is hard to be optimistic regarding the possibilities for Korean unification. However, the expansion of multi-level contacts since President Kim Dae Jung (1998-2003) launched the sunshine policy in a typically functionalist fashion to promote cooperation in order to improve relations provides evidence of a mutual will to develop closer relations and contributes to peaceful coexistence, although contradictory developments have occurred in the process. While the sunshine policy shows clear similarities with previous administrations' policies, what has been new is its consistent implementation; after all, contacts continued even when armed incidents occurred, showing that North Korean attempts to obstruct the policy were doomed to fail. This pattern has continued also under President Roh Moo-hyun (2003-) whose "policy for peace and prosperity" is strikingly similar to the sunshine policy. If peaceful coexistence is created, it would become a great step forward in relations but to transform them into a state resembling that of pre-unity Germany and Yemen requires an opening of far more extensive contacts than the current ones. Due in particular to the closed nature of North Korean society, it is at present unrealistic to expect any such development.

That socio-cultural contacts which have been most apparent in academia and education, sports and religion have expanded significantly both qualitatively and quantitatively since 1998 has been an important sign of improved relations manifesting a mutual will to develop closer ties, The process did not begin entirely from scratch. The art troupes' performances in September 1985 during the first family reunions in P'yôngyang and Seoul marked the beginning of substantial North-South socio-cultural exchanges. Contacts then began to expand somewhat during the 1990s. In addition, a legal framework for socio-cultural exchanges and cooperation was established in 1989-1990.

That socio-cultural contacts from 1998 onwards have taken place when armed incidents have occurred has contributed to securing peace, in accordance with the functionalist view that bringing states actively together reduces the risks of conflicts. However, whether socio-cultural contacts are the most realistic way to overcome the Cold War structure on the Korean Peninsula in the future in an effort to coexist peacefully is virtually impossible to determine since inter-Korean relations are affected by internal and external economic and political factors that tend to reduce their impact. It should be noted, however, that since socio-cultural contacts took place in North Korea in 1992 and 1993 when the North's nuclear program caused severe tensions, they had contributed in any event to securing peace prior to 1998.

Besides these contributions to secure peace, socio-cultural contacts have brought with them three specific outcomes that should not be underestimated. Firstly, human exchanges through South Korean humanitarian aid to North Korea which began in 1995 due to the food crisis, and which expanded from 1998 onwards, have been the first contacts to be continuously pursued in spite of setbacks in relations. In fact, while the numbers of South Koreans involved in humanitarian aid has been low but has risen, these contacts have contributed to reducing tensions, thus reconfirming the functionalist view that promoting contacts contributes to securing peace. They have also created more positive mutual impressions by encouraging North and South Koreans to get to know each other better and have made it possible for South Koreans to distinguish between the North Korean government and the North's citizens.

Secondly, the five joint publications that were published from 1998-2002 show that the two Koreas can cooperate if there is mutual will to do so. Given the tense relations, it is remarkable that one joint report from the unification conferences held 1995-1999 was published in 2000. Equally remarkably, joint research projects resulted in a joint dictionary of computer terminologies published in 1999 and a language study in 2002. The symbolical value of the photo book published in 1998 and the history volumes in 2000 should not be underestimated either. Taken together, these achievements should create a "can-do spirit" that could be extended into other fields if there is sufficient will on both sides.

Thirdly, the influx of South Korean influences into North Korea has provided knowledge about the South. Those influences began with South Korean songs reaching North Korea already in 1989, but songs have continued to be introduced and have remained popular. The June 2000 first inter-Korean summit led to further influence through exposure to South Korean products. That most North Koreans know that South Korea is better off economically and that an unknown number of people have, by purchasing South Korean products, been able to compare their quality with that of domestic products can only have reinforced the public's discontent with the government's poor economic performance. Recent influence on education in the North has also been significant. These outcomes have by providing knowledge of each other, as well as creating mutual confidence and a "can-do-spirit", contributed with the potential to, in the long-run, transform relations into a state of peaceful coexistence and, eventually, to contribute to unification.

Another important outcome of the inter-Korean summit was the family reunion subject since the issue involves millions of Koreans, although, as of July 2004, only about 10,000 people of advanced ages have benefited from them. Besides the important humanitarian dimension, family reunions provide knowledge about each other. But the North Korean government's fears that the reunions will bring in foreign influences with negative consequences on society have contributed to making them irregular and thus meeting places have been moved from the capitals to distant Mt. Kûmgang. Consequently, family reunions have been less important than humanitarian aid in terms of influence and will have less long-term impact on relations than the three specific outcomes.

However, the significance of the inter-Korean summit and the 15 June Declaration must not be exaggerated: although it also led to an activation of official talks and socio-cultural contacts, the basic characteristic of North-South relations being tense has remained. Military issues in particular have hardly been discussed and the nuclear issue throws a dark shadow over relations.

In fact, the impact of socio-cultural contacts on relations must, in spite of these remarkable outcomes, not be overrated. Firstly, contacts have been insignificant compared to those between pre-unity Germany and Yemen. In Germany, the most important socio-cultural contact were ordinary East German's wide access to West German TV which gave them knowledge of West German society and enabled comparison with their own socio-political system. Large-scale mutual visits were also significant. The most important socio-cultural contact in Yemen appears to have been informal meetings between Yemenis abroad. Family reunions, informal meetings along the border and large-scale migration from South to North Yemen showed that people-to-people contacts were extensive. That unification was a common wish indicates that North and South Yemenis knew each other well.

In sharp contrast, most inter-Korean socio-cultural contacts have been irregular one-time events and have, with just a few exceptions, involved extremely few people such as politicians, scholars, journalists, religious workers, aid workers and media people whereas the general public only have had the opportunity to go to Mt. Kûmgang on "pre-arranged tours".

Consequently, among the, as of late 2004, 800,000-900,000 South Korean visitors to North Korea, only a tiny minority can have got more than a rather superficial impression. Nonetheless, the opportunity to travel is important since it would have been impossible unless the North Korean government had permitted it, partly as a sign of willingness to create peaceful coexistence. In fact, a positive change in recent years is that socio-cultural events have increasingly been held on the Korean Peninsula which have enabled more substantial contacts than the previous ones held in third countries. That experiences of "the other Korea" are superficial apply particularly to North Korea due to the far lower number of visitors to South Korea, but socio-cultural contacts have yet not been a one-sided communication alone.

The low number reflects North Korea's unwillingness to expose its citizens to external influences that, in spite of tight social control, could undermine the socio-political system: visits to South Korea no doubt have a more direct impact on people than the influx of influences from the South. But North Korea has not rejected such contacts that bring economic benefits, including the Mt. Kûmgang project, and has undertaken policies to minimize the impact of foreign influences. Yet, South Korean influences explain why North Koreans complain that they cannot go to the South while South Koreans visit the North. Actually, whereas "value integration" in terms of a feeling of a common ethnic identity, language, culture, history and set of customs and traditions, should be stronger given the joint historical legacy, a desire to live in peace, freedom and prosperity have reached at least some North Koreans, thanks to the sunshine policy. This distinguishes it from previous administrations' pursuit of mainly structural integration.

Even if one estimates the socio-cultural contacts' diffusion effects on the basis of the performances' audiences, TV ownership ratios and watchers of TV-relayed events, this has been limited. Public interest in South Korea in unification issues is limited and, while it apparently is higher in North Korea, the TV ownership ratio is lower and no statistics were available on the audience for the performances reported on in this book. Nonetheless, such events have spread knowledge of each Korea. In addition, the ability to apprehend each other's culture on a few occasions confirm that some common cultural characteristics remain.

Secondly, the commercialization, politicization and distortion of some socio-cultural events weaken their impact on relations. That South Korea has regularly paid large sums of money to stage joint events undermines, along with abuses of them presenting political messages and distorting actual conditions, their cultural content. Unfortunately, such characteristics appear to have been "a necessary evil" to accomplish them at all. In this way, cooperation may actually strengthen division.

In brief, it is improbable that inter-Korean socio-cultural exchanges and cooperation have significantly contributed to restoring national homogeneity. On the contrary, heterogeneity has been reconfirmed. But the experience is mixed: the level of heterogeneity should not be exaggerated. This confirms the view that it would be preferable to regard such a situation not as something bad that should be changed, but as simple differences due to the division of a socialist North Korea and a capitalist South Korea. The common experiences of homogeneity that do exist should be utilized as a starting point for creating a socio-cultural community through expanded contacts. However, such a community cannot be equalized with the restoration of homogeneity.

On the contrary, such a community would have to recognize the importance of "diversity" to function properly. In fact, the terms "homogeneity" and "heterogeneity" are too broad and simple terms to characterize the two Korean states that contain both characteristics making them diverse societies. Koreans in both the North and the South have to realize this crucial fact both to create peaceful coexistence and to, eventually, unify Korea assuming that either goal is fully achievable.

7.2 Obstacles to Korean unification

While there are positive impacts of socio-cultural contacts on inter-Korean relations, the development of inter-Korean relations clearly shows that mutual distrust is the major impediment to forming closer relations. Mutual distrust not only reduces the positive impact of the functionalist approach on relations by preventing further expansion, but is also the main explanation why the thaw in relations during the years 1971-1972, 1984-1985 and 1990-1991 did not last long and that the degree of the thaw beginning in 1998 must not be overrated. In addition, North Korea's nationalistic stance in particular makes it improbable that the North would attempt to realize the benefits of international cooperation in terms of raising domestic welfare levels, although the government should be aware of those. The huge economic gap between the two Koreas makes it unrealistic to expect that a state of interdependence that would weaken the nation state will develop. On the contrary, North Korea will likely become increasingly dependent economically on South Korea which could undermine the socio-political system but, as long as strong social control remains, such a scenario remains unlikely.

Mutual distrust is in turn a major explanation for the obvious lack of will towards unification amongst the North and South Korean governments, which contradicts the expressed target to unify Korea. North Korea's unification policy is affected by fears among the leading classes that unification will cause retaliation from the ordinary people, but also for the South Korean government, it is easier to manage a state of division than to pursue policies aiming at changing the status quo. The lack of interest in unification issues expressed by young South Koreans in opinion surveys conducted in 2000-2002, shows that they regard national division as the natural state of affairs which further reduces the will for unification. While data implies that North Koreans are more interested, this is not reflected in government policies. Besides mutual distrust and the lack of will as well as interest, a fourth obstacle is that the North's direct and the South's indirect unification policies are mutually exclusive. The recent steps taken to reduce the differences are unlikely to significantly reduce the fears that these diametrically opposed systems create on both sides. In addition to those four political obstacles, the estimated huge costs of unification and the huge economic gap in the South's favour, that far exceeds those between pre-unity Germany and Yemen, are two economic impediments affecting the South's unification policies.

In spite of these six obstacles, it could be argued, given the fact that Korea was unified from 668-1945 and that the two states still share common cultural characteristics, that such a foundation would facilitate unification. However, both the account of inter-Korean relations and the opinion surveys show that differences caused by the two socio-political systems undermine the joint historical legacy making "socio-political differences" a seventh obstacle. While it is reasonable to assume that when the Korean War-generation dies out mutual distrust will diminish, there is no guarantee that its replacement by the post-division generation that comprises the vast majority of the two Koreas' populations will facilitate unification. On the contrary, since this generation in South Korea regards a divided Korea as a natural state of affairs it could perpetuate division. The longer the time that passes, the more differences will be seen to develop making unification more difficult.

The position of North Korean defectors in South Korean society is the only available model to assess how North and South Koreans can join together in any semblance of unity. Unlike the brief socio-cultural events, their lives involve such daily realities as securing employment and receiving social recognition that are important for human dignity.

Although successive South Korean governments since 1962 have enacted legislation to help defectors adapt, they have experienced great difficulties in South

Korea as a result of the different socio-political systems. Lack of relevant skills and experience in making own initiatives are primary factors that impede integration: defectors have difficulties competing on the highly competitive South Korean labour market. Defectors' new lives in South Korea have often differed from their own expectations, causing frustration. In spite of both states speaking Korean, even language causes difficulties for defectors. The division has led to socio-political differences that weaken the positive impact of socio-cultural contacts on relations, regardless of whether defectors have experienced such contacts or not.

However, while economic and political realities are more important for South Koreans in their daily lives than contacts with their Northern compatriots, there are indications of common cultural characteristics remaining that could facilitate the development of closer relations and, eventually, unification. In fact, continuous human exchanges through aid work and joint publications could not have been accomplished otherwise. That common cultural characteristics remain is also clear from a few socio-cultural events. In particular, music concerts but also family reunions and the affinity shown by South Koreans towards North Koreans during the 2002 Pusan Asian Games are more convincing examples than the 2001 opinion survey on accommodation of North Korean culture, showing that most respondents could comprehend it.

Besides the socio-political differences caused by division, what also causes difficulties to North Korean defectors' integration is South Koreans' superior attitudes towards them: they face discrimination and contempt. Consequently, to change such attitudes is of the utmost importance to minimize the social impact of defectors being "marginal men" – i.e. neither North nor South Koreans. The defectors position is thus strikingly similar to that of East Germans and South Yemenis who became second-class citizens following on German and Yemeni unification in 1990. Such a situation does not bode well for either rapprochement or unity. Recent opinion surveys show that Koreans' negative views of each other have diminished thanks to the sunshine policy, but the deeply rooted hostile views will not easily disappear. On the contrary, in the case of defectors, competition over employment and other daily issues may actually reinforce them.

In addition to mutual distrust, lack of will for unification, lack of interest, mutually exclusive unification policies, the costs of unification, the economic gap and the broad term "socio-political differences", Korean unification is affected by the geopolitical context. Recent data shows that the United States, China, Japan and Russia prefer a divided, rather than a unified, Korea. Since this view is reflected in their policies towards Korea, the impact is, of course, negative rather than positive. Actually, Korean unification could affect the regional political situation to their disadvantage.

Japan is regarded as the country that most opposes unification: a unified Korea could become an economic competitor, although that would not happen immediately. On the contrary, the opinion among North Korean defectors in 2000 was that the United States and South Korean governments were the main obstacles. This is not surprising given that North Korea has consistently regarded the United States as the partner to discuss the conclusion of a peace agreement to end the Korean War with, instead of South Korea which undermined its own position by not signing the 1953 armistice agreement. But the prospects for the signing of a North Korea-United States peace agreement seem distant.

To make the situation even more complex, South Korea's strategic position is important for the United States by serving the dual role of keeping a watching eye on both China and Russia. For China, North Korea serves as a buffer zone between itself and the US presence in South Korea because of its troops there. While Russia plays a minor role in the Korean question, it does not want to be excluded from it.

The most positive sign of their policies towards the two Koreas is the wish to maintain peace and for a peaceful and gradual unification. The wish for peace can contribute to securing peaceful coexistence on the Korean Peninsula. The most worrying sign is that the major regional powers – China and the United States – may become rivals in the unification process which would make it even more complicated than is currently expected.

The enumerated obstacles raise the question what could in fact change the current situation? Domestic factors are more important than international ones but both need, as was the case in Germany and Yemen, to concur for unification to occur. Opinion surveys conducted since 1996 show that changes in the North Korean socio-political system are more important but also South Korea has to change: the development of inter-Korean relations confirms the view that the two Korean states are the main enemies to unification. That South Korea has a National Security Law and claims the whole Korean territory in its constitution must annoy North Korea, but to change these provisions is a most difficult task. There are no signs of a change of government in North Korea which, however, is no guarantee for change since the people around Kim Jong Il would like the system to remain intact as long as it works to their own advantage. Yet, since North Korea shows a high degree of unity politically that has been undermined economically, socially and culturally, there is a potential for social change.

The opinion among North Korean defectors that a regime change is necessary for unification seems to be realistic given that Kim Jong Il has, since 2002, deliberately abused the nuclear issue to cause obstacles in inter-Korean relations while economic and socio-cultural contacts continue. Such contradictory patterns reconfirm the lack of will for unification. Since a dismantlement of the nuclear program would greatly weaken North Korea's bargaining position and six-party talks so far have failed to reach a final solution, it is unlikely that the current situation will end shortly. But the North's behaviour is unpredictable; only time will tell whether the seemingly promising agreement of 19 September, 2005 will contribute to solve the issue.

Uncertainties regarding North Korea have created the paradoxical situation that, in spite of its self-reliant, nationalistic juche ideology and its hostility towards South Korea, the United States and Japan, it is nonetheless dependent on large amounts of humanitarian aid from these nations to maintain its socio-political system. At the same time, China is playing an important role as the main supplier of energy and food to the North and, indeed, as a mediator in the nuclear issue. Such a situation confirms that maintaining peaceful division is far more important than unification, although opinion surveys persistently show that unification is a common wish among South Koreans. Policy changes are, at present, hard to detect.

7.3 Lessons from German and Yemen unification

The main lesson for Korea from German and Yemeni unification in 1990 is that unification may take place unexpectedly and require ad hoc policies to implement. Although South Korea is less affluent than West Germany was and is incapable of absorbing North Korea, its larger economy will still have to lead the process towards unification. Therefore, the long-term consequences have to be considered well in advance. From this point of view, the expansion of inter-Korean economic ties is important.

That South Korea has carefully studied the German experience implies that there is an awareness of the practical and specific dimensions of unification. But the probability that the economic situation in North Korea is worse than is commonly acknowledged, as was the case in East Germany, is high. German unification has been far more expensive than expected and the gap between eastern and western Germany has not yet been eradicated. The Yemeni experience shows that hopes for better economic development in unity may fail to materialize due to internal chaos and unforeseeable external developments. The extent of social and cultural differences between the two Korean states should not be underestimated either, although available data shows a somewhat mixed picture.

While German and Yemeni unification took place unexpectedly and at a remarkable pace, it was the combination of long-term improvements in relations and favourable historic accidents that enabled unity. Relations between the two Germanys showed ups and downs but developed more smoothly than was the case between the two Yemeni states, which still had better and far more extensive relations than North and South Korea have ever had. The tendency in both Germany and Yemen was a gradual expansion and improvement of relations that facilitated the unification processes in 1989-1990, when a "now-or-never" development towards unity began. It was particularly important that West Germany through "change through rapprochement" had brought East Germany closer in both economic and human terms since it undermined loyalty towards the party.

Characterizing unification of Germany as "absorption" and of Yemen as "agreement" is basically correct, but neither term gives full justice to the unification processes and the factors that enabled it. In particular, the Yemeni way of unification, which ideally appears to be positive, should rather be described as "power-sharing" followed by division, civil war and power monopolization by North Yemen, which already dominated the country by being more populous.

Yemeni unification differs from Germany's also by being decidedly political "from above" whereas popular participation "from below" played an important role in the German case. On the basis of post-unity developments, "from below" appears to be a better approach, but, considering the development of inter-Korean relations, "from above" is a course more likely to be followed by the two Korean states. On the other hand, in Germany unification "from below" coexisted with politics pursued "from above" showing that a combination of these approaches is preferable to excluding popular participation, as the two Yemens did.

The Yemeni experience shows that "agreement" is an idealistic way of unification that does not work when there is mutual distrust between the two halves of the divided nation in addition to uneven population ratios. On the other hand, pre-unity developments reconfirm that expansion of contacts is necessary to bring divided states closer to each other.

To give credit to the unifications of Germany and Yemen, a distinction must be drawn with the political unification accomplished in 1990 and "human union", that is unifying citizens who had long lived in different socio-political systems. The latter process is far more difficult and will still take considerable time to accomplish in Germany. The difficulties of the, as of late 2004, 6,300 North Korean defectors in adapting to life in South Korea implies that, in spite of common cultural characteristics, it will be hard to create human union also in a divided Korea.

A similarity between German and Yemeni unification is that both took place very rapidly. In Germany, East Germany's weak economy, the erosion of the party's power and the end of Soviet patronage enabled such a unification. Given the strong Soviet influence over East Germany, unification could not have taken place otherwise. That TV provided knowledge about West Germany created "value integration".

This was particularly the case in political terms: East Germans wanted to live in peace, freedom and prosperity. West Germany realized that it must utilize this "now-or-never" opportunity to unify Germany on its own terms through the fastest way possible which was absorption. In contrast, it is unlikely that the party's power in North Korea will erode. Its social control is also stronger than that of the party in East Germany. In addition, neither China nor Russia exert the same degree of influence over North Korea as the Soviet Union did over East Germany.

Also in Yemen, "a now-or-never" opportunity developed in 1989 due to the end of Soviet patronage in South Yemen and was encouraged by hopes for common oil exploration. Given the often tense relations, Yemen could not have unified so quickly if the two presidents had not decided to unify the nation within six months. However, the unification process did not include a full-scale merger of the different political and economic systems leaving such issues largely to be dealt with afterwards. In particular, the armed forces were not integrated. It became an overwhelming task to handle political and economic integration while overcoming preunification tensions. Such conditions eventually caused the 1994 civil war that made South Koreans re-evaluate the Yemeni way of unification in a far more cautious direction than the previously positive one.

A "now-or-never" opportunity may develop also in Korea, but to follow Yemen's laissez-faire approach to unification would be highly dangerous, particularly if a decision was made not to unify the armed forces when strong tensions have long dominated inter-Korean relations. Consequently, the German model of unification appears to be a better one since it largely integrated the political and economic systems during the unification process. But this was easier to do in Germany than in Yemen since West Germany dictated the terms of unification based on its superior economy and dominated the entire unified country.

Because of the huge economic gap between the two Koreas, there will also be one dominating and one dominated part in unified Korea, which, due to the incomparably larger number of people integrating, will create worse tensions than those so far experienced by North Korean defectors. In fact, a notable difference is that the more even population ratio in Korea means that a relatively higher share of the population will have to be integrated into the unified country's socio-political system.

In Germany, the post-unification problems were never threatening the state since the economic and political systems had previously largely been integrated, in sharp contrast to Yemen. Another striking contrast is that German unification was achieved without any bloodshed whereas South Yemeni politicians had been killed during the unification process. That they continued to be so afterwards reconfirms the extent of mutual distrust. Integration of the economic and political systems between the two Koreas will, due to the limited contacts, take longer time than they did in Germany and Yemen. If Korean unification could take place peacefully, it would be a remarkable achievement that would facilitate human union.

Lessons from Yemeni unification are also that unification should take place gradually to reduce tensions and that it must be achieved peacefully and democratically. From this point of view, the gradual approach taken through the sunshine policy is the only realistic one in the Korean case. On the other hand, the two Yemens' leaders had to consider the special conditions ripe for unification implying that a gradual one at this stage would have been harder to accomplish. Only time can tell if such a situation will develop in Korea.

7.4 Towards closer inter-Korean relations and a unified Korea?

How can socio-cultural exchanges and cooperation contribute to consolidating the present development towards peaceful coexistence on the Korean Peninsula and, eventually, unify the nation? Above all, contacts need to be expanded and regularized to contribute to secure a state of *relative* peaceful coexistence. In other words: peace is threatened by continuous tensions but will only occur verbally and through occasional military incidents. That the two Koreas maintain increasingly active socio-cultural and economic contacts, in spite of the nuclear issue, implies that it should be possible to create such a state. The more regularized contacts become, the less likely it is that incidents occur. Economic contacts, in particular, may reinforce the socio-cultural potential to transform inter-Korean relations by providing knowledge about South Korea, especially if a situation where ordinary North Korean citizens begin to challenge government policies should develop. Regularized contacts that are unhindered by ups and downs in relations will also create mutual confidence, as is already the case in terms of humanitarian aid. If confidence could be created also in politics, it would be a remarkable achievement.

To end division, political and economic changes must take place in both Koreas as well as in the geopolitical context. If such a state is reached, socio-cultural contacts would have been important by providing knowledge of each other; German unification shows that socio-cultural contacts in this respect are important for the unification of a divided nation. While both Koreas can learn from German and Yemeni unification, no geopolitical change of the same magnitude as the end of the Cold War will benefit the process. It is unrealistic to expect an end of the Cold War structure on the Korean Peninsula, unless the two Korean states change their present policies simultaneously. It is also an indisputable fact that no country can play the same role as the Soviet Union did in 1989-1990 when it could have prevented German unification but was unwilling to do so. Another crucial difference is that North Korea is a far more rigid state than East Germany and South Yemen ever were and will not easily promote other changes than those that improve the functions of its poorly working socio-political system.

With this background, the South Korean government's target to create peaceful coexistence to facilitate unification in the long run is the most realistic policy possible and must continue. It is likely that North Korea will continue to obstruct rapprochement but policy changes should not be ruled out. For South Korea, maintenance of policy consistency is of the utmost importance, including after President Roh Moo-hyun retires (in 2008).

Considering the degree of mutual distrust and the huge economic gap, the difficulties to create closer contacts should not be underestimated but, as developments so far indicate, the more they expand the more difficult they are to hinder. However, that North Korea is a closed society and fears that South Korean influences undermine the foundations of its socio-political system makes patience indispensable in all of South Korea's contacts with the North.

While consolidating, expanding and evaluating the North-South exchanges pursued are possible tasks to perform, it is an entirely different one to prepare for unification; only time will tell whether the sunshine policy opens the way for unification. Although this study confirms that both Koreas have carefully investigated the experiences of German unification, the German case has made unification more difficult due to the lessons of the huge economic costs involved in a richer country with a far smaller pre-unity economic gap and a more favourable population ratio. Unification has also been an economic burden and human union has not yet been achieved. Also the Yemeni civil war has caused concerns.

Consequently, South Korean companies' policy to invest in North Korea to reduce the economic gap prior to unification deserves some credit and goes in line with the functionalist view that bringing states closer together promotes peace. There is at present no alternative to the gradual approach towards unification through the sunshine policy which has induced North Korea, while still creating military incidents and pursuing a nuclear program reflecting its security concerns, to cautiously open up. Also the pursuit of "economic management improvement measures" since 1 July, 2002 indicates that North Korea is attempting to make its socio-political system reform while simultaneously preserving it.

In spite of the signs of weakened state control due to the North's economic crisis since the mid-1990s, few people leave North Korea and even fewer defect, showing that state control is pervasive. Consequently, the inflow of foreign influences in recent years through the North Korea-China border are, at the moment, unlikely to result in a change of the socio-political system. However, they may reinforce the potential for changes that the human exchanges through South Korean humanitarian aid to North Korea, joint North-South publications and the influx of South Korean influences create. But changes will not occur by themselves: there is apparently no political will in either North or South Korea, even to develop relations that would resemble those of pre-unity Germany and Yemen.

At the moment, both Koreas prefer to preserve the present state of affairs rather than to implement policy changes whose consequences are difficult to forecast. Yet Kim Dae Jung deserves credit for being the first South Korean president to not only initiate a more active policy approach towards North Korea but also to consistently implement it. The policy with continuous expansion of socio-cultural exchanges and economic cooperation as important features must continue, but a few policy amendments are desirable.

Firstly, it is necessary to reconsider the sacred target of "restoring homogeneity" by acknowledging that division has changed Korean society forever. Only eventual unification will tell to what extent homogeneity still exists but even if cultural characteristics remain, the different socio-political systems have certainly changed social values.

Secondly, the creation of a socio-cultural community where diversity is acknowledged should be considered. To implement this task, knowledge of each other is most important which means that continuous contacts and tolerant attitudes towards North Korean defectors are of the utmost importance. Improved knowledge is the most important way to eradicate the superior attitudes that South Korea's economic superiority creates.

Thirdly, these policy goals must be pursued with a long-term approach which reinforces the need for contacts. At the same time, awareness that unforeseen developments may take place is extremely important: how unification takes place cannot be forecast. It is certain, however, that domestic socio-cultural, political and economic factors must match with favourable international developments if Korea is to unify. The sooner such a state of affairs is reached, the less difficult unification will become as an ultimate goal.

Chronology

1839	The British occupy Aden.
1905	A border is established between North and South Yemen.
1910-1945	Korea becomes a Japanese colony.
1918	North Yemen becomes independent.
1945	Korea is divided.
1948	The Republic of Korea and the Democratic People's Republic of Korea are established.
	South Korea enacts the National Security Law.
1949	The Federal Republic of Germany and The German Democratic Republic are established.
1950-1953	The Korean War rages.
1957	North Korea proposes media exchanges.
1958	North Korea proposes the formation of one Korean team for the 1960 Olympics.
1960	North Korea proposes a confederation.
	North Korea proposes the establishment of a joint publishing institute.
1961	North Korea proposes media exchanges.
	Pro-South and pro-North Korean residents in Japan jointly hold "The Cultural Festival For Peaceful Unification Through the Promotion of Cultural Exchanges" in Tokyo.
August	The Berlin Wall is built on 13 August.
1962 April	"The Special Law to Support Men of National Merit and Defectors to the South" is enacted.
1965	North Korea proposes joint film production and a joint theatre contest.
1966	North Korea suggests exchanges of journalists and scientists.
1967	West Germany drops the Hallstein doctrine and introduces Ostpolitik.
	South Yemen becomes independent.
1970	First inter-Yemeni summit in Kuwait.
March, May	First meeting of the East and West German heads of government on 19 March in East Germany and on 21 May in West Germany.
1972 July	North and South Korea sign the 4 July Communiqué.
October	Border war between North and South Yemen.

November	Second inter-Yemeni summit in Tripoli, Libya 26-28 November. Presidents declare their intention to unify Yemen.
December	East and West Germany sign the Basis of Relations Treaty on 21 December.
1973 September	East and West Germany become UN members.
1975	Korean South-North Coordinating Committee talks are broken (began in 1972).
1976 April	South Korea proposes to exchange and exhibit old arts objects and archaeological materials.
1977 February	Third inter-Yemeni summit in the border regions.
August	Fourth inter-Yemeni summit is held in Sanaa.
October	North Yemen president Ibrahim al-Hamdi is assassinated.
1978	North-South Korea Red Cross talks are broken.
June	North and South Yemen presidents are assassinated.
1979 January	"The Special Law to Compensate Brave Defectors to the South" is enacted.
February	Second Yemeni war breaks out but ends in March.
March	Fifth inter-Yemeni summit held in Kuwait 28-30 March. Presidents promise to work towards unity.
1980	North Korea presents a new proposal for a confederation.
1981 November	South Korea proposes to arrange an exchange exhibition of ancient relics.
	Korean Christian scholars abroad meet with North Koreans in Austria at "The Dialogue between North Korean and Foreign Christians Abroad for the Fatherland's Unification".
December	Sixth inter-Yemeni summit held in Aden. Presidents announce concrete measures to implement unification.
	East and West German heads of government meet 11-13 December, in East Germany.
1982	South Korea calls for a Provisional Agreement on Basic Relations with North Korea.
January	A draft constitution of the proposed Yemen Republic is approved.
December	"The Dialogue between North Korean and Foreign Christian Scholars Abroad for the Fatherland's Unification" is held in Finland.
1984 March	Reverend Matheo visits North Korea.
November	South Korea proposes cultural exchanges.
December	"The Dialogue between North Korean and Foreign Christian Scholars Abroad for the Fatherland's Unification" is held.
1985 March	Mikhail Gorbachev comes into power in the Soviet Union.

September	First family reunions in Seoul and P'yôngyang 20-23 September. Art troupes perform.
1986 January	Civil war breaks out in South Yemen.
June	North and South Korean Christian churches meet for the first time at the "North-South Council on Peace and Unification" in Switzerland.
July	Seventh inter-Yemeni summit is held in Tripoli.
1987 September	SED chief Erich Honecker makes an official visit to Bonn 7-11 September.
1988	Ch'ôndogyo sends sacred books to North Korea.
May	Eighth inter-Yemeni summit is held in Sanaa 3-4 May. Agreement on oil and gas exploration signed.
June	South Korea proposes exchanges of cultural and arts personalities on 3 June.
July	The Buddhist monk Taewôn visits North Korea. South Korean President Roh Tae Woo announces in the 7 July Declaration his willingness to open exchanges with North Korea.
October	South Korea opens for the public forbidden materials on North Korea and lifts the ban on indirect trade with the North. Reverends Chang Ik and Chông Ûi-ch'ôl visit North Korea.
November	"The Committe for Exchanges between Buddhists in North and South Korea" is formed. North and South Korean Christian churches meet in Switzerland.
1989	South Korea launches the Korean National Community Unification Formula. Law-maker Sô Kyông-wôn and student representative Im Su-kyông are imprisoned after illegal visits to North Korea.
February	Hyundai Group Chairman Chung Ju Yung visits North Korea. South Korean Reverends visit North Korea and celebrate mass.
March	South Korea sets up The Council to Promote Exchanges and Cooperation between North and South Korea.
May	Hungary opens its borders with Austria on 2 May.
June	The Guidelines for Inter-Korean Exchanges and Cooperation are forged on 12 June. The Buddhist monk Sin Pôpt'a visits North Korea.
July-August	Reverend Yi Tae-gyông visits North Korea 29 July-12 August.

October	The Buddhist monk Taewôn visits North Korea.
	SED chief Erich Honecker resigns on 18 October.
November	The Berlin Wall falls on 9 November.
	West German Chancellor Helmut Kohl presents a "Ten-point Plan for German Unity" on 28 November.
	Ninth inter-Yemen summit in Aden 29-30 November. Presidents sign an agreement on unification.
December	The end of the Cold War is announced.
1990	Direct trade begins between North and South Korea.
February	Full international acceptance of German unification is reached at a NATO and Warsaw Pact states conference.
	The Roh Tae Woo Government announces the five basic principles to activate North-South cultural exchanges.
March	East Germany's first democratic elections are held on 18 March.
	North and South Korea participate in "The Foundation Meeting of the Association of Asian History" in Japan 15-18 March.
April	An accord proclaiming the Yemen Republic and principles for the transitional period is signed.
May	Yemen reunifies on 22 May.
July	A West-East German currency union goes into effect on 1 July.
	North and South Korea participate in "The First Christians Tokyo Seminar" 10-13 July.
August	The Roh Tae Woo Government enacts and promulgates the Inter-Korean Exchanges and Cooperation Act on 1 August.
	North and South Korea participate in "The Third International Scientific Conference on Korean Studies" in Japan 2-5 August.
	Bonn and East Berlin sign the Unification Treaty on 31 August.
September	The first inter-Korean Prime Ministerial talks are held.
	North and South Korean art troupes perform traditional music and dance.
	The Soviet Union, the United States, France and the United Kingdom agree on guarantees for full German sovereignty.
	Yemeni workers are expelled from Saudi Arabia.
	North and South Korea participate in "The Second International Scientific Conference on Dialogue, Peace and Cooperation in the Asia-Pacific Region" in the Soviet Union 4-6 September.

October	Germany reunifies on 3 October.
	North and South Korea participate in "The Third International Symposium on a Northeast Asian Joint Economic Community" in China 9-12 October.
	"The North-South Film Festival" is held in the United States 10-14 October.
	The first inter-Korean football matches are played in P'yôngyang 11 October and Seoul 23 October.
	The Seoul Traditional Musical Band visit P'yôngyang 14-24 October.
December	North and South Korean Christian churches meet in Switzerland.
	The first post-unity German elections are held on 2 December.
	The P'yôngyang National Music Band visits Seoul 8-13 December.
1990-1992	North and South Korea hold publishers meetings abroad.
1990-1994	Transfers of public sector funds from western to eastern Germany approach DM 600 billion.
1991	The Kohl Government launches the Eastern Recovery Program.
	North and South Korea participate in "The Symposium on Traditional Theatre in Asia" in China.
January-February	North and South Korean scholars participate in "The Conference on Economic Development and Cooperation in the Northeast Asian Region" in China 28 January-1 February.
February	North and South Korea participate in "The Seventh WCC General Meeting" in Australia.
March	"The North-South Church Scholars' Symposium" is held in the United States.
	Permission is given for the formation of a unified Korean team for the World Table Tennis Championships.
	The music series "Echo of the Korean People" is performed in Japan.
	North and South Korea participate in "The 15th Conference of the Association of Korean Studies in Europe" in France 22-26 March.
	North and South Korea participate in "The Northeast Asia Security Conference" in China 23-25 March.
April	The Buddhist monk Sin Pôpt'a again visits North Korea.
April-May	A joint "Korea" team participates in the 41st World Table Tennis Championships in Japan 24 April-6 May.

May	Permission is given for the formation of a unified Korean team for the World Junior Soccer Championships.
North and South Korean artists take part in "The International Arts Exhibition" in Japan 2-5 May.
Televised try out youth soccer games are played in Seoul 8 May and in P'yôngyang 12 May.
North and South Korea participate in "The Second Asian History Meeting" in China 20-28 May.
North and South Korea participate in "The North-South Paintings and Writings Exhibition" in China 27-29 May.
North and South Korea participate in "The Northeast Asian International Conference" in Japan 27-29 May.
North and South Korea hold the meeting "Simplification of the Romanization of Han'gûl for Mechanization" in Denmark 27-31 May.
May-June	North and South Korea participate in the first conference "Peace in Asia and the Role of Women" in Japan 28 May-4 June.
North and South Korea participate in "The Seventh International Scientific Symposium on Unification of the Korean Peninsula" in Japan 31 May-2 June.
June	North and South Korea participate in "The First North Korea-United States Scientific Conference" in the United States 3-7 June.
A joint "Korea" team participates in the 6th World Junior Soccer Championships in Portugal 14-30 June.
June 1991-June 1992	The first joint North-South research project – *Nambukhan ônô pigyo yôn'gu* [*A Comparative Study of Language in North and South Korea*] begins. The study is published in 2002.
July	North and South Korea participate in "The Northeast Asia Environment Conference" in Mongolia.
North and South Korea participate in the celebrations of the 250th anniversary of the introduction of Buddhism to the Soviet Union.
North and South Korea participate in "The Second Christians Tokyo Seminar" 9-12 July.
North and South Korea participate in "The Foundation Meeting of the Civilian Association for Economic Development and Cooperation in the Northeast Asian Region" in China 17-19 July.
North and South Korea participate in "The Conference on Young Scholars in Korean Studies" in China 29-31 July.

August	Students meet at P'anmunjôm 12 August.
North and South Korea participate in "The International Scientific Conference on Korean Studies" in China 12-14 August.
North and South Korea participate in "The Unified North-South Traditional Dance, Customs and Arts Festival" on Sakhalin Island 17-18 August.
North and South Korea participate in "The 1991 International Science and Technology Contest" in China 19-24 August.
North and South Korea participate in "The '91 International Scientific Conference on Electronics, Intelligence and Telecommunications" in China 21-23 August.
North and South Korea participate in "The International Scientific Conference on Northeast Asia's Economic and Technological Development" in China 29-31 August.
August-September	North and South Korea participate in "The Seminar on Northeast Asian International Cooperation" in China 27 August-1 September.
September	North and South Korea become UN members.
Students meet at P'anmunjôm 4 September.
September-October	Reverend Kwak Sôn-hûi visits North Korea 24 September-1 October.
October	North and South Korea participate in the first preliminary meeting of "The Northwest Pacific Action Plan" in Russia.
October-November	Ch'ôndogyo representatives meet at "The Fourth Asian Religionists' Peace Conference" in Nepal 28 October-2 November.
"The Joint Buddhist Mass Praying for the Unification of the Fatherland" is held in the United States during "The North-South Buddhists' Joint Meeting" 28 October-4 November.
November	North and South Korea participate in "The International Symposium on a Northeast Asian Economic Bloc" in Japan 22 November.
North and South Korea participate in the second conference "Peace in Asia and the Role of Women" in Seoul 25-30 November.
December	North and South Korea sign the Agreement on Reconciliation, Non-aggression and Exchanges and Cooperation 13 December.
North and South Korea sign the Joint Declaration on the Denuclearization of the Korean Peninsula 31 December.

1992 January	Daewoo Group chairman visits North Korea. KNCC Director Reverend Kwôn Ho-gyông visits North Korea 7-13 January.
February	The 13 December agreement is ratified. North and South Korea participate in "The International Scientific Conference on Economic Cooperation in Northeast Asia" in Japan 3-5 February.
April-May	North and South Korea participate in "Northeast Asia Economic Forum" in P'yôngyang 28 April-4 May.
May	North and South Korea participate in "The Eighth International Scientific Symposium on Unification of the Korean Peninsula" in Japan 17-18 May. North and South Korea participate in "The North Pacific Conference on Security and Cooperation" in Canada 22-23 May.
June	North and South Korea meet at "The North-South Conference on the Spelling of Han'gûl in Roman Letters" in France 16-17 June. North and South Korea participate in "The Hawaii 6 Nations International Scientific Conference" 23-25 June.
July	North Korean Deputy Prime Minister visits South Korea. North and South Korea participate in "The International Scientific Conference on Comparative Research on Development in the Northeast Asian Region" in China 10-12 July.
August	North and South Korea participate in "The Unification Arts Festival" on Sakhalin Island 16 August. North and South Korea participate in "The 1992 UN Arms Reduction Conference" in China 17-19 August. North and South Korea take part in "The Fourth International Scientific Conference on Korean Studies" in China 20-22 August. North and South Korea participate in "The Forum on Economic Cooperation in the Northeast Asian region" in Russia 25-28 August.
August-September	North and South Korea participate in "The Celebrations of the 40th Anniversary of the Establishment of Self-Government of Koreans in Yônbyôn" in China 23 August-3 September.
September	North and South Korea participate in the third conference "Peace in Asia and the Role of Women" in P'yôngyang 1-6 September. "The National Music Festival" is held in New York 26 September.

October	North and South Korea participate in the second preliminary meeting of "The Northwest Pacific Action Plan" in China.
	North and South Korea participate in "The Third Christians Tokyo Seminar" 20-22 October.
1993 April	North and South Korea participate in "The Second Symposium on the Unification of the Korean Peninsula" in the US 14-21 April.
	North and South Korea participate in the conference "Inheritance and Development of Korean Culture in Northeast Asia" in China 15-17 April.
	North and South Korea participate in "The Second General Directors' Meeting of the Civilian Association for Economic Development and Cooperation in the Northeast Asian Region" in China 18-20 April.
	North and South Korea participate in the fourth conference "Peace in Asia and the Role of Women" in Japan 24-29 April.
	North and South Korea participate in "The Korean People's Music Concert" in Japan 26 April.
May	North and South Korea participate in "The Third Meeting of the Planning and Management Conference" held in P'yôngyang 9-10 May.
May-June	North and South Korea participate in "The Excavations of Parhae Relics in the Maritime Provinces of Siberia" in Russia 27 May-13 June.
August	North and South Korea participate in "The International Scientific Conference on Koguryô Culture" in China 11-14 August.
	North and South Korea participate in "The Seminar on Language and Philosophy Towards Unification" in China 28-31 August.
October	North and South Korean Ch'ôndogyo directors meet.
	North and South Korea participate in "The Unified Korea Arts Exhibition" in Japan 12-23 October.
	North and South Korea participate in "The Second Asia Solidarity Conference on Comfort Women" in Japan 21 October.
	North and South Korea participate in "The Seventh General Meeting of the East Asian Athletic Council" in P'yôngyang 24-25 October.
November	North and South Korea participate in the third preliminary meeting of "The Northwest Pacific Action Plan" in Thailand.

	North and South Korea participate in "The P'yôngyang Conference on Japan's Management of its Post-war Days" 6-9 November.
	North Korea participates in "The Second Expert Meeting on Resources, Industry and Environment" in Seoul 8-11 November.
December	South Korea permits imports of non-political and non-ideological works from North Korea for sale.
	"The Law to Protect North Korean Defectors" is enacted.
1994 February	North and South Korea participate in "The International University Students Peace Seminar" in Moscow 14-17 February.
	North and South Korea participate in "The Fourth International Scientific Conference on Korean Studies" in China 20-22 February.
March	Representatives of Ch'ôndogyo meet in China 10 March.
	North and South Korea participate in "The UNESCO Comparative Research Seminar on the Protection of Northeast Asia Biological Sphere" in China 13-23 March.
April	Taejonggyo leader An Ho-sang meets his North Korean counterpart in China.
May	North and South Korea participate in "The International Conference for Establishing a Standard Spelling of Han'gûl in Roman Letters" in Sweden on 20 May.
	Civil war breaks out in Yemen on 21 May, when the South declares independence.
May-June	North and South Korea participate in "The 4th Christians Tokyo Seminar on Peaceful Reunification of the Fatherland and Missionary Work" 31 May-2 June.
June	North and South Korean students participate in "The Second World Student Leaders' Science and Peace Conference" in China 21-26 June.
	North and South Korea participate in "The Association of East Asian Athletic Meeting" in Taiwan 27-28 June.
July	Civil war in Yemen ends with the South's defeat on 7 July.
	Kim Il Sung dies on 8 July.
	North and South Korea participate in "The International Scientific Conference On Economic Development and Cooperation in the Northeast Asian Region" in China 16-25 July.
August	North and South Korea participate in "The International Scientific Conference on Northeast Asian Historical Research" in China 1-5 August.

	North and South Korea participate in "The First Conference on the Next Generation of Politicians in East Asia" in Malaysia 3-8 August.
	North and South Korea participate in "The International Scientific Conference on Computerization of the Korean Language" in China 6-8 August.
	North and South Korea participate in "The Second UNESCO Research Seminar on the Preservation of the Biological Sphere in the Northeast Asian Region" in South Korea in 14-21 August.
	North and South Korea participate in "The Scientific Conference on The Prospects for Cooperation Among the Northeast Asian Countries in the 21st Century" in China 18-19 August.
September	"The North-South Korea-China Photo Exhibition" is held in China 26-30 September.
October	North Korea and the United States sign the Agreed Framework on 21 October.
1995	13 Daewoo technicians became the first South Koreans since 1953 to settle in North Korea.
	North Korea accepts an offer of rice aid from South Korea.
	North and South Korea participate in the UNESCO-sponsored conference on the East Asian Biosphere held in Seoul.
	North and South Korea participate in "Germany and Korea: Meeting Within Division, 1945-1995 Cold War and Afterwards" in Germany.
February	North and South Korean students participate in "The Third World University Students' Peace Seminar" in Beijing 5-9 February.
March	North and South Korea participate in "The Fourth International Christian Conference on Peace on and Reunification of the Korean Peninsula" in Japan 28-31 March.
April	North and South Korea sign the "Memorandum of Understanding on Environmental Principles" for the UNDP-supported project "Tumen River Area Development Program".
	Taejonggyo leader An Ho-sang visits North Korea 11 April.
May	North and South Korea participate in "The East Asian Conference on the Protection of National Parks and Nature" in China.

	The Chogye sect Director Song Wôl-chu meets the head of the North Korean Federation of Buddhists Pak T'ae-ho in China.
	Catholic priest Kim Sang-jin and three pastors visit North Korea 28-30 May.
June	North and South Korea participate in "The Fourth General Meeting of the Council of American Korean Churches Peaceful Unification 70 Year" in the United States 26-28 June.
July	North and South Korea participate in "The Third Asian Solidarity Conference on Comfort Women" in Japan 3-5 July.
	North and South Korea participate in "The International Scientific Conference on Northeast Asia in the 21st Century" in China 18-21 July.
	North and South Korea participate in "The 50th Anniversary of Liberation Meeting" in the United States 19-24 July.
July-August	The first joint unification conference abroad is held in China 31 July-1 August.
August	North and South Korea participate in "The Fourth World Women's Conference" in China.
	The Buddhist monk Toan visits North Korea.
	North and South Korea participate in "The International Scientific Conference on Korean Language Standards" in China 3-4 August.
	North and South Korea participate in the conference "Reappraisal of the Primitive and Old Civilizations in Northeast Asia" in Japan 4-6 August.
	North and South Korea participate in "The '95 International Scientific Conference on Electronics, Intelligence and Telecommunications" in China 7-12 August.
	Reverend Kwak Sôn-hûi visits North Korea 15-22 August.
September	North and South Korea participate in "The Fourth Northeast Asian and Pacific Environmental Forum" in Japan.
	North and South Korea participate in "The International Scientific Conference on Computerization of the Korean Language" in China 14-16 September.
October	North and South Korean students meet at "The Northeast Asia Youth Leaders' Conference" in China 8-11 October.
	North and South Korea participate in "The General Meeting of Korean Christians in Japan" 9-11 October.

	North and South Korea participate in "The Scholars Conference of Environment and Development in East Asia" in Thailand 20-22 October.
October-November	North and South Korea participate in "The Foreign North-South Catholics' Seminar in New York" 27 October-2 November.
1996	The Daewoo Group sets up a joint-venture in North Korea.
January	North and South Korea participate in "The Sixth Northeast Asia Economic Forum" held in the US 18-19 January.
January-February	North and South Korea participate in "The International Ecumenical Conference for Peace and Solidarity in Northeast Asia" in Macao 29 January-2 February.
February	North and South Korea participate in "The Niigata Northeast Asian Economic Conference" 7-9 February.
	North and South Korea participate in "The Korean Peace Arts Exhibition" in Japan 8-13 February.
	North and South Korea participate in "The North-South's Religionists' Conference for the Unification of the Fatherland" in China 26-29 February.
April	The Chogye sect Vice-director Sin Pômt'a visits North Korea.
	North and South Korea participate in "The Fifth Symposium on the Unification of the Korean Peninsula" in the US 19-20 April.
	North and South Korea participate in "The Seminar on the North Korean Economy" in the US 22-23 April.
May	North and South Korea participate in "The '96 International Scientific Conference for the Unification of the Fatherland" in the United Kingdom 5-6 May.
	North and South Korea participate in "The Scientific Conference on the Prospects for Economic Cooperation at the Gulf of Pohai" in China on 8 May.
June	North and South Korea participate in "The Scientific Conference on Peace and Economic Cooperation in Northeast Asia" in China 1 June.
	North and South Korea participate in "The Fifth Christians Tokyo Seminar on Peaceful Reunification of the Fatherland and Missionary Work" 5-7 June.
August	North and South Korea participate in "The Scientific Conference on Northeast Asia in 21st Century" 1-4 August in China.

	North and South Korea participate in "The '96 International Scientific Conference on Korean Unification" in the United Kingdom 5-6 August.
	North and South Korea participate in "The International Scientific Conference for Korean Language Scholars" in China 5-9 August.
	North and South Korea participate in "The Third International Scientific Conference on Computerization of the Korean Language" in China 12-14 August.
	North and South Korea participate in "The Scientific Conference on the Present Conditions of and Prospects for Korean Studies" in China 19-20 August.
	North and South Korea hold a scientific conference on life-time education and education through correspondence in China 22-23 August.
September	A North Korean submarine runs aground on the east coast. The second joint North-South unification conference abroad is held in China 13-15 September.
December	North Korea apologizes for the submarine incident.
1997 February	Korean Workers' Party Secretary Hwang Jang-yop defects.
March	North and South Korea participate in "The North-South American Church Conference" in the United States 17-19 March.
April-May	North and South Korean womens' teams have contacts at the World Table Tennis Championships in the United Kingdom 24 April-5 May.
May	Catholic priest Kim Sang-jin visits North Korea 28-30 May.
	North and South Korea participate in "The North-South Korean Religious Leaders' Conference" in China 30-31 May.
June	North and South Korea participate in "The North-South Catholics' Seminar" in China 4-7 June.
	North and South Korea participate in "The German Churches' Day" 17-22 June.
	North and South Korea participate in "The Women's International Peace Symposium" 17-23 June.
	"The Regulations on Management of Socio-Cultural Projects Between North and South Korea" are enacted on 27 June.
June-July	"The Joint Conference for Peace and Harmony on the Korean Peninsula" is held in China 30 June-1 July.

July	North and South Korea participate in "The International Korean People's Photo Seminar and Exhibition" in China. "The Law on the Protection and Resettlement of North Korean Defectors" is enforced on 14 July. North and South Korea participate in "The Third International Scientific Conference on Koguryô Culture" in Japan 20-21 July.
August	North and South Korea participate in "The World Reformist Churches Federation General Meeting" in Hungary 8-20 August. North and South Korea participate in "The Seventh Northeast Asia Economic Forum" in Mongolia 17-21 August. The third joint North-South unification conference abroad is held in China 29-30 August.
September	North and South Korea participate in "The Fourth Seminar of World University Students for Peace" in China 13-17 September. Korean Broadcasting System (KBS) completes a documentary on North Korea on 14 September. Korean National Council of Churches' (KNCC) Director Kim Tong-wan visits North Korea 23 September. General Federation of Korean Churches chairman Chi Tôk meet representatives of North Korea in China 25-26 September.
October-November	North and South Korea participate in "The North-South Peace Arts Exhibition" in Japan 28 October-1 November.
December	The *Joong Ang Ilbo* Unification Culture Research Centre gets permission to visit North Korea for a cooperation project 10 December.
1998	North and South Korea participate in the symposium "Women and Sexual Violence".
January	The Yônbyôn Scientific Technical College Supporters' Association gets permission to found a Scientific and Technical College in the Najin-Sônbong region.
February	South Korean President Kim Dae Jung implements his new "sunshine policy". North and South Korea participate in "The UN Conference on Arms Reduction in Southeast Asia" in Indonesia 16-18 February. North and South Koreas participate in "The Scientific Conference on Security in Northeast Asia" in the United Kingdom 16-20 February.

	North and South Korea participate in "The Niigata Northeast Asian Economic Conference" 17-19 February. The fourth unification conference abroad is held in Beijing 20-21 February. North and South Korea participate in "The Tenth Conference on Arms Reduction and Peace in the Asia-Pacific Region" in Nepal 20-24 February.
March	Business with and travel to North Korea are facilitated. North and South Korean Buddhists meet in China. The third North-South Catholic meeting is held in China. North and South Korea participate in "The North-South Churches' Conference on Unification and Sharing" in Australia 16-18 March. The Measures to Activate Civilian Organizations' Humanitarian Assistance to North Korea are enacted on 18 March.
April	Failed North-South government talks are held in China. The Sports Art, the Korean Welfare Foundation and the Korean Culture Foundation get permissions for cooperation projects with North Korea. The Sports Art makes the documentary "P'yôngyang Report" that is shown on TV.
May	Sisterhood ties are set up between the South's Sônggyungwan University and the North's Koryô Sônggyungwan University. Children's Arts Troupe "Little Angels" perform in North Korea 2-12 May. Bishop Ch'oe Ch'ang-mu and six priests from the Catholic National Committee of Reconciliation visit North Korea 15-22 May and hold mass in P'yôngyang.
May-June	KNCC Director Kim Tong-wan visits North Korea 26 May-2 June. Joint North-South photo exhibition held in Seoul 29 May-11 June. The photo book *Paektu-esô Halla kkaji 'lensû-ro pon choguk* [*From Mt. Paektu to Mt. Halla – The Fatherland Seen from the Lens*] is published.
June	The Korean Welfare Foundation becomes the South's first non-governmental organization (NGO) to pursue cooperation with North Korean counterparts 5 June. 500 cows are delivered to North Korea on 16 June. A North Korean submarine is caught on the east coast 22 June.
July	Armed North Korean agent found dead on the east coast 12 July.

	The fourth North-South Catholic meeting is held 13-15 July.
Pulgasari becomes the first North Korean film shown in South Korean cinemas 22 July.
North and South Korea participate in "The Eighth Northeast Asian Economic Forum" in Japan 28-29 July.
July-August	North and South Korea participate in "The Symposium on Forced Arrests by the Japanese in War-time" in Japan 30 July-1 August.
August	A delegation from The Korean Cultural Network Research Centre visits North Korea 4-11 August.
Representatives of Ch'ôndogyo visit North Korea 11 August.
North Korea launches its first multistage missile on 31 August.
September	*An Chung-gûn Shoots Hirobumi Itoh* becomes the first North Korean film shown on South Korean TV.
The religious Korea Neighbour-Loving Association delivers milk cows to North Korea.
The Korean Sharing Movement launches a campaign for exchanges of books between North and South Korea.
Joint North-South photo exhibition held in Pusan 4-12 September.
The fifth North-South Catholic Meeting is held in China 14-18 September.
October	North and South Korea participate in "The Fifth Asian Solidarity Conference on Comfort Women" in China.
North and South Korea participate in "The Sixth Christians Tokyo Seminar".
The North Korean drama *Im Kkôk-chông* is shown on South Korean TV.
A Northeast Asian Forestry Forum is initiated through NGO cooperation.
"The Enforcement Ordinance of the New Legislation on the Settlement of and Support for North Korean Defectors" is enacted.
North and South Korea participate in "The Sixth Christians Tokyo Seminar on Peaceful Reunification of the Fatherland and Missionary Work" 8-10 October.
500 cows are delivered by Chung Ju Yung, who also meets North Korean leader Kim Jong Il 29 October.
The joint "Yoon Yi-sang Unification Concert" is held in P'yôngyang on 31 October.

November	North Korean speedboat evades pursuit along the western shore.
	Representatives of "The North-South Childhood Friends" visit North Korea and exchange pictures.
	Tourist tours to Mt. Kûmgang in North Korea are launched 18 November.
December	North Korean spy boat is sunk off the southern coast.
1999	Seoul Broadcasting Station (SBS) TV makes and shows *The Homecoming of Dr. Cho Kyông-ch'ôl.*
February	South Korean civilian organizations are allowed to provide direct aid to North Korea on 10 February.
April	The Buddhist Association for the Peaceful Unification of the Fatherland and the North Korean Federation of Buddhists meet in China.
	The sixth North-South Catholic meeting is held in China 5-7 April.
	The joint conference "The Role of Religionists for the Unification of Korea" is held in China 25-27 April and announces "The 1999 Beijing Declaration".
May	The seventh North-South Catholic meeting is held in China 2-3 May.
	Ministers Kim Myung-gi and Eun Hi-kon from the Korean Methodist Church Association visit North Korea 18-25 May.
May-June	Two officials of the Buddhist Fraternities Association visit the North Korean Federation of Buddhists 25 May-1 June.
June	A South Korean housewife is detained by North Korea at Mt. Kûmgang but is freed.
	North-South West Sea battle ends with the South's victory on 15 June.
	The American section of the Buddhist Association for the Peaceful Unification of the Fatherland gives a welcome dinner for the North Korean soccer team 17 June.
June-July	Failed North-South official talks on family reunions held in Beijing.
July	The joint conference "Situation and Future of the Korean Race toward the New Millennium" is held in China 22-24 July.
	The joint seminar "The Role of Youth for Establishing a Unified Fatherland" is held in China 25-29 July.
August	The SN21 Enterprise gets permission for a cooperation project with North Korea.
	The first North-South workers' football matches are played in P'yôngyang.

	"The North-South Ch'ôndogyo Leaders' Meeting" is held in China.
	At "The Fourth International Seminar on the Computerisation of the Korean Language" held in China 13-15 August a joint dictionary is published.
August-September	11 South Korean artists and painters visit North Korea 31 August-7 September.
September	The Hyundai Asan gets permission for a cooperation project with North Korea.
	North and South Korea hold the meeting "Womens' Exchanges in Relation to Assistance to North Korea" in the North.
	"The Unification Basketball Games" are played in P'yôngyang and broadcast on TV 23-24 September.
	A joint conference on protection of forests in North Korea is held in China 27 September.
October	Reverend Chu Pong-t'aek from the Korean Missionary Association for National Unification visits North Korea.
	Representatives of the Chingak sect visit North Korea.
	Ministers Kim Myung-gi and Eun Hi-kon from the Korean Methodist Church Association visit North Korea.
	The South Korean government allows public access to North Korea's satellite TV broadcasts on 22 October.
	"The Fifth Conference on Unification Issues" is held in China 26-27 October.
November	The Buddhist Association for the Peaceful Unification of the Fatherland and the North Korean Federation of Buddhists meet in Beijing.
December	Korean Peninsula Energy Development Organization and Korea Electric Power Corporation sign an agreement on constructing light-water reactors in North Korea.
	The joint "Peace and Friendship Concert 2000" is held in P'yôngyang on 5 December.
	The joint "National Unification Concert" is held in P'yôngyang on 20 December.
	"The Unification Basketball Games" are played in Seoul 23-24 December.
2000 February	North Korean art is exhibited at "The Grand Arts Exhibition for World Peace" in Seoul 10-21 February.
March	President Kim Dae Jung launches the "Berlin Declaration".
	The seventh North-South Catholic meeting is held in China 27-29 March.
April	A joint mass is held in P'yôngyang on 23 April.

May	Representatives of Ch'ôndogyo hold working-level talks in China 1-2 May.
	The P'yôngyang Students Youth Troupe performs in Seoul 24-27 May.
May-June	The P'yôngyang Circus Troupe performs in Seoul 27 May-11 June.
June	Seoul National University Press buys the copyrights and publishes the book *Pukhan-ûi munhwajae-wa munhwa yujôk* [*North Korea's Cultural Treasures and Cultural Remains*].
	First inter-Korean summit is held in P'yôngyang 13-15 June.
	A five-point Joint Declaration is announced on 15 June.
	Five North Korean films are shown at "The Fifth Hwanghae Arts Festival" in Inch'ôn 16-18 June.
July	The Korean Culture Network Research Centre gets permission for a cooperation project with North Korea.
	An inter-Korean auto rally is held at Mt. Kûmgang 3-4 July.
	North and South Korea play table-tennis in P'yôngyang 28 July.
	First inter-Korean ministerial talks held in Seoul 29-31 July.
August	South Korean media representatives visit North Korea 5-12 August, and sign an agreement on media cooperation.
	North and South Korea participate in "The International Scientific Conference on the Position of the Korean Language in the World" in China 11-13 August.
	Buddhists simultaneously hold mass to pray for unification on 15 August.
	First round of family reunions (since 1985) take place in Seoul and P'yôngyang 15-18 August.
	The North Korean Symphony Orchestra performs in Seoul 18-24 August.
August-September	Second inter-Korean ministerial talks are held in P'yôngyang 29 August-1 September.
September	Kôn'guk University Press publishes *Pundan-ûl nômô t'ongir-ûl hyanghae* [*Beyond Division Towards Unification*].
	The documentary "From Mt. Paektu to Mt. Halla" is shown by KBS TV.
	63 former North Korean agents are repatriated on 2 September.

	50 members of Chochongryun (Japan) visit South Korea 22-27 September.
	109 South Korean tourists visit Mt. Paektu and P'yôngyang 22-28 September.
	First inter-Korean economic talks (since 1985) are held in Seoul 25-26 September.
	First North and South Korea's defence ministers' talks are held on Cheju Island 25-26 September.
	Third inter-Korean ministerial talks are held on Cheju Island 27-30 September.
September-October	North and South Korea march together at the opening and closing ceremonies of the Sydney Olympics 15 September-1 October.
October	A National Unification Concert is held in P'yôngyang.
	The sacred fire for South Korea's National Athletic Games is put on at Mt. Kûmgang 1 October.
	SBS TV makes the first Southern broadcast from North Korea 9-10, 13-14 October.
	Ch'ôndogyo representatives visit North Korea 9-13 October.
	The Asia-Europe Meeting held in Seoul expresses its support for peace on the Korean Peninsula 20 October.
	The UN General Assembly adopts the first inter-Korean joint resolution on Peace, Security and Reunification on the Korean Peninsula 31 October.
November	North and South Korea hold "The Ancient History Symposium on the 100th Anniversary of the Korean Society for the Promotion of Learning" in Tokyo.
	Second Inter-Korean economic talks are held in P'yôngyang 8-11 November.
	119 members of Chochongryun visit South Korea 17-22 November.
November-December	Second round of family reunions take place in Seoul and P'yôngyang 30 November-2 December.
December	South Korea's *Defence White Paper* annoys North Korea.
	North and South Korea participate in "The Seventh Christians Tokyo Seminar".
	Fourth inter-Korean ministerial talks are held in P'yôngyang 12-16 December.
	The pro-North Korean Kûmgangsan Opera Troupe in Japan performs in Seoul 15-17 December.
	North and South Korea participate in "The International Scientific Conference on Korean Womens' Life in North Korea, South Korea and China" in China 19-20 December.

	The inter-Korean Economic Cooperation Committee (KECC) meets for the first time in P'yôngyang 28-30 December.
2001 January	The Korean Methodist Church gets government permission for a project.
February	A joint performance of *Ch'unhyang* is made in P'yôngyang.
	A short-run marathon race is held at Mt. Kûmgang.
	A conference in the series "The Computerization of the Korean Language" is held in China 22-24 February.
	Third round of family reunions take place in Seoul and P'yôngyang 26-28 February.
March	US-South Korea summit held.
	Joint mass is held at Mt. Kûmgang.
	"The North-South Joint Exhibition and Scientific Debate Forum on the Forced Integration of Korea into the Japanese Empire" takes place in P'yôngyang 1-6 March.
	Letters are for the first time exchanged by divided family members at P'anmunjôm on 15 March.
	The South Korean Council of Religionists for Peace and the North Korean Council of Religionists announce a joint statement against the distortion of Japanese history on 28 March.
April	Representatives of the Korean Council of Religionists for Peace visit North Korea.
	North and South Korea participate in "The 20th Conference of the Association of Korean Studies in Europe" in London 4-8 April.
	South Korean singer Kim Yôn-ja performs at "The April Festival in North Korea" 5-12 April.
	80 members of Chochongryun visit South Korea 6-11 April.
May	South Korean journalists visit North Korea to cover the EU visit.
	"The Joint Holding of Labour Day" takes place at Mt. Kûmgang on 1 May.
June	North and South Korea participate in "The 23rd Moscow International Film Festival".
	North and South Korea agree to set up an Information Technology Scientific College in P'yôngyang.
	A KBS team visits North Korea for filming on the occasion of the first anniversary of the inter-Korean summit.

	"The Traditional Clothes Exhibition" opens in P'yôngyang 2-5 June.
	The KNCC and the NKCF participate in the German Churches' Day in Frankfurt and hold mass to commemorate the first anniversary of the summit, 11-17 June.
	"The National Unification Debate Forum" is held at Mt. Kûmgang on the occasion of the first anniversary of the summit 14-16 June.
	The joint photo exhibition "From Mt. Paektu to Mt. Halla" opens in P'yôngyang 14-24 June.
	Representatives of Ch'ôndogyo meet in P'yôngyang 20-22 June.
July	Unification rally takes place at Mt. Kûmgang.
	"The North-South Peasants' Meeting for National Unification" is held at Mt. Kûmgang 18-19 July.
August	The Mt. Kûmgang motorcycle touring takes place.
	The joint photo exhibition "From Mt. Paektu to Mt. Halla" opens in Seoul 14-23 August.
	"The Grand National Festival for Unification" takes place in P'yôngyang on 15-21 August and causes controversy.
September	Ch'ôndogyo representatives visit North Korea.
	Fifth inter-Korean ministerial talks are held in Seoul 15-18 September.
November	Sixth inter-Korean ministerial talks are held at Mt. Kûmgang 9-14 November.
	North and South Korea exchange fire in the demilitarized zone (DMZ) 27 November.
November-December	North and South Korean Catholic Churches hold a joint Holy Communion for the Korean people and seminar on An Chunggûn in P'yôngyang 27 November-4 December.
2002	Unification costs in Germany amount to 600 billion euros.
January	US President George Bush defines North Korea, Iran and Iraq as "the axis of evil" on 29 January.
February	US-South Korea summit is held in Seoul on 20 February.
April	President envoy Lim Dong Won visits P'yôngyang 3-6 April.
April-May	Fourth round of family reunions take place at Mt. Kûmgang 28 April-3 May.
May	Cheju Island residents visit North Korea 10-15 May.
	"The North-South Arts Peace Exhibition" is held in Seoul 15-25 May.
	"The Joint Prayers Meeting for Peaceful Unification in Mt. Kûmgang" takes place 16-18 May.

June	The inauguration ceremony and matches from the Soccer World Cup are televised on North Korean TV. "The National Festival for Unification on the Occasion of the Second Anniversary of the 15 June Declaration" takes place at Mt. Kûmgang 14-15 June. North-South naval clash in the Yellow Sea on 29 June.
July	North Korea announces the 1 July Economic Improvement Measures. North and South Korea participate in "The Tokyo Christian's Meeting" 22-25 July.
July-August	Hanyang University teaches information technology in P'yôngyang.
August	"The Joint Conference on Standardizing Linguistic Information" is held in Beijing. Seventh inter-Korean ministerial talks are held in Seoul 12-14 August. "The National Festival for Unification" is held in Seoul 14-17 August. Second KECC meeting is held in Seoul 27-30 August.
September	KBS and Munhwa Broadcasting Corporation (MBC) report from P'yôngyang in advance of the Asian Games. "The Students and Arts Troupe of Koreans in Japan" performs in South Korea on 4 September (Seoul) and 6 September (Chônju). "Unification Soccer Games" are played in Seoul on 7 September. Fifth round of family reunions take place at Mt. Kûmgang 13-18 September. A South Korean T'aekwôndo team performs in P'yôngyang 14-17 September. The KBS symphony orchestra makes a return visit to P'yôngyang 16-22 September. "The 2002 MBC Special Concert in P'yôngyang" is held on 27 and 29 September.
September-October	North Korea participates in the Asian Games held in Pusan 29 September-14 October. North and South Korea march together at the opening and ending ceremony.
October	North and South Korea participate in "The International Scientific Conference on Modern Illumination of Traditional Korean Culture" in China. North and South Korea participate in "The Scientific Meeting on New Conditions and Plans for Creating Peace on the Korean Peninsula in the 21st Century" in China.

National Foundation Day is jointly celebrated for the first time at Tan'gun's tomb in P'yôngyang on 3 October.
A South Korean film is shown in P'yôngyang on 11 October.
"The North-South Youth and Students' Meeting" is held at Mt. Kûmgang 12-14 October.
"The South-North Womens' Unification Meeting" is held at Mt. Kûmgang 15-17 October.
North Korea admits that, in spite of the 1994 Agreed Framework, it has continued its nuclear program on 17 October.
Eight inter-Korean ministerial talks are held in P'yôngyang 19-22 October.
A North Korean T'aekwôndo team performs in Seoul 23-26 October.

November	Third KECC meeting held in P'yôngyang 6-9 November.
	Cheju Island residents visit North Korea 25-30 November.
December	United States cuts off oil supplies to North Korea, which reactivates its Yôngbyôn nuclear reactor.
2003 January	North Korea declares its withdrawal from the non-proliferation treaty on 10 January.
	Ninth inter-Korean ministerial talks are held in Seoul 21-24 January.
February	North and South Korea march together at the opening and ending ceremony of "The 5th Asian Winter Games" held in Japan 1-8 February.
	Fourth KECC meeting held in Seoul 11-14 February.
	Sixth round of family reunions takes place at Mt. Kûmgang 20-25 February.
March	North Korea participates in "The March First Joint National Unification Event" in Seoul 1-2 March.
	"The North-South Youth Red Cross Friendship Tree Planting Event" is held at Mt. Kûmgang 21-23 March.
	"The North-South Harmony Prayers Meeting" is held at Mt. Kûmgang 23-25 March.
	"The Sixth North-South and Foreign Scholars Unification Conference" is held in P'yôngyang 26-27 March.
March-April	"The Conference on Exchanges between Christian Churches" is held in P'yôngyang 29 March-2 April.
April	"The Mass of the Groundbreaking of the P'yôngyang Theological School" is held 5-9 April.
	Three-party nuclear talks are held in China 23-25 April.
	Tenth inter-Korean ministerial talks are held in P'yôngyang 27-29 April.

May	"The 1 May North-South Workers' Unification Meeting" is held in P'yôngyang. Buddhists announce a joint prayer on 1 May. The North-South Peace Arts Exhibition is held in Seoul 15-25 May. Fifth KECC meeting is held in P'yôngyang 19-23 May.
June	Railways are ceremonially connected in the DMZ 14 June. A groundbreaking ceremony of the Kaesông Industrial Zone is held 30 June. Seventh round of family reunions take place at Mt. Kûmgang 27 June-2 July.
July	Eleventh inter-Korean ministerial talks are held in Seoul 9-12 July. North and South Korea exchange fire in the DMZ 17 July.
July-August	The Teachers' Trade Union visit North Korea 29 July-2 August.
August	"The KBS Amateurs Song Contest" is held in P'yôngyang 11 August. "The 15 August National Meeting for Peace and Unification" is held in P'yôngyang. "The Scientific Forum on the name of Korea in English" is held in P'yôngyang 18-26 August. North Korea participates in "The Summer Universiad Contest" held in Taegu 21-31 August. North and South Korea march together at the opening and ending ceremony. 256 Cheju Islanders visit North Korea 25-30 August. Sixth KECC meeting is held in Seoul 26-28 August. Six-party nuclear talks are held in China 27-29 August.
September	"The North-South Young Students Representative Meeting" is held in North Korea 1-3 September. 114 South Korean tourists travel by the North's Air Koryô from Seoul to P'yôngyang in a joint tour project on 15 September. Eighth round of family reunions take place at Mt. Kûmgang 20-25 September. "The Youth Relics Exploration" take place in North Korea 22-26 September. "The Scientific Conference to Examine the Truth of the Ukisima Incident" takes place in P'yôngyang on 29 September.
September-October	"The Joint North-South Foundation Day Event" is held in North Korea 30 September-5 October.

October	North and South Korea participate in the conference "Study on Popular Korean Songs Before Liberation" held in China 6-7 October.
	South Koreans participate in events 6-9 October. "The Ryugyông Chung Ju Yung Sports Stadium" is inaugurated. SBS relays "The Unification Concert" and "The Unification Basketball Games".
	"The Medical Science Discussion Forum" is held in P'yôngyang 14 October.
	Twelfth inter-Korean ministerial talks are held in P'yôngyang 14-17 October.
	"The North-South Media Committee Meeting" is held in North Korea 15-19 October.
	The conference "The Sense of Joint National Community in Korean History" is held in P'yôngyang 20-27 October.
	"The Cheju Island National Peace Festival" is held 23-27 October.
November	Seventh KECC meeting is held in P'yôngyang 5-8 November.
	North and South Korea participate in "The Scientific Meeting on the Unified Development of the Korean Language and Investigation of Dialects" held in China 6-9 November.
	"The Mt. Kûmgang Tourism 5th Anniversary Event" is held at Mt. Kûmgang 19 November.
2004 February	Thirteenth inter-Korean ministerial talks are held in Seoul 3-6 February.
	"The Joint Scientific Conference on the Return of Cultural Assets Plundered by the Japanese Imperialists" is held in P'yôngyang 24-28 February.
	Second round of six-party talks is held in Beijing 25-28 February.
March	Eighth KECC meeting is held in Seoul 2-5 March.
	"The North-South Foreign Youth Students' Representative Meeting" is held in China 20-23 March.
March-April	The ninth round of family reunions take place at Mt. Kûmgang 29 March-3 April.
April	The South Korean Youth Red Cross visits Mt. Kûmgang and participates in "The Friendship Tree Planting Event" 4-6 April.
April-May	"The North-South Workers' 1 May, 2004 Unification Meeting" is held in P'yôngyang 30 April-3 May.

May	"The Sixth Medical Science Discussion Forum" is held in P'yôngyang 3 May.
Fourteenth inter-Korean ministerial talks are held in P'yôngyang 4-7 May.
"The Seoul Meeting of the International Solidarity Association To Urge A Cleansing of Japan's Past" is held 20-24 May.
First North-South Korean General talks are held at Mt. Kûmgang 26 May.
June	Ninth KECC meeting is held in P'yôngyang 2-5 June.
"The Joint North-South Scientific Conference on the Modern Nationalist Movement" is held in Seoul 2-5 June.
Second North-South Korean General talks are held at Mt. Sôrak 3-4 June.
"The June 15 National Meeting" is held in Inch'ôn 14-17 June.
"The Joint North-South Photo Exhibition" is held in P'yôngyang 14-20 June.
North and South Korea participate in "The Symposium on the Iron Silk Road" held in Seoul 17-18 June.
Third round of six-party talks is held in Beijing, 23-26 June.
"The North-South Peasants Unification Meeting" is held at Mt. Kûmgang 26-28 June.
July	Tenth round of family reunions is held at Mt. Kûmgang 11-16 July.
"The North-South Educators' Meeting for the Implementation of the 15 June Joint North-South Declaration" is held at Mt. Kûmgang 18-20 July.
468 North Korean defectors arrive in South Korea 27-28 July.
August	North and South Korea march together at the opening and ending ceremony of the Olympic Games held in Athens 13-29 August.
September	"The Joint Commemorative Photo Exhibition and Scientific Conference on the Registration of Koguryô Relics as World Cultural Heritage" is held at Mt. Kûmgang 11-12 September.
November	"The Mt. Kûmgang Tourism 6th Anniversary Event" is held at Mt. Kûmgang 19-20 November.
Religionists take part in the inauguration ceremony of the jointly built Singyesa temple at Mt. Kûmgang on 20 November.

October	North and South Korea participate in the conference "Study on Popular Korean Songs Before Liberation" held in China 6-7 October.
	South Koreans participate in events 6-9 October. "The Ryugyông Chung Ju Yung Sports Stadium" is inaugurated. SBS relays "The Unification Concert" and "The Unification Basketball Games".
	"The Medical Science Discussion Forum" is held in P'yôngyang 14 October.
	Twelfth inter-Korean ministerial talks are held in P'yôngyang 14-17 October.
	"The North-South Media Committee Meeting" is held in North Korea 15-19 October.
	The conference "The Sense of Joint National Community in Korean History" is held in P'yôngyang 20-27 October.
	"The Cheju Island National Peace Festival" is held 23-27 October.
November	Seventh KECC meeting is held in P'yôngyang 5-8 November.
	North and South Korea participate in "The Scientific Meeting on the Unified Development of the Korean Language and Investigation of Dialects" held in China 6-9 November.
	"The Mt. Kûmgang Tourism 5th Anniversary Event" is held at Mt. Kûmgang 19 November.
2004 February	Thirteenth inter-Korean ministerial talks are held in Seoul 3-6 February.
	"The Joint Scientific Conference on the Return of Cultural Assets Plundered by the Japanese Imperialists" is held in P'yôngyang 24-28 February.
	Second round of six-party talks is held in Beijing 25-28 February.
March	Eighth KECC meeting is held in Seoul 2-5 March.
	"The North-South Foreign Youth Students' Representative Meeting" is held in China 20-23 March.
March-April	The ninth round of family reunions take place at Mt. Kûmgang 29 March-3 April.
April	The South Korean Youth Red Cross visits Mt. Kûmgang and participates in "The Friendship Tree Planting Event" 4-6 April.
April-May	"The North-South Workers' 1 May, 2004 Unification Meeting" is held in P'yôngyang 30 April-3 May.

May	"The Sixth Medical Science Discussion Forum" is held in P'yôngyang 3 May. Fourteenth inter-Korean ministerial talks are held in P'yôngyang 4-7 May. "The Seoul Meeting of the International Solidarity Association To Urge A Cleansing of Japan's Past" is held 20-24 May. First North-South Korean General talks are held at Mt. Kûmgang 26 May.
June	Ninth KECC meeting is held in P'yôngyang 2-5 June. "The Joint North-South Scientific Conference on the Modern Nationalist Movement" is held in Seoul 2-5 June. Second North-South Korean General talks are held at Mt. Sôrak 3-4 June. "The June 15 National Meeting" is held in Inch'ôn 14-17 June. "The Joint North-South Photo Exhibition" is held in P'yôngyang 14-20 June. North and South Korea participate in "The Symposium on the Iron Silk Road" held in Seoul 17-18 June. Third round of six-party talks is held in Beijing, 23-26 June. "The North-South Peasants Unification Meeting" is held at Mt. Kûmgang 26-28 June.
July	Tenth round of family reunions is held at Mt. Kûmgang 11-16 July. "The North-South Educators' Meeting for the Implementation of the 15 June Joint North-South Declaration" is held at Mt. Kûmgang 18-20 July. 468 North Korean defectors arrive in South Korea 27-28 July.
August	North and South Korea march together at the opening and ending ceremony of the Olympic Games held in Athens 13-29 August.
September	"The Joint Commemorative Photo Exhibition and Scientific Conference on the Registration of Koguryô Relics as World Cultural Heritage" is held at Mt. Kûmgang 11-12 September.
November	"The Mt. Kûmgang Tourism 6th Anniversary Event" is held at Mt. Kûmgang 19-20 November. Religionists take part in the inauguration ceremony of the jointly built Singyesa temple at Mt. Kûmgang on 20 November.

2005 February	North Korea claims that it has nuclear weapons on 10 February.
July-August	The first session of the fourth round of six-party talks is held in Beijing 26 July-7 August.
September	The second session of the fourth round of six-party talks is held in Beijing 13-19 September. An agreement is reached on 19 September.
November	The first session of the fifth round of six-party talks is held in Beijing 9-11 November.

Bibliography

Ahn, Yinhay. "The Kim Il Sung Constitution and the Change of the Kim Jong-il System in North Korea". *International Journal of Korean Unification Studies* 8 (1999).
— "North Korea in 2001: At a Crossroads". *Asian Survey* 42 (2002), 1.
— "North Korea in 2002: A Survival Game". *Asian Survey* 43 (2003), 1.
Amnesty International. *Republic of Korea (South Korea): Long-term Prisoners Still Held under the National Security Law*. London, May 1998.
— *Republic of Korea (South Korea): Amnesty International Calls for Prisoner Releases and a Halt to National Security Law Arrests*. London, July 1998.
Ash, Robert F. "Economy". In *The Far East and Australasia 2005*. London: Europa Publications Ltd., 2004.
Association of Korean Studies in Europe. *Conference Programme*. London: University of London, 2001.
Bae, Jung-ho, Kim, Kook Sin, Shin, Sang-jin, Yun, Ik-chung and Choi, Choon-heum. *Nambukhan siljilchôk t'onghap-gwa chubyônguk hyômnyôk yudo pangan*. [*A Plan for Real North-South Unity and Inducement for Cooperation from the Surrounding Countries.*] Seoul: T'ongil yôn'guwôn [Korea Institute for National Unification: KINU], 2002.
Barclays Capital Asian Special Report. "What Rating for a Unified Korea?". 13 July, 2000.
Beal, Tim. *North Korea: The Struggle Against American Power*. London and Ann Arbor: Pluto Press, 2005.
Brown, David G. "North Korea in 1998: A Year of Foreboding Developments". *Asian Survey* 39 (1999), 1.
Chanda, Nayan and Shim, Jae Hoon. "Trouble on the Tracks". *Far Eastern Economic Review (FEER)*, 28 September, 2000.
Chang, Yong-hun. "Asian Geimsû Puk ch'amga, simnijôk naengjôn kujo haech'e ch'ôt pal". ["North Korea's Participation in the Asian Games, First Step to the Dissolution of the Mental Cold War Structure".] *T'ongil Han'guk* (2002), 11.
Chang, Yu-jông. "Nambuk hapchak 3D animation 'keûrûn koyangi Dingka', Hananet-esô chigûm sangyông chung". ["The North-South Joint 3D Animation 'The lazy cat Dingka' is Now Shown at Hananet".] *Minjok 21* (2002), 1.
Cheon, Seong Whun. "Pukhan haengmunje". ["The North Korean Nuclear Issue".] In T'ongil yôn'guwôn, *T'ongil hwangyông-mith Nambukhan kwangye chônmang: 2003-2004*. [*The Unification Environment and the Prospects for Relations Between North and South Korea: 2003-2004*.] Seoul: T'ongil yôn'guwôn, 2003.

— "Pukhan haengmunje". ["The North Korean Nuclear Issue".] In T'ongil yôn'guwôn, *T'ongil hwangyông-mith Nambukhan kwangye chônmang: 2004-2005*. [*The Unification Environment and the Prospects for Relations Between North and South Korea: 2004-2005.*] Seoul: T'ongil yôn'guwôn, 2004.

Cho, Han Bum. *NGOs-rûl t'onghan Nambuk sahoe munhwa kyoryu hyômnyôk chûngjin pangan yôn'gu*. [*A Study on a Plan for Promotion of Socio-Cultural Exchanges and Cooperation between North and South Korea Through NGOs.*] Seoul: Minjok t'ongil yôn'guwôn, 1998.

— *Nambuk sahoe munhwa kyoryu hyômnyôg-ûi p'yôngga-wa palch'ôn panghyang*. [*An Evaluation of and Development Directions for Socio-Cultural Exchanges and Cooperation between North and South Korea.*] Seoul: T'ongil yôn'guwôn, 1999.

— *Nambukhan haksul kyoryu hyômnyôk chûngjin pangan yôn'gu*. [*A Study on a Plan for Promotion of Scientific Exchanges and Cooperation between North and South Korea.*] Seoul: T'ongil yôn'guwôn, 2000.

— *Nambukhan sahoe munhwa kongdongch'e hyôngsông pangan yôn'gu*. [*A Study on a Plan for the Formation of a North-South Korean Socio-Cultural Community.*] Seoul: T'ongil yôn'guwôn, 2002.

— "Chôngsang hoedam ihu sahoe munhwa kyoryu-ga Pukhan sahoe-e mich'in yônghyang". ["The Influence of Socio-Cultural Exchanges on North Korea After the Summit Meeting".] In *Nambuk kwangye palchôn-gwa hanbando p'yônghwa chôngch'ak*. [*The Development of Inter-Korean Relations and Securing Peace on the Korean Peninsula.*] Seoul: T'ongil yôn'guwôn, 2002. Conference report.

— "NGOs and Inter-Korean Socio-Cultural Exchanges and Cooperation". *International Journal of Korean Unification Studies* 11 (2002), 1.

— "Sahoe munhwa punya". ["The Socio-Cultural Field".] In T'ongil yôn'guwôn, *T'ongil hwangyông-mith Nambukhan kwangye chônmang: 2002-2003*. [*The Unification Environment And The Prospects For Relations Between North and South Korea: 2002-2003.*] Seoul: T'ongil yôn'guwôn, 2002.

— "Sahoe munhwa punya". ["The Socio-Cultural Field".] In T'ongil yôn'guwôn, ibid., 2003.

— "Sahoe punya". ["The Social Field".] In T'ongil yôn'guwôn, ibid., 2004.

— Fax, 16 March, 2005.

Cho, Han Bum, Kim, Kyu-Ryoon, Kim, Sung-Chull and Kim, Hyông-sik. *Pichôngbu kigu(NGO)-rûl t'onghan Nambukhan kyoryu hyômnyôk chûngjin pangan yôn'gu*. [*A Study on A Plan for The Promotion of Exchanges and Cooperation Between North and South Korea Through Non-Governmental Organizations (NGOs).*] Seoul: T'ongil yôn'guwôn, 2000.

Cho, Min. *T'ongil kwajông-esô mingan tanch'e-ûi yôkhal*. [*The Role of Civilian Organizations in the Unification Process.*] Seoul: Minjok t'ongil yôn'guwôn, 1996.

— "Chôngch'i punya". ["Politics".] In T'ongil yôn'guwôn, ibid., 2002.

— "Chôngch'i punya". ["Politics".] In T'ongil yôn'guwôn, ibid., 2003.

Ch'oe, Hak-chu. "Nambukhan sahoe munhwa kyoryu-ŭi ŏje-wa onŭl". ["Socio-Cultural Exchanges Between North and South Korea Yesterday and Today".] *Pukhan* (October 2000).
Ch'oe, Tae-sôk and Yi, Sang-suk. "Pukhan-ŭi taehak saenghwal-gwa sae sedae-ŭi kach'igwan". ["Attending College in North Korea and Values of the New Generation".] In Minjok hwahae hyŏmnyŏk pŏmkungmin hyôbŭihoe [Nationwide Association for National Reconciliation and Cooperation], *Pukhan chumin-ŭi ilsang saenghwal-gwa taejung munhwa*. [*North Korean Citizens' Daily Life and Popular Culture*.] Seoul: Orŭm, 2003.
Choi, Jinwook, Kim, Sung-Chull, Park, Jong Chul, Park, Hyeong Jung, Suh, Jae Jean, Lee, Kyo-Duk, Cheon, Seong Whun, Chon, Hyun Joon and Hong, Kwan Hee. *Nambuk kwangye-ŭi chinjôn-gwa kungnaejôk yônghyang.* [*The Development of inter-Korean Relations and its Domestic Influence.*] Seoul: T'ongil yôn'guwôn, 2003.
Choi, Soo Young. "Kyôngje punya". ["Economics".] In T'ongil yôn'guwôn, ibid., 2002.
— "Kyôngje punya hoedam". ["Economic Talks".] In T'ongil yôn'guwôn, ibid., 2004.
Choi, Soo Young, Lim, Kang Taeg and O, Seung-Yol. *Nambukhan nongôp kyoryu hyômnyôk pangan yôn'gu.* [*A Study on a Plan for Cooperation and Exchanges Between North and South Korea in Agriculture.*] Seoul: T'ongil yôn'guwôn, 2000.
Choi, Sung-jin. "White Cloak Diplomacy: North Korea Emerges from Isolation, Forging Ties Abroad". *Korea Now*, 8 April, 2000.
Chon, Hyun Joon. "Taenam tonghyang". ["Policies towards South Korea".] In T'ongil yôn'guwôn, ibid., 2002.
Chôn, U-t'aek. "Namhan-e innûn t'alpukja-dûr-ŭi simnijôk kaltŭng-mith kû-e taehan hae-gyôl pangan". ["Mental Tensions of North Korean Defectors in South Korea and a Plan to Solve Them".] In T'ongil yôn'guwôn, *T'alpukja-ŭi poho-mith kung-nae chôgûng kaesôn pangan.* [*A Plan for an Improvement of the Protection of and Adaptation to South Korean Society by North Korean defectors.*] Seoul: T'ongil yôn'guwôn, 1999.
Chôn, Ûn-ju. "Nambuk yôsông t'ongil taehoe-rŭl mach'imyô...: Nambuk yôsông hamkke ch'un p'yônghwa-wa taedong ch'um". ["Ending the North-South Women's Unification Meeting: North-South Women Danced the Dance of Peace and Together".] *T'ongil Han'guk* (2002), 11.
Chông, Sông-san. "Pukhan-ŭi yesul hyônhwang". ["The Present Conditions of Arts in North Korea".] In Minjok t'ongil yôn'guwôn, *1997 nyôndo ch'och'ông seminar kyôlgwa pogosô.* [*A Report of the Results from the 1997 Invitation Seminars.*] Seoul: Minjok t'ongil yôn'guwôn, 1998.
Chông, T'ae-hôn. "Nambuk yôksahak kyoryu hyônhwang-gwa palchôn-ŭl wihan cheôn". ["Present Conditions of North-South Exchanges in History and Suggestions for Its Development".] *Yôksa pip'yông* 65 (Winter 2003).

Chông, Un-jong. "Sisa nondan – Taegu U taehoe-ga namgin munjejôm: simgakhan Nambukhan munhwa ijilhwa hyônsang". ["Current Issues Rostrum – Problems Remaining from the Taegu U: Serious Cultural Heterogeneity between North and South Korea".] *Pukhan* (October 2003).

Chosun Ilbo. NKchosun.com, http://nk.chosun.com/schedule/schedule.html?ACT=year&year=1=2000&year2=2003. Accessed 28 January, 2005.

Chung, Chung-gil and Jeon, Chang-gon. "The Farmers' Market in North Korea: The Seed of Capitalism?". *East Asian Review* 12 (2000), 1.

Chung, Ok-nim. "The Role of South Korea's NGOs: The Political Context". In L. Gordon Flake and Scott Snyder (eds), *Paved with Good Intentions: The NGO Experience in North Korea.* Westport, Connecticut: Praeger Publishers, 2003.

Crock, Stan, Moon, Ihlwan and Dexter, Robert. "The 'Wrong Signal' on Containing Nukes?". *BusinessWeek*, 3 October, 2005.

Dong-a Ilbo. "Nambuk kwangye-ûi wigi". ["The Crisis in inter-Korean Relations".] 18 February, 1997.

Dresch, Paul. *A History of Modern Yemen.* Cambridge: Cambridge University Press, 2000.

— E-mail, 28 February, 2005.

Eberstadt, Nicholas. *The End of North Korea.* Washington, DC: The AEI Press, 1999.

The Economist. "Encounter in Pyongyang". 17 June, 2000.

— "Hugs for Koreans: But not Yet for the North Korean Leader". 19 August, 2000.

— "The Koreas Start a Slow March, not Yet in Lockstep". 30 September, 2000.

— "Times Change, so Why not Laws?". 6 November, 2004.

— "China and North Korea: Managing Chaos". 19 February, 2005.

Europa Publications. *The Far East and Australasia 1998, 2000, 2002, 2005.* London: Europa Publications, 1997, 1999, 2001, 2004.

— *The Europa World Year Book, 2001 (vol. 2).* London: Europa Publications, 2001.

— "Yemen: Introductory Survey". In *The Europa World Year Book, 2001 (vol. 2).* London: Europa Publications, 2001.

— "Yemen". In *The Middle East and North Africa, 2005.* London: Europa Publications, 2004.

Flake, Gordon and Snyder, Scott (eds). *Paved with Good Intentions: The NGO Experience in North Korea.* Westport, Connecticut: Praeger Publishers, 2003.

Flockton, Christopher. "The German Economy since 1989/90: Problems and Prospects". In Klaus Larres (ed.), *Germany since Unification: The Domestic and External Consequences.* Houndmills and London: Macmillan Press Ltd., 1998.

Foley, James A. *Korea's Divided Families: Fifty Years of Separation.* London and New York: RoutledgeCurzon, 2003.

Foster-Carter, Aidan. "History". In *The Far East and Australasia 1998, 2000, 2002, 2005.* London: Europa Publications, 1997, 1999, 2001, 2004.

— "The Koreas: Peace in our Time?". N.p., September 2000.

German, Richard and Taylor, Elizabeth. "Yemen: Economy". In Europa Publications, *The Middle East and North Africa, 2005*. London: Europa Publications, 2004.
God dei sinmun. "Cheje, enôji pojangsi Pungmi chôngsanghwa". ["North Korea-United States Normalization When the System and Energy are Guaranteed".] http://news.hot.co.kr/2003/08/24/200308241614374113.shtml. Accessed 6 June, 2005.
Greenlees, Donald and Hiebert, Murray. "Nuclear No-No". *FEER*, 16 September, 2004.
Grinker, Roy Richard. *Korea and its Futures: Unification and the Unfinished War.* New York: St. Martin's Press, 1998.
Ha, Yong-Chool. "South Korea in 2000: A Summit and the Search for New Institutional Identity". *Asian Survey* 41 (2001), 1.
— "South Korea in 2001: Frustration and Continuing Uncertainty". *Asian Survey* 42 (2002), 1.
Ham, Pyông-su, Kil, Un-pae, Yi, Chong-wôn and Ch'oe, Wôn-gi. *NGO-rûl t'onghan Nambukhan ch'ôngsonyôn kyoryu hyômnyôk pangan yôn'gu.* [*A Study on a Plan for Exchanges and Cooperation between Youth in North and South Korea Through NGOs*.] Seoul: T'ongil yôn'guwôn, 2000.
Han, Man-gil. "T'alpuk ijuja-ûi Namhan sahoe chôgung munje-wa chaesahoehwa pangan". ["The Issue of North Korean Defectors' Adaptation to South Korean Society and a Plan for Resocialization".] *T'ongil yôn'gu nonch'ong* 5 (1996), 2.
Han'guk munhwa yesul chinhûngwôn. [Korean Culture and Arts Foundation]. "2000nyôn kukak kwallyôn haengsa-mith minsok yesulche". ["Events Related to Korean Music and Folk Arts Festivals during 2000".] http://www.kcaf.or.kr/yearbook/2001/kukak/umak-kukak22.htm. Accessed 6 June, 2005.
Harrison, Selig S. "A Path to Peace: President Kim's Policies Foster Improved Inter-Korean Relations". *Newsreview*, 3 April, 1999.
— *Korean Endgame: A Strategy for Reunification and US Disengagement.* Princeton: Princeton University Press, 2002.
Hart-Landsberg, Martin. "Korean Unification: Learning from the German Experience". *Journal of Contemporary Asia* 26 (1995), 1.
Hebbelstrup, Søren. E-mail, 28 April, 2002: 4 May, 2004.
Hong, Kwan Hee. "Nambuk changsônggûp hoedam". ["North-South General Level Talks".] In T'ongil yôn'guwôn, ibid., 2004.
Hudson, Michael C. "Bipolarity, Rational Calculation and War in Yemen". In Jamal S. al-Suwaidi (ed.), *The Yemeni War of 1994: Causes and Consequences.* London: Saqi Books, 1995.
Huh, Moon Young. "Taenam tonghyang". ["Trends towards the South".] In T'ongil yôn'guwôn, ibid., 2003.
Hwang, Byung-ki. "Direction of Inter-Korean Musical Exchanges". *Korea Focus* 9 (2001), 4.
Hwang, Ho-gon. "Nambuk sûp'och'û kyoryu". ["North-South Sports Exchanges".] *T'ongil Han'guk* (1989), 2.

Hwang, In Kwan. "Korean Reunification in a Comparative Perspective". In Young Whan Kihl (ed.), *Korea and the World: Beyond the Cold War*. Boulder: Westview Press, 1994.

— "Yôngse chungnip t'ongil pangan-ûi yuyongsông: t'ongil sôngsasik'il hwanggûm-ûi chungganch'i". ["The Usefulness of Unification Through Permanent Neutrality: The Golden Mean to Accomplish Unification".] *T'ongil Han'guk* (2004), 9.

Hwang, Jang-jin. "A Monumental Step Forward: Two Koreas Recognize Common Ground in Reunification Plan". *Korea Now*, 17 June, 2000.

Hwang, Jang-yop. "Strategy for Peaceful Korean Unification". *Korea Focus* 7 (1999), 1.

Hyôn, Sông-il. "T'ongir-ûl wihan Namhan-ûi chôngch'i sahoejôk pyônhwa panghyang". ["The Directions of Social Changes in South Korean Politics Towards Unification".] In Yi Yông-sôn (ed.), *T'ongir-ûl wihae Namhan-do pyônhae-ya handa – Pukhan ch'ul-sin hakcha-dûr-ûi chujang-gwa Namhan hakcha-dûr-ûi nonp'yông. [Also South Korea Must Change for Unification – Assertions by Scholars of North Korean Origin and Comments by South Korean Scholars.]* Seoul: Orûm, 1998.

Inter-Korean Agreement, 13 December, 1991. N.p. Unoffical translation.

The Internet Hankyoreh, "Nambuk kongdong haksul hoeûi 20il put'ô P'yôngyang sô kaech'oe". ["North-South Joint Scientific Conference Opens in P'yôngyang from the 20th"]. http://www.hani.co.kr/section009000000/2003/09/009000000200309151426706.html. Accessed 6 June, 2005.

Jeong, Young Tai. "Kunsa tonghyang". ["Military trends".] In T'ongil yôn'guwôn, ibid., 2003.

Jonsson, Gabriel. "Betydelsen av Göran Perssons besök i Nord- och Sydkorea". ["The Significance of Göran Persson's Visit to North and South Korea".] *Yoboseyo* 41 (2001), 3.

Juhlin, Sven. "NNSC och dess förändrade roll under 1990-talet". ["The Neutral Nations Supervisory Commission and their Changed Role During the 1990s".] Lecture at Stockholm University, 22 March, 2000. Minutes available from the author.

Kang, Il-gyu, Kim, Ch'ôl-hûi, Kim, Young-Yoon and Yi, Ûn-gu. *Nambukhan chigôp kyoyuk hullyôn punya-ûi kyoryu-mith hyômnyôk pangan yôn'gu. [A Study on a Plan for Exchanges and Cooperation between North and South Korea in Vocational Education and Training.]* Seoul: T'ongil yôn'guwôn, 2000.

Kang, Il-gyu, Ok, Chun-p'il and Yi, Ûn-gu. *Nambukhan p'yônghwa kongjon-gwa Nambuk yônhap ch'ujin-ûl wihan chigôp kyoyuk hullyôn punya-ûi yôn'gye pangan yôn'gu. [A Study on a Plan for Connecting Vocational Education and Training for Peaceful Coexistence Between North and South Korea and North-South Unity.]* Seoul: T'ongil yôn'guwôn, 2001.

Kang, Sôk-sûng. "Nambukhan-ûi munhwa yesul chôngch'aeg-ûi t'uksông pigyo-wa kyoryu silt'ae-e kwanhan yôn'gu". ["A Study of Characteristics of North and South Korea's Culture and Arts Policies and Actual Conditions of Exchanges".] *Pukhan hakbo* 28 (2003).

Kang, Won-tack. "Bridging the Divide: A Survey on the Mt. Kumgang Tour". *East Asian Review* 12 (2000), 1.

Kihl, Young Whan (ed.). *Korea and the World: Beyond the Cold War.* Boulder: Westview Press, 1994.

Kil, Ûn-pae, Yi, Chong-wôn and Ch'oe, Wôn-gi. *Nambukhan p'yônghwa kongjon-ûl wihan ch'ôngsonyôn-ûi sahoe munhwajôk tongjilsông chûngjin pangan yôn'gu.* [*A Study on a Plan for Peaceful Coexistence between North and South Korea by Promoting Socio-Cultural Homogeneity Among the Youth.*] Seoul: T'ongil yôn'guwôn, 2001.

— *Nambukhan-ûi silchiljôk t'onghab-ûl wihan ch'ôngsonyôn kyoryu hyômnyôk chedohwa pangan yôn'gu.* [*A Study on a Plan for Institutionalization of Youth Exchanges and Cooperation for Real Unity between North and South Korea.*] Seoul: T'ongil yôn'guwôn, 2002.

Kim, Chae-in and Chang, Hye-gyông. *Yôsông pichôngbu kigu-rûl t'onghan Nambukhan kyoryu hyômnyôk hwalsônghwa pangan yôn'gu.* [*A Study on a Plan for Activation of Inter-Korean Exchanges and Cooperation through Women's NGOs.*] Seoul: T'ongil yôn'guwôn, 2000.

Kim, Chae-in, Chang, Hye-kyông and Kim, Wôn-hong. *Nambuk yônhap tangye-esô-ûi yôsông chôngch'aek ch'ujin pangan.* [*A Plan for Women's Policies in the Phase of North-South Unity.*] Seoul: T'ongil yôn'guwôn, 2001.

Kim, Chin-so. "Sahyangga". ["Songs of Thoughts of Home".] In *Han'guk minjok taepaekkwa sajôn*, vol. 11. [*A National Encyclopedia of Korea.*] Sôngnam: Han'guk chôngsin munhwa yôn'guwôn [Academy of Korean Studies], 1991.

Kim, Choong-hwan. "Toward the End of Agony". *Han'guk-Sûweden hyôphoe sosik* (2003), 7.

Kim, Dae Jung. *Tasi, saeroun sijag-ûl wihayô: saranghanûn chôlmûn-i-wa chongyông-hanûn kungmin-tûr-ege pach'inûn iyagi.* [*For a New Beginning: Stories Dedicated to Beloved Young People and Respected Citizens.*] Seoul: Kimyôngsa, 1998. (1993).

Kim, Hak-sông. *Tong sôdok injôk kyoryu silt'ae yôn'gu.* [*A Study on the Actual Conditions of Human Exchanges Between East and West Germany.*] Seoul: Minjok t'ongil yôn'guwôn, 1996.

Kim, Hoo-ran. "Geumgang: Mountain of One's Dreams". *Korea Now*, 11 December, 2004.

Kim, Hwan-sik. "Nambuk haksaeng mannam-ûn sunsuhae ya handa". ["Meetings between North and South Korean Students Must Be Pure".] *T'ongil Han'guk* (1996), 6.

Kim, Kook Sin. *Yemen t'onghap sarye yôn'gu.* [*A Case Study of Yemen Unity.*] Seoul: Minjok t'ongil yôn'guwôn, 1993.

— "Yemen t'ongil pangsig-i hanbando t'ongir-e chunûn sisajôm". ["Suggestions from the Yemeni Way of Unification to Korean Unification".] In Minjok t'ongil yôn'guwôn, *Yemen t'ongir-ûi munjejôm* [*Problems of Yemen Unification.*] Seoul: Minjok t'ongil yôn'guwôn, 1994.
— "Togil, Pet'ûnam, Yemen t'ongil sarye". ["The Unification of Germany, Vietnam and Yemen".] In Minjok t'ongil yôn'guwôn, *Pundanguk t'onghap-gwa p'yônghwa hyôpchông* [*Reunification of Divided Countries and Peace Agreements.*] Seoul: Minjok t'ongil yôn'guwôn, 2001.
— "Han-mi kwangye". ["Relations between South Korea and the United States".] In T'ongil yôn'guwôn, ibid., 2002.
Kim, Min-gon. "Kyoyuk ch'amgwandan-ûro P'yôngyang-e tanyô wa sô". ["Travelling to P'yôngyang with an Inspection Tour".] *Minjok hwahae* (2003), 09/10.
Kim, Pyông-no. "Nambuk munhwa yesul-mith sûp'och'û kyoryu-ûi hyônhwang-gwa kwaje: pôp chedo changbi sigûphada". ["The Present Conditions of and Tasks for North-South Cultural, Arts and Sports Exchanges: Fitting Out a Legal System Urgent".] *T'ongil Han'guk* (2000), 7.
Kim, Pyông-no, Park, Jung Chul, Lee, Woo-Young and Cheon, Seong Whun. *Nambukhan t'onghab-ûl wihan chonggyo kyoryu hyômnyôg-ûi chedohwa pangan.* [*A Plan on Institutionalization of Religious Exchanges and Cooperation for Unity between North and South Korea.*] Seoul: T'ongil yôn'guwôn, 2002.
Kim, Samuel S. "North Korea in 1999: Bringing The Grand Chollima March Back In". *Asian Survey* 40 (2000), 1.
— "North Korea in 2000: Surviving through High Hopes of Summit Diplomacy". *Asian Survey* 41 (2001), 1.
Kim, Sang-hwan. "Nambuk sahoe munhwa kyoryu-ûi sônggwa-wa munjechôm". ["Results of and Problems with Socio-cultural Exchanges between North and South Korea".] *Pukhan* (April 2001).
Kim, Sang-ch'ôl. "Pukhan chumin-ûi chonggyo saenghwal: Nambukhan chonggyo chôngch'aek-gwa kidokkyo-rûl chungsim-ûro". ["Religion among North Koreans: Emphasis on Religious Policies in North and South Korea and Christianity".] In Minjok hwahae hyômnyôk pômkungmin hyôbûihoe [Nation-wide Association for National Reconciliation and Cooperation], ibid., 2003.
Kim, Soo Am. "T'alpukja munje-ûi taeûng-gwa chôngch'aek taean: choyonghan wegyo t'onghan ch'egyejôk poho sigûphada". ["How to Face the North Korean Defectors Issue and Policy Alternatives: The Urgency of Systematic Protection Through Quiet Diplomacy".] *T'ongil Han'guk* (2004), 9.
Kim, Su-hyôn. "Chôt Nambuk hakcha kongdong yôn'gusô palgan". ["First North-South Scholars' Joint Scientific Report Published".] http://www.hani.co.kr/section-005000000/2002/02/005000000200202182246032.html. Accessed 6 April, 2005.
Kim, Tu-hyôn. "58 nyôn man-ûi pungnyôk tongp'o pangmnun-ûro t'ongil yôlgi kadûkhan Taegu". ["Taegu Filled with Unification Fever due to the First Visit by Northern Compatriots in 58 Years".] *Minjok hwahae* (2003), 09/10.

Kim, Young Choon. "Puk-il kwangye". ["North Korea-Japan Relations".] In T'ongil yôn'guwôn, ibid., 2004.
Kim, Young Yoon. "Kyôngje punya". ["Economics".] In T'ongil yôn'guwôn, ibid., 2003.
— "Kyôngje punya". ["Economics".] In T'ongil yôn'guwôn, ibid., 2004.
Kim, Young Yoon and Choi Soo Young, *Understanding North Korea's Economic Reforms.* Seoul: Korea Institute for National Unification, Centre for the North Korean Economy, 2005.
Kim, Yông-gi. "T'ongir-ûi hanûr-ûl yôlda – 2003 kaech'ônjôl minjok kongdong haengsa". ["Opening Unification's Heaven – 2003 National Foundation Day Joint Events".] *Minjok hwahae* (2003), 11/12.
Ko, Sang-tu. "Pukhan naebu-ûi chôngch'i kaltûng kwalli pangan". ["A Plan on Managing the Internal Political Discords in North Korea".] In Moon, Chung-in, Ko, Sang-tu, Chin, Yông-chae, Pak, Han-gyu and Yi, Tong-yun, *Nambukhan chôngch'i kaltûng-gwa t'ongil. [Political Discords between North and South Korea and Unification.]* Seoul: Orûm, 2002.
Ko, Yong-gwôn. "Nambuk sahoe munhwa kyoryu hyômnyôg-ûi hyônhwang-gwa kwaje". ["Actual Conditions of and Tasks for North-South Socio-Cultural Exchanges and Cooperation".] In Kunsan taehakkyo hyôndae inyôm yôn'guso & T'ongil munje yôn'gu hyôbûihoe [Kunsan University: Research Institute on Modern Thoughts and Research Association of Unification Issues], *Nambukhan kyoryu hyômnyôg-ûi hwalsônghwa pangan. [Proposals for a Vitalization of Exchanges and Cooperation between North and South Korea.]* Kunsan: Kunsan taehakkyo hyôndae inyôm yôn'guso, 2002. Conference report.
Korea Focus. "Lessons of Yemen's Reunification". Vol. 2 (1994), 4.
Korea Institute for National Unification. *Exploring New Areas for Multilateral Inter-Korean Cooperation.* Seoul: KINU, 1998. Conference report.
— *The Unification Environment and Relations Between North and South Korea; 1999-2000.* Seoul: KINU, 2000.
— *International Organizations' Assistance to North Korea and Inter-Korean Cooperation.* Seoul: KINU, 2001.
— *Korea Institute for National Unification 2002, 2004.* Seoul: KINU, 2002, 2004. Brieflets.
Korea Now. "Full Tilt on the Diplomatic Front: N.K. Warms Up to International Community to Stay Clear of Total Collapse". 25 March, 2000.
— "Text of the N-S Accord". 17 June, 2000.
— "Welcoming N.K. into the Fold: Two Koreas Enter Unprecedented Diplomatic Heights as Foreign Ministers Step Up Contacts". 29 July, 2000.
— "To Smooth Over Ideological Friction: Seoul Repatriates 63 Imprisoned North Koreans in Goodwill Gesture". 9 September, 2000.
The Korean Classical Literature Institute. *The Story of Hong Gil dong.* Seoul: Baek Am Publishing Company, 2000.
Kostiner, Joseph. *Yemen: The Tortuous Quest for Unity, 1990-94.* London: Royal Institute of International Affairs, 1996.

Kunsan taehakkyo hyôndae inyôm yôn'guso & T'ongil munje yôn'gu hyôbûihoe [Kunsan University: Research Institute on Modern Thoughts and Research Association of Unification Issues]. *Nambukhan kyoryu hyômnyôg-ûi hwalsônghwa pangan.* [*Proposals for a Vitalization of Exchanges and Cooperation between North and South Korea.*] Kunsan: Kunsan taehakkyo hyôndae inyôm yôn'guso, 2002. Conference report.

Larres, Klaus. "Germany in 1989: The Development of a Revolution". In *Germany Since Unification: The Domestic and External Consequences*, ibid.

Lawless, Richard I. "Yemen: History". In Europa Publications, *The Middle East and North Africa, 2005*. London: Europa Publications, 2004.

Lawrence, Susan V. "North Meets South". *FEER*, 29 April, 1999.

Lee, Hong Yung. "South Korea in 2002: Multiple Political Dramas". *Asian Survey* 43 (2003), 1.

— "South Korea in 2003: A Question of Leadership?". *Asian Survey* 44 (2004), 1.

Lee, Hun Kyung."Nambuk munhwa kyoryu-ûi hyônhwang-gwa munjejôm". ["Present Conditions and Problems of North-South Cultural Exchanges".] In Minjok t'ongil yôn'guwôn, *T'ongil munhwa-wa minjok kongdongch'e kônsôl.* [*Building a Common Unified Culture and Nation.*] Seoul: Minjok t'ongil yôn'guwôn, 1994.

Lee, Keumsoon. *T'alpukcha munje haegyôl pangan.* [*A Plan to Solve the North Korean Defectors Issue.*] Seoul: T'ongil yôn'guwôn, 1999.

— "Assisting North Korea by Intergovernmental Agencies and Non-Governmental Organizations: Current State and Implications". In Korea Institute for National Unification, *International Organizations' Assistance to North Korea and Inter-Korean Cooperation.* Seoul: KINU, 2001.

— "Taebuk chiwôn". ["Assistance to North Korea".] In T'ongil yôn'guwôn, ibid., 2002.

— "Taebuk chiwôn". ["Assistance to North Korea".] In T'ongil yôn'guwôn, ibid., 2003.

— *Taebuk indojôk chiwôn-ûi yônghyangnyôk punsôk.* [*An Analysis of the Influence of Humanitarian Aid to North Korea.*] Seoul: T'ongil yôn'guwôn, 2003.

— "Taebuk chiwôn". ["Assistance to North Korea".] In T'ongil yôn'guwôn, ibid., 2004.

— E-mail, 19 May, 2004.

Lee, Keumsoon, Kang, Sin-ch'ang, Kim, Pyông-no, Kim, Soo-Am, An, Hye-yông, O, Seung-Yol, Yun, Yô-sang, Lee, Woo-Young, Lim, Soon-Hee and Choi, Euichul. *Pukhan it'al chumin chôgûng silt'ae yôn'gu.* [*A Study on the Reality of Adaptation of North Korean Defectors.*] Seoul: T'ongil yôn'guwôn, 2003.

Lee, Keumsoon, Choi, Euichul, Suh, Jae Jean, Lim, Soon-Hee, Lee, Woo-Young and Kim, Soo-Am. *White Paper on Human Rights in North Korea.* Seoul: KINU, 2004.

Lee, Keumsoon, Choi, Euichul, Lim, Soon-Hee and Kim, Soo-Am. *White Paper on Human Rights in North Korea.* Seoul: KINU, 2005.

Lee, Ki-baek. *A New History of Korea.* Seoul: Ilchokak, Publishers, 1984. Translated by Edward W. Wagner with Edward J. Shultz.
Lee, Kwang-ho. "Latest Round of Six-Party Talks", *Vantage Point* 28 (December 2005), 12.
Lee, Kyo Duk. "Taenam tonghyang". ["Trends toward South Korea".] In T'ongil yôn'guwôn, ibid., 2004.
Lee, Woo-Young. *T'ongil kwajông-esô mass media-ûi yôkhal.* [*The Role of Mass Media in the Unification Process.*] Seoul: Minjok t'ongil yôn'guwôn, 1996.
— *Pukhan munhwa-ûi suyong silt'ae chosa.* [*An Investigation of the Actual Conditions of Accommodating North Korean Culture.*] Seoul: T'ongil yôn'guwôn, 2001.
— "Simin sahoe-esô pon ch'amyô chôngbu-ûi taebuk chôngch'aek". ["Views of the Civil Society of the Participatory Government's North Korea Policy".] In Uri minjok sôro topki undong p'yônghwa nanum sent'ô [Korean Sharing Movement Peace Sharing Centre], *Ch'amyô chôngbu 1nyôn, Nambuk kwangye chindangwa palchôn panghyang.* [*One Year of Participatory Government, A Diagnosis of North-South Relations and Development Directions.*] Seoul: Uri minjok sôro topki undong p'yônghwa nanum sen'ô, 2004. Conference report.
Lee, Woo-Young, Lee, Keumsoon, Suh, Jae Jean, Choon, Hyun Joon and Choi, Choon-heum. *Pukhan it'al chumin munje-ûi chonghapchôk chôngch'aek pangan yôn'gu.* [*A Study on a Plan for a Comprehensive Policy on the North Korean Defectors Issue.*] Seoul: T'ongil yôn'guwôn, 2000.
Lee, Woo-Young, Son, Gi-Woong and Lim, Soon-Hee. *Nambukhan p'yônghwa kongjon-ûl wihan sahoe munhwa kyoryu hyômnyôg-ûi hwalsônghwa pangan.* [*A Plan for Vitalization of Socio-cultural Exchanges and Cooperation for Peaceful Coexistence between North and South Korea.*] Seoul: T'ongil yôn'guwôn, 2001.
Lim, Kang Taek. "Kyôngje punya". ["Economics".] In T'ongil yôn'guwôn, ibid., 2002.
Lim, Soon Hee. *Pukhan-ûi taejung munhwa: silt'ae-wa pyônhwa chônmang.* [*Popular Culture in North Korea: Actual Conditions and Prospects for Change.*] Seoul: T'ongil yôn'guwôn, 2000.
— "Isan kajongmunje". ["The Divided Families Issue".] In T'ongil yôn'guwôn, ibid., 2003.
— "Isan kajongmunje". ["The Divided Families Issue".] In T'ongil yôn'guwôn, ibid., 2004.
Lintner, Bertil. *Great Leader, Dear Leader: Demystifying North Korea under the Kim Clan.* Chiang Mai: Silkworm Books, 2005.
— "Nordkorea ger upp kärnvapen: Kompromiss nådd i förhandlingarna – men flera frågetecken kvarstår". ["North Korea Gives Up Nuclear Weapons: Compromise Reached in Negotiations – But Many Question Marks Remain".] *Svenska Dagbladet*, 20 September, 2005.
Lundin, Tomas. "Murens fall gav tysk baksmälla: 15 år efter att Berlinmuren öppnades önskar nästan en fjärdedel av västtyskarna att den stod kvar". ["The Fall of the

Wall Caused German Hangover: 15 Years After the Opening of the Berlin Wall Almost a Quarter of West Germans Wishes That It Should Have Remained".] *Svenska Dagbladet*, 9 November, 2004.
McAdams, A. James. *Germany Divided: From the Wall to Reunification.* Princeton: Princeton University Press, 1993.
McCormack, Gavan. "Pyongyang Waiting for the Spring". http://www.nationinstitute.org/tomdispatch, 24 February, 2005. Accessed 3 March, 2005.
Marsh, David. *Germany and Europe – The Crisis of Unity.* London: Heinemann Limited, 1994.
Ministry of Unification. *Kim Dae-jung's Policies on North Korea: Achievements and Future Goals.* Seoul: Ministry of Unification, 1999.
— *P'yônghwa pônyông chôngch'aek haesôl charyo.* [*An Explanation of the Policy for Peace and Prosperity.*] http://www.unikorea.go.kr/kr/uninews/uninews_policyfocus.php, 10 March, 2003. Accessed 25 April, 2003.
Minjok hwahae hyômnyôk pômkungmin hyôbûihoe. [Nation-wide Association for National Reconciliation and Cooperation]. *Pukhan chumin-ûi ilsang saenghwal-gwa taejung munhwa.* [*North Korean Citizens' Daily Life and Popular Culture.*] Seoul: Orûm, 2003.
Minjok t'ongil yôn'guwôn [KINU]. *T'ongil hwangyông-gwa Nambukhan kwangye: 1991~1992.* [*The Unification Environment and Relations Between North and South Korea: 1991~1992.*] Seoul: Minjok t'ongil yôn'guwôn, 1991.
— Ibid., *1992~1993.* Ibid., 1992.
— Ibid., *1993~1994.* Ibid., 1994.
— Ibid., *1994~1995.* Ibid., 1994.
— Ibid., *1995~1996.* Ibid., 1995.
— Ibid., *1996~1997.* Ibid., 1996.
— Ibid., *1997~1998.* Ibid., 1997.
— Ibid., *1998~1999.* Ibid., 1998.
— *1997 nyôndo ch'och'ông seminar kyôlgwa pogosô.* [*A Report of the Results from the 1997 Invitation Seminars.*] Ibid., 1998 (b).
— *Pundanguk t'onghap-gwa p'yônghwa hyôpchông* [*Reunification of Divided Countries and Peace Agreements.*] Ibid., 2001.
Mitrany, David. *A Working Peace System: An Argument for the Functional Development of International Organization.* London: The Royal Institute of International Affairs, 1943.
— *The Functional Theory of Politics.* Bristol: Western Printing Services Ltd., 1975.
Moon, Chung-in, Ko, Sang-tu, Chin, Yông-chae, Pak, Han-gyu and Yi, Tong-yun. *Nambukhan chôngch'i kaltûng-gwa t'ongil.* [*Political Discords between North and South Korea and Unification.*] Seoul: Orûm, 2002.
von Morr, Hubertus. Speech held at the conference "Inter-Korean Relations and Peace Building on the Korean Peninsula" in Seoul, 14 June, 2002. Minutes available from the author.

Mun, Nan-yông. "NGO Ch'onghoe-e tanyô-wa-sô – segye-nûn hanada". ["Coming back from a NGO General Meeting – The World is One".] http://www.wfwp.or.kr/kukjea/ngo8.htm. Accessed 6 June, 2005.
Newsreview. "Cruising into History". 21 November, 1998.
— "A Mountain of Memories: Tourist Bask in the Grandeur of Mt. Kumgang – and Pray for Reunion with Separated Families". 28 November, 1998.
— "Stalemate: Family Reunion Talks Stalled Again". 10 July, 1999.
— "Kudos for KEDO: Contract Signed to Facilitate Construction of N-reactors in N.K.". 18 December, 1999.
— "Inter-Korean Full Court Press: N.K. Basketball Giant visits Seoul for Historic Games". 25 December, 1999.
O, Ki-sông. *Nambukhan munhwa t'onghamnon: munhwa-ûi kujo punsôg-e ûihan t'onghap kwajông yôn'gu.* [*A Theory of Cultural Integration between North and South Korea: A Study of the Unity Process Based on an Analysis of Cultural Structures.*] Seoul: Kyoyuk kwahaksa, 1999.
— "Nambuk kyoryu hwalsônghwa-rûl wihan mingan tanch'e-ûi yôkhal – sahoe munhwa kyoryu-rûl chungsim-ûro". ["The Role of NGOs in Activating North-South Exchanges – Emphasis on Socio-Cultural Exchanges".] *T'ongil munje-wa kukche kwangye* (December 1999).
Ok, Tae Hwan and Kim, Soo Am. *The Initial Phase of Unified Korea.* Seoul: KINU, 1998.
Paek, Yông-ch'ôl. "Hyanghu t'ongil chôngch'aek panghyang IV". ["The Future Directions of Unification Policies IV".] In Minjok t'ongil yôn'guwôn, ibid., 1998b.
Paek, Yông-ok. *Kukje kigu-rûl t'onghan Nambuk kyoryu hyômnyôk chûngdae pangan yôn'gu.* [*A Study on a Plan for Enlarging Exchanges and Cooperation between North and South Korea Through International Organizations.*] Seoul: Minjok t'ongil yônguwôn, 1994.
Pak, Nan-hûi. "Han'guk kasu-ro-sô-nûn ch'ôûm-ûro Kim Chông Il wiwônjang mannago on Kim Yôn-ja". ["Kim Yôn-ja is the First Korean Singer to Have Met Chairman Kim Chông Il".] *Yôsông Chosôn* (April 2001).
Pak, Sang-bong. "Nambuk munhwa kyoryu-ûi hô-wa sil". ["Emptiness and Results of Cultural Exchanges between North and South Korea".] *Pukhan* (October 2000).
Park, Jong Chul, Kim, Young-Yoon and Lee, Woo-Young. *Pukhan ith'al chumin-ûi sahoe chôgûng-e kwanhan yôn'gu: Silt'ae chosa mith kaesôn pangan.* [*A Study of North Korean Defectors' Adaptation to Society: An Investigation of Actual Conditions and Plans for Improvements.*] Seoul: Minjok t'ongil yôn'guwôn, 1996.
Park, Kyung-Ae. "North Korea in 2003: Pendulum Swing between Crisis and Diplomacy". *Asian Survey* 44 (2004), 1.
Park, Tong Whan. "South Korea in 1998: Swallowing the Bitter Pills of Restructuring". *Asian Survey* 39 (1999), 1.

Park, Young Ho, Kim, Kyu-Ryoon, Suh, Jae Jean, Lim, Kang Taeg, Cho, Min and Huh, Moon-Young. *T'ongil sinario-wa t'ongil kwajôngsang-ûi chôngch'aek pangan: ironchôk model-gwa chônmunga insik chosa.* [*Unification Scenarios and a Plan for Unification Policies: A Theoretical Model and An Investigation of Specialists' Cognitions.*] Seoul: T'ongil yôn'guwôn, 2002.

Pfennig, Werner. "From Division through Normalization to Unification: A Comparative View on Developments in Germany and Korea". *Korea Observer* 32 (2001), 1.

Pohl, Manfred. "Farewell to Model? German Experiences with Unification and Its Implications for Korean Strategies". In Korea Institute for National Unification, *Exploring New Areas for Multilateral Inter-Korean Cooperation.* Seoul: KINU, 1998, ibid.

Pond, Elizabeth. *Beyond the Wall: Germany's Road to Unification.* Washington, DC: The Brookings Institution, 1993.

P'yônghwa-rûl mandûnûn yôsônghoe. [Women for World Peace.] "Kôrô on kil". ["Our Path".] http://www.peacewomen.or.kr/new_wmp/makepeace/walking_peace.htm. Accessed 6 June, 2005.

Quinones, Kenneth. "Chôegûn Pukhan-ûi silsang". ["The Recent State of Affairs in North Korea".] In Minjok t'ongil yôn'guwôn, ibid., 1998b.

Rhee, Kang Suk. "Korea's Unification: The Applicability of the German Experience". *Asian Survey* 33 (1993), 4.

Rosamond, Ben. *Theories of European Integration.* Houndmills: Macmillan Press Ltd., 2000.

Ryu, Chae-gyu. "Nambuk ch'eyuk kyoryu-ûi ôje-wa onûl: Nambuk, 'son e sonchapko' At'ene kanda". ["North-South Sports Exchanges Yesterday and Today: North and South Korea Walk Hand-in-Hand To Athens".] *T'ongil Han'guk* (2004), 8.

Savada, Andrea Matles (ed.). *North Korea: A Country Study.* Washington, DC: Library of Congress, 1994.

Savada, Andrea Matles and William Shaw (eds). *South Korea: A Country Study.* Washington: Library of Congress, 1992.

Schloms, Michael. *North Korea and the Timeless Dilemma of Aid.* Münster: LIT Verlag, 2004.

Segye p'yônghwa t'ongil kajông yônhap. [The Family Federation for World Peace and Unification.] "Nam-gwa puk, kûrim-ûro mannatchi" ["North and South Korea Met Through Paintings".] http://www.tongil.or.kr/main2/boardnews/boardcontent.html?&no=794&code= WEB. Accessed 6 June, 2005.

Shim, Jae Hoon. "Spring Thaw?: South Korea Tries a New, Gentler Approach to North". *FEER*, 11 June, 1998.

— "Kim the Cool: South's Reaction to North's Intrusion Signals New Maturity". Ibid., 9 July, 1998.

— "Fire, Backfire: Missile Test Threatens Overtures to Pyongyang". Ibid., 10 September, 1998.

— "A Crack in the Wall". Ibid., 29 April, 1999.

Shim, Jae Hoon and Adrian Edwards. "No Turning Back". Ibid., 22 June, 2000.
Shin, Sang-jin. "Taebuk p'oyong chôngch'aeg-ûi hyoyulchôk ch'ujin-ûl wihan chubyôn anbo wegyo hwangyông chosông pangan". ["A Study on Creating a Regional Security and Diplomatic Environment to Efficiently Pursue an Inclusive Policy towards North Korea".] In T'ongil yôn'guwôn, *Nambukhan hwahae hyômnyôk ch'okjin pangan*. [*A Study on Promotion of Reconciliation and Cooperation between North and South Korea.*] Seoul: T'ongil yôn'guwôn, 2000.
Sim, Choi Hong. *Fragrance of Spring: The Story of Choon Hyang*. Seoul: Pojinchae Ltd., 1992. (1970).
Sin, Chun-yông. "Ilche-ûi chosôn kangjôm pulpôpsông-e taehan Nambuk kongdong charyo chônsihoe: Nambuk kongdong taech'ô-ro wanjônhan ilche ch'ôngsanûl". ["The North-South Joint Exhibition on the Forced Integration of Korea into the Japanese Empire: Clear Up the Japanese Occupation Entirely Through a Joint North-South Stand".] *Minjok 21* (2001), 4.
Smith, Hazel. "'Opening Up' by Default: North Korea, the Humanitarian Community and the Crisis". *The Pacific Review* 12 (1999), 3.
Snyder, Scott. "The NGO Experience in North Korea". In Flake, Gordon and Snyder, Scott (eds), ibid.
Son, Gi-Woong. *Nambukhan hwangyông punya kyoryu hyômnyôk pangan yôn'gu: tajachôk yangjachôk chôpkûn*. [*A Study on a Plan for Exchanges and Cooperation between North and South Korea in the Environmental Field: A Multilateral and Bilateral Approach.*] Seoul: Minjok t'ongil yôn'guwôn, 1996.
— "Changgwangûp hoedam". ["Ministerial Talks".] In T'ongil yôn'guwôn, ibid., 2004.
Son, Gi-Woong, Kang, Kwang-gyu and Kim, Kyông-sul. *Nambuk hwangyông enôji hyômnyôk hwalsônghwa chôllyak yôn'gu.* [*A Strategic Study on Activation of North-South Cooperation in Environment and Energy.*] Seoul: T'ongil yôn'guwôn, 2002.
Song, Byung-Nak. *The Rise of the Korean Economy*. New York: Oxford University Press, 2003. (1990).
Song, Chông-mi. "Cheju, 'p'yônghwa-wa t'ongir-ûi sôm'-ûro – Cheju minjok t'ongil p'yônghwa ch'eyuk munhwa ch'ukchôn mak olla". ["Cheju, Towards an Island for Peace and Unification – Just Returning from The Cheju Island National Unification, Peace and Culture Festival".] *Minjok hwahae* (2003), 11/12.
South Korea – Constitution. http://www.oefre.unibe.ch/law/icl/ks00000.html.
Steininger, Rolf. "The German Question, 1945-95". In Larres, ibid.
Suh, Byung Moon. "Hyanghu t'ongil chôngch'aek panghyang I". ["The Future Directions of Unification Policies I".] In Minjok t'ongil yôn'guwôn, ibid., 1998b.
Suh, Jae Jean. "The Reunion of Separated Families under the Kim Dae-Jung Government". *The Journal of East Asian Affairs* 16 (2002), 2.
— *North Korea's Market Economy Society from Below.* Seoul: KINU, 2005.

Suh, Jae Jean, Choi, Euichul, Lee, Woo-Young, Lee, Kum-Sun, Lim, Soon-Hee and Kim, Su-Am. *White Paper on Human Rights in North Korea 2003*. Seoul: KINU, 2003.

Suh, Jae-Jung. "Assessing the Military Balance in Korea". *Asian Perspective* 28 (2004), 4.

Suwaidi, al-Jamal S. (ed.) *The Yemeni War of 1994: Causes and Consequences*. London: Saqi Books, 1995.

Tang, Shiping. "A Neutral Reunified Korea: A Chinese View". *The Journal of East Asian Affairs* 13 (1999), 2.

Taylor, Paul. "Introduction". In Mitrany, ibid., 1975.

T'ongil yôn'guwôn [KINU]. *T'alpukja-ûi poho-mith kung-nae chôgûng kaesôn pangan*. [*A Plan for an Improvement of the Protection of and Adaptation to South Korean Society by North Korean Defectors*.] Seoul: T'ongil yôn'guwôn, 1999.

— *Nambukhan hwahae hyômnyôk ch'okjin pangan*. [*A Study on Promotion of Reconciliation and Cooperation between North and South Korea*.] Seoul: T'ongil yôn'guwôn, 2000.

— *T'ongil hwangyông-mith Nambukhan kwangye-wa chônmang*. [*The Unification Environment and the Prospects for Relations between North and South Korea*.] Seoul: T'ongil yôn'guwôn, 2000.

— *T'ongil hwangyông-mith Nambukhan kwangye: 2001-2002*. [*The Unification Environment and Relations between North and South Korea: 2001-2002*.] Seoul: T'ongil yôn'guwôn, 2001.

— *T'ongil hwangyông-mith Nambukhan kwangye chônmang: 2002-2003*. [*The Unification Environment And The Prospects For Relations Between North and South Korea: 2002-2003*.] Seoul: T'ongil yôn'guwôn, 2002.

— "Purok: 2002nyôndo chuyo sakôn ilchi". ["Appendix: A Diary of Major Events in 2002".] In T'ongil yôn'guwôn, ibid., 2002.

— *T'ongil hwangyông-mith Nambukhan kwangye chônmang: 2003-2004*. [*The Unification Environment And The Prospects For Relations Between North and South Korea: 2003-2004*.] Seoul: T'ongil yôn'guwôn, 2003.

— "Purok: 2003nyôn Nambuk kwangye ilchi". ["Appendix: A Diary of North-South Relations in 2003".] In T'ongil yôn'guwôn, ibid., 2003.

— *T'ongil hwangyông-mith Nambukhan kwangye chônmang: 2004-2005*. [*The Unification Environment And The Prospects For Relations Between North and South Korea: 2004-2005*.] Seoul: T'ongil yôn'guwôn, 2004.

— "Purok: 2004nyôn chuyo sagôn ilchi". ["Appendix: A Diary of Major Events in 2004".] In T'ongil yôn'guwôn, ibid., 2004.

T'ongilbu. [Ministry of Unification.] *T'ongilbu 30nyônsa*. [*A 30-year History of Ministry of Unification*.] Seoul: T'ongilbu, 1999.

Uri minjok sôro topki undong p'yônghwa nanum sent'ô [Korea Sharing Movement Peace Sharing Centre]. *Taebuk indojôk chiwôn, kyoryu hyômnyôg saôp-gwa Pukhan-ûi pyônhwa*. [*Humanitarian Aid to North Korea, Exchange and Cooperation Projects and Changes in the North*.] Seoul: Uri minjok sôro topki undong p'yônghwa nanum sent'ô 2003. Conference report.

— Ch'amyô chôngbu 1nyôn, Nambuk kwangye chindan-gwa palchôn panghyang. [*One Year of Participatory Government, A Diagnosis of North-South Relations and Development Directions.*] Seoul: Uri minjok sôro topki undong p'yônghwa nanum sent'ô, 2004, ibid.
de Vylder, Stefan, Axelsson Nycander, Gunnel and Laanatza, Marianne. *De minst utvecklade länderna och världshandeln.* [*The Least Developed Countries And World Trade.*] Göteborg: Novum Grafiska AB, 2001.
Wagner, Helmut and Kang, Myoung-Kyu. "Introduction". In Helmut Wagner and Myoung-Kyu Kang (eds), *Korea and Germany: Lessons in Division.* Seoul: Seoul National University Press, 1990.
Wagner, Helmut and Kang, Myoung-Kyu (eds). *Korea and Germany: Lessons in Division.* Seoul: Seoul National University Press, 1990.
World Bank. *World Development Report 2004: Making Services Work for Poor People.* New York: Oxford University Press, 2003.
Yang, Sung Chul. "The Lessons of United Germany for Divided Korea". In *Korea and the World: Beyond the Cold War*, ibid., 1994.
Yang, Young-shik. "Kim Dae-jung Administration's North Korea Policy". *Korea Focus* 6 (1998), 6.
Yi, Chong-sôk. "Pukkyông nambuk haksul hoeûi kaeyo mith ch'amga sogam". ["A Summary of and Impressions from Participating in the North-South Scientific Meeting in Beijing".] In Minjok t'ongil yôn'guwôn, ibid., 1998b.
Yi, Chu-ch'ôl. "Haeppyôt' chôngch'aek 5nyôn-ûl p'yônggahanda: sahoe munhwa kyoryu, ije hyônsil alge twae". ["Evaluating Five Years of Sunshine Policy: Now the Reality Becomes Known".] *T'ongil Han'guk* (2002), 12.
— "Pukhan chumin-ûi Namhan pangsong suyong silt'ae-wa ûisik pyônhwa". ["North Korean Citizens' Reception of South Korean Broadcasting and Changes in Consciousness".] *T'ongil munje yôn'gu* 40 (2003), 2.
Yi, Ki-bôm. "Indojôk chiwôn, kyoryu hyômnyôg-ûl t'onghan Nambuk kwangye-ûi palchônchôk chônmang". ["Prospects to Develop inter-Korean Relations Through Humanitarian Aid, Exchanges and Cooperation".] In Uri minjok sôro topki undong p'yônghwa nanum sent'ô [Korea Sharing Movement Peace Sharing Centre], *Taebuk indojôk chiwôn, kyoryu hyômnyôg saôp-gwa Pukhan-ûi pyônhwa. [Humanitarian Aid to North Korea, Exchange and Cooperation Projects and Changes in the North.*] Seoul: Uri minjok sôro topki undong p'yônghwa nanum sent'ô, 2003, ibid.
— "Nambuk ôrin-i-ga hamkke hanûn t'ongil madang-ûl". ["The Ground for Unification Made by North-South Children Together".] *Minjok hwahae* (2004), 1/2.
Yi, Sông-mu. "Pundan ihu ch'oech'o, Nambuk yôksa hakcha P'yôngyang sangbong". ["The First Meeting Between North and South Korean Historians Since the Division in P'yôngyang".] *Minjok 21* (2001), 4.

Yi, Yông-sôn (ed.). *T'ongir-ûl wihae Namhan-do pyônhae-ya handa – Pukhan ch'ul-sin hakcha-dûr-ûi chujang-gwa Namhan hakcha-dûr-ûi nonp'yông.* [*Also South Korea Must Change for Unification – Assertions by Scholars of North Korean Origin and Comments by South Korean Scholars.*] Seoul: Orûm, 1998.

Yonhap News. *2000, 2001, 2003 Pukhan yôngam.* [*2000, 2001, 2003 North Korea Yearbook.*] Seoul: Yonhap News Ltd., 1999, 2000, 2002.

— "Pukhaek t'agyôl 6kaehang kongdong sôngmyông chônmun". ["The Full Text of the 6-point Joint Agreement to Settle the North Korean Nuclear Issue".] http://bbs.yonhapnews.co.kr/ynaweb/printpage/News_Content.asp. 19 September, 2005. Accessed the same day.

Yoon, Suh-kyung. "Dollars and Sentiments". *FEER*, 22 June, 2000.

Index

Abd al-Fattah, Ismail 36
Aden 33, 34, 35, 36, 38, 40, 42, 44, 235, 236, 238
Agreed Framework 57-8, 85, 217, 245, 259
Ahn, Yinhay 83
Air Koryô 90, 260
Ali, Abdullah Salih 36, 39, 40, 41, 42, 44, 45
Ali, Nasir Muhammad 36, 37, 39: fn. 57
Ali, Salim Rubay 35
"Alliance 90", 25
An, Chung-gûn 119, 125, 251, 257
An, Ho-sang 127, 244, 245
APEC 116
Arab Cooperation Council 38
Arab League 35, 36
Arirang 84, 114, 120, 132, 138, 143
Armistice Agreement 55, 68, 75, 216, 217, 228-9
Asia-Europe Meeting 77, 255
Asian Games 83, 84, 89, 90, 102, 108, 119, 120-21, 137, 228, 258, 259
Athens Olympics 94, 262
Australia 71, 122, 123, 239, 250
Austria 21, 122, 216, 236, 237
"Axis of evil" 82, 85, 91, 257

Bangkok 764, 116
Beijing 58, 65, 67, 84, 86, 87, 91, 92, 103, 104, 105, 109, 110, 111, 112, 113, 114, 116, 117, 119, 123, 124, 126, 127, 129, 133, 134, 136, 142, 179, 181, 245, 252, 253, 258, 261, 262, 263
Berlin 13, 14, 16, 17, 18, 19, 22, 25, 26, 31, 131, 238
"Berlin Declaration" 69, 72, 253
Berlin Wall 13, 23, 24, 28, 32, 235, 238
Bid, Ali Salam al 40, 42, 44
Biermann, Wolf 18
Bonn 16, 18, 19, 20, 26, 31, 237, 238
Brandt, Willy 14, 15, 18, 20

Britain *see* United Kingdom
Buddhism 3, 77, 89, 121, 125-6, 237, 238, 240, 241, 246, 250, 252, 253, 254, 260
Burma 62
Bush, George 81, 82, 95, 257

Cambridge University 59
Canada 101, 112, 242
CDU 25
Chang Ik 122, 237
Changch'ung Cathedral 122, 124
Cheju Island 75, 83, 90, 213, 255, 257, 259, 260, 261
Chi, Tôk 124, 249
Chin, Yo-han 80
China 9, 52, 55, 57, 59, 60, 65, 69, 70, 71, 72, 76, 77, 84, 85, 86, 87, 88, 90, 93, 102, 105, 108, 109, 110, 111, 112, 113, 114, 115, 116, 117, 119, 124, 129, 135, 136, 139, 140, 142, 144, 145-6, 153, 156, 157, 162, 170, 177, 178, 181, 184, 190, 215-16, 217-18, 219, 221, 228-9, 231, 234, 239, 240, 241, 242, 243, 244, 245, 246, 247, 248, 249, 250, 251, 252, 253, 254, 255, 256, 258, 259, 260, 261
Chindo 103
Chingak sect 126, 253
Cho, Han Bum 1, 4, 81, 84, 120, 121, 135, 137, 139, 140, 141, 202, 208, 212
Cho, Kyông-ch'ôl 119, 252
Cho, Yông-hûi 122
Chochongryun 107-108, 109, 255, 256
Ch'oe, Chang-mu 124, 250
Ch'oe, Hak-chu 102
Ch'oe, Yong-gôn 101
Chogye sect 126, 246, 247
Choi, Jinwook 1, 54, 88
Chosun Ilbo 73
Chôn, U-t'aek 162

Ch'ôndogyo 121, 126-7, 237, 241, 243, 244, 251, 253, 254, 255, 257
Chông, Un-jong 121
Chông, Ûi-ch'ôl 122, 237
Ch'ôngjin 180
Chônju 258
Chu, Pong-t'aek 125, 253
Chun, Doo Hwan 9, 51, 56, 60
Chung, Ju Yung 61, 67, 90, 237, 251, 261
Chung, Mong Jun 72
Chung, Oknim 183
Ch'unhyang 80, 256
Ch'usôk 133
CIA 78
Civil war (South Yemen) 37, 38, 39, 237
Clinton Administration 217
CNN 139
Cold War 2, 13, 26, 38, 41, 69, 73, 79, 82, 98, 114, 120, 135, 140, 141, 216, 218, 223, 233, 238, 245
COMECON 16, 30
Comfort women 128, 129, 142, 243, 246, 251
Computerization of Korean 65, 79, 117, 245, 246, 248, 253, 256
Confucianism 3, 187, 216
Czechoslovakia 22

Daewoo 52, 58, 62, 63, 156, 242, 245, 247
Denmark 116, 117: fn. 28, 240
Der Spiegel 18
DMZ 56, 61, 75, 82, 87, 139, 153, 257, 260
Dong-a Ilbo 58
Dresch, Paul 33, 37

East Germany 38, 53, 146, 149, 153, 185, 187
The Economist 73, 77-8
Edwards, Adrian 72
Egypt 38
El Salvador 62
EU 80, 256
Eun, Hi-kon 124, 252, 253
European community 16

FAO 180
Financial Times 15
Finland 122, 236
Flockton, Christopher 30

Foley, James A. 9, 185, 186
Four-Party talks 217
France 12, 16, 27, 109, 117, 238, 239, 242
Frankfurt 125, 257
Fukuoka 123
Functionalism 4-6, 49, 58, 94, 95, 98, 148, 149, 212, 223, 224, 226, 233
The Fund for inter-Korean Cooperation 98, 103, 179, 180, 183

Geneva 50: fn. 1, 57, 85, 128: fn. 43, 185, 217
Germany 1, 3, 4, 7, 8, 11-12, 41, 42, 43, 44, 45, 46-7, 49, 53, 54, 55, 57, 59, 62, 63, 64, 66, 95, 96, 98, 101: fn. 7, 102, 104, 114, 125, 130, 138, 148, 154: fn. 4, 163, 179, 187, 207: fn. 18, 210, 211, 215, 219, 223, 225, 227, 228, 229, 230-32, 233, 234, 235, 236, 238, 239, 245, 248, 257
  Basic Law (West Germany) 25, 26
  Basis of Relations Treaty/Basic Treaty 3, 15, 18, 19, 29, 236
  "change through rapprochement" 14, 230
  constitution 13, 17, 24
  currency union 24, 25, 26, 29, 238
  division 12-20
  Eastern Recovery Program 31, 239
  Hallstein doctrine 13, 14, 235
  national homogeneity 13, 20
  number of visitors 13, 14, 17, 21
  ten-point plan for unity 24, 238
  two-plus-four talks 27, 29
  unification 20-33
  unification treaty 26, 29, 32, 238
Ghashmi, Ahmad al 25
Gorbachev, Mikhail 20, 22, 26, 27, 236
Grinker, Roy Richard 2, 3, 4, 8, 144: fn. 66, 162, 170
Gulf War 42

Hamburg 18
Hamdi, Ibrahim al- 35, 236
Hamhûng 144
Han, Man-gil 162, 163, 167
Hanawôn 156-7, 158, 177
Hanbok 3
Han'gûl 116, 117, 240, 242, 244

Hankook Ilbo 46, 190, 220
Hanyang University 84, 258
Harrison, Selig S. 54, 60, 61, 78, 216
Hart-Landsberg, Martin 28, 29, 30
Hawaii 112, 242
Honecker, Erich 13: fn. 2, 15, 18, 20, 21, 22, 23, 237, 238
Hong, Ki-mun 101
Hong, X-hee 147
Hong Kong 101, 142
Hudson, Michael C. 41
"Human union" 33, 45, 188, 231, 232, 233
"Human unity" 20, 46, 179
Hungary 20, 21, 22, 29, 31, 124, 237, 249
Hwang, Byung-ki 132
Hwang, In Kwan 29, 41, 43, 201, 216
Hwang, Jang-yop 58, 63, 248
Hyesan College of Education 116
Hyôn, Sông-il 1, 201
Hyundai 52, 61, 63, 65, 68, 72, 237
Hyundai Asan 106, 253

IAEA 86, 92
Ihwa Women's University 138
Im, Su-kyông 52, 102, 128, 237
Inch'ôn 94, 119, 141, 254, 262
Indonesia 62, 114, 116, 249
Inter-Korean Economic Cooperation Committee 75, 78, 83, 87, 93, 256, 258, 259, 260, 261, 262
Inter-Korean Exchanges and Cooperation Act 98, 100, 102, 238
Inter-Korean Joint Resolution in the UN 77, 255
Inter-Korean Ministerial Talks 74-5, 82, 83, 87, 92, 254, 255, 257, 258, 259, 260, 261, 262
International Federation of the Red Cross 180, 181
International Olympic Committee 101
Iran 82, 257
Iraq 38, 42, 82, 86, 257
Israel 40
Italy 71

Japan 9, 16, 56, 57, 65, 68, 70, 71, 75, 79, 84, 85, 86, 87, 88, 89, 92, 93, 94, 102, 103, 104, 107, 108, 109, 110, 111, 112, 115, 116, 120, 122, 123, 125, 127, 128, 129, 132,135, 139,142, 146, 148, 184, 190, 201, 206, 215-16, 218-19, 221, 228, 229, 235, 238, 239, 240, 241, 242, 243, 244, 245, 246, 247, 249, 251, 255, 256, 258, 259, 261, 262
Joong Ang Ilbo 105, 259
Jordan 38
Juche 53, 66, 70, 88, 95, 229
Juhlin, Sven 55

Kaesông 88, 89, 118
Kaesông Industrial Complex (Zone) 83, 87, 93, 260
Kang, Jeong-gu 82
Kang, Myoung-kyu 19: fn. 13, 28
Kangnûng 170
KBS Symphony Orchestra 84, 258
KBS TV 77, 80, 84, 89, 119, 131, 133, 145, 249, 254, 256, 258, 260
KEDO 58, 63, 86, 253
Kelley, James 85
Kim, Choong-hwan 201
Kim, Dae Jung 4, 9, 49, 50, 58, 59, 60, 61, 64, 67, 68, 69, 72, 82, 95, 97, 105, 132, 135, 148, 183, 217, 223, 234, 249, 253
Kim, Hyông-dôk 162
Kim, Il Sung 9, 51, 52, 53, 58, 81, 82, 92, 102, 104, 131, 132, 134, 135, 142, 144, 168, 181, 190, 206, 207, 208, 244
Kim, Jong Il 9, 61, 67, 69, 71, 72, 79, 81, 82, 86, 102, 131, 132, 134, 142, 144, 145, 147, 186, 205, 206, 207, 208, 219, 220, 229, 251
Kim, Kook Sin 20, 29, 32, 207: fn. 18
Kim, Myung-gi 124, 252, 253
Kim, Pyông-no 3, 121
Kim, Samuel S. 68, 72
Kim, Sang-hwan 133, 134
Kim, Sang-jin 124, 246, 248
Kim, Soo Am 7, 176
Kim, Sôn-jôk 127
Kim, Tong-wan 124, 249, 250
Kim, Young Sam 9, 52, 57, 58, 60, 181
Kim, Yôn-ja 144, 145, 256
Kim Il Sung Constitution 70
Kim Il Sung University Library 125

Kisa famine 184
Ko, Yong-gwôn 1, 80, 103, 135, 137, 138, 202, 212
Koguryô 94, 108, 109, 110, 243, 249, 262
Kohl, Helmut 23, 24, 25, 26, 28, 30, 31, 32, 44, 238, 239
Korea Development Institute 53
Korea Electric Power Corporation 63, 86, 220
Korea Institute for National Unification 54, 66, 76, 115, 147, 162, 174, 191, 210, 213
Korea Neighbour-Loving Association 141, 182, 251
Korea Now 74
Korea Youth Development Institute 196, 199, 206, 208
Korean Central News Agency 134
Korean Central TV 144, 147
Korean Photographers' Association 99
Korean Sharing Movement 129, 141, 182, 251
Korean War 7, 49, 50, 55, 57, 73, 97, 100, 151, 154, 185, 201, 227, 229, 235
Korean Welfare Foundation 106, 141, 250
Korean Workers' Party 58, 77, 78, 133, 248
Koryô 110, 126, 140
Koryô Sônggyungwan University (Kaesông) 118, 250
Koryô University 120
Kostiner, Joseph 40, 41
Kôn'guk University Press 113, 254
Krenz, Egon 22, 24
Kumsusan Memorial Palace 181
Kunsan 2: fn. 3
Kuwait 35, 36, 42, 235, 236
Kwak, Sôn-hûi 122, 124, 241, 246
Kwôn, Ho-gyông 122, 242
Kyebaek 177, 178

Larres, Klaus 29
Lee, Hong-Yung 120, 121
Lee, Keumsoon 162, 170, 183
Lee, Woo-Young 142, 190, 191, 203
Leipzig 22
Libya 236
Lim Dong Won 82, 257
"Little Angels" 64, 103, 107, 250

London 27, 79, 109, 113, 256
Los Angeles 101, 125

Macao 123, 247
de Maiziére, Lothar 25, 26
Malaysia 113, 245
Malta 26
Manchuria 184
Mangyôngdae 64, 81, 82
Marsh, David 15, 25, 28, 29, 30, 32
Matheo 122, 236
MBC 80, 84, 258
McAdams, James A. 21
McCune-Reischauer System 9
Mettke, Jörg 18
Mielke, Erich 23
Ministry of Defence 78, 154, 155, 159
Ministry of Education
    North Korea 118
    South Korea 107: fn. 15, 131: fn. 45
Ministry of Health and Welfare 155, 159
Ministry of Labour 160
Ministry of Unification 79, 98, 118, 140, 153, 156, 160, 161, 166, 171, 201, 207
Mitrany, David 4-6
Modrow, Hans 24
Mongolia 112, 115, 116, 141, 240, 249
von Moor, Hubertus 33
Moscow 27, 101, 102, 109, 119, 244, 256
Mt. Halla 64, 77, 80, 105, 110, 250, 254, 257
Mt. Kûmgang 57, 61, 62, 64, 67, 68, 76, 77, 80, 81, 82, 83, 84, 88, 89, 91, 92, 93, 94, 106, 107, 113, 124, 129, 131, 139, 140, 186, 224, 225, 252, 254, 255, 256, 257, 258, 259, 260, 261, 262
Mt. Myohyang 182
Mt. Paektu 64, 77, 80, 90, 105, 110, 119, 133, 250, 254, 255, 257
Mt. Sôrak 92, 262
Mun, Ik-hwan 52, 102, 128
Muslim Brotherhood (North Yemen) 40

Najin-Sônbong 111, 118, 124, 249
Nam, Hae-gûn 122
Namp'o 89, 141

National Security Law 52, 64: fn. 23, 69, 82, 94, 102, 118, 134, 149, 199, 202, 229, 235
NATO 27, 238
Nepal 114, 126, 241, 250
Netherlands 129
New York 100, 104, 119, 123, 124, 242, 247
Newsreview 63, 66
Niigata 112, 247, 250
Nordpolitik 50, 52, 56, 59, 60
North Korea
  Arirang Festival 139
  constitution 154
  economic management improvement measures 211-12, 220, 233-4, 258
  fears for unification 66, 171, 206, 227
  "food migrants" 69
  impact of socio-cultural exchanges 98, 142-9, 234
  missiles/weapons of mass destruction 68, 77, 78, 82, 86, 114, 216, 217, 218, 251
  nuclear program 52, 57, 58, 63-4, 85-7, 88, 91-2, 95, 108, 111, 114, 129, 133, 148, 184, 212, 216-17, 218, 219, 224, 225, 229, 232, 233, 259, 263
  "Our way of socialism" 138
  "pragmatic socialism" 211, 220
  South Korean influences 76, 98, 142-9, 151, 206, 208, 224, 234
  unity 208, 220, 229
  views of unification 206-207, 227
  visitors to South Korea 66, 76, 79, 83, 106-108, 136
North Korean defectors 8, 9, 70, 92, 102, 120, 136, 145, 147-8, 151, 179, 187-8, 189, 208, 220, 227-8, 229, 231, 232, 234, 235, 236, 244, 249, 251, 262
  adaptation to life in South Korea 162-179
  attitudes towards unification 206-207, 220
  background 153
  Chinese characters 157, 164, 168, 169
  marginal man 162, 170, 187, 228
  numbers 152-3
  studies of 162, 163-6, 166-171, 171-4, 174-8
  support for 154-161
North-South Korea
  4 July Joint Communiqué 55-6,101, 134, 190, 215, 235
  15 June Declaration *see* Joint Declaration
  Basic Agreement 57, 59, 60, 68, 99, 134, 179, 241
  "can-do spirit" 130, 224
  characteristics of socio-cultural exchanges and cooperation 97, 130-140, 149, 226
  common culture/cultural legacy 2-3, 130, 143-4, 164, 165-6, 186-7, 188, 196, 200, 205, 220, 225, 226, 227, 228, 231
  confederation 51, 53, 59, 60, 95, 114, 122, 134, 235, 236
  consequences of unification 54-5
  costs of unification 53-4, 60, 95, 197, 198, 200, 207, 210-11, 216, 227, 228
  development of socio-cultural exchanges and cooperation 97, 100-108
  diffusion effects of socio-cultural contacts 97, 137, 148, 226
  divided families/family reunions 1, 8-9, 50, 55, 56, 57, 61, 67, 68, 69, 72, 73-4, 75, 76, 77, 78, 79, 81, 82, 88-9, 93, 95, 99, 102, 106, 107, 108, 125, 132, 135, 138, 139, 143, 145, 146, 147, 148, 151, 152, 184-7, 188, 189, 202, 212, 223, 224-5, 228, 237, 252, 254, 255, 256, 257, 258, 259, 260, 261, 262
  economic gap 62, 95, 163, 198, 201, 220, 227, 228, 232, 233
  formula for unification 198, 201, 209-210, 213
  gradual unification 33, 51, 53-4, 95, 191, 210, 218, 219, 220, 221, 229, 232, 233
  heterogeneity 1-3, 84, 100, 101: fn. 6, 102, 116, 134, 168, 169, 187, 188, 190, 195, 198, 199, 200, 201, 202, 203, 204, 226

homogeneity 1-3, 80, 84, 97, 103, 104, 113, 115, 121, 129, 130, 137, 139, 143, 144, 148, 151, 167, 168, 187, 190, 193, 194-5, 199, 200, 202, 205-206, 207, 220, 226, 234
Joint Declaration/15 June Declaration 72, 73, 74, 75, 80, 81, 82, 84, 94, 95, 107, 139, 225, 254, 258, 262
joint publications 65, 105, 110, 113-14, 116, 117, 130, 149, 151, 224, 228, 234, 240, 250, 253, 254
law 78-9
legal foundations of socio-cultural exchanges and cooperation 97, 98-100, 148, 223
lessons from German and Yemeni unification 230-32
main tasks for unification 199, 202, 212, 214-15, 220
military power 78
military talks 75, 92, 255, 262
mutual distrust 55, 73, 94, 95, 130, 170, 190, 197, 201, 226, 227, 228, 233
nationalism 1, 55, 183, 201, 216, 226-7, 229
obstacles to unification 191, 198, 200-201, 207, 210-11, 219, 220, 226-30
peace treaty 78, 199, 202, 217, 228-9
Red Cross 56, 66, 73, 79, 100, 102, 141, 180, 181, 182, 185, 236
socio-cultural diversity 2, 3, 132, 137, 144, 226, 234
socio-cultural exchanges and cooperation 1-4, 7-9, 56, 64-6, 67, 76-7, 79-81, 83-4, 89-91, 93-4, 95, 148-9, 188, 189, 190, 191, 202, 223-6
trade 52, 56-7, 58, 62-3, 76, 81, 85, 87-8, 93, 237, 238
types of socio-cultural exchanges and cooperation 97, 108-130
unification and great powers 9, 190, 198, 199, 200, 201, 215-19, 220, 221, 228-9
unification policies 49, 50-55, 58-61, 95, 146, 227, 228
North-South Prime Minister Talks 57, 103, 238

North-South Summit 50, 72-3, 74, 78, 79, 80, 95, 97, 106, 107, 118, 119, 121, 125, 135, 137, 139, 146, 147, 152, 182, 224, 225, 226, 254, 256, 257
Northern Limit Line 68, 82, 83, 87, 92
NPT 86, 91, 92, 259

O, Ki-sông 1, 2, 80, 104, 138, 146, 205
Ok, Tae Hwan 7
Osaka 123, 128
Ostpolitik 14, 15, 18, 20, 235
Ottawa 27
"Outposts of tyranny" 91

Paek, Nam-sun 60-61, 71
Paek, Yông-ch'ôl 134
Paekche 178: fn. 36
Pak, Ch'ang-tûk 122
Pak, Sang-bong 130, 132, 133, 134
Pak, T'ae-ho 126, 246
Pak, Yông-sin 101
P'anmunjôm 74, 79, 99, 118, 139, 241, 256
Parhae 109, 140, 243
Paris 27
Park, Chung Hee 9, 50, 56, 60, 101
Park, Jung Chul 162, 171
Park, Young-Ho 1
Party of Democratic Socialism 25
Peaceful coexistence 2, 15, 35, 36, 37, 59, 60, 95, 137, 140, 189, 202, 212, 219, 221, 223, 224, 225, 226, 229, 232, 233
Persson, Göran 80
Pfennig, Werner 33
Phillipines 58, 71, 116, 129
Pohl, Manfred 27, 28, 33, 54
Poland 15, 20, 22, 29, 116
Policy for peace and prosperity 88, 89, 96, 223
Portugal 103, 240
Potsdam agreement 12
Pusan 77, 83, 105, 120, 121, 228, 251, 258
Putin, Vladimir 219
Pyôn, Chin-hûng 80
P'yôngyang 52, 61, 64, 65, 67, 68, 71, 72, 73, 75, 76, 77, 79, 80, 81, 82, 83, 84, 87, 88, 89, 90, 92, 93, 94, 95, 101, 102, 103, 107, 111, 118, 119, 120, 124, 125, 126, 127, 128, 129, 133,

139, 140, 143, 144, 182, 186, 205, 208, 223, 237, 239, 240, 242, 243, 244, 250, 251, 252, 253, 254, 255, 256, 257, 258, 259, 260, 261, 262

Reagan, Ronald 27
Research Institute for National Unification 162
Rhee, Kang Suk 3, 9, 16, 20, 29, 54, 62
Rice, Condoleeza 91
Rodong Sinmun 144
Roh, Kil-yong 116
Roh, Moo-hyun 9, 86, 89, 94, 96, 223, 233
Roh, Tae Woo 9, 51, 52, 53, 56, 59, 60, 98, 102, 237, 238
Russia 9, 57, 59, 86, 87, 109, 111, 112, 115, 116, 135, 153, 190, 215-16, 217, 218, 219, 221, 228-9, 231, 241, 242, 243
Ryu, Yôl 132

Sahyangga 132
Sakhalin Island 103, 241, 242
Samson Venus 180
Samsung 156
Samsung Electronics 76, 133
Sanaa 34, 35, 37, 44, 236, 237
Saudi Arabia 39, 42, 43: fn. 66, 44, 238
SBS TV 64, 77, 90, 119, 133, 252, 255, 261
Schmidt, Helmut 18
Second-class citizens 31, 33, 47, 163, 170, 187, 228
Seoul 64, 66, 68, 72, 73, 74, 75, 76, 77, 79, 80, 82, 83, 84, 87, 89, 90, 92, 93, 94, 102, 103, 105, 107, 111, 119, 120, 126, 128, 130, 131, 134, 135, 143, 144, 146, 155, 186, 196, 199, 208, 223, 237, 239, 240, 241, 244, 245, 250, 253, 254, 255, 256, 257, 258, 259, 260, 261, 262
Seoul National University (Press) 110, 114: fn. 24, 116, 254
Shanghai 109
Shim, Jae Hoon 72
Shin, Sang-jin 216
Siberia 109, 145, 165, 184, 219, 243
Sin, Chae-ho 169
Sin, Pômt'a 126, 247

Sin, Pôpt'a 125, 237, 239
Singapore 116
Singyesa 94, 262
Sinûiju 75
Sirhak 79
Six-party talks 86-7, 91-2, 219, 229, 260, 261, 262, 263
Smith, Hazel 70
Snyder, Scott 182
Social Democrats 24, 25
Socialist Unity Party 13, 14, 15, 19, 20, 21, 22, 23, 237, 238
Sokch'o 67
Son, Gi-Woong 115
Song, Wôl-chu 126, 246
South Korea
    7 July Declaration 98, 102, 127, 130, 237
    15 August Liberation Day Celebrations 81-2, 140, 145, 257
    accommodation of North Korean culture 191-6, 200, 220, 228
    anti-communism 135, 203, 220
    constitution 154, 229
    humanitarian aid/assistance to North Korea 8, 58, 66, 76, 81, 85, 87, 88, 93, 95, 98-9, 100, 122, 123, 124, 126, 127, 129, 135, 136, 141, 146, 151-2, 179-84, 188, 189, 224, 225, 228, 229, 232, 234, 245, 250, 252
    impact of aid 182-4
    interest in unification 196-200, 208-209, 214, 220, 227
    mutual security treaty with the United States 216
    NGOs and unification 97-8, 140-42, 148, 180-84, 188, 250, 251
    reasonability of unification 197, 200, 209
    three-stage model for unification 58-9
    time for unification 197, 209, 210
    views of North Korea 189-91, 213, 220
    views of unification 189-90, 196-215, 220
    visitors to North Korea 64, 76, 106-107
South-North Coordinating Committee 56, 101, 236

Soviet Union 12, 14, 15, 16, 20, 21, 22, 26, 27, 29, 34, 37, 38, 39, 46, 47, 52, 53, 59, 61, 102, 112, 125, 138: fn. 58, 219, 231, 233, 236, 238, 240
Sô, Kyông-wôn 52, 237
Sông, Tong-chun 143
Sônggyungwan University (Seoul) 118, 250
Sôngt'a 126
Stasi 23
Steininger, Rolf 32
Stockholm 86, 117
Stoph, Willy 15
"Structural integration" 3, 146, 226
Suh, Byung-Moon 66
Suh, Jae Jean 9, 185, 186, 208, 211, 212
Suh, Jae-Jung 78, 216
Sunshine policy 60-61, 64, 68, 79, 82, 86, 95, 96, 97, 135, 141, 148, 149, 197, 200, 214, 220, 223, 226, 228, 232, 233, 249
Supreme People's Assembly 71, 101, 128
Sweden 55, 80, 86, 244
Switzerland 101, 122, 216, 237, 239
Sydney Olympics 76-7, 255

Taegu Universiad 89, 132, 137, 260
Taejonggyo 127, 244, 245
Taesông kongsa 155, 156
Taewôn 125, 237, 238
Taiwan 60, 120, 142, 244
Tan'gun 84, 90, 127, 177, 259
"Team Spirit" 56
Thailand 115, 116, 120, 243, 247
Three-way talks 86, 259
Toan 125, 126, 246
Tokyo 68, 101, 109, 110, 112, 123, 128, 129, 235, 238, 240, 243, 244, 247, 251, 255, 258
Tonghak Rebellion 127
Tripoli 35, 37, 236, 237
Tumen River 111, 116, 136, 245

Ulbricht, Walter 13, 14, 15
Ulsan 138
UN 16, 43: fn. 68, 50, 51, 52, 57, 60, 77, 88, 113, 114, 236, 241, 242, 249, 255
UNCHR 128: fn. 43, 129
UNDP 111, 115, 116, 142, 180, 245
UNEP 115

UNESCO 115, 244, 245
UNICEF 180, 181
Unification
    absorption 7, 9, 12, 27, 28, 29, 30, 46, 53-4, 59, 60, 134, 191, 210, 230, 231
    agreement 7, 9, 12, 40, 41, 45, 46, 213, 230, 231
    communization 34, 78, 214
    from above 41, 46, 230-31
    from below 29, 41, 46, 230-31
    neutrality 216, 218, 219
"Unification Basketball Games" 65, 90, 106, 119, 120, 253, 261
Unification Soccer Games 83, 119, 258
United Kingdom/Britain 12, 16, 26, 27, 33, 59, 71, 114, 120, 235, 238, 247, 248, 249
United States 9, 12, 16, 26, 27, 34, 39, 42, 55, 56, 57, 59, 61, 63, 68, 69, 70, 71, 78, 81, 82, 83, 85-6, 87, 88, 91, 92, 95, 102, 111, 112, 113, 116, 122, 123, 125, 126, 135, 147, 153, 162, 168, 170, 182, 183, 184, 201, 205, 206, 211, 215-17, 218, 219, 220, 221, 228-9, 238, 239, 240, 241, 243, 245, 246, 247, 248, 252, 256, 257
    Troops 114, 134, 198, 199, 201, 202, 217, 218, 229

"Value integration" 3, 4, 9, 16, 20, 98, 146, 149, 179, 225-6, 231
Vatican 122
Vietnam 7, 92

Wagner, Helmut 19: fn. 13, 28
Warsaw Pact 13, 27, 238
Warsaw University 116
Washington 68, 217
von Weisaecker, Richard 33
West Germany 50, 54
West (Yellow) Sea 67, 68, 82, 92, 140, 183, 184, 252, 258
Westpolitik 14
WFP 180, 181
Woosung 180
Wôn, Hong-gu 101
Wôn, Tong-sôk 104: fn. 11

Yang, Young-Shik 61
Yemen 1, 7, 8, 11-12, 46-7, 49, 55, 62, 95,
    96, 130, 148, 163, 187, 207: fn. 18,
    210, 215, 219, 223, 225, 227, 228,
    229, 230-32, 233, 234, 235, 236,
    237, 238
  civil war 44-5, 46, 47, 230, 231, 233,
    234
  constitution 35, 36, 37, 40, 45, 236
  Council of Ministers 45
  division 33-8
  General Popular Congress 42, 44, 45
  "historic accident" 38, 41, 46
  mutual distrust 44, 46, 231, 232
  oil exploration 37, 38-9, 43, 47, 231
  Opposition Coordination Council 45
  Presidential Council 42, 44, 45
  unification 38-46
  war 35, 36, 235, 236
Yemen Council 36, 37
Yemeni Reform Grouping 42, 44, 45
Yemeni Socialist Party 35, 38, 42, 43, 44, 45
Yi, Chong-sôk 133
Yi, Chu-ch'ôl 121
Yi, Hyo-jae 128
Yi, Hyôn-bok 116
Yi, In-mo 135
Yi, Ki-bôm 183
Yi, Tae-gyông 122, 237
Yi dynasty 140
Yoon, Yi-sang 64, 143, 251
Yô, Yôn-gu 128
Yôn, Hyông-muk 57
Yônbyôn (Yanbian) 65, 70, 104, 109, 110,
    114, 115, 117, 118, 136, 144, 242,
    249
"Yônbyôn songs" 144
Yôngbyôn (nuclear reactor) 86, 259
Yun, To-hyôn 84

For Product Safety Concerns and Information please contact our EU
representative GPSR@taylorandfrancis.com
Taylor & Francis Verlag GmbH, Kaufingerstraße 24, 80331 München, Germany

www.ingramcontent.com/pod-product-compliance
Lightning Source LLC
Chambersburg PA
CBHW071346290426
44108CB00014B/1457